Iranian Intellectuals in the Twentieth Century

D1263934

*Published with the assistance of a grant
from the Iran-America Foundation*

Iranian
Intellectuals
20th *in the*
Century

Ali Gheissari

University of Texas Press ⭗ Austin

Requests for permission to reproduce material from this work should
be sent to Permissions, University of Texas Press, P.O. Box 7819,
Austin, TX 78713-7819.

∞The paper used in this publication meets the minimum require-
ments of American National Standard for Information Sciences—
Permanence of Paper for Printed Library Materials,
ANSI Z39.48-1984.

Library of Congress Cataloging-in-Publication Data
Gheissari, Ali, 1954–
Iranian intellectuals in the twentieth century / by Ali Gheissari.
—1st ed.
p.   cm.
Includes bibliographical references (p.   ) and index.
ISBN 0-292-72804-2 (pbk. : alk. paper)
1. Iran—Intellectual life—20th century.   2. Intellectuals—Iran—
Political activity.   3. Political culture—Iran.   I. Title.
DS266.G44   1998
955.05′086′31—dc21   97-6742

To Anna,
and to Rana, Soraya, and Mariam

CONTENTS

⌐ PREFACE ⌐

THE IDEA FOR THIS BOOK—TO PORTRAY THE MAIN IDEOLOGI-
cal tendencies found among Iranian intellectuals, particularly those in the
political opposition—was initially conceived before the Iranian revolution of 1979. The advent of the revolution and the role of intellectuals in
the early articulation of its goals have only magnified these ideologies
and made their analysis more germane.

It is a relatively easy task to collect the material for the study of the
circulation of ideas in modern Iran; the difficulties arise when one tries
to apply some method of analysis. I like to think that these difficulties are
inherent in the subject and that the barriers they pose are altogether real,
but I have also come to realize that I have often been searching for particular formations or trends, when the manifest reality of the Iranian intellectual and ideological landscape during the last 150 years or so pro-
hibits speaking with accuracy of clear and consonant trends. Instead,
formations often resulted from a subtle movement of ideas that at first
glance may have been too rudimentary or haphazard to be categorized as
a definable trend. There were many ruptures and institutional discontinuities, not only on the intellectual scene, but also in politics and society,
and in the usage of language.

This study is not intended to be a comprehensive history of Iranian
intellectuals in the twentieth century and, although it refers to literary
works, it is not a sociology of literature. It also is not a probe into the
roots of the Iranian revolution, although it discusses certain important
points in modern Iranian history that led up to that event. It rather tries
to illustrate certain components of modern Iranian political culture as
perceived and developed by intellectuals and as revealed in the wealth of
material found in their political and literary writings.

By "political culture," I mean the complex set of intersubjective and
meaningful norms and symbols shared by members of a community over
a given time span. It includes the broad array of intellectual and ideological values that influence not only the planned orientations of an individ-

ual or group, such as political affiliations and styles of political behavior, but also the more subjective concerns, such as concepts of legitimacy and the criteria for determining what constitutes virtue.

From the mid–nineteenth century to the present, several themes and preoccupations have remained at the core of Iranian political culture and ideological history. In this work I have tried to highlight at least two of them: autocracy and attitudes toward the influence of the West. Although the origins of both themes can be traced back to pre–modern times, in their recent forms they have involved distinctly new concepts and new means of representation. Here the study of the intelligentsia as a social type or group has a particular significance, because in spite of many contradictions, its members were most closely associated with modernity—both formally, in terms of their appearance and manners, and theoretically, in their constant efforts to articulate the historical relevance of modernity.

An intellectual is by definition an educated person dealing in the life of the mind. In the period under consideration in the present study, by *intellectuals*, I also refer broadly to those who, though differing in ideological motivations and in solutions to social problems, try to maintain what they regard as an up-to-date vision, seek social and political change, and identify with the objective spirit of the modern world, i.e., with change both as a necessity and as historically inevitable. This group, in all its diversity, tended to direct its attention to transforming society to the benefit of the ordinary, and mainly deprived, majority of the population whose hard life, it was assumed, gave them a higher degree of historical and moral significance than the affluent few. In this view a more humane, rational, and just world would ultimately replace the present corrupt society.

As far back as the early nineteenth century, Iranian intellectuals, though they shared characteristics with other social groups, regarded themselves as differing in outlook and teleology from the rest of society. They aspired to lead the people toward a vision that would restore their confidence and identity and offer a political solution to the question of social justice. They thought of Iranian society as stagnant and its political order as anachronistic, and it was their duty to revive the one and update the other. Such a paradigmatic constitution, no matter how rudimentary and full of discrepancies, was an integral part of the general process of modernity.

The theoretical populism of intellectuals was often colored by an underlying distrust of established authority, though distrust of the state did not prevent them from becoming civil servants. In the mid-1920s, for example, many intellectuals supported the emerging Pahlavi state and, like army officers and bureaucrats, were later dependent on it. But unlike the other two groups, they doubted the legitimacy of the regime and also developed a preoccupation with the intrusion of Western influence.

In this book I shall argue that the failure of scattered reforms from above in nineteenth-century Qajar society precipitated the formation of a nationalist ideology that was primarily conceptualized to challenge despotism and arbitrary rule, and that eventually led to the Constitutional movement of 1905. In this movement the modernist intelligentsia and a significant section of the ulama collaborated to promote social justice. However, the Constitutional movement did not succeed in an overall institutionalization of its principles in the political culture, nor did Pahlavi state nationalism, with its stress on modernization and the transformation of urban space and typology. The marked increase in political activity in the 1940s, the introduction of the "intellectual element" in literary works, and various arguments on the crisis of Iranian modernism will also be discussed and analyzed. Debates on strategies of self-awareness constituted a major preoccupation among the intelligentsia during the years following the coup d'état of 1953. In the ensuing years the Pahlavi regime's legitimacy was increasingly called into question, leading the opposition away from reform and ultimately resulting in the revolution of 1979. The book also offers some observations on certain ideological expressions in the postrevolutionary period.

In the preparation of this work I have been fortunate to benefit from the knowledge of several friends and colleagues. First I should remember the late Hamid Enayat, my mentor at Tehran University and Oxford. I am also grateful to Ervand Abrahamian, Anna Enayat, Michael Gilsenan, John Gurney, Homa Katouzian, Hasan Kayali, Timothy McDaniel, Michael Meeker, Roger Owen, Vali Nasr, Darius Rejali, and Hossein Ziai, who gave me the benefit of their ideas and criticism over the years. I am particularly indebted to my friend Mohsen Ashtiany, who patiently read the drafts and gave me his most helpful comments. I would further like to express my sincere appreciation to the late Albert Hourani, and to Iraj Afshâr, Simin Dâneshvar, Mohammad-Reza Shafi'i Kadkani, and especially my brother Mohammad Gheissari in Tehran who, in a variety of ways, were always inspiring and supportive. My thanks are also due to Colin Wakefield of the Bodleian Library for his cordial assistance during the early stages of my research; to Hâj Mohammad Shahriâri, who always met my odd bibliographical requests in good spirit; to Margaret Ševčenko for editing the final version of the manuscript; to Ali Hossaini, formerly the Humanities Editor of the University of Texas Press, for his keen interest; and to Leslie Tingle and Helen Hyams for professional assistance and copyediting the text. However, the responsibility for all shortcomings remains entirely mine. My wife, Anna Alevra Gheissari, and my family provided me with unbounded support, and I wish to dedicate this work to them in gratitude and affection.

A.G.
January 1997

NOTE ON
⟶ TRANSLITERATION ⟵
AND DATES

THE SYSTEM OF TRANSLITERATION USED HERE RENDERS CON-
sonants according to the system adopted by the *International Journal of
Middle East Studies*, but omits diacritical marks, with the exception of
the hamza ('), the ayn ('), and Â and â for long alif. Vowels are rendered
to reflect the sound in English that most closely approximates modern
Persian pronunciation. Established words and names in English are An-
glicized. Personal names are rendered in accordance with the transliteration rules outlined here, except when cited in sources in European languages. All translations are by the author unless otherwise stated.

In the text, dates are all in the Common Era unless they refer directly
to Persian texts. In the notes and bibliography, dates are given in the Islamic solar (*shamsi*) calendar current in Iran and are followed by the corresponding date in the Common Era separated by a slash. Dates prior to
the official adoption of the solar calendar in Iran (legislated by the Majles
on 11 Farvardin 1304/31 March 1925) are given in the Islamic lunar
(*gamari*) calendar followed by A. H. (*anno Hegirae*) and the corresponding date in the Common Era. On 20 Esfand 1354/10 March 1976 an
"imperial calendar" was introduced that begins with the foundation of
the Achaemenian Empire in 559 B.C.E.; hence the Persian New Year
1355/1976 corresponds to 2535. Although the new measure was reversed
on 11 Shahrivar 1357/2 September 1978 in the wake of the revolution,
most works published in Iran during that period bear the imperial date.
Those dates are followed here by the more familiar Islamic *shamsi* dates
in square brackets and the corresponding date in the Common Era.

LIST OF
— BIBLIOGRAPHIC —
ABBREVIATIONS

EI	*Encyclopaedia of Islam.*
EI2	*Encyclopaedia of Islam* (New Edition).
EIr	*Encyclopaedia Iranica.*
IJMES	*International Journal of Middle East Studies.*
IS	*Iranian Studies.*
Jarâ'ed	Mohammad Sadr-Hâshemi. *Târikh-e Jarâ'ed va Majallât-e Iran* (A History of the Iranian Press and Periodicals). 4 Vols. 1st edition, Isfahan, 1327–1331/1948–1952; reprinted Isfahan, Enteshârât-e Kamâl, 1364/1985.
MEJ	*Middle East Journal.*
MES	*Middle Eastern Studies.*
Moshâr	Khân-Bâbâ Moshâr. *Mo'allefin-e Kotob-e Châppi-e Fârsi va Arabi az Âghâz-e Châpp tâ Konoun* (Persian and Arabic Books in Print and Their Authors from the Beginning of the Print Industry in Iran to the Present). 5 Vols. Tehran, 1340–42/ 1961–63.
Press and poetry	M. A. Tarbiyat and E. G. Browne. *The Press and Poetry of Modern Persia.* Cambridge: Cambridge University Press, 1914.
Rejâl	Mehdi Bâmdâd. *Sharh-e Hâl-e Rejâl-e Iran dar Qarn-e 12 va 13 va 14 Hejri* (Iranian National Biography in the Nineteenth and Twentieth Centuries). 6 Vols. Reprinted Tehran: Zavvâr, 1357/1978.
S/N	Yahyâ Âryanpour. *Az Sabâ tâ Nimâ: Târikh-e 150 Sâl Adab-e Fârsi* (From Sabâ to Nimâ: A History of 150 Years of Persian Literature). 2 Vols. (Tehran, 1350/1971), 4th

edition, Tehran: Jibi, 1354/1975; 3rd additional volume, published posthumously, as *Az Nimâ tâ Rouzegâr-e Mâ: Târikh-e Adab-e Fârsi-ye Mo'âser* (From Nimâ to Our Time: A History of Contemporary Persian Literature). Tehran: Zavvâr, 1374/1995.

~ I ~

Introduction: Modern Intellectualism in Iran

Iran has excellent mothers, delicious food, awful

intellectuals, and beautiful plains . . .

—SOHRÂB SEPEHRI[1]

Ideological History in Perspective

THE IRANIAN REVOLUTION OF 1979 AND THE SUDDEN FALL OF
the Pahlavi monarchy took many people, political activists among them,
by surprise. It is true that toward the end of Mohammad-Reza Shah's
reign the credibility gap between the people and the state had widened,
but in that period the intellectual opposition was concerned mainly with
transcending its self-avowed "theoretical poverty" regarding the analysis
of contemporary society in order to define an effective challenge to the
authority of the state. As revolutionary events unfolded, popular dissent
gained momentum and brought down the monarchy surprisingly rapidly.
In these circumstances, intellectuals found themselves following rather
than leading the events. Here a particularly puzzling factor for the intellectuals was that on the whole they were unable to articulate a "historically logical" sequence linking Iranian society under the Shah to the increasingly dominant Islamic features of the revolution, because these

events ran so counter to the conceptual premises that underlay the intelligentsia's determinist and formalist approach to historical time—namely, the idea of a linear progress of reason in history, in which the role of traditional phenomena remains hopelessly vague. Intellectual discourse thus had to resort to such favorite stopgaps as "anachronistic" and "hegemonic" in order to describe events that contradicted its presuppositions.

The preoccupation with theoretical poverty and the urge to conceptualize social realities were long-standing concerns of intellectuals that can be traced back to several decades before the revolution. As they saw it, comprehension of present circumstances in accordance with a foreordained teleology concerning history and matters historical called for a suitable taxonomy of the society's historical status.[2] Showing interest in social research and pondering predictable ways to analyze Iran's recent history had become the objective of intellectuals since the coup d'état of 1953, and especially since the early 1960s. Many historians and social scientists, as well as poets and writers, tried to conceptualize modern history in accordance with a social theory that claimed to be capable of transcending the cleavage between facts and values, or between realities and ideals. Historical analysis was expected to produce not only a theoretical self-consciousness but also a terminological framework suitable for both analyzing social formation and guiding praxis.

These ideas were structured around and determined by changes that had taken place regarding the idea of the individual, including the concept of the self.[3] Along with an emphasis on the importance of historical consciousness, a significant ideological characteristic of many Iranian intellectuals prior to the revolution of 1979 was a teleological vision that, shunning as always any piecemeal notion of political practice, tended to undermine the self by rendering it secondary to a presupposed spirit of the whole; this was a departure from earlier modernist attitudes of the Constitutional value system, which had a more individualistic bent. Before the revolution, the intelligentsia and the radical political opposition more generally had adopted a utopian perspective with an overlay either of Marxist Leninism or militant Shi'ism, which regarded the individual merely as an inseparable part of a supreme whole whose worth was to be measured in terms of his or her place in such a totality.[4] The fusion of these attitudes hampered the institutionalization of the normative and practical underpinnings of modernity and made the political culture of the opposition on the eve of the revolution seem symbolic and metaphoric rather than practical.

Images of the self in these circumstances often consist of several distinct yet interrelated layers. These include the personal or private self-image, the less abstract and less personal typological self-image, and the national self-image.[5] At the level of the personal or private self-image, temporal authenticity and internal consistency are often imagined by the individual in accordance with the individual's own set of acquired values, criteria of virtues, and other internalized cultural standards. In the public sphere, the private self-image is usually conditioned to display forms of social representation that do not always maintain the same attributes as those privately held by the person. The typological self-image, which by its very nature has objective representation and augments social and cultural diversity in a society, is an objectification of the private self-image; its function is to regulate socialization. Finally, the national self-image, or *nation-view*, represents what individuals, privately or collectively, perceive about their overall or common mode of being as a nation and includes the situation of a given society and culture and its place in the world; it has a historicist aspect. For instance, modern Iranian intellectuals view their situation in certain terms such as the encounter with the West and Western culture, "conspiracies" of power politics, and changes in traditional structures. In modern Iran, questions of self-definition and of nation-view have been continuously problematic.

Encounters with the West during the first half of the nineteenth century ended a period of relative isolation and made many Iranian reformers, notably those who were associated with the royal court, realize the need to introduce modern technology and administration, but their efforts in this regard were unsuccessful and, in the minds of ordinary people, modernization and reformism from above soon became associated with failure. The major obstacle to reform has generally been identified as the arbitrary and autocratic structure of the state, which, benefiting from occasional sanctions by traditionalist ulama, was resistant to change. Western influence in Iran continued to grow, however, and with it public awareness of the importance of the West and the status of Iran in regional politics.

Political writings of the time emphasized Iranian nationalism, especially as the country's pre-Islamic history became more widely known. One of the manifestations of these nationalist sentiments was the effort to write "pure" Persian and to purge the language of "alien," primarily Arabic, words. The literature of this period, in addition to taking a critical stance vis-à-vis the West and emphasizing Iranian nationalism, also called for political reform. The quest for institutionalized justice, as manifested, for example, in the demands for the establishment of a council of grievances (*'edâlat-khwâneh*), which became more pronounced during the latter part of the nineteenth century, and the challenge to absolutism and despotism were themes in this literature, which contrasted despotism (*estebdâd*) and absolutism (*motlaqiyat*) with Constitutionalism (Mashrutiyat). This reformist dimension also challenged certain patriarchal elements in traditional culture by demanding equal opportunity in education and insisting on individual rights.

The Constitutional movement of 1905 won the support of certain members of the ulama, some of whom even became its active advocates and were instrumental in mobilizing the public in favor of the movement. But overall, the Constitutional movement had a secular trait, a feature that was also evident in various literary and political publications of the period. The prime concern of the anti-Constitutionalists, which instead of Mashruteh (Constitutionalism) insisted on Mashru'eh (i.e., a regime based on the Shari'a), was to safeguard tradition, rather than to promote theocracy. The notion of *law*, at first a unifying theme and a general demand of the Constitutionalists, soon led to divisions within their ranks, because of the fundamental difference between a system of law primarily derived from the Shari'a that was acceptable to the ulama and the European constitutional model favored by the modernists. Education and judicial practice, both of which had traditionally been under the ulama's control, were also objects of dispute.

Not surprisingly, the collaboration between the ulama and the modernists was short-lived and the Constitutional movement ultimately failed to institutionalize its basic conceptual premises (such as individual rights and representation) in the political culture. Instead, traditional patterns of submission to authority returned under the Pahlavi state. Both factions of the Constitutional movement were responsible for this failure. The modernists' crude identification of traditional phenomena as reactionary alienated traditional society, a hostility that culminated during the recent revolution in the negative reaction of the Islamic revivalists to the whole Constitutional legacy.

Many of these ideological processes were reflected in the literature of each period. The transformation in literary consciousness in Iran, which assumed a clear form in the late nineteenth century, initially had a greater stylistic impact on prose than on poetry. Although both genres shared new social and political orientations and terminology, poetry retained its traditional patterns and meters. But during the first two decades of the twentieth century, social and political poetry, in comparison with prose, displayed clear allusions to universal sentiments with a greater degree of elegance, verve, and clarity of diction. It was also in this period that the novel became accepted among intellectuals as a distinct literary genre, as translations of European works (either directly from the original or through their earlier Arabic translations) begun in the mid-nineteenth century grew in popularity and influence. However, it was not until after the Constitutional movement that Iranian writers began to turn out translations with some degree of professional competence and then began themselves to try their hand at writing fiction—novels, plays, and short stories—for a new class of reading public. From the start, these works were written to serve the cause of modernism. Novels were viewed as vehicles for enlightenment and were written to convey some message. The earliest novels in particular often had the character of advice literature, and their readers had mostly modernist aspirations. In the post-Constitutional period and the early years of the Pahlavis, historical and social novels displayed a sense of nostalgia for the all-powerful state and a concern with social problems, including the position of women in society.

In the 1920s and 1930s the production of "intellectual literature," both poetry and prose, continued, and by the 1940s it had taken on a socialist tone. Especially after the fall of Reza Shah and with the rise in influence of the pro-Soviet Tudeh Party among the youth, the spread of the intellectual element in literature increased. Modernism, nationalism, and democratic ideas; criticism of certain aspects of traditional culture, such as religion, patriarchy, and nepotism; criticism of the country's political establishment; and a critical attitude toward the West were the main attributes of the intellectual element and were recurrent themes of this literature.

The Tudeh Party had a twofold impact on Iranian writers and intellectuals. Its more positive or affirmative influence included stressing the importance of the intellectual element, advocating socialist ideas, and putting forward a categorical assurance regarding long-term historical ends. A more negative influence was the party's tendency to follow the Soviet line without question, even when it went against the country's interests, an attitude that alienated many intellectuals, who found the pretext of internationalism offensive. By the 1960s the so-called intellectual literature represented mainstream modernism. Although after the coup d'état of 1953, as a reaction to the officially stated Iranism of the day, explicit nationalism decreased in the intellectual literature, patriotism and the desire to be both politically and culturally independent remained strong.

Beginning in the early 1960s, the gap increased considerably between the younger generation of intellectuals and the state, on the one hand, and the traditional opposition (mainly the National Front and the Tudeh Party), on the other. The old opposition offered no clear response to the Shah's programs for reform. Many intellectuals felt unable to deal with the new realities or to conceptualize recent developments; some had very little concrete empirical knowledge of the country and its problems. They criticized superficial Westernism (*gharbzadegi*) and endorsed self-assertion and returning to one's authentic identity. Along with a show of commitment to systematic research, however, in this period an extremist and radical tendency to endorse the armed struggle also emerged among the younger generation of dissenting intellectuals, which continued through the revolution and beyond.

Theoretical and Methodological Issues

Modern intellectualism in Iran began to appear in the course of the nineteenth century and was primarily marked by a paradigm shift in the theoretical approach to reality. At the same time it was also a by-product of modern education. The opening of the first polytechnic institute (Dâr al-Fonoun) in the mid-nineteenth century provided one of the earliest venues for this new intellectual modernism. At the outset the very idea of an "intellectual" was problematic. It functioned as a typological demarcation, both implicitly and explicitly. Before the nineteenth century, learning was not altogether confined to Islamic seminaries; the Persian court tradition and Persian literature were also involved in the circulation of learned discourse. But neither took a partisan view in opposition to Islam, which was a cultural given and a way of life. Generating knowledge continued to be an engagement of Islamic colleges within their own agenda, though during the first half of the nineteenth century, theological debates at times ran over into the public domain. Examples are the Osouli-Akhbâri, Sheikhi, and Bâbi controversies on topics such as theology, gnosis, the use of human reason (*ʿaql*) and independent judgment in jurisprudence and the authority of the Shiʿi jurists, salvation history, and the nature of historical time.[6] However, apart from the institutional discourse of the Islamic learning current in the seminaries, and independent of any established genre of Islamic scholarship such as *tafsir* (interpretation), an intellectual language gradually developed that had links with the state, though it was not necessarily subservient to the state's quotidian interests or demands. This was the language of state officials and reform-minded courtiers.

Several factors contributed to its development. One was the recovery of centralized authority by the Qajar state (r. 1779–1925) toward the closing years of the eighteenth century. Although after the fall of the Safavid dynasty in the 1730s, a number of attempts were made to restore political authority in Iran, these attempts were either primarily nomadic and entangled in warfare, like the rule of Nâder (r. 1736–1747) and the relatively short tenure of the Afshârids in Khorâsân, or confined to certain parts of the country, like the government of Karim Khân Zand (r. 1750–1779) in Shiraz over central and southern Iran. Both of these were local and did not succeed in expanding their authority over Iran as a whole. It was not until the end of the eighteenth century that the first Qajar shah, Âqâ Mohammad Khân, began to restore a central authority that ultimately included most of the provinces of what had been the Safavid empire (c. 1501–1722).

The life of Âqâ Mohammad Khân (r. 1779–1797) was spent mostly on campaigns, but his nephew and successor Fath-Ali Shah (c. 1797–1834) enjoyed an established authority and a court with all its revived institutions. One group of the elite that at that time became associated with the established political authority sought to emulate the traditions of the Persian court and court literature. This sense of continuity in Persian institutions and the *idea* of Iran was not entirely new. Intellectuals idealized certain Iranian institutions in and around the royal court and fostered the idea of national consciousness. The Persian literati of Fath-Ali Shah's time included courtiers, poets and writers, administrators and chroniclers, Sufis and clerics.[7] The tradition of court patronage continued in this period and Fath-Ali Shah's own writings can in fact be regarded as an indicator of a broader trend. The current nationalist discourse of such circles had as its reference point, or paradigm, earlier periods and the tradition of high literature in Iran. These processes contributed to the diversity of literary and intellectual life during the first half of the nineteenth century.

Prose and verse, political writings by state bureaucrats, legal texts produced by the jurists, and a variety of theological, philosophical, and Sufi texts were written in an often-turgid style, but occasionally there were lucid and elegant exceptions.[8] Authors used the allusive style they regarded as a sign of high culture and learning or, in Sufi literature, as an indispensable ingredient of the esoteric quality of their texts. In philosophy, the turgid style of the Safavid era continued into the Qajar period.

The second stage in the development of the nationalist discourse in the royal court coincided with defeats at the hands of Russians in the 1810s and 1820s that touched off patriotic sentiments among reform-oriented courtiers. Abbas Mizrâ (1789–1833), Fath-Ali Shah's heir, was one such early figure. He, together with several like-minded officials, tried during the reign of Fath-Ali Shah to institute a program of rapid modernization of the army in order to restore Iran's land and revenues that had been lost to Russia. These and other early reformist ideas were primarily articulated within the court, and it was not long before they met with resistance from conservative elements at court; several of these reforms had to be abandoned.

Combined with the burdens of autocracy, such failures were gradually translated in the popular consciousness into a general notion of governmental incompetence. The resulting polarization between the notion of the people (*mellat*) and the state (*dowlat*) resulted in a *situational movement* in the making of the modern intellectual, which had more than just immediate or passing bearings on policy making. A significant consequence of this situational movement was a paradigm shift in the very act of intellectual practice. In other words, intellectualism as a volition began to be defined by individual intellectuals as a distinct stance, and possibly an act, with sociopolitical concerns and manifestations. Subsequently a segment of the nonmodern intellectual class in its broadest sense, which included the literati, the Sufi circles, the high-ranking officials, and the ulama, began to consider both the necessity and the desirability, including the justness, of social and political reforms or, at least, of change. Although none of these preferences were complete or irreversible, this situational transformation soon turned into a significant typological demarcation that separated the modern type from the nonmodern type. Before long, typological differences extended to further separations in life-style, manners, reading preferences, and self-image.

As the modern intellectual discourse became better known, it came to be identified as the most up-to-date channel for representing sociopolitical concerns. People from different walks of life and with different intellectual backgrounds (including the ulama and the philosophers), turned to this emerging modern intellectual discourse when the occasion demanded. This is not to argue that intellectual typology succeeded in absorbing all intellectual potentialities; the point, however, is that the quest for social justice and administrative reform became increasingly represented through the medium of modern intellectual discourse. This situation has direct methodological bearings for our analysis of the extent of intellectualism in the society. Intellectualism offered a new kind of continuously developing discourse that claimed the ability to articulate contemporary sociopolitical issues and demands. Therefore, people from other typologies, while retaining their own identity and self-image, could resort to intellectual discourse or, at times, to intellectual manners and forms, in order to express their own points of view. In other words, intellectual mannerisms and forms opened new vistas to different social types. The so-called religious-radical alliance of the late nineteenth century and the Constitutional movement of the early twentieth century referred to by some historians[9] can be explained in this light.

The ulama resorted to modern discourse to make their points. They accepted it as the political language of the day. Although the ulama regarded contemporary matters that involved the Europeans as temporary topics and not worthy of their earnest intellectual attention, they viewed their involvement in current affairs as their religious duty and social work as being "for God's sake" (*fi sabil Allâh*). Their awareness of modern affairs was often cursory and did not extend beyond the needs of their various constituencies. The structure and quality as well as the number of the ulama's theoretical and analytical writings show this lack of enthusiasm, but this sort of detachment and apathy was before long replaced by an equally superficial literature in opposition to Europe and things European, including the entire concept of modernity, or what they perceived it to be. Modernity was conceptualized as an *external phenomenon*. A similar attitude also persisted during the recent revolution in, for example, the use of the leftist intellectual vocabulary in Islamic political rhetoric. In other words, as long as the modern intellectual discourse could assist the spread of the ideological message, whatever that was, other groups (or types) would readily turn to it.

This does not mean that other groups or types had become intellectuals or had absorbed all aspects of the intellectual paradigm and discourse. A significant factor in this situation is the existence of a paradigmatic field in which different paradigms coexist. The ulama did not have to be "intellectuals" before they could begin to use intellectual discourse. In a paradigmatic field, values of each paradigm are in circulation in that field; that is how, in any given field, knowledge of different paradigms becomes possible and accessible to others, no matter how relative or limited such knowledge may be. As a whole, the paradigmatic field constitutes the given cultural milieu of a society. The mere awareness of other paradigms in a given field makes them, for all practical purposes, accessible. Again, from a methodological point of view, we can argue that several situations may arise in a paradigmatic field. In order to claim familiarity with a paradigm or a given cultural repertoire, or to consider oneself as having access to it, one's knowledge and motivation need not necessarily be based on empirical or documentary grounds.

In other words, people do not have to rely exclusively on an acquired body of direct knowledge and information regarding the paradigm or repertoire in question. Awareness of its existence and of its relationship to their own paradigm or to paradigms with which they are more familiar will provide them with enough confidence to regard the paradigms or repertoires in question as being accessible. This is also the case with paradigms of their own culture and typology, such as their assumed familiarity with and accessibility to their national literary and artistic heritage: people may not know minute details of such art or literature, but at any given moment, they regard that heritage as theirs and as accessible.

Intellectuals and the Problem of Classification

One methodological question in the study of intellectuals is how narrowly we should define their typological domain. If we categorize as intellectuals those who follow a modern vision, receive a modern education and identify themselves with the kind of knowledge that is the product of modern institutions, and subscribe to the modern style of criticism, then we have a problem in explaining the so-called religious intellectuals. Some who identified themselves with modern institutions also pointed to the merits of traditional seminaries and cautioned their fellow modernists against ignoring them. A dilemma arises from a fairly rigid interpretation of perspective. In the case of intellectuals, like any other social group, typological demarcations and variations of vision and perspective are not to be treated as fixed analytical or interpretive boundaries. Instead we are concerned with the multiplicity of attributes and preferential criteria. A given perspective is maintained not only through assertive axiology and conceptual cohesion, but also by an ability and willingness to occasionally avoid acting in predictable ways. Such multiplicity should not therefore be viewed as an anomaly with respect to cultural integrity and identity formation.

By the emergence of modern intellectualism in the nineteenth century, the modern secular and nationalist intellectual discourse had gradually become the standard medium for issues concerning the social and political aspects of the modern world, to such an extent that it was also used by intellectuals of the more traditional (or nonmodern) typology. For instance, a significant segment of the ulama supported the Constitutional movement without feeling the need for articulating and developing any exclusive discourse of their own pertaining to the conceptual principles or political objectives of the movement. As long as the intellectual discourse assumed the task of communicating the project of modernity, which included diverse areas of practice, for all practical purposes it furnished everyone with the necessary and contingent means of expression. That is why different components and even different versions of the intellectual discourse have been used by different social types in their experience of modernity.

This does not mean that other social groups made no effort to develop their own expressions of modernity, but only that in doing so they relied on the intellectual discourse and, at the same time, maintained their own image of authenticity. For instance, throughout the twentieth century, the ulama's reliance on the modernist discourse of the intellectuals was proportionately greater than their commitment to actively developing a new discourse that, both conceptually and terminologically, would correspond to their paradigm. One indication of this was their slim theoretical and textual contribution to the Constitutional movement, compared to their public visibility and political involvement. This also holds for those members of the ulama who, at different stages and in varying degrees, were critical of Constitutionalism. None of the notable authorities, such as Âkhound Mohammad-Kâzem Khorâsâni and Mirzâ Mohammad-Hosein Nâ'ini, who supported the Constitutional movement, or Sheikh Fazlollah Nouri, who came to oppose it, left any sophisticated theoretical contribution to the subject, as if too much intellectual involvement with mundane politics was beneath them and they did not wish to invest their scholarly energies in writing about such affairs. Nâ'ini's defense of Constitutionalism, which is one of the most articulate accounts of the compatibility of Islamic tenets and the modern state, is in essence formalistic and circumstantial.[10]

Nâ'ini intended to produce an argument for the adoption of Constitutionalism in Iran and wrote a simple and straightforward manifesto to support it. On the other hand, Nouri's later opposition was by and large caused by a personal grudge against individuals—notably against Seyyed Abdollâh Behbahâni, a leading pro-Constitutionalist mujtahid in Tehran—and particular events of the day, as can be seen in his communiqués, released while he was protesting at the Abd al-Azim sanctuary south of Tehran. The contrast is more glaring in the case of Khorâsâni, who is widely regarded as a major figure of Koranic exegesis and interpretation; he was a pro-Constitutionalist mujtahid residing in the 'Atabât whose political writings are also limited to telegrams and communiqués.

Writing about modern politics with a sense of theoretical involvement and personal commitment was a preoccupation of intellectuals that corresponded to the specific paradigm shift and to the situational transformation of the intelligentsia into a social type for whom politics appeared, in Max Weber's term, as a "vocation."[11] The ulama, on the other hand, were never convinced of the necessity or, more particularly, the legitimacy of such a paradigm shift. Consequently, their support for the popular movement and Constitutionalism was circumstantial rather than philosophical or intellectual.

~ 2 ~

Intellectuals in
the Constitutional Period

IT IS COMMONPLACE AMONG STUDENTS OF IRANIAN SOCIETY to trace any discussion of the significance or impact of modernity back to the nineteenth century, which is regarded as a period representing both the climax or most authentic phase of traditionalism and the beginning of the modern period. It was in reaction to the realities of the nineteenth century that modern ideas, such as ideas about social justice, and modern ways of life and of social interaction were established. But the arrival of new ways of life and commerce in Iran and the exposure to modern ideas, especially by the affluent and educated, are often misrepresented by contemporary scholars as being the antithesis of traditionalism; they see the triumph of modernity and the climax of traditionalism as mutually exclusive. It is inaccurate, however, simply to assume that the nineteenth century was a kind of prelude setting the stage for the twentieth. Many problems that confront twentieth-century Iran had their origins, or were already in place, in the nineteenth century.

From the perspective of intellectual history and the sociology of ideas, the nineteenth century seems to be a mixture of intellectual stagnation and vitality. For instance, in the late nineteenth century, the influential Muslim activist al-Afghani subscribed to the idea that a major factor contributing to the general backwardness of Muslim societies compared with the modern West was the decline of philosophy. For al-Afghani and his followers, any meaningful and enduring reform depended on a philosophical revival. A similar argument would be put forward in the twentieth century by many Muslim intellectuals and Western Orientalists. In a recent study of the history of political ideas in Iran, for example, it is even argued that Iran had no tradition of independent political philosophy, but only various political ideas invariably dominated by, and subservient to, the paradigms of either religion or autocracy, or both.[1]

It is true that although important debates and exchanges took place, such as the Osouli-Akhbâri controversy over the practice of independent juridical extrapolation (*ijtihâd*) in Islamic jurisprudence (*fiqh*) and the subsequent line of the Sheikhi school in Shi'ism, which adhered to a "literalist" (Akhbâri) rather than "rationalist" (Osouli) approach in exegesis and interpretation, philosophizing was on the decline in the nineteenth century.[2] Yet it was also a period when modern Western ideas were introduced, and one of the most important legacies of these ideas, both before and after the Constitutional movement of 1905, was the spread of a modern rationality that grew out of ideas associated with the Enlightenment. Over time, this new rationality reshaped Iranian society, notwithstanding all the inevitable ambiguities that surrounded its reception and its uneven distribution both across the society at large and in the context of individual personalities with allegedly modernist reputations. Parliamentary democracy came to be viewed as the most desirable form of political organization for society, free trade and economic nationalism were championed, and a gradual move toward a modified and moderate form of Europeanization became the goal.

These ideas and orientations, which began to emerge in the general context of Qajar society and in the Constitutional movement in particular, continued to have a significant impact on the political culture and the world outlook of the intelligentsia and are reflected, for example, in the ways in which national consciousness and patriotic sentiments were articulated in a Constitutional ideology and in the role given to Islamic institutions and a revised Shi'i discourse in popularizing national aspirations.

What is defined as "modern," however, never really became a standard or definite pattern of action, impression, or experience rooted in the society, and the experience of modernity varied. Thus, for instance, although liberals claimed to want a parliamentary democracy, in practice they showed little resistance to, and in fact even welcomed, the establishment of Pahlavi's autocracy after the almost two decades of social insecurity and political chaos that had followed the Constitutional movement, and a prevailing theme in the expression of social aspirations, political discourse, and the literature of that period, especially after the First World War, remained the quest for a centralized and powerful state.

Europeanization of manners and other forms of fashion were adopted equally cautiously and did not always occur at the expense of traditional attitudes or behavior. Similarly, in literature, the most successful patriotic poetry and prose of the Constitutional period, such as the writings of Mohammad-Taqi Bahâr, Iraj Mirzâ, and Abu al-Qâsem Âref of Qazvin, combined traditional patterns with modern ideas.

The uneasy coexistence of modernity and tradition lies behind many of the contradictions that characterized individual Iranian reformists and the reform movement as a whole. Even the intelligentsia itself, though a distinctly new social group, was never entirely free of the constraints of traditionalism. The word *intellectual* (in current Persian, *rowshanfekr*, literally, enlightened-minded) was in the nineteenth century more often *monavvar al-fekr* (with the same literal meaning);[3] it was used to refer to a wide variety of people who, despite differences in their social and cultural backgrounds, shared a common commitment to reform. The heterogeneity of this early group contrasts sharply with the predominantly middle-class intelligentsia of the Pahlavi era. But both differed from earlier literati, such as court secretaries or Sufi poets and writers, who were traditionally involved in the development of language. From the 1820s to the 1920s, members of the new intellectual class included courtiers and statesmen such as Amir Kabir, Sepahsâlâr, and Amin al-Dowleh; Muslim activists such as al-Afghani; royal princes such as Abbas Mirzâ, Soleymân Mirzâ Eskandari, and Iraj Mirzâ; and merchants such as Hâj Zein al-Âbedin Marâgheh'i and Abd al-Rahim Tâlebuf, all of whom were preoccupied with the ideas of social reform and the necessity of political change.

One of the earliest references to "intellectuals" was made by Mirzâ Âqâ Khân Kermâni, a radical activist and an admirer of the *philosophes* of the French Enlightenment, whom he describes as "*monavvar al-'oqoul*" (the enlighteners of minds) and "*râfe' al-khorâfât*" (the refuters of superstitions).[4] He writes, "If [only] ten learned [men] and philosophers emerge within a nation, they can be more fruitful to that nation than ten million ignorant and *mostaz'af* [impoverished] people."[5] Kermâni's reference to *monavvar al-'oqoul* appears to have introduced the term, which later became *monavvar al-fekr* and eventually gave way to *rowshanfekr*.[6]

During the Constitutional period, intellectuals were often also referred to as *motejaddedin* (modernists) or *ma'âref-parvarân* (educators). In contrast to the recent trend, in which intellectualism has become a term of abuse in the official propaganda of the Islamic regime, during the Constitutional movement, it was given particular status and value and lent prestige to the person so designated. Being a *monavvar al-fekr* was regarded as identical with being a nationalist, a reformist, a Constitutionalist, and, later, a modernist. Some of the ulama and their students at seminaries also began to view *monavvar al-fekr* as a positive attribute. In a pamphlet first published in Istanbul in 1910, Sheikh Asadollâh Mamaqâni, who had earlier been a pupil of Âkhound Khorâsâni, a prominent mujtahid in Najaf, after criticizing the political passivity of some of the ulama and theology students sitting in the quiet atmosphere of their schools, remarks that living in seclusion prevents people from being *monavvar al-afkar*, a quality he regarded as a prerequisite to achieving political and economic progress in the country and in Islam.[7]

Not everyone approved the term, however. The poet and literary scholar Bahâr ascribes the term *monavvar al-fekr* in his *Sabk-Shenâsi* (Stylistics), along with a number of other words and expressions, to the last quarter of the nineteenth century and points to it as an example of the decadence of Persian in that period, ascribing this decline to the influence of the daily press of the time, especially *Habl al-Matin* (Secure Cord), published in Calcutta, and *Iran-e Now* (New Iran), *Sharq* (The Orient), *Barq* (Lightning), and *Showrâ* (Council), published in Tehran. He argues that the pressure to publish on a daily basis left writers with no time for eloquence and style and their tendency to imitate European and Turkish writers reduced their originality even further. As a result, Bahâr argues, an unprecedented number of new terms, made from combining words of different linguistic origins and with different grammatical structures, had found their way into the Persian language and had gradually become current in everyday usage. *Monavvar al-fekr* was one such neologism.[8]

Bahâr's reference to the role of journalists and the daily press testifies to the considerable increase in the number of journals and newspapers in the Constitutional period; several writers and poets even became professional journalists. It was during this period as well that modern intellectuals began to develop into an independent group, detached from the traditional sources of support such as religious institutions and the court. As a result of these two developments in the course of the nineteenth century, the initiative for developing the language gradually shifted away from both court secretaries (*ahl-e divân*) and, broadly, mystic or gnostic writers and poets (*ahl-e ʿerfân*) and was assumed by the newly emerging intellectuals who were professional writers (*rowshanfekrân-e ahl-e qalam*).[9]

The literature of the Constitutional movement exemplifies this development of writing with a social and political orientation. Political poetry, satire, and critical journalism constituted a remarkable body of

Persian literature in the late nineteenth century and the Constitutional period. Authors such as Ali-Akbar Dehkhodâ, Nasim-e Shomâl, Iraj Mirzâ, Bahâr, Âref, Farrokhi Yazdi, and Mirzâdeh Eshqi all produced critical and patriotic work that testifies to the vitality and importance of that literature. The fact that each, perhaps with the exception of Dehkhodâ, was first and foremost a poet, suggests that in its early phase, poetry was an effective literary medium. Poetry's effectiveness lay mainly in the fact that it was still composed in accordance with traditional meters familiar to the public and its themes and overall imagery were structured around familiar topics of current concern—social justice, political integrity, and a quest for cultural enlightenment and general prosperity, for example.[10]

The reformist ideals of the Constitutional movement also found their expression in a generation of critical tracts (*resâleh*), clandestine papers (*shab-nâmeh*), and the press (*rouz-nâmeh* and *majalleh*). Political writings, such as newspapers, leaflets, tracts, and pamphlets, enjoyed a growing popularity among the literate public who became the new patrons for writers. New ideas were introduced and debated. Periodicals with varying foci and ideological stances, such as *Habl al-Matin* (Secure Cord), *Nasim-e Shomâl* (Northern Breeze), and *Sour-e Esrâfil* (The Trumpet-Call of Isrâfil [the Angel of Resurrection]) in the Constitutional period and *Bahâr* (Spring), *Ra'd* (Thunder), *Barq* (Lightning), *Shafaq-e Sorkh* (Red Twilight), *Toufân* (Storm), *Now-Bahâr* (New Spring), and *Daneshkadeh* (The Place of Knowledge) in the post-Constitutional period, were among the more influential publications.

In many cases, the authors of this literature were political activists writing from exile. Their works were occasionally published with the financial support and sponsorship of some of Iran's merchant families, many of whom lived abroad, tending their commercial offices in the major cities of India, Russia, and the Ottoman Empire.[11] In addition to importing goods and capital, these merchants also helped the spread of modernism by providing an extended social network through which some ideas and fashions current in foreign cities could gradually reach Iran. In the 1930s, at the climax of Reza Shah's Westernization programs, many of these families were welcomed back to Iran and their image was presented to the urban public as a desirable example of modernity. In turn, they soon filled the newly opened cafés, regularly attended thés dansants and soirees at the Grand Hotels, sent their children to piano classes, and joined the tennis clubs. However, around the turn of the century, the three main exchange and communication routes between

Iran and the outside were Bushire-Bombay, Rasht-Baku, and, most important, Tabriz-Istanbul.[12]

While ideas of nationalism and liberal democracy had come to Iran through Ottoman Turkey and British India, respectively, the more radical socialist and communist ideas were imported from Russia (via the Rasht-Baku circuit mentioned above). The earliest contacts between Russian and Iranian intellectuals can be traced back to Fath-Ali Âkhoundzâdeh and, later, to ʿAbdol-Rahim Tâlebof. Iranian workers in the Caucasus, mainly in and around the oilfields, were a conduit for these ideas, as were Iranian merchants, who by the late nineteenth century had established commercial bureaus in Baku, Tiflis, and other trading centers in the Caucasus.[13] There was also considerable contact between Iranian merchants and intellectuals living in Ottoman Turkey (mainly in Istanbul) and their compatriots in southern Russia (in Baku, Tiflis, and elsewhere in the southern Caucasus).[14]

As a result of the importation of socialist theory and ideology, the language of political discourse in Iran was further changed. New expressions were added to and sometimes even replaced the terminology inspired by the European traditions of economic liberalism and parliamentary democracy, and the ideas they conveyed soon presented a challenge to Western liberalism. For instance, before the Constitutional movement, the term *enqelâb* (revolution, literally, inversion[15]) had a somewhat negative connotation. Supporters of Constitutionalism often outlined their programs as necessary to "avoid revolution," by which they meant crisis or chaos,[16] and were more apt to use the French term *révolution* to refer to a radical sociopolitical transformation of which they approved.[17] Later, after the establishment of the Parliament (Majles), and also following the circulation of socialist ideas, use of the term *enqelâb* for the revolution became associated with radicalism and progress. Literary circles began to talk of a "literary revolution" in poetry and prose; in 1909, a periodical entitled *Yâdegâr-e Enqelâb* (Memorial of the Revolution) was founded by Moʿtamed al-Islam Rashti in Qazvin; after the victory of the Constitutionalists, it was moved to Tehran.[18] This was followed in 1915 by *ʿAsr-e Enqelâb* (Age of Revolution) and later *ʿAhd-e Enqelâb* (Epoch of Revolution). The socialist poet and journalist Mohammad Farrokhi Yazdi wrote that *enqelâb* was the inevitable and justified means to secure freedom and social justice; in a *rubâʿi* (quatrain), he referred to himself as an *enqelâbi* (revolutionary).[19]

Along with revolution, a popular theme in the literature of the time, especially in the post-Constitutional period, was a desire for the establishment of a powerful central state capable of unifying and protecting the country, often accompanied by a romantic account of the country's ancient glories. Even after the spread of Islam in Iran, the pre-Islamic culture continued to constitute a rich reserve of symbols and myths for writers and ordinary people alike.[20] For pioneering reformists, ancient Iran was not merely a depository of myths but a historical period during which Iran had enjoyed power and a high culture, both clearly absent in contemporary society.

Western Orientalists, travelers, colonial agents, and other foreigners played an important role in this revival of interest in ancient Iran. In the 1840s, Henry Rawlinson (1810–1895), a British military officer interested in the history of Mesopotamia, succeeded in reading the inscriptions at Bistoun, the first time that an ancient Persian inscription had been deciphered.[21] He presented a copy of his translation to Mohammad Shah (r. 1834–1848), who apparently received it with enthusiasm and interest. The Qajars, who earlier in their rule had stressed their Turkic origins,[22] now sought to trace their lineage back to Iran's own past. An indication of this tendency can be found in, for example, Fath-Ali Shah's several rock reliefs and inscriptions, in the pre-Islamic Persian style, at Firouzkouh, Kâzeroun, Tâq-e Bostân, and Cheshmeh Ali in Rey. He also gave tribal and Islamic names to his eldest sons but began to shift to pre-Islamic Persian names for the younger ones.[23] The Qajars also began to imitate ancient ceremonies. An account of Âqâ Mohammad Khân's coronation, in 1796, relates that he was dressed in an arm band and fittings, held a sword, and wore a crown described as Tâj-e Kiâni, the legendary crown of ancient Iranian kings, inlaid with jewels.[24] Before then, an Iranian shah wore a turban or hat decorated with feathers and precious stones, rather than a crown.[25]

For the reformists, the accuracy of knowledge concerning Iran's past was less important than the potential impact a revival of the past could have in shaping the present. Ancient Iran became yet another ideological element the reformists could use to criticize the backwardness of the country. In 1874, Mirzâ (Mohammad-) Ebrâhim Khân Badâye'-Negâr, a court chronicler who was a contemporary of Mohammad Shah and Nâser al-Din Shah (r. 1848–1896), wrote as follows:

It has been four hundred years since the New World was discovered. At the beginning people there numbered two million and all were savage and in the shape of beasts and brutes. Now it has nearly a hundred million people, with so much wealth and strength and prestige and grandeur that one can say they have become the first people and the first state on earth. Here comes the last [in the line], the state of Iran, with at least eight thousand years of precedence. There it is, the country of Keyqobâd, and Jamshid, and Fereydoun. Now, what has happened to make it the most humiliated state on earth, trampled underfoot by everyone, even [by] the Afghans and the Turkmans?[26]

The passage exemplifies the typical themes of a reformist orientation: comparing the weakness of Iran's present with its glorious past and with the successes of the West and wondering what was actually responsible for that state of affairs.

In the Qajar period, modern notions of nation and nationalism also came in from the West. The words used for these terms in Persian include *mihan, vatan, keshvar, mellat, qowm,* and *umma* for nation; *mihani, vatani, keshvari, melli,* and *qowmi* for national; and *mihani, vatani,* and *melli* for nationalist. But they do not always fully correspond to their English equivalents.[27] *Mihan, vatan,* and *keshvar* mean native country or fatherland and denote geographical space; *mihani* and *vatani* could be considered to be the same as patriotic. *Keshvar* refers to a country with certain territorial borders. *Mellat* refers to the mass of people who inhabit the fatherland, except those who were at the service of the state (*dowlat*). There has been a long-standing conceptual difference and tension between the terms *dowlat* (the state) and *mellat* (the nation or the people), reflecting the larger historical reality of the despotic structure of political power.

Classifying the country's population into *melli* and *dowlati* emphasizes their respective relationships to the established power.[28] Such a conceptual dichotomy has not been a general trait of Iranian political culture, however. During the tenure of "popular" governments, such as those of Amir Kabir and Sepahsâlâr in the nineteenth century and Mosaddeq in the twentieth, there was a considerable improvement in the relationship between the people and the state, thus refuting the fatalistic view of the irreconcilability of Iranians with the phenomenon of *dowlat,* as such. A similarly simplistic but widely held notion is the idea that religion, Shi'ism in particular, has often been responsible for alienating people from the state. Although Shi'ism has strong theoretical principles that tend to undermine the state, in reality it was primarily the despotic deeds of governments that undermined the loyalty of the people.

Prior to the period under consideration, terms such as *mihan, vatan,* and *umma* were also widely used to express religious, mystical, or even

mythical meanings of country and community. Classical Persian literature and folklore provide a rich reserve of examples of such usage.[29]
During the Qajar period and on the eve of the Constitutional movement, *mellat* and *vatan* became the subject of patriotic poetry, in such accessible forms as the street ballad and prose, including political satire,
plays with social content, critical essays, and journalism.[30] This growing
public articulation and celebration of national consciousness, expressed
in terms of a general spirit of patriotism, reinforced the drive for reform.
Individual reformists and statesmen, such as Abbas Mirzâ, Amir Kabir,
Sepahsâlâr, and Amin al-Dowleh, assisted the movement in its early
stages, convinced that the prolonged scientific and technological stagnation of the country was a major obstacle to progress. To the best of their
abilities, and according to the opportunities open to them, they sought
to alter that course. Foreign military advisers were engaged to train and
reorganize the Persian army in accordance with modern standards, and
Western technicians were recruited.[31]

Amir Kabir and Sepahsâlâr pushed for the construction of the Dâr al-
Fonoun, a modern polytechnic institute founded in 1851,[32] and the establishment of a printing house and an official newspaper, *Vaqâye'e Ette-
fâqiyeh* (News), whose first issue appeared in 5 Rabi' II 1267 A.H./7
January 1851.[33] Amir Kabir realized that the rigid political structure was
at the center of many of the country's problems and, during his short
tenure as prime minister (1848–1851) before falling victim to a court
conspiracy, was contemplating certain fundamental reforms to the system.[34] Pioneering reformists in Iran, despite their ideological differences,
were united in their support for change. They identified as a national
cause opposition to despotism, independence from the intervention and
influence of foreign interests, reform, and progress.

Simultaneously, another reformist trend developed whose prime fo-
cus centered on the subjective, spiritual, and cultural life of Iranians and
that regarded the invasion of foreign influences as being at the core of
corruption, then as always throughout the country's eventful history.
Compared to some other Middle Eastern societies, such as Ottoman
Turkey or Egypt, Iran was relatively isolated from the modern West.
Apart from occasional contacts between European diplomats and the
Persian royal court, for example, in the Safavid period (1501–1722) and
during the rule of Nâder (1736–1747), European influence had not been
a factor in Iran until the early part of the nineteenth century, beginning
in the reign of Fath-Ali Shah (r. 1797–1834).[35]

Another factor mitigating Iran's exposure to external cultural influences was its relatively rural character.[36] Ottoman and some Arab societies were, by comparison, far more urban[37] and, in addition, their cities held sizable communities of foreigners[38] and people of different religions, especially Christians and Jews, both of whom were particularly likely to be exposed to Western ideas and to advancing modern industries and techniques.[39] In Iran, Christians and Jews were usually on the margin of the society, and foreigners were always isolated.[40]

The initial reception given to the Europeans was not, however, hostile. When Henry Martyn (1781–1812), a British missionary, went to Iran in 1811 to finish his earlier Persian translation of the Bible (a completed copy of which was presented to Fath-Ali Shah by the ambassador Sir Gore Ouseley in 1812), he was well received, especially in Shiraz, and was referred to as "Mollâ Martyn." Sir Robert Ker Porter's *Travels* provides an early account of Martyn's residence in Shiraz:

> [*Henry Martyn*] *dwelt there nearly a year; and on leaving its walls, the apostle of Christianity found no cause for "shaking off the dust of his feet" against the Mahomedan city. The inhabitants had received, cherished, and listened to him; and he departed thence amidst the blessings and tears of many a Persian friend. Through his means, the Gospel had then found its way into Persia; and as it appears to have been sown in kindly hearts, the gradual effect hereafter, may be like the harvest to the seedling. But, whatever be the issue, the liberality with which his doctrines were permitted to be discussed, and the hospitality with which their promulgator was received by the learned, the nobles, and persons of all ranks, cannot but reflect lasting honour on the government, and command our respect for the people at large.*[41]

Henry Martyn's colorful, if dubious, refutations of Islam led several of his opponents, including Mirzâ Mohammad-Ebrâhim, a mujtahid in Shiraz, to produce tracts of varying quality in defense of their own religion.[42] Among the more intelligent responses to Martyn was *Irshâd al-Muzellin fi Ithbât-i Nobuwwat-i Khâtam al-Nabi'in* (Directing the Misguided to the Path by Proving the Prophethood of the Seal of the Prophets), a tract by the prominent Sufi Mollâ Mohammad-Reza Hamedâni, known as Kowsar-Alishâh,[43] which probably was written at the request of Fath-Ali Shah.[44]

It was not long, however, before tolerance was replaced by zealotry, even xenophobia. The wars with Russia during the reign of Fath-Ali Shah that, despite the efforts of Crown Prince Abbas Mirzâ, had resulted in a series of defeats in 1813 and 1828, and the resulting loss of territory, made the Persian court realize the country's backwardness in military and technological matters.[45] In addition, these defeats affected the Iranian view of the West. The previous mixture of self-confidence and relative tolerance was replaced by a sense of resignation regarding Western progress in modern industry and material achievements. Continued political and economic setbacks also contributed to the evaporation of the earlier spirit of tolerance. An early example was the assassination of A. S. Griboyedov, the Russian ambassador in Tehran, and the slaughter of nearly all members of his staff, on 6 Sha'bân 1244 A. H./11 February 1829, at the hands of a mob that attacked the embassy as a result of anti-Russian agitation.[46] Toward the end of the century there was public protest against the tobacco concession granted to the Regie Company, signed at Tehran on 20 March 1890, which resulted in its cancellation in December 1891.[47] On these occasions, rejection of Western political and economic encroachment was accompanied by a passionate rejection of Western social and cultural forms combined with an idealized version of Iranian history and culture. The Return Movement in Persian literature in the first half of the nineteenth century is another example of this reaction. Its prime concern was to revive and uphold classical standards.[48]

Among the nationalist reformers, a return to ancient roots was simply a necessary step toward regaining cultural integrity, without which modern progress would be virtually impossible. Purification of Iranian culture from foreign elements appeared to be the first task. The initial targets were in fact not Western but Arabic-influenced elements that had been incorporated into the language and religion in Iran. Attempts to purify the language appeared earlier than direct attacks on religion, not least because of the fear of public reaction. For example, two of Fath-Ali Shah's sons, 'Abbâs Mirzâ and Jalâl al-Din Mirzâ, were both noted for having strong nationalist feelings.[49] Jalâl al-Din Mirzâ wrote a book in three volumes on the history of Iran from the time of Keyoumars (the first legendary king) until the death of Nâder and the end of the Afshârids (mid-eighteenth century), entitled *Nâmeh-ye Khosrovân* (The Book of Kings). It represents one of the earliest attempts during the Qajar period to purify the language from foreign, mainly Arabic, words and to simplify the style of writing.[50] Another early figure was the poet Yaghmâ, who was also known for his prose style, which was distinguished by his use of Persian vocabulary.[51]

Another "language purifier" was Mirzâ Reza Khân Afshâr Qazvini, councillor and chargé d'affaires to the Persian embassy at Istanbul and the author of *Parvaz-e Negâresh-e Pârsi* (The Principal Method of Writing Persian), published in 1883; it was a manual designed to show its users how to write various kinds of letters using only allegedly pure Persian phraseology. The current equivalents of many recommended words were also given by the author in the margin of each page.[52] Other prominent figures in this effort to purify the language were secular reform-minded critics, authors, and political activists like Mirzâ Fath-Ali Âkhoundzâdeh, Mirzâ Âqâ Khân Kermâni, Hâj Zein al-Âbedin Marâgheh'i, 'Abdol-Rahim Tâlebof, Mirzâ Malkam Khân, and Mirzâ Yousef Khân Mostashâr al-Dowleh. Âkhoundzâdeh went so far as to advocate changing the way Persian was written by replacing the Arabic alphabet with the Latin one.[53]

Ironically, it was not long before these early efforts to purify the Persian language from Arabic words fell prey to another extreme, namely, the excessive use of European, mainly French, terms. Perhaps French vocabulary was viewed as an inevitable, and therefore justifiable, vehicle of modernity.

The Concept of Mashrutiyat (Constitutionalism)

Where the term *Mashrutiyat* comes from is unclear. Many authors contemporary to the movement used the term in its literal sense of "conditional";[54] others argued that it derived not from the Arabic word *shart* (condition), but from the French word *le charte* (charter), which had entered Iran via Ottoman Turkey.[55] In his Persian lexicon, Ali-Akbar Dehkhodâ, a veteran of the Constitutional movement, writes: "The term *mashrutiyat* was used neither in Arabic nor in Persian. . . . [T]his word came into the Persian language via the Ottoman Turks, and indicates the rule of law; it is synonymous with the French word '*constitution.*'"[56] Still others objected to the term *mashruteh* being identified with the French word *constitution*, maintaining that the former was a mistaken translation of the latter, and that the term *constitution* should have been retained in its original French form in order to prevent intentional misinterpretation by the reactionaries.[57] Taqi-zâdeh reports that one of the ulama of Tabriz, Âqâ Mirzâ Sâdeq Âqâ, suggested that the original French term *constitution* should be used in Iran. He reasoned that if the Arabic term *mashruteh* (which can be used to mean conditional) were to be employed by the ulama, they might come up with the idea that the new regime should be under the condition of having no freedom or of being under the rule of the ulama.[58] Today, the etymology of *mashruteh* is still the subject of discussion in Iran as it is in Turkey.[59] Whatever it means, the idea behind it was to challenge *motlaqiyat* (absolutism) and *estebdâd* (despotism), and for that reason it was a fundamental element in the reformist consciousness as a whole.[60]

Before the Constitutional movement, the majority of programs for reform had been initiated from above and had failed to accomplish their aims. The single biggest obstacle to reform was the arbitrary structure of political power in Qajar Iran. Reform measures were vulnerable to arbitrary intervention that could either delay them or eliminate them altogether. Since most reform initiatives were dependent on, and identified with, the person of the reformer, when that person was no longer in power, his plans were summarily abandoned. That is why the history of reform in Iran over the last 150 years or so has been marked by repeated ruptures. The result was to stigmatize reformism as an abject failure. Until the advent of the Constitutional period, the Iranian people remained disillusioned and doubtful about the possibility of success of any official plan for reform.[61] Thus, achieving any long-term or fundamental change would require, among other things, overcoming this stigma.

Many explanations have been offered as to why the Constitutional movement began in the first place. Analyses inspired by Soviet Marxism argue that it was simply another step in the continuous anticolonialist campaign of the "Eastern peoples" based on the class struggle. However, as a result of bourgeois influence, the movement eventually suffered setbacks.[62] After the recent revolution in Iran, it became the official opinion that Constitutionalism was originally a religious movement that was gradually manipulated and corrupted by an unholy alliance between Western colonialists, through their local agents in Christian missions and Masonic secret societies, and secular intellectuals infatuated with Western values.[63]

Although Constitutionalism involved a fragile alliance between reformist intellectuals and some of the ulama,[64] the degree to which the Constitutionalist movement was assisted by the clergy is a matter of debate.[65] Among mainstream Iranian historians, the role of the secular reformists has received more systematic attention than that of the ulama. Reformist members of the ulama included Seyyed Mohammad Tabâtabâ'i; the preacher Âqâ Seyyed Jamâl al-Din Isfahani, active inside Iran; and some residents in the 'atabât, the Shi'a centers of Iraq, such as Âkhound Mohammad-Kâzem Khorâsâni, Hâj Sheikh 'Abdollâh Mâzandarâni, and the most articulate of all, Mirzâ Mohammad-Hosein Nâ'ini, but their role in the Constitutional movement has been underplayed by some historians. For instance, Kasravi admits that the leadership was in the hands of the ulama, but the main credit, he insists, goes to "the unknown masses."[66] Malekzâdeh, on the other hand, stresses the significance of certain reformist and revolutionary personalities and leaders who were active in political societies (*anjomans*), most of whom came from within the ranks of the ulama or had clerical backgrounds.[67]

Âdamiyat explains the movement primarily in terms of the contribution made by the secularist intellectuals who had embraced Western-style ideas of reform, progress, and social change. According to Âdamiyat, the "Mashrutiyat national movement" can be classified as part of the "freedom-seeking movements of the urban middle class," its main ideological elements consisted of political democracy and parliamentary liberalism, and its major supporters were "the intelligentsia, both reformist and revolutionary, progressive merchants, and the enlightened clergy." The intelligentsia were all from the ranks of modern educated people who favored Western-style political reasoning, opposed old political principles, and advocated a parliamentary system for Iran, and their intellectual standpoint was based on, and inspired by, the "ideas of the Great French Revolution."[68]

Âdamiyat views merchants' collaboration with the intelligentsia and their participation in the Constitutional movement as being a result of increases in their prosperity and security, caused by the growth in trade and other economic activities. This in turn led them to seek to achieve a more prestigious social position and wider opportunities. The involvement of the merchants was particularly significant because the bazaar was the economic center of every town and was controlled by the major merchants (*tujjâr*) and various guilds (*asnâf*).[69] On the question of the ulama's participation in the movement, Âdamiyat writes that, because of the "influence, inspiration, and popularity of the ideas of the freedom-seeking intellectuals, the clergy leaned towards Constitutionalism and, as a result, gave a religious interpretation and fundamental justification to the concept of Mashrutiyat.[70] Âdamiyat adds that, by participating in the movement, the ulama wanted to establish clerical supremacy, and he maintains that they did not believe in a parliamentary system or in rational politics.[71]

The real significance of the contribution of the pro-Constitutionalist ulama was in the way they tried to elaborate a Constitutional theory in accordance with a new approach to Islamic and, more specifically, Shi'i principles. The intellectual background for such a contribution had been laid down in earlier debates in Islamic political theory.[72] Nevertheless, the ulama's participation in the Constitutional movement and their support of the secular reformists during the early phases of that movement should not be interpreted to mean that they were fully influenced by and had absorbed the Western-style ideas and motifs of the intellectuals. On the contrary, the ulama had neither absorbed those ideas nor, as Âdamiyat argues, were in favor of such notions. They were not, in the narrow sense of the term, "intellectuals," and they did not come into contact with Constitutional ideas via the same channels as the intellectuals had. What bound them to the movement, and for a time made them allies with the secular reformists, was their belief in the necessity of overcoming the political incompetence of the Qajar state.

Challenging absolutism and arbitrary rule had to be accompanied by necessary measures and proposals as to how arbitrary political power should be controlled and regulated. It was around this theme that the idea of law applied to preserve social justice came into being. Unsurprisingly, therefore, the first demand articulated by Constitutionalists, as well as by those who had reformist aspirations, was for the establishment of a council of grievances ('edâlat-khwâneh, literally, house of justice).[73] Although both groups were united in this, it was also on the question of law that differences emerged between them.

The secular reformists based their conception of law on legacies of the French Revolution.[74] Most tended to dissociate religion from politics; some, such as Mirzâ Fath-Ali Âkhoundzâdeh, roundly rejected religion in general and Islam in particular. Still, in the early phases of the Constitutional movement, the overall attitude of such modernists toward Islam was a combination of acceptance, caution, tolerance, and pragmatism. This approach is clear in the works of Mirzâ Malkam Khân (1833–1908), one of the best known of the secular reformers.[75] Malkam was in many ways typical of the newly emerging intellectuals, with his preference for Western ideas and values. His view of Islam suggests that he did not grasp the implications of its fundamental role in Persian society, nor its inherent tension with modernity. Instead, he saw Islam simply as instrumental in bringing about a program of political action.[76] Commenting to the English poet and traveler Wilfred Blunt on his own earlier reform activities, Malkam admitted that he simply "determined to clothe my material reformation in a garb which my people would understand, the garb of religion."[77]

One serious drawback to this pragmatic, somewhat cavalier, approach to religion was that neither Malkam nor his fellow reformists were able to develop and sustain a coherent theory of national reform. Malkam's newspaper, *Qânoun* (Law), did, however, have an important impact on the educated and intellectual elite of Iran and was effective in the promotion of Constitutionalist ideas. In 1888 Malkam was involved in a scandal over the Lottery Concession in London. As a result, he was dismissed by Nâser al-Din Shah and recalled to Tehran. He ignored the summons, stayed in London, and became engaged in the politics of opposition to the Iranian regime. The publication of *Qânoun*, financed by the fortunes made in the lottery affair, may have been Malkam's way of restoring his damaged reputation in Iran. The first issue of *Qânoun* appeared in London on 20 February 1890; in all, there were forty-one issues, about one per month.[78]

The pro-Constitutional ulama approached the question of law in society and the role of religion from an altogether different perspective. The ulama and those who became known as the Islamic reformists believed in the necessity of law, but of a kind that had to be not only compatible with Islam but also entirely derived from it. The ulama viewed Islam as an eternal and universally valid source of legislation. Accordingly, their task was to discover from the Koranic teachings appropriate laws suitable for present-day society. For them the stagnation and backwardness of Islamic societies, as compared with Western Christian countries, was a result, not of adhering to Islamic law, but of paying inadequate attention to Islam. The ulama believed that catching up with European civilization could come only through religious revival. The progress and developments that had already taken place in Christian countries constituted a theme in several tracts and treatises written by the ulama in support of Mashrutiyat.[79] Modernization, for the clerical faction supporting it, was to be undertaken in order to enable Muslims to stand up to European countries; it was not viewed as something that would weaken their own culture or religion. On the contrary, it would be a buttress, strengthening it by new means and methods.

By the late nineteenth and early twentieth centuries, Islamic revivalism captured the attention of many within the Islamic societies. Figures like al-Afghani, Sheikh Mohammad 'Abdoh, Mohammad Rashid Reza, 'Abdol-Rahman Kawâkebi, and Ali 'Abdol-Razzâq made substantial contributions to the ideological foundations of this movement.[80] Of these revivalists, al-Afghani was the most influential; he inspired several anti-European movements in the Middle East.[81] In Iran his ideas influenced both the ulama and the emerging secular reformists. One of the basic themes in al-Afghani's approach to Islam was the importance of *'aql*

(reason). He viewed philosophy as necessary for the survival and historical continuity of cultures and civilizations, and 'aql as the very essence of
philosophical practice.[82] The backwardness of Islamic societies, as compared to the progress of Christian societies, was primarily caused by the
suspension of philosophical reasoning:

> *If philosophy does not exist in an umma [community], but all the members*
> *of that umma held to particular sciences those sciences would not survive in*
> *that umma for [even] one century, for, without the spirit of philosophy, it*
> *would be impossible for that umma to derive any result from those sciences.*
> *It has been sixty years since the Ottoman state and the Egyptian khedives*
> *opened [modern] schools in order to teach the new sciences [to their people],*
> *but so far they have not benefited from those sciences, the reason being that*
> *in these schools the "philosophical" sciences are not taught. And since there*
> *is no spirit of philosophy, these sciences have borne no fruit for them. Un-*
> *doubtedly if during these sixty years there had been a spirit of philosophy*
> *in those schools they could have made themselves independent from the*
> *belâd-e farang [the West] and they could have tried to reform their coun-*
> *tries in accordance with science, and would not have had to send their chil-*
> *dren every year to European countries in order to be educated. . . . The first*
> *defect in every decaying umma has occurred in the philosophical spirit [of*
> *that umma] and then that defect has penetrated into its sciences, manners,*
> *and institutions.*[83]

Al-Afghani urged Islamic societies, for their own survival, to promote
and revive philosophical reasoning in their contemporary teachings and
discourse. Toward the end of his famous treatise, entitled *Haqiqat-e
Mazhab-e Neycheri* (The Truth of Naturalist Doctrine), he notes three
conditions for bringing about "the elevation of communities to stages of
perfection and to their complete and true bliss." These are, first, the
purification of people's *lowh-e 'oqoul* (minds) from the burden of super-
stition; second, respect for human individuality and status; and third,
reestablishment of religious faith on the basis of *'aql va dalil* (reason and
proof) and abstention from blind imitation.[84]

Al-Afghani's adherence to philosophy sometimes put him at odds
with religion. For instance, in his discussions with some European Orientalists who thought that the "unscientific Arab mentality" was to
blame for Islamic decline, al-Afghani responded that the main cause
should be sought, not in race, but in religious prejudice. He maintained

that "all [religions] resemble one another. No agreement and no reconciliation are possible between these religions and philosophy. Religion imposes on man its faith and its belief, whereas philosophy makes him free totally or in part."[85]

In his search for ways to make philosophy more concrete and accessible, and thus transform it into a social force, al-Afghani did not hesitate to turn to religion, for he was clearly aware of its social function and political potential. In his lectures and teachings in Muslim countries, he betrayed no doubts about religion, and he used Islam for political mobilization. In this respect, his approach was similar to Mirzâ Malkam Khân's. In fact he was a frequent contributor to *Qânoun*. In al-Afghani's case, however, it was the style of his political practice, more than its content, that proved problematic. His approach involved a near-obsession with daily politics. This style, despite achieving some immediate successes, was harmful to the development of a cultural tradition capable of generating a concrete political consciousness in response to modern realities, especially in a country like Iran, whose recent history had been marked by ruptures.

The obsession with agitation and short-term politics remained a salient characteristic of many modern Iranian intellectuals and political activists. Hence, "the main weakness of Islamic modernism" can be identified as the

> *excessive concern with politics at the expense of facing some fundamental issues in the relationship between Islam and the modern world. This was perhaps an inevitable requirement of the fight against imperialism in the nineteenth century. But what proved later to be more harmful was some of the modernists' special style of politicking. Since the Muslim masses at that time were much more ignorant than they are today, and the literate and enlightened elite who had the capacity to lead their struggle for independence was tiny and powerless, some modernists, and most notably Jamal ad-Din, often saw their best chance of achieving their progressive ideals in appealing to traditional rulers. When this did not work, they resorted to conspirational politics (Jamal ad-Din is reported to have expressed his belated regret that instead of such manoeuvers with Sultans and Amirs, he had not directly appealed to the people themselves). Subsequent generations of modernists inherited all these weaknesses from the pioneers. Thus intellectual renaissance was sacrificed to political activism, and clique intrigues took the place of the political education of the masses.[86]*

Another characteristic of al-Afghani's thinking that had enduring effects was its strong anti-European bias, which was largely a reaction to the colonial practices of the Europeans. Combined with a charismatic personality, he was able to advance two of his aims: a more rapid mobilization of Muslims in order to catch up with the technological achievements of Christian countries and the undermining of Nâser al-Din Shah, whom he blamed both for being too passive and powerless in his relationships with European powers and for being overly enchanted with European (*farangi*) material culture. But this effectiveness must be measured against the larger and more negative influence al-Afghani had on political thought in his own and later times. It is undeniable that during the colonial period, Western Christian organizations attempted to enhance Western influence through missionaries; nevertheless, the real aim of European expansionism was not religious but economic. It was derived from the systematic function of industrial capitalism, which al-Afghani must surely have known. His encounters with merchants would have been sufficient to acquaint him with the effects of Western capitalism and its expansion, but he also had the advantage of a close acquaintance with sophisticated intellectuals in the Middle East as well as in Europe. Yet by interpreting, or rather misinterpreting, the reality of Western politics in religious terms, he encouraged a rigid xenophobia among Muslims, and especially among Iranians, who had comparatively little direct knowledge of the West.

After an earlier close relationship with the Qajar court, al-Afghani became disillusioned regarding the possibility of reform originating from the court, and it was he who inspired and subsequently endorsed the assassination of Nâser al-Din Shah in 1896. This vacillation between extreme tactics did nothing to help the public to understand the structural obstacles to reform and the rigidity of political power in Iran. It also failed to encourage the Muslim society to attain more direct knowledge of the historical exigencies of contemporary Western civilization and thus prolonged a rigid, hostile attitude in popular sentiments toward the West.

As pointed out above, during the Constitutional period, the necessity of applying and preserving law in the society was a general, unifying theme. Gradually, however, this same theme led to division. Since the image of law for the secular reformists was derived primarily from the tradition of the French Enlightenment and the Revolution that followed, a modern notion of individual rights lay at its core. The main source of law for the reformist Shi'a thinkers was the Shari'a and the principles of Islamic jurisprudence (*fiqh*), in which the notion of justice ('*adl*) theoretically had a central place. It was possible for these two divergent theoretical and ideological lines to coexist as long as their advocates were campaigning against despotism and the arbitrary power of the court, but once the Constitutional revolution had occurred in 1905, the differences between them came to the surface.

In their support of Constitutionalism, the ulama justified certain political concepts as being in accordance with Shi'i tenets. In the later pro-Constitutional arguments by the ulama, special attention was paid to the role of reason ('*aql*), which, though distinct from the modern concept of rationality, also differed from its more traditional and scholastic versions. Here, as before, reason was employed to reflect upon and search for verdicts regarding present questions by taking into account contemporary exigencies. The problem was that the new exigencies could not be accommodated within the traditional criteria of religious reasoning. Problems arising from colonialism, technological stagnation, limitations caused by traditionalism, and the need for administrative reform created a situation that inevitably influenced the entire process of reflection and reasoning among both the pro-Constitutionalist ulama and their successors.

This new mood can be clearly distinguished in the approach of the reformist ulama to issues such as administrative reform, the application of law in society, and the preservation of the rights of individuals. In this context, the role of some prominent mujtahids, such as Âkhound Khorâsâni, Mirzâ-ye Nâ'ini, Sheikh Hâdi Najmâbâdi (although he had died before the Constitutional movement began, his ideas were nevertheless influential), and others who were active both within the country and from the 'Atabât, is cardinal.[87] Their influence extended to the younger generation, some of whom later produced tracts and treatises in support of Constitutionalism, as well as on more specific issues concerning civil reform.

An example of a little-known tract of this kind, written by a reformist *talabeh* (theology student), is *Maslak al-Imam fi Salâmat al-Islam* (The Doctrine of Imam for the Well-Being of Islam), by Hâj Sheikh Asadollâh Mamaqâni, first published anonymously in 1910 in Istanbul.[88] In it, the author outlines the necessary qualities and duties of a mujtahid as a Muslim leader and then compares the relative state of contemporary Christian and Muslim societies. He is bitterly dismayed at the backwardness and misery of Muslim societies compared with the progress and prosperity of the Christian ones. Although a devout Muslim, he is at the same time a nationalist and a critic of several aspects of Iranian life. He regards certain segments of the population as unproductive and includes among them some of the clergy, servants of the Holy Shrines, reciters of elegies and preachers, and wandering dervishes, as well as the wealthy and the landlords, peasants who have run away from their villages in order to avoid taxes, and women; he holds these people responsible for the backwardness of the country and of Islamic civilization and is confident that progress and Islam are compatible.

The author's prime concern is to convince Islamic countries that they must promptly develop their economies through adopting modern technology, especially the railway (*"shemandofer,"* from the French *chemin de fer*), to raise their military power to a level suitable for defense against Christian armies.[89] In addition, Iran in particular should restore its educational system and build up its administrative organization. He suggests one improvement of the educational system as being the foundation of a grand Islamic polytechnic (*dâr al-fonoun-e moʿazzam-e Islami*) with a well-defined program (*proghrâm*).[90] He comments in some detail about the departments and curriculum this proposed polytechnic should have. He suggests instituting an educational center (*howzeh-ye ʿelmi-ye*) in either Mashhad or Qom, preferably the latter because it is closer to the capital, with a curriculum that includes classical and religious subjects alongside the new sciences—the natural sciences, economics, and politics—as well as European languages and other subjects. His proposals for governmental reorganization are likewise derived from his understanding that the society can no longer function properly without an up-to-date system of administration. Although he does not mention the term *despotism*, it is clear that he has it in mind, because the rigidity and arbitrariness of despotic rule are incompatible with educational and administrative reforms. Nevertheless, he is in favor of piecemeal change, provided that it results in a strong state.

He regards women as among the victims of a bad, or even nonexistent, educational system:

One important segment of [the population of] our country [is] the unfortunate women who, if calculated in accordance with correct statistics, perhaps number more than 8.5 million. These poor and unfortunate creatures have no knowledge of science and industry, nor do they know what science is or what technology means. Except for causing their husbands or their guardians thousands of troubles and enormous expense, they have no good skills which would be useful for the country. This very inactivity of the female class has bred moral corruption and bad habits among them. This is all too obvious in them but it also affects the Muslim and Iranian children who are growing up with their ignorance and immorality. These children too will grow up to be like them: impolite and ill-mannered, of no use to the world of religion or that of the country, except corrupting the Islamic el-ement. It was for this reason that the Pride of the Universe [the Prophet Mohammad] ordered that "seeking knowledge is a duty for all Muslim men and Muslim women."[91]

The subject of women and their civil rights, and the necessary steps toward the improvement of their position in the society, received wide coverage in the periodicals and some of the literary works of the period. On the eve of the Constitutional movement, those who addressed the question of women normally did so in relation to the major issue of the day, despotism and arbitrary rule. For instance, the historian Nâzem al-Islam Kermâni reports that in early 1905, in the course of a conversation with the leading mujtahid Seyyed Mohammad Tabâtabâ'i about the gen-eral problems of the country and the urgent need for educating the people, he suggested to Tabâtabâ'i that the Constitutionalists should "make some effort toward the education of the country's girls and clothe them with science and art because, until girls are educated properly, boys will not grow up well."[92] At this point, Âqâ Mirzâ Seyyed Mohammad-Sâdeq, son of Tabâtabâ'i, who headed the Madraseh-ye Islam, the school founded by his father, entered the discussion and pointed out several ba-sic problems. He noted the need for ensuring safety for girls during their journey from their homes to school and back, the necessity of providing good female teachers for them, and the importance of correcting their behavior. But the main problems, in Mohammad-Sâdeq's view, were, first, that there had to be a good police force in the city so that anyone who tried to disturb the girls would be arrested and, second, that female teachers would need to be trained, since it was not appropriate to appoint men to teach girls. At the end, Tabâtabâ'i concluded that "one should never expect reform and discipline until the Iranian govern-ment is constitutional and has constitutional laws, and this despotism is removed."[93]

The goal of bringing about an end to despotism by replacing it with a parliamentary system was not shared equally by all members of the ulama. Even before divisions arose between the pro-Constitutional ulama and the secular reformists over the question of law, there were diverging opinions within the ulama over parliamentary process. Not all members who opposed despotism and arbitrary rule embraced the Constitutional movement. Some traditionalist and conservative figures, such as Sheikh Fazlollâh Nouri, Mirzâ Abul-Qâsem the Imam-Jomʿeh (leader of the Friday Prayer) of Tehran, Mollâ Mohammad Âmoli, and Mirzâ Hasan Mujtahid Tabrizi, defended *mashruʿiyat* (meaning laws prescribed by the *shariʿa*) instead of *mashrutiyat*. They did so partly because they were afraid that the *mashrutiyat* would mean the beginning of the collapse of traditional structures and partly to protect their own privileges. *Mashruʿiyat* was a term that was intentionally put forward to represent both a literal and a theoretical alternative to *mashrutiyat*, in order to attract the loyalty of the ordinary people away from a political solution to the problem of despotism and autocracy.

In terms of the significance of their activities, in both scope and quality, the pro-Constitutional ulama had a greater contribution than those in the opposite camp. Some of them even began with a critical review of certain Shiʿi notions regarding political life and legitimate authority. In the *Maslak al-Imam*, Mamaqâni identifies as a source of political stagnation in Iran the opinion held by some ulama about the question of unjust government and its meaning.[94] He asserts that this opinion had such a strong effect on people that they considered anyone who had worked for the government to be a sinner who could legitimately be ostracized by the community.[95] Such an attitude, the author argues, discourages participation by learned people in the affairs of the state, leaving the way open for the incompetent and oppressors. This situation, he declares, has caused much weakness in Islam.[96] He elaborates on the question of the meaning of unjust rule or unjust authority (*saltanat-e jâʿereh*) and asks whether it is at all possible today for a political authority to be just. In keeping with general Shiʿi opinion, he states that during the period of the Occultation of the Twelfth Imam, no other rule or authority is just or could be justified, and thus anyone who cooperates with such an authority is standing against divine rule. Nevertheless, the author maintains that if an employee of an unjust state shows good intentions and seeks to protect the welfare of Muslims, his services can and should be honored. In order to support this point in the face of its obvious divergence from his earlier uncompromising statement, he refers to the [First] Imam himself, reminding the reader how, at the time of the dominant usurper and the unjust government, the Imam had praised the services of those officials who worked for the welfare of the community.

It is clear that behind these arguments and counterarguments lies a simple practical motive, namely, to combat the prevailing passivity and lack of participation of Muslims in political affairs. The author urges people to develop the economy and strengthen the military in order to resist the pressures of Western countries. He further argues that "protection of an Islamic country and the dignity of Muslims comes before, and is more important than, all religious duties; and [anyone] who ignores this Divine Command will be punished on the Day of Judgment."[97]

One of the most remarkable examples of this line of argument is in Nâ'ini's systematic treatise, *Tanbih al-Umma va Tanzih al-Milla* (Awakening the Community and Purifying the Nation). In this text, Nâ'ini asserts that the religious questions (*omour-e shar'i*) have already been clarified in the Koran. For the clarification of public, social, and/or non-religious questions (*omour-e 'orfi*), one must consult the experts in these areas. Determining the relationship between the people and the ruler belongs to *omour-e 'orfi*. Although as a Shi'i thinker, Nâ'ini considered the only and truly just rule to be that of the Twelfth Imam, in practice, during the period of Occultation before the reappearance of the Imam, he believed that it was not only possible but even legitimate to regulate the relationships between the people and the government in accordance with certain laws and instructions.[98]

What is noteworthy here is that the pro-Constitutionalist ulama focused their attention on the removal of despotic and absolutist rule; most of them—even the more conservative and traditional members of the anti-Constitutionalist ulama—opposed the formation of an Islamic government. For instance, the so-called "*mashruteh-ye mashru'eh*" (Constitutional government in accordance with the laws of the Shari'a) of Sheikh Fazlollâh Nouri, in which he endorsed the autocratic Qajar rule, was mainly in support of a traditional separation between the Shari'a, as a speciality of the ulama, and the *omour-e 'orfi*, as part of the wider *omour-e dowlati*, or duties of the state; it did not advocate a theocratic Islamic government.[99]

With the deposition of Mohammad-Ali Shah and the restoration of the Majles in the summer of 1909, most of the politically active ulama considered their task done and contended that, unless there was another emergency, they should no longer involve themselves in politics, but instead leave the *omour-e 'orfi* to *ahl-e 'orf* (those interested and engaged in public affairs). On the other hand, soon after the Constitutional revolution, the majority of secular reformers assumed that they had ideological control over the movement and showed little concern for either the actual or the potential impact of losing the support of the ulama. As the extremism of the modernists increased, the ulama grew suspicious of the ideals of the movement, disillusioned about its course, and worried about its outcome.

For example, during the last days of Mozaffar al-Din Shah, the Constitutionalist camp was busy drafting an additional article to the Constitution granting equal rights for members of all religions. The ulama opposed this measure and insisted that in an Islamic society followers of recognized religions other than Islam should not enjoy equal rights with Muslims and should pay a capitation tax (*jizya*). Knowing that Crown Prince Mohammad-Ali Mirzâ was against them and their ideas, the Constitutionalists were anxious to ratify the draft and quickly obtain the ailing Shah's signature. It has been reported that Sultan Mahmoud Mirzâ (a student of the Dâr al-Fonoun) rose from the crowd that had gathered in the compound of the Majles and, in a loud voice, told the leading mujtahid Seyyed ʿAbdollâh Behbahâni that, if the article were not ratified the same day, people would pull him around the town by his turban tied around his neck. Apparently "Seyyed ʿAbdollâh kept quiet and the bill was passed."[100]

The consequences of modernist reforms in neighboring Ottoman Turkey had also weakened the traditional function of religion. Moreover, the ulama were critical of the free press and regarded it as a direct challenge to their authority and social prestige. As a result of these developments, some of those ulama who had at first shown remarkable readiness and tolerance for the adaptation and legitimation of the Constitutional ideas in accordance with religious principles and who had effectively advocated Constitutionalism to the people began to withdraw their support. The execution of the prominent mujtahid Sheikh Fazlollâh Nouri, which followed the restoration of the Majles in 1909, greatly added to the ulama's anxiety.[101] It was also reported that, out of sheer disillusionment, Nâʿini ordered the withdrawal from circulation of the remaining copies of his tract and "threw them into the Tigris."[102] Among further signs of disillusionment reference can also be made to Hâj Âqâ Mujtahid Shirâzi (1882–1930), who, in 1912, cautioned against the dangers of "anarchy" and the rise of a new "oligarchy."[103] Such a break was a setback in the further development of both the theory and the practice of Constitutionalism in Iran and before long it paved the way for the return of autocracy.[104]

The secular reformists' understanding of law and the methods of its application in society led them to advocate the idea of a parliament or national assembly and the separation of powers; the rights of the individual were to be fully preserved and protected. Although liberalism and belief in individual rights has often resulted in parliamentary ideas and attitudes, everyone who advocates a parliamentary system is not necessarily either a liberal or a believer in individual rights. The major weakness in the political understanding of some of the secular leaders of the Mashrutiyat and intellectuals of that period resulted from their neglect, or perhaps ignorance, of the prerequisites and principles that need to be in place before rights and liberties can be guaranteed. Their zealous, if formalistic, approach to parliamentary institutions and organizations led them to believe that as soon as a Majles was formed by the deputies of the people, other improvements would inevitably follow. But events unfolded differently. The notion of individual rights formally enshrined in the text of the Constitution[105] was never fully established in the political culture.

In principle, the Constitutional movement was a major challenge not only to a despotic government but also to the tradition of submission to authority. This challenge, however, suffered several setbacks in the course of the post-Constitutional period. Because of internal struggles, famine, and insecurity, as well as foreign power politics, in the form of both direct intervention and the many side effects that followed the First World War, real opportunities to engage in Constitutionalism were few.[106] Instead of a Constitutional government, the response to the crises of the early decades of the twentieth century was the establishment of the autocratic Pahlavi state, which reduced the chances for institutionalizing the Constitutionalist reforms even further. Institutionalization of reform measures has always been difficult to achieve within modern Iranian political culture. Although the executive powers and the functions and responsibilities of the parliament were all well defined in the text of the Constitution, in practice the state, whenever it desired, violated these codes and principles. The long-standing tradition of despotic power undercut efforts to institutionalize the conceptual achievements of the Mashrutiyat movement.[107] Advocates of Constitutionalism were able to articulate a typically modern approach to the individual's civil rights, but they did not succeed in building the necessary institutions to guarantee them. When political anarchy and territorial disintegration threatened, the Constitutionalists seemed willing to submit to the security of autocracy.

This tendency to forsake the conceptual and normative achievements of a new political movement in the moments of crisis and unrest that often follow constitutes a major analytical question of the modern Iranian political culture. Frequent references to the Constitutional "political heritage" are common, but in practice, this heritage has been so regularly undermined that it became merely an imaginary witness devoid of historical reality.

Shortly before the recent revolution in Iran, the contemporary writer Houshang Golshiri proclaimed that after nearly eighty years, intellectuals were still struggling to realize the ideals of the Constitutional movement and were still in the same stage as their counterparts were at the turn of the century: "Here, for whatever reason, such as rupture of previous intellectual and cultural movements or trends, or the influence of foreign elements, the result was that each cultural trend survived only for a few years or a decade, but was severed later by an axe or a sickle, and after a few years one had to begin all over again from scratch." [108]

The same kind of concern was also expressed through a curious metaphor by an Iranian columnist writing in Paris a few years after the revolution who, while utterly puzzled by the discontinuities in Iran's history, noted that "the historical parable of our country is similar to the anecdote of a taxi-meter, for anyone who comes [to power], turns the meter back to zero, sets everything on fire, and blows away the ashes in contempt." [109] This sense of discontinuity has remained a preoccupation of Iranian intellectuals throughout the twentieth century.

– 3 –

Intellectuals
and State Nationalism,
1921–1941

THE CONSTITUTIONAL MOVEMENT REPRESENTED A CHALLENGE
to the traditional structures of Iranian society mainly by its emphasis on
the individual, its criticism of autocratic and patriarchal norms, and its
preference for a liberated and modern system of values,[1] at least until social and political disarray led to a reaction. Then most Iranians responded
to the crisis by demanding a return to a strong central state capable of
restoring order and security in the country and by looking for a strong-
willed patriot who would be their savior (*nâji*). A popular image of the
time showed the broken ship of the homeland amid a stormy sea, or the
epic hero Kâveh the Blacksmith holding his "Kâviâni Banner" to salvage
the integrity of the country.

Newspapers, pamphlets, and a variety of historical and social novels
and patriotic poetry produced during the 1920s and 1930s dealt repeatedly, and sometimes exclusively, with the various options for national
policy and cultural direction, pondering which might best suit modern
Iran. The consensus was that Iran needed an up-to-date state that could
enforce law and protect the nation's territorial integrity. Opinions differed mainly on the question of the degree to which Western measures
should be accommodated.

One line of argument, advocated mainly by intellectuals exposed to
European influences, stressed the preservation of "Iranian values" and at

the same time equated modernism with Westernism. This group included Seyyed Hasan Taqizâdeh (1878–1970), a veteran Constitutionalist activist whose Persian journal *Kâveh*, named after the legendary figure, which appeared in Berlin during the First World War, later became a platform for advocating Europeanization. The paper's first series (1916–1919) was pro-German in its coverage of the war, but a short-lived postwar series (1920–1921) was devoted entirely to literature, history, and culture. In an editorial by Taqizâdeh in the first issue of this second series, *Kâveh* set as its goals to "spread European civilization in Iran," to "protect Iranian nationality and national integrity," and to "refine and preserve Persian language and literature." To secure these objectives, the editor recommended an "unconditional acceptance and promotion of European civilization" and an "absolute concession" to European educational, scientific, and industrial norms and manners. In short, "Iran must become Europeanized, in appearance and in essence, physically and spiritually."[2]

Other even more enthusiastically Western approaches were also put forward. One advocate was Hâj Mirzâ Hasan Khân Mohtasham al-Saltaneh Esfandiâri, a midlevel statesman during the late Qajar period who later came to prominence during the reign of Reza Shah.[3] In the aftermath of the Constitutional movement, his appointments, often based on favoritism rather than merit, took him to Europe. He became an assistant to the prime minister in the cabinet of Mirzâ Ali-Asghar Khân Atâbak and was among the representatives of the government in the first Majles. Later he headed the ministries of Justice, Foreign Affairs, Finance, and Arts. He also became a deputy and eventually the speaker of the Majles. He wrote his now almost forgotten booklet, a long essay entitled *ʿElal-e Badbakhti-e Mâ va ʿAlâj-e Ân* (Causes of Our Misery and Its Cure), in 1921.[4] It captures the climate of opinion of the period, and it is a good example of the kind of reform manifesto that was printed after the Constitutional movement had ended.

Mohtasham al-Saltaneh begins by stressing his patriotism and assuring the reader that his recommendations for change all stem from his love of nation and goodwill. His inquiries had led him to believe that since the creation of man, there had always been a conflict between knowledge and ignorance, and between justice and injustice. This conflict has been at the core of all political corruption and social rebellion. Sensible nations, in order to avoid chaos, turned to consultative government (*hokoumat-e showravi*) as the best social system because its maintenance

depends on "knowledge and justice" alone.[5] Knowledge could be promoted by building schools and libraries and introducing compulsory
education; justice could be maintained through meritocracy.

After the Constitutional movement, he continues, successful Western
models of consultative government were not copied in Iran, and as a result, national "ignorance," economic weakness, and "capitulation"[6] resulted.[7] The increase in number of political societies (*anjomans*) and the
later mushrooming of parties served only to arouse internal anguish.[8]
Mohtasham al-Saltaneh urges writers and journalists to enhance the image of the Majles in public opinion[9] and cautions them to avoid insulting
the ulama because these men possess qualities beneficial to the public
interest, as their leadership in the Constitutional movement demon-
strates.[10] The author occasionally quotes from the Koran and uses Arabic
poems and proverbs to support his arguments. In advising the journalists
to abstain from the current vindictive journalism (especially against the
ulama), however, he quotes from Jules Simon on the necessity of ethical
principles for the spiritual development of humanity and other reforms.[11]
He also criticizes the ideological attacks on the "aristocracy" and "capitalism" as blind imitation of a Western vogue, since such concepts have
no reality in the Islamic society of Iran. "What capital and what capitalist?" he writes. "I only wish we had a few capitalists, as others do, who
could generate some social activity, so that we would not have to keep
on begging in this manner from foreign capitalists."[12]

Mohtasham al-Saltaneh refutes the validity of applying Marxist class
theory to Iranian society, arguing that the relationship between landlords
and peasants was never as antagonistic in Iran as it was in Europe or in
Russia before the Bolshevik takeover. "Revolutionizing" the Iranian
peasantry would cause "unimaginable" harm to the peasants themselves
and would be a crime "greater than murder."[13] Regarding the industrial
worker, it would also be "ridiculous" if, "on the basis of mere illusion
we try to invent something that does not exist" in Iran:[14] "The term
worker is current in Europe (*Farangestân*) and in Russia because there exist factories, mines, railroads, telegraph and telephone cables in abun-
dance, capitalist[s], capital, worker[s] in enormous numbers, etc., etc. It
is clear to everyone that if we spoke of a worker it would only make us a
laughingstock."[15]

The author also complains about the current fashion among the youth
of arguing with their elders and urges them to respect the older generation and their wisdom.[16] He also rejects the fashionable notion that religion is obsolete—the young should pursue scientific knowledge, but

they should also adhere to Islam.[17] True Islamic teachings contain such qualities and moral virtues as "simplicity," "equality," and "charity," as manifested in the biographies of the Prophet and the First Imam, Ali.

Turning to the state of the country as a whole, the author lists, as manifestations of backwardness, moral depravity; wide illiteracy; lack of genuine Islamic observance, especially in Tehran; disregard for justice; an idle Constitutional government; a massive excess of imports over exports; capital outflow from the country; constraints on domestic and foreign trade; lack of railways and good roads; and untapped natural resources.[18]

Mohtasham al-Saltaneh then offers his fourfold remedy: reassertion of the Islamic identity,[19] improvement of public education,[20] administration of social justice,[21] and development of the national economy.[22] Islam, in the author's opinion, would be the "best barrier" against further "calamities".[23] "Historical texts" contain ample evidence that "so long as Muslims acted in compliance with Islamic teachings, they were masters of the world," but as soon as they abandoned those teachings, they plunged into their present wretched state.[24]

Regarding the country's education, he is adamant that national weakness can be cured by fighting ignorance and illiteracy, provided that schooling does not alienate people from their own roots and religion.[25] He proposes, first, expanding primary schools and high schools so that all social classes could benefit and supplementing their curricula with courses on the sciences and religious ethics;[26] second, employing good "teachers from abroad" to train well-qualified indigenous students in a "fixed period of time" for "various skills";[27] and third, sending abroad a select group of graduates (they should be "mature and firm in their religious beliefs"), under the supervision of a "learned religious" person. After their studies, these students would return home and be put in charge of their areas of speciality, so that there would be no further need to hire foreign instructors or to send students abroad.

Mohtasham al-Saltaneh further recommends that scientific achievements should be rewarded annually and specialists should be encouraged to accept practical and professional employment rather than be absorbed by the bureaucracy.[28] He suggests that the government should benefit from the education students in theological seminaries receive by recruiting these men into appropriate state functions. The government should send a select group of students to the Shi'i centers of Iraq (*'atabât*) annually for the completion of their studies, with the purpose of later appointing them to the judiciary.[29]

The state should also form an organization made up of people who are learned in foreign languages to translate scientific and other current texts into Persian.[30] Teaching foreign languages, however, should be confined to "political schools" and institutions of higher education, as it is not necessary for ordinary students to "waste their time learning European languages" when they should be learning "mathematics and natural sciences."[31]

Mohtasham al-Saltaneh then turns to the question of implementation of justice. He begins by quoting a series of passages from the Koran and Ali ibn Abi Tâlib's *Nahj al-Balâgah* (The Road to Eloquence), as well as verses from Persian poets (e.g., Nezâmi), on the virtues of justice. He regrets that, notwithstanding the Constitutional movement, there is not much evidence of social justice in Iran, though even Ardeshir Bâbakân, the founder of the ancient Sassanid dynasty, said that no realm would survive without ʿadl (justice) and siâsat (administration of the polity). Without security and legal protection, the economy also stagnates, as it has in Iran.[32] To remedy this situation, Mohtasham al-Saltaneh urges the government to organize a Justice Ministry (ʿadliyeh) on reliable and well-defined legal foundations, and then respect its independence. Certain qualified mujtahids should contribute by supervising the preparation and the subsequent publication of the necessary legal texts into Persian. The ulama should also assist the state in appointing qualified judges; if they fail to do so, they will "undoubtedly greatly regret it."[33]

The fourth and last of Mohtasham al-Saltaneh's remedies deals with the economy, without which no polity can succeed.[34] Among other things, the author recommends developing natural resources and cutting the importation of unnecessary goods in order to save much-needed hard currency ("It is said that some Iranian women wear imported stockings costing ten tumâns a pair and [imported] shoes costing twenty tumâns a pair"[35]). Although private companies play an important role in economic development, it is the government that should assume responsibility for spending on infrastructure.[36]

The ulama and journalists are invited to convey his proposed remedies to the people, now adrift in a sea of "poverty and confusion."[37] Majles deputies should ensure its survival by abandoning their obstructionist attitude toward government. "How can the government possibly govern," Mohtasham al-Saltaneh asks, "if it is changed three to four times a year?"[38]

Mohtasham al-Saltaneh's ideas, which were shared by many of his fellow intellectuals as they were to be instituted by the Pahlavi state, had a lasting impact on Iranian society. During the decade that followed the Constitutional movement, the political incompetence and corruption of the Qajar court continued unabated, and urgent matters of national interest went unattended, until finally, in 1921, there was a coup d'état, backed by the Cossack Brigade, which was a more organized and disciplined unit within the army. The prolific journalist Seyyed Ziâ' al-Din Tabâtabâ'i became prime minister, and he appointed Reza Khân, the brigade's commander, as minister of war. It was not long, however, before Reza Khân seized power, pushed Seyyed Ziâ' aside, and in 1923 himself became prime minister. Amid growing opposition to the Qajars, on 9 Âbân 1304/1 November 1925 the Majles decreed that the dynasty had ended,[39] and the next month a Constituent Assembly proclaimed Reza Khân as the first shah of a new dynasty. He was crowned on 25 April 1926.[40]

Over the twenty years of Reza Shah's effective rule, the face of Iranian society changed considerably, especially in the cities. He had the backing of important groups, at least in the early years. The intelligentsia regarded him as a secular patriot capable of putting an end to political divisions and social chaos, isolating the forces of traditionalism, and limiting the power of the ulama. Many Shi'i leaders saw in him a strong patriot capable of suppressing the radical elements whose secularism and anticlericalism had made the ulama both disillusioned and suspicious about the future course of Constitutionalism. Reza Khân's decisiveness and his commitment to modernization also impressed the country's politicians and civil servants. His humble origins freed him from any connection with an established aristocracy, and this further contributed to his popularity even with establishment members, who no longer trusted anyone from their own circles.

While he was building up his power, therefore, Reza Shah benefited from broad popularity. With the support of the intellectuals, he further secularized the entire state machinery, isolated the ulama from some of their traditional areas of influence and income, such as education and juridical power, and tried to position them within the new administrative system.[41] His campaign against the more radical trends embraced by the intellectuals, especially socialist and Marxist ideologies, was supported by the ulama. Later in his rule, Reza Shah was able to manipulate these various social groups—for example, playing the ulama and the intellectuals off against one another—without much fear of the emergence of a united front of forces hostile to his rule. Not surprisingly, this allowed him ever-greater, and more arbitrary, use of power.

Over time, the shah's impact on Constitutionalist principles was as negative as his influence on modernization was positive. Ironically, before becoming shah, he had briefly considered the possibility of forming a republic, but he quickly abandoned the idea when it became clear that it would neither gain him any further support nor inspire a united social movement. On the contrary, the possibility of an Iranian republic caused alarm among various groups, especially the ulama. The recent Westernization measures of Turkey under Kemal Atatürk were fresh in their minds, and they regarded the formation of a republic as a serious threat to traditional religion. Reza Khân's critics, on the other hand, suspected that his interest in a republic was nothing but a charade, so they, too, opposed it. Before a real crisis developed, Reza Khân intervened and suppressed the "republican uproar" (*ghowghâ-ye jomhouri*). He visited the religious leaders and assured them that he would never permit a republic in Iran, thus securing their support. His overthrow of the Qajar dynasty and founding of his own were greatly facilitated by the ulama's seal of approval.[42]

By using events such as the republican affair, Reza Khân managed to suppress signs of opposition or objection to his power. As monarch, he ran the day-to-day affairs of state using the same autocratic authority he had wielded so effectively to establish himself in power. He kept the Majles alive, but gradually rendered it ineffective; dissident elements either were replaced by loyal ones or were constantly harassed. To reconcile the discrepancy between his constitutionally sanctioned title of monarch and his actual autocratic leadership, Reza Shah distanced himself from the traditional sources of legitimacy, i.e., religion and tribe, and turned instead to a carefully crafted version of nationalism that celebrated Iran's pre-Islamic heritage. This source of legitimacy could be promoted as being older than Islam and broader than any single tribe. By stressing the institution of kingship and the panorama of Iranian history and culture, Reza Shah generated a deluge of nationalistic rhetoric and sentiment. He named the new dynasty Pahlavi, a reference to the ancient language of the pre-Islamic Sassanids. Heroes of the past were honored; ancient names and symbols were given to many public places and people began to give their children old Persian names. The Iranian Academy, Farhangestân, was founded to purify the language of foreign loanwords.[43] Emphasizing patriotic sentiments was a measure by which the Pahlavi state expected to curb foreign influence and reduce ethnic prejudices and religious obscurantism in the country.

To secure his objectives of national homogeneity, a strong military, a functional administrative state, and the integration of certain Western socioeconomic ideas and principles, Reza Shah adopted a policy of rapid modernization somewhat similar to the one that Atatürk was using to modernize the newly founded Republic of Turkey. Personally, also, they were not unlike: neither had any significant formal education, both were infatuated with the material advances of modern Western civilization, and each tried to introduce certain aspects of such developments to his country by introducing factories, railroads, hospitals, and new educational institutions. In the case of Iran, a whole new system of government administration was also put in place.[44] Their attitudes differed toward the intellectual elite, however. According to Abrahamian, "whereas Mustafa Kemal conscientiously channeled the enthusiastic backing of the intelligentsia into the Republican party, Reza Shah gradually lost his initial civilian support, and, failing to secure social foundations for his institutions, ruled without the assistance of an organized political party. Thus whereas Mustafa Kemal's authority rested firmly on Turkey's intelligentsia, Reza Shah's state hovered somewhat precariously, without class foundations, over Iran's society."[45]

By the time Reza Shah had fully consolidated his power, Iran was nothing less than a dictatorship. Politicians and intellectuals who had at first praised the shah's ability and energy in uniting the country and restoring order soon became disillusioned as his arbitrary interventions into state affairs and his autocratic style of policy making continued. Critics had branded the autocracy of the Qajars as *estebedâd* (despotism or tyranny) but used the French *dictateur* and *dictature* to describe Reza Shah's regime and later that of Mohammad-Reza Shah.[46] The state was now both the source and the symbol of a new claim to authority.

In Iran, especially before the Constitutional movement, authoritarianism underlay many social and political relationships.[47] Family, group, religious, tribal, and political relationships were all authoritarian in character, and submission was the defining characteristic of any relationship within them. In Islam harmony and felicity are attainable only through unconditional submission to the will of God. In Sufi teachings, and in the tradition of Islamic ethics in general, submission is regarded as a virtue.[48] An omnipresent goodness is acknowledged in return for acquiescence and submission to one's fate. In Shi'i Islam, for instance, the practice of *taqiyya* or concealment of truth, coupled with an apparent submission to the dominant authority, was devised as a measure of prudence and self-preservation in the face of a superior and usurping power. The Iranian attitude toward authority was influenced by this Sufi and

Shi'i background. It led to an ability to accept a ruler while simultaneously rejecting the legitimacy of his rule and helps to explain the attitude of the people as Reza Shah's reign wore on. Even when the majority of the people, and intellectuals in particular, had become critical of the state, they adopted a pragmatic attitude (whether from fear, apathy, or cynicism) toward further modernization. At the same time they withdrew their trust in the regime, thus undermining its legitimacy.

The modernization the Pahlavi regime undertook defined modernism as the imitation of certain Western developments and institutions. Most of the country's political, economic, and even social apparatus was overhauled. The conscription law of 1926 laid the foundation for the creation of a modern national army, in which discipline and military dress, accompanied by a special blend of nationalist discourse, played a crucial role.[49] Civil service reforms begun in 1926 changed the entire structure of the state machinery. The new Ministry of Justice was founded in 1927 and was headed by a graduate of Geneva University, Ali-Akbar Dâvar. New roads and telegraph lines and the installation of wireless stations greatly improved communications.[50] A trans-Iranian railroad, from the Persian Gulf to the Caspian Sea, was begun, financed by the state monopolies through indirect taxation on such consumer essentials as tea and sugar.[51] State industries were built for refining sugar, manufacturing textiles, and processing food, chemicals, and tobacco. Major towns were at least partially modernized by reconstruction and new public buildings.[52] There were improvements in the country's educational system as well. Modern schools, offering similar education to both sexes, were expanded, and standard school texts were introduced.[53] Tehran University was opened in 1935. In addition, students were sent abroad for further training on a regular basis.[54]

Modernization measures reached far into the private lives of the citizenry. A 1929 law required all Iranian civilian men to replace their traditional costumes and clerical garb with standard Western-style clothing,[55] which was considered more functional and more appropriate for modern living and which reduced the appearance of ethnic heterogeneity and class stratification in public life. After 1935, men were required to wear European hats as well. In the following year, women were prohibited from wearing veils (*châdor*) in public.[56]

These more intrusive measures met with scattered resistance in several parts of the country. For example, in July 1935, in opposition to the imposition of the "Pahlavi hat," traditionalists in Mashhad took to the streets and subsequently gathered in the courtyard of the old Gowharshâd Mosque adjacent to the Shrine of Imam Reza. The government responded by sending forces who stormed the sanctuary and, after inflicting injuries and some loss of life, managed to disperse the crowd. Unveiling, too, was unpopular with some women, who simply refused to appear in public places. When Reza Shah fell from power, many of them returned to the veil. Modernism had already influenced people before the Pahlavi regime, but the government's policy of dictating uniform dress caused negative reactions by those who viewed it as a violation of their self-image and social status. In the words of one observer, "[F]or women who were endeavouring to lead an active life, working or studying, this policy [of unveiling] was doubtless welcome, but for many women who still lived in a secluded milieu, the change came as an unwelcome shock for which they were not prepared, arousing great opposition. Thus when Reza Shah left the country in 1941, the combination of male conservatism, hostility to the regime and the sense of social unease experienced by many women brought the return of veiling and former styles of dress in some sections of the country."[57]

Most of the state's development measures were focused on the urban centers, while the country's agriculture and the general situation of the peasantry remained virtually unaltered.[58] In keeping with the general policy of the state toward centralization, provincial officials were appointed from Tehran; some could not even communicate in the language of the local people. Although this approach originally was taken in order to protect territorial integrity in the face of growing threats by various ethnic separatist movements, in later years it gradually widened the gap between the state and the countryside.

Another significant factor about the Pahlavi modernization program is that it succeeded in drawing a considerable number of people with modern education into the state bureaucracy. Hitherto independent offices and their functionaries were also drawn into working with the new administrative system. These included the notary public and registry offices that arranged civil contracts of all kinds, which were made directly accountable to the newly created ministries of Justice and Interior. While depriving the ulama of some traditional functions, such as running the Islamic courts (*mahâkem-e sharˁ*) and the schools at the primary level (*maktab*), the state left the administration of the registry offices to them, but made them accountable by requiring licensing and permissions.

This measure gave the state more control over civil contracts and served to make them more uniform. In the Qajar period, many government officials worked out of their homes, making the performance of the duties of their office a very personal matter, with little or no differentiation between public duties and private status. The Pahlavi modernization measures also freed the government from the almost impossible task of transferring into a central archive the records of all existing contracts, since these had previously been arranged in private offices.[59] The new system also provided the state with extra income in terms of royalties and stamp duties, because the private seal of each individual officeholder was no longer an adequate endorsement for a document or a contract to be officially binding. For this purpose, official government stamps now had to be purchased.

Over the course of time, these arrangements had an important impact on the overall state administration and contributed to the formation of a new bureaucratic culture. The new institutions for higher education, such as Tehran University, facilitated both the promotion of traditional bureaucrats within the state administrative system and the entry of new members into it; the administration now required from applicants an appropriate academic degree from a secular institution. Bureaucrats were thus likely to have spent a few years in the specifically modern atmosphere of the university, exposed to new modes of discourse, principles, and codes of conduct.

The development of the modern state not only facilitated social mobility and helped the growth of the middle class, it also brought about further changes in popular conceptions of the self—changes that had already begun to appear during the post-Constitutional period. Some of the implications of the new ascendancy of the individual, as well as different aspects of social change, were the subjects of numerous books, plays, and poetry in the post-Constitutional years and beyond. An examination of this literature and its imagery provides a clear sense of the experience of modernity in Iran. The production of historical and social novels provides a link between the reformist works of the Constitutional period and the so-called intellectual literature of the later periods. However, this literature is largely snubbed or ignored by contemporary writers and has attracted little scholarly analysis.[60]

The novel emerged in Iran as a direct consequence of modern urban living, an increase in literacy, and the resulting interest in reading among the middle class. The early novels, in particular, at times focused on contemporary questions, supplying the reader with a form and context through which the new spirit of the social world could be reconstructed and observed. As a means of introducing and popularizing modern themes and topics, the novel supplemented the press, and, in fact, several novels were initially published in installments as series in periodicals and newspapers.

Before the introduction of the novel, social, cultural, and political issues had been written about mainly in political poetry and in sometimes satirical journal articles. The early novelists carried on the tradition of political commentary, emphasizing the importance of a strong, modern state, national integrity, and social equality; a didactic tone is pervasive in these early novels. But even as they instructed their readers on reformist topics, they did so in ways that increasingly departed from past patterns, which proved unsuited to the modern idiom. Whether textual or oral, religious or secular, prosaic or poetic, traditional forms seemed to be a poor medium for relaying modernist messages. For instance, popular stories such as *Mosayyeb-Nâmeh*,[61] *Amir Arsalân*,[62] and *Shirouyeh Nâmdâr*[63] and popular storytelling such as epic recitation (*naqqâli*)[64] had little relevance to the promotion of modernist causes. Similarly, religious practices, whether carried out privately, as in, for example, omen (*estekhâreh*) and augury (*fâl*),[65] or in gatherings for *ta'ziyeh* performances,[66] held little interest for readers of modern literature.[67] Popular classical texts such as the *Kelila va Dimna* and the *Golestân* did not fare much better either, since young readers found them irrelevant to the problems of the modern world.

Publishing grew as an important channel of communication, as literacy spread with the expansion of the educational system. Other, more ephemeral, factors contributing to the popularity of new literature include the development of a distinctively modern type of privacy[68] and the concomitant emergence of a new conception of leisure time.[69] Whereas the premodern mentality served to privatize and retain a transcendental other (such as the notion of imaginary witness in *'erfan*, or gnostic, literature), modern privacy is structured to regulate the relationship between personal matters and the objective world. In a modern context there were now certain institutionalized fragments of time specifically defined and allocated for the individual to spend privately, though not necessarily in private, as a feature of modern leisure time. As a form of entertainment, as well as enlightenment, the novel was well suited to this new way of passing time. It was a portable companion for increasingly mobile individuals, whether in their own room (yet another invention of modern life[70]) or in other places—at work, in waiting rooms, or on business trips, where reading a novel during the free hours was considered preferable to interaction with the local people.

The impact of the novel on everyday life was far-reaching. Not only intellectuals, high school and university students among them, but also government employees, housewives, and even army officers could be found reading fashionable works and exchanging ideas about them. The introduction of the novel changed not only what people read, but how they read. As the demand for novels grew, certain bookshops in major cities began, in addition to selling books, to lend them for a fee.[71] This encouraged people to read for long stretches of time—a kind of reading markedly different from the traditional random perusal of the Koran or of such classical writers as Khayyâm, Rumi, Sa'di, and Hâfez, which one would dip into from time to time. Novels were also typically read only once, whereas older books were read or recited over and over again.

The historical novel in Iran grew out of translations of books with historical content into Persian, a practice that had increased considerably from the second half of the nineteenth century onward. Because knowledge of European languages was not widespread and the supply of books and access to material in foreign languages was very limited, translators catered to people's demand for information. New scientific discoveries, historical and geographical information, political commentaries, biographies of famous personalities, topics in health care and hygiene, articles on morality and ethics, and, of course, novels were translated and read.

The impact of translation on the cultural life of the urban communities, and more specifically on that of the intellectual elite, was not wholly positive. The majority of works in translation were originally written either in French or Arabic, which limited the number and kind of views on current issues or opinions that were available. In a great many cases, translated works were the only *available* channel of information on the West, a trend that continued well into the later periods, and when knowledge of the West rests so fully on such an arbitrary selection of sources, it cannot help but be skewed and distorted.

Another serious drawback to the passion for translation was that, in rendering modern Western ideas into Persian, Iranian writers and translators often developed a kind of inferiority complex. This state of mind was not confined to general impressions of Western ideas and texts; it also shaped expectations concerning the actual and potential functions of the translated ideas and texts. As a result, a metaphysic of translation gradually developed among the intelligentsia. Beneath the seemingly confident project of translation, a reification gradually grew, shared by both the translator and the reader—each having, in this context, an abstract identity for the other—regarding the status of the text and all the expectations surrounding it. Some Iranian writers and critics were aware

of this situation. For example, as early as during the Constitutional period, in a short preface to his *Mokâlemeh-ye Sayyâh-e Irani bâ Shakhs-e
Hendi* (Discourse of an Iranian Traveler with an Indian Notable),
Mu'ayyed al-Islam, the editor of the influential newspaper *Habl al-Matin*,
expressed these reservations: "The Europeans have been translating
books of literature and novels of foreign countries, but from [this act of]
translation they do not demand the improvement of their national ethics
or the removal of their moral shortcomings. Their purpose is to achieve
sufficient information and to inquire about the states and habits of that
[particular foreign] nation. This can be beneficial for a nation [only] if it
has already been freed from itself and is intending to engage in others."[72]

Nevertheless, translators continued to be active and their work
broadly read.[73] In time the translators themselves began to try their hand
at novel writing, using native historical subjects, but influenced by the
norms and spirit of the European models. A classic nineteenth-century
example of a translator turned novelist is Mohammad-Ali Shirâzi (Naqib
al-Mamâlek), who was the first to translate into Persian the works of the
Arab historian and author of historical novels Georgi Zaidan (d. 1914).[74]
Naqib al-Mamâlek was a private secretary to Nâser al-Din Shah and was
also known as the court storyteller (*naqqâl-bâshi*); one of his routine
functions at court was to tell "bedtime stories" to the shah. The princess
Tourân Âghâ Fakhr al-Dowleh, sitting in an adjacent room, wrote down
the tales.[75] The story of *Amir Arsalân*, perhaps the most famous of these
transcriptions (first completed in 1292 A.H./1875),[76] has the same textual spirit as Naqib al-Mamâlek's translations of Zaidan. This influence
extends from imitation of normative imagery, such as intersubjective
codes of conduct and value judgments, to the adoption of more objective settings from contemporary life, albeit anachronistic vis-à-vis the
time of the novel. A similar pattern can also be noted in the Persian poetry of the early twentieth century.[77]

Translators throughout the Middle East favored works by Dumas,
Hugo, Chekhov, and Byron because they regarded them as patriotic and
their work helped to import ideas of European nationalism. A revival of
historical topics indicative of bygone eras of material and cultural power,
such as Pharaonic Egypt, the Central Asiatic origins of the Turks, or the
Persian Empire, was a deliberate attempt by writers to urge their compatriots to overcome the country's present state of weakness. One effect
of the novels' championing of nationalist sentiments was to increase the
political involvement of the middle classes, who absorbed this fervor as
they read.

In their glorification of the national heritage, authors of historical novels were seldom hostile to Islam. Although there was a tendency to hold a "foreign" element responsible for the manipulation or degeneration of the "genuine Iranian spirit," the criticism was normally directed toward the imposition of an Arabic as opposed to Islamic influence. A relatively short historical drama entitled *Namâyesh-e Dâstân-e Khounin yâ Sargozasht-e Barmakiân* (The Unfortunate Tale or the Fate of the Barmakids), written by Seyyed ʿAbdol-Rahim Khalkhâli (b. Khalkhâl 1251/ 1872-1873, d. Tehran 30 Khordâd 1321/20 June 1942), illustrates this tolerance toward Islam.[78]

Khalkhâli was a well-known Constitutionalist activist in Tehran who had collaborated with Seyyed Mohammad-Reza Shirâzi in the publication of *Mosâvât* (Equality), a pro-Demokrât Party paper and was an organizer of the Anjoman-e Komiteh-ye Bidâri-e Iran (Society for the Awakening of Iran), a political society of Constitutionalist activists.[79] His small lending library and bookshop, Ketâb-khwâneh-ye Kâveh (Kâveh Library), was frequented by intellectuals and political activists in Tehran during the Constitutional period. In 1915, he began publication of *Parvin* (Pleiades), a biweekly journal devoted to the sciences, literature, and ethics. In an introduction he wrote in June–July 1925, the author gave some historical background for his play, which takes place in the Umayyad and early Abbasid periods (45–235 A.H. /665–850). Once more under the yoke of an alien rule and suffering enormous deprivation, the Iranians sought revival. The author singles out Abu Muslim Khorâsâni[80] and the Barmakid dynasty as examples of Iranian patriots who work tirelessly to free Iran from alien rule.[81] The Barmakid role in securing the caliphate for Hâroun, and after him for his younger son Maʾmoun, "the greatest and wisest of all Abbasid caliphs," whose mother was of Persian descent, is highly praised by the author.[82] The "true story" of this family, he claimed, had never been told, either by Arabs or by Iranian historians; to set the record straight, the author, inspired by "an extreme love for [his] country," had written the story of the Barmakids for those "interested in the independence [or integrity] of Iran."[83]

The play has five relatively short acts (*pardeh*) with about twenty characters. The court is split into pro-Arab and pro-Persian factions, but, owing his power to the Barmakids, the ruling caliph, Hâroun al-Rashid, places his trust in them. The drama begins with a conversation between Fazl ibn Rabiʿ and the Arab poet Abu al-ʿAtâhia about the increasing influence of the Persians at the Abbasid court. The former complains that a "bunch of fire-worshipping Persians," who are now "pretending to be true Muslims," have infiltrated the entire administrative body of the caliphate and are effectively in control of the Islamic empire, yet "no one is aware of their real intentions"; even worse, Hâroun himself is deceived by them. In order to safeguard Arab supremacy, the two men vow to use whatever means are at their disposal to overcome the popularity of the Barmakids. Fazl, wishing to regain the office he had lost to Yahyâ Barmaki, promises handsome rewards to Abu al-'Atâhia in return for his composing and distributing anti-Persian poems. To increase their chances of undermining the Barmakids, Fazl further instructs the poet to select a few attractive female slaves from the Jewish merchant, the opportunist Mollâ Pinâs, for delivery to Hâroun's elder son, Amin. The hope is to recruit Amin and create a united front in order to isolate the influence of the pro-Persian party.

It is later revealed that Ja'far Barmaki and Hâroun's sister, 'Abbâsa, in defiance of Hâroun's wishes, had consummated their marriage and as a result had two sons. In a joint conspiracy in which Amin's mother, Zubaida, takes an active part, they secretly place a note (*shab-nâmeh*)[84] in the caliph's bedroom.[85] Angered by the revelations, Hâroun, who had already become concerned about the increasing popularity and influence of the Barmakids, orders the elimination of both 'Abbâsa and Ja'far. The drama ends with a scene in which Hâroun's servant and executioner Masrour is about to carry out his master's orders against the disillusioned Ja'far, whose last words are: "O, God of Iran! Ja'far is being sacrificed for Iran! Lord save Iran! Lord keep the blood-stained hands of the aliens away from Iran! O, Iranians! This is the work of aliens' domination! Do not abandon [your] independence! Do not be deceived by the aliens."[86] Khalkhâli's play is a typical example of the openly nationalistic content of this kind of historical narrative. The audience could not fail to grasp the message that political sovereignty was the ultimate protection of indigenous talent.

The literary genres of novel and drama were effective means of reaching modern audiences. Mu'ayyed al-Islam refers to the novel (*roumân*) in the introduction to his *Mokâlemeh-ye Sayyâh Irani bâ Shakhs-e Hendi* as being an effective and engaging genre for communicating urgent sociopolitical messages.[87] A biweekly publication made its appearance in Tehran that was exclusively devoted to drama, called *Rouznâmeh-ye Tiâtr* (The Theater), edited and written by Mirzâ (Mohammad-) Reza Khân Tabâtabâ'i Nâ'ini (1873–1931). Its first issue appeared on 4 Rabi' I 1326 A.H./6 April 1908 and the last (No. 12) on 21 Jamâdi I 1326/21 June

1908; it was suppressed as a result of the anti-Constitutionalist pressures of Mohammad-Ali Shah, which led to the suppression of the Majles on 23 Jamâdi I 1326/23 June 1908. The paper consisted of pieces in dramatic form that were critical of autocracy.[88]

Another reference to the novel can be found in a book on general ethics addressed to youth—a group regarded as especially vulnerable to European enchantments—by (Mohammad-) Hasan Jâberi Ansâri entitled *Âftâb-e Derakhshandeh* (The Glittering Sun), published in 1923.[89] (Mohammad-) Hasan (ibn Hâj Mirzâ Ali ibn Mahmoud) Jâberi (1870–1945) studied first under his father. At seventeen, he began clerical work for Mirzâ Habibollâh Khân Ansâri (Moshir al-Molk) and then worked for the Qajar prince and governor Zell al-Sultan in Isfahan, where in 1328 A.H./1910 he entered the Ministry of Justice (*'Adliyeh*). He was appointed head of the Penal Court (*Mahkmeh-ye Jazâ'i*), but following the political turmoil of 1911, he resigned from public service and devoted his time entirely to journalism and historical writings. Among his works is the famous text *Târikh-e Isfahan Nesf-e Jahân* (Isfahan, [the city which is worth] One Half of the World: A History), a history of Isfahan "from the beginning of Islam."[90] Mu'ayyed al-Islam's support of reform and Jâberi's advocacy of restraint toward modernism in fiction are indications of the overall influence of modernist imagery and mores in Iranian society by the early 1920s.

In the preface to *Âftâb-e Derakhshandeh*, Jâberi complains about a prevailing sense of apathy among the younger generation toward their past. Although he laments their preference for "stories about love or deceit" (*roumân-hâ-ye 'eshq-bâzi yâ neyrang-sâzi*), he decides to adopt the genre of *roumân* himself in order to attract their attention.[91] He wants to encourage modern youth to "gain some pride" and "appreciate the value of their religious knowledge and [their] Divine Book," and to prevent them from believing that "the sun of science only shines from Western Europe."[92] The book is constructed around conversations between two fictional characters: Mahjour (literally, despondent or forlorn), the twelve-year-old son of an old sage named Dabir Vâlâ, and Maghrour (meaning haughty and arrogant), the son of Dastour A'lâ, a notable. Both characters are students at Dâr al-Fonoun who become rivals for the love of Rakhshandeh (Luminous), an "attractive sixteen-year-old descendant of an ancient conqueror." Mixed into the plot are discussions on meteorology and the cosmos, replete with references to Kant and Newton, Herschel and Laplace, as well as to the Koran and to classical literary and philosophical figures.[93] Maghrour, a modernist type with an arrogant confidence in European science and standards, often ridicules Mahjour's belief in the universal validity of Islamic imperatives concerning both scientific generalities and codes of conduct.

Their discussions also include detailed comparisons of modern manners with religious instructions and traditional habits. In each case, Mahjour confidently produces up-to-date explanations in support of the scientific justifiability of the latter.[94] These vary from rules of personal hygiene, such as Mahjour's practice of washing his hands before meals and avoidance of cutlery (recommended by Maghrour, but objected to by Mahjour for being, among other things, affordable only for certain "chair-sitting" demagogues of the bureaucracy), to conversions from traditional to European dress and the resultant need for new accessories such as "thirty tumâns for a pair of *poutins* [Fr. *bottine*, boots]" and "braces for two tumâns."[95] Mahjour further objects to a current vogue in which families spend "five hundred toumâns annually" on the "*tiâtr* (theater), *sinâmou* (cinema), *telgerâf* (telegraph), *kâfeh* (café) and *qahveh-khwâneh* (coffeehouse)," and parents show a willingness to spend another five hundred tumâns to have their children "learn a language alien to Arabic and Persian."[96] Mahjour continues: "If [being] civilized depends on drinking *wisky* at ten tumâns a bottle, or sitting in golden *doroshkeh* [Rus. *drozki*, carriage] or on a golden chair, or spending one tumân for *tovâlet* [Fr. *toilette*, makeup], or thirty tumâns an hour for a syphilitic woman, or gambling away one thousand liras [pounds sterling (?)], or being abusive to religious saints who used to break their fasts on only one date and used to give whatever they had to the poor, I am repulsed by such civility.[97]"

To counterbalance the seemingly modern habits to which Maghrour proudly subscribes, Mahjour produces a range of instructions of traditional or religious origin, such as the digestive benefits of having sweets as "*desser*" (dessert) or using toothpicks after a meal.[98] Meanwhile, Mahjour's knowledge and debating skills were reported to Derakhshandeh and have added to her secret love for him.[99] Another long conversation on cosmology follows in which Mahjour, with his passionate admiration for the Creator, refers to the marvels of the galaxy that were "specifically described to Jâberi" (the actual author) by "Prince Arfaʿ al-Dowleh," who was a token modernist known for his travels in Europe, as part of the latter's recollections of the "observatory at Paris."[100] He also refers to Camille Flammarion's ideas on the "colourful atmosphere of some stars." [101] It is further stated that all this seemingly new information is in fact compatible with the allegorical accounts of the Prophet, which he had observed through a "*teleskoup*" (telescope) within his soul.[102]

Toward the end of the book, Mahjour bids a sentimental farewell to Derakhshandeh and departs for a suddenly planned official journey to "*Ourup*" (Europe). When he reaches Istanbul, he is informed that he has been excluded from the entourage because of budgetary cutbacks; the real reason is an old rivalry between his late father and Dastour A'lâ, who was heading the delegation. After buying a diamond diadem for Derakhshandeh, Mahjour returns home without delay. Meanwhile, his mother has arranged a wedding for him. Out of respect for his mother's wishes and to protect the reputation of the unseen young bride, he reluctantly goes ahead with this marriage.[103] The book ends with a long appendix in which further reference is made to Jâberi, the author. His works are introduced in detail and his remedies are praised.[104] For instance, both Mahjour and Maghrour agree that Jâberi's earlier recommendations concerning the necessity of organizing a modern army and restoring order in the country were followed by "Mr. Sardâr Sepah" (the future Reza Shah).[105]

To the historical novels were soon added social and critical novels with a deliberate, and at times crude, attempt at realism and the portrayal of the problems and aspirations of ordinary people. One favorite topic was alienation from city life, particularly the perfunctory character of life in Tehran. The implicit contrast here was with a much older tradition in the Middle East of the city as the source of a good and full life, in the moral sense. As urban life came to be identified with modernization and, further, with the specific modernizing programs of the state, the reputation of the old cities changed. So, too, did the urban space itself. The northern towns, such as Rasht, Tabriz, and Qazvin, were particularly exposed to Russian influence. A widely traveled British visitor wrote in 1931: "Tabriz is far more Russian than Persian and our Hotel there was more like an Inn in Poland than a Persian Caravanserai; it was called the hotel Europa." [106]

The Russian and Ottoman impact was also visible in Tehran from the late nineteenth century onward,[107] as part of a more general tide of modernism and Europeanization that swept across the Middle East.[108] Changes in clothing as well as in manners and styles of speech were accompanied by new streets, shops, and clubs; hence increased references to *parc*, *hôtel*, *restaurant*, *café*, *club*, and *cinéma*. More foreign, mainly French, loanwords that found their way into the language and still remain in modern Persian are *concert, terreur, censeur, politique, commission, démocrate, radical, gendarme, danse, classe* (in every sense of the term), *diplôme, diplomatie, programme, chance,* and *théâtre.* For some, these changes were indications of the loss of community, the disintegration of *Gemeinschaft,* and the growth of alienation. Because the state so thoroughly identified the city as its domain and its prime target for modernization, critics of the new urban life-style were almost ipso facto critics of political authority, and the factors responsible for urban degeneration and the crisis of culture came to be understood as political in nature. One implication of this politicization of the issue of urban alienation is that it prevented, or at least lessened, pessimism and bleak attitudes about the prospects of metropolitan life. At the same time, it seemed to offer the possibility that modern anomie could be resolved by political action.

Although earlier works (especially the historical novels) recommended a strong state as a necessary precondition for the restoration of national integrity and self-respect, a sense of disillusionment, helplessness, betrayal, and fatalism gradually surfaced in some later writings, notably in social novels such as Moshfeq Kâzemi's *Tehran-e Makhouf* (Tehran, City of Horrors)[109] and Mohammad Mas'oud's *Tafrihât-e Shab* (Nocturnal Pleasures).[110] These authors turned their attention to issues concerning the social situation of women that, despite being addressed almost exclusively by male authors, touched on real aspects of daily life, such as social discrimination and public prejudice, topics hitherto untackled in literary works.

The new novels were less restrained about traditionally avoided subjects like gender relations, with the result that the notoriety that was attached to the publisher or author often surrounded works of sentimental and dramatic content. The first edition of some of the works by Sâdeq Hedâyat published in Iran, for example, were regarded as unsuitable for teenagers on the grounds that they were "pessimistic"; this apprehension turned to near-hysteria when the author himself committed suicide. In the case of works by Mohammad Mas'oud, a warning was often printed on the cover and title page prohibiting their sale to persons under eighteen, and in some cases under twenty-five, years of age. Obviously, these printed warnings only served to titillate the public, but in terms of artistic imagery and literary refinement, the actual dramatic and erotic content of this literature was minimal. "Shocking" stories were seldom narrated explicitly; instead, oblique references and coy circumlocutions left most of the action to the reader's imagination. Compared to such classical works as Nezâmi's *Khosrow va Shirin* or Gorgâni's *Vis va Râmin*, written for an entirely different audience and often genuinely erotic, the modern texts were tame indeed.[111]

Among the most common themes of this literature was loss of the security of a traditional life; the characters were cast adrift in an unstable and insecure environment. Typical victims were women and ex-villagers, the two groups most in danger of being harmed by the loss of traditional ways, or at least so regarded by some male authors.[112] The real agenda of these stories was to discuss the ever-increasing sense of disjointedness that had come to prevail in a society that, after decades of uncertainty and material hardship, was now moving toward modernity. Their obsession with modernism, whether positive or negative, prevented these authors from considering the problem in terms of a wider ambiguity. Instead, they concentrated on people such as women and peasants, allegedly pure and innocent and therefore defenseless in a hostile milieu whose norms they did not understand.

These novels reflected many important features of the post-Constitutional period and helped to mold what became the Iranian modern mentality. Later literature began to tackle more difficult social issues, but many of the humanist and romantic ideals of the Constitutional movement remained in place. As the state tightened its grip on social life, however, this humanist dimension encountered problems; it could not provide a vision for transcending such circumstances. This crisis led both to the introduction of certain ideological, mainly socialist, standards and to an emphasis on a structural transformation of literary production; a new notion of the self emerged at the core of literary thinking and expression, accompanied by remarkable changes in the form of prose and in poetry. The personae of the author came to the fore: social realities now had to percolate down through the self of the author. In other words, the simple, and at times superficial and naive, attentiveness of the early novels to the reader was gradually replaced by the self-conscious supremacy of the author. This transformation as a whole can be described in terms of the introduction of an intellectual element to literary consciousness, which from the 1940s onward became a dominant feature.

– 4 –

Politics and Literature, 1941–1953

IN HIS MEMOIRS, GENERAL HASSAN ARFA RELATES TWO ANEC-
dotes to illustrate the extent of public disregard for law and government
after Reza Shah, under Allied pressure, abdicated and left the country in
September 1941. According to the first, once, while the general's wife
was being driven to downtown Tehran, her chauffeur turned the wrong
way into a one-way street, and when she objected he replied, "O well, it
does not matter now; Reza Shah is gone."[1] According to the second,
told to the general by an Englishman about a traveler who had been held
up by a bandit, "After having taken all his belongings, the robber noticed
a paper in the pocket of his victim, and asked him what it was. 'A
telegram, announcing Reza Shah's return,' said the traveller calmly. The
brigand, abandoning his booty, fled at once without asking for any
details."[2]

As these two vignettes show, the political climate of Iran did indeed
change abruptly with the shah's abdication. Rules, regulations, and political authority were so closely associated with the person of the ruling
sovereign that any change in leadership was bound to result in lawless-
ness, but at the same time, as the sixteen years of autocratic rule gave way
to frequent changes in government, a haphazard, sometimes chaotic,
combination of civil liberties ensued, allowing intellectuals to enjoy a period of cultural and political criticism.

Debates went on across the ideological spectrum, thanks to this relative freedom of expression, both in the press and in organized political
parties. Inspired by Soviet Marxism, the left offered an analysis of the
world and a blueprint for a future society. Nationalists, both moderate

and extremist, publicized their agenda. And Islamic groups examined questions concerning the interaction between Islam and modern Iranian society. Topics such as the nature of Iranian modernism and the relationship with the West were once again current themes of discussion. A free press also allowed an increase in the number of translations from European languages and this, too, contributed to the overall broadening of the intellectual vision. As a result, an array of literary and political views developed. Although pioneers in modern literary style like Sâdeq Hedâyat (1903–1951), in prose, and Nimâ Yushij (1896–1959), in poetry, had begun writing during the Reza Shah years, it was in the 1940s that modern literature began to assume its present form.

Iran had been a key area for the Allied forces during the Second World War,[3] and, although the Allies had declared that they would not interfere in the country's internal affairs, in practice intervention was inevitable. During the occupation, several prime ministers and cabinets succeeded each other in running the country.[4] In 1941–1942 alone, there were three governments: Ali Mansour (Mansour al-Molk)[5] was replaced by Mohammad-Ali Foroughi (Zakâ' al-Molk II), who was trusted by the Allies (mainly the British) and who had been active in arranging for Reza Shah's departure and the succession of his twenty-two-year-old son, Mohammad-Reza Pahlavi. Foroughi succeeded in passing the Tripartite Treaty[6] through the Majles, despite some determined opposition, before he, too, was required to step down in March 1942. His replacement, Ali Soheili, lasted only until July; then Ahmad Qavâm (Qavâm al-Saltaneh) became the new prime minister.

During this period political parties developed into a significant channel for political ambitions and sometimes for articulating political ideas.[7] Many older members of the intelligentsia had been supporters of the Constitutional movement but had also felt compelled to back the Pahlavi state when chaos threatened in the years following the First World War. In contrast, many of the young intellectuals and political activists had grown up under the autocracy of Reza Shah's reign and were eager to enjoy political freedom. Compared to the previous period, this group was also significant in size, thanks in part to the expansion of education. Politics remained an urban affair, with the royal court and foreign diplomatic missions among the centers of news, but with the Majles also becoming a lively arena for debate.

The role of the press in shaping public opinion was comparable to that in the Constitutional period.[8] In contrast to the activities of the political societies (*anjoman*s) of the Constitutional period, in the 1940s, members of many political parties, especially the left-leaning Tudeh Party, had a considerable influence on the journalism of the day.[9] Almost every aspect of the press improved, from circulation to style and substance, although in some cases the usual sloganeering and vindictiveness remained.

The bazaar continued to be, as in the Constitutional period, a focal point for internal politics and a natural constituency of the ulama. Without relinquishing many of its traditionalist orientations, the bazaar also evolved into an important stage for secular party politics, particularly for groups affiliated with the National Front coalition. The streets surrounding the Majles, the bazaar, the university, and the Marble Palace, at the center of the city, were often the site for political rallies and large meetings,[10] whose frequency inspired the introduction of a new loanword, *miting* (meeting). A particularly popular spot was the Bahârestân Square opposite the Majles, because it had several main avenues (such as Sarcheshmeh and the long stretch of Nâderi-Estânbul-Shâhabâd) leading into it. Another significant location was Nâderi Avenue in Tehran. It encapsulated on a small scale the kind of interplay between economics, politics, and culture that was a hallmark of the transition to modernity. The street, lined with newly opened shops vending European-style sweets and pastries, cafés, restaurants, pharmacies, stationery stores and booksellers, cinemas and theaters, tailors and barber shops, fashionable dressmakers, and dance studios, represented a new type of urban space that people regarded as being modern. With the British, Soviet, Turkish, German, French, and Italian embassy compounds and housing for the foreign staff and their families located nearby, there was a ready market for the street's European-style goods and services. Groceries stocked such exotic items as sausage, olives, mustard, mushrooms, and artichokes, suitable for European dishes but hardly ever used in Persian cuisine.[11] Many black-market consumer goods, from clothing and sports gear to cosmetics and kitchenware, were available in the alley behind the British Embassy, heightening the overall "European" reputation of the area.

Many Armenians, Jews, and Zoroastrians resided in the Nâderi Avenue quarter and gave it an atmosphere very different from that of predominantly Muslim neighborhoods. Some members of the Armenian community who had migrated to Iran in the aftermath of the Russian Revolution opened modern businesses for which demand was increasing, such as auto repair shops; photography studios; liquor stores; delicatessens; sandwich, pastry, and piroshki shops; and music and dance studios. Among the area's residents and customers one could hear Armenian and Turkish being spoken along with newly acquired Persian.[12]

This cosmopolitan air attracted local intellectuals, who frequented the European-style cafés such as Café Nâderi and Café Firouz, which were very different from the traditional *qahveh-khwâneh* (coffeehouse) with its exclusively male patronage. Café Nâderi was an extension of the restaurant of the then-fashionable Hotel Nâderi. Some of the shops that opened in the area in the 1940s have thus far survived the ravages of time and are still operating today.

After Reza Shah's abdication, several political parties sprang up, of which three are representative: the leftist Tudeh Party, the right-wing National Will Party, and the centrist National Front, a coalition of several political parties and groups. Although the results of the 1943 elections favored the conservative faction, the Tudeh Party and the National Front had greater influence on Iranian intellectuals both during that period and after. A mention can also be made of Hezb-e Demokrât (Democrat Party), founded in 1946 by Ahmad Qavâm (Qavâm al-Saltaneh). It was more of an association of old-guard aristocratic politicians (including Muzaffar Firouz, Mohammad Farmânfarmâ, ʿAbdol-Qâsem Amini, and Sardâr Fâkher Hekmat) and anti-British and non-Tudeh radical intellectuals (including Mohammad-Taqi Bahâr, Mahmoud Mahmoud, and Hasan Arsanjâni), who at times had diverse political opinions and leanings.[13] It is also worth noting that Mohammad-Reza Shah distrusted this party and was often suspicious that its more senior and influential members (like Qavâm and Firouz) would, independent of him, enter negotiations with the representatives of one of the superpowers.

Following Qavâm's fall from power in 1948, Hezb-e Demokrât, too, soon disintegrated. This and other examples that came later, such as Hezb-e Mardom (People's Party) and Hezb-e Melliyoun (Nationalists' Party), which appeared following a royal decree in 1958 urging a two-party system, indicate that the upper middle class had readily tacked on the royal court, did not see any reason to form a meaningful and viable political party, and was basically cynical about the whole parliamentary process. The Shah's own experiment with the Hezb-e Rastazhiz (Resurrection Party) in the mid-1970s was likewise an indication of the reality of most political parties in Iran, which for the most part were devoid of institutional and conceptual underpinnings. An exception was perhaps the Tudeh Party, which, at least for the 1940s, activated the considerable political and ideological potential of the younger generation of Iranian intellectuals.

The Tudeh Party was grounded in the Marxism imported from Russia in the Constitutional period. After the Bolshevik Revolution, socialist ideas gained a wide following among Iranian activists, who admired the Russian revolutionaries and especially Lenin (1870–1924). The February 1921 treaty signed by the Socialist government, which cancelled the previous Tzarist concessions in Iran, further increased the popularity of the new Soviet regime.[14] The existence of pro-socialist sentiments in Iran is confirmed by the many references in the literature and journalism of the 1920s and 1930s.[15]

The Iranian intelligentsia were also exposed to Marxism by Taqi Arrâni (1902–1940), a graduate of Berlin University, whose thinking had a determinist and natural-science orientation similar to the ideology of the Second International.[16] Arrâni's ideas so influenced many younger members of the Group of Fifty-Three, which later formed the nucleus of the Tudeh Party, that he is considered their spiritual leader.[17] Members of this group were arrested in 1937 on charges of communist activity, but were released, along with most political prisoners, shortly after Reza Shah's departure from the country.

Hezb-e Tudeh-ye Iran (The Party of the Iranian Masses) was formed in late September 1941 and held its first provincial congress in June 1942. In the beginning, it defined itself as a mass organization based on a broad union of workers, peasants, artisans, and intellectuals. It did not officially declare socialism and Marxism as its ideology, not only because a 1931 law forbidding the formation of associations with "collectivist ideology" was theoretically still in force, but also because, as a newly formed party, it did not want to alienate people with religious sentiments who might otherwise become members. Moreover, although the Tudeh Party's pro-Soviet stance was evident from the beginning, neither the party nor its Soviet supporters wanted to heighten suspicion among the Western forces, since that might jeopardize Allied assistance to the Russian front.[18]

During the war years, the main propaganda efforts of the party, reflected largely in its newspapers, first *Siâsat* (Politics), then *Rahbar* (Leader), and later *Mardom* (People), were focused on anti-Fascist and pro-peace campaigns. At the same time, the party spent much of its energy trying to convert Iranian intellectuals with nationalist aspirations who, preoccupied with the idea of fighting British influence and imperialist intervention, had developed pro-German tendencies. In the words of a later author, the party "sought to divert the Anglophobic element of Iranian nationalism from a pro-German orientation to an anti-Fascist one."[19] The early constituencies of the Tudeh Party outside Tehran were located in Azarbâyjân, Gilân, and Mâzandarân, northern provinces that had a history of political activity. Âzarbâyjân and Gilân, from the turn of the century until the establishment of the Pahlavi state, were among the most politically active areas of Iran and their proximity to Russia guaranteed exposure to socialist ideas. Two other important constituencies of the Tudeh Party were in Isfahan and Abadan, both of which had a substantial industrial working-class population—Isfahan emerged in the 1940s as a major center for textile production and Abadan expanded with the growth of its large oil refinery.[20]

The groundwork for political activity and party organization was laid at the First Conference (held in Tehran on 17 Mehr 1321/9 October 1942), which was attended by 120 delegates representing intellectuals, workers, professionals, and artisans from Tehran and the provinces.[21] Conference delegates called for the restoration of civil liberties, in accordance with the Iranian Constitution, and the cancellation of the "antidemocratic" laws of Reza Shah, including the 1931 law banning communist activities. They recommended the creation of a democratic government that would be representative of the people, reformed electoral laws and restoration of political rights for women, the redistribution of state and crown lands to peasants and the purchase of the large private estates by the government to be distributed among the peasants, an eight-hour day for workers, and legal recognition of trade unions.[22] Delegates also stressed the principle of "democratic centralism," a trademark of Stalinist ideology. Two areas in which the Tudeh Party's activism was particularly effective were the organization of trade unions and the publication of radical journals and newspapers that stressed the urgency of economic, social, and political change. Party members also played a role in the December 1942 bread riots in Tehran.[23] On the whole, the popularity of radical ideology persisted among the youth; when the first party congress convened in Tehran in August 1944, there were 168 delegates representing 25,800 members.[24]

By 1946, internal rifts and strains had begun to appear. Party intellectuals, notably Eprim Eshâq and Khalil Maleki, voiced doubts and concerns over various policy and organizational issues. Eshâq, a young Assyrian economist who had studied at Cambridge, was especially outspoken. His pamphlets, *Cheh Bâyad Kard?* (What Is to be Done?) and *Hezb-e Tudeh-ye Iran Sar-e Du Râh* (The Tudeh Party of Iran at a Crossroads) were both critical and controversial.[25] Eshâq argued that the party's emphasis on gaining members had reduced the quality of its membership and suggested that party intellectuals should occasionally expel opportunist elements, thus forcibly maintaining the party as a pioneering organization faithful to its original principles. He further proposed that the party should reassure people regarding its patriotic loyalties by demonstrating that it was not a blind follower of Moscow. A key step, according to Es-hâq, would be to establish relationships with the labor unions of capitalist countries. None of these recommendations were accepted by the leadership, and subsequently Eshâq left the party.[26]

Khalil Maleki had been a prominent member of the Group of Fifty-Three.[27] As a Tudeh Party member, he decried the undemocratic behavior of the party leadership and protested against their political and moral dependency on the Soviet Union. He eventually formalized his criticisms into an extended essay.[28] Members of Maleki's faction (mainly young intellectuals) considered themselves constructive critics and party "reformists." They insisted on a democratic electoral procedure and on teaching theory to young cadres. They urged the leadership to convene the second party congress, which had been intentionally delayed in the aftermath of the collapse of the separatist movement in Âzarbâyjân. Although the reformist group was well represented in the local central committee at a provincial conference in Tehran (convened in July 1946), the debates continued and finally resulted in a major party split in early 1948.[29]

The second party congress was held soon after, in April. Anvar Khâmeh'i was the leader of the third faction critical of the party leadership. But unlike Eshâq or Maleki, Khâmeh'i was in favor of establishing closer ties with the Soviet Union. He denounced Maleki's group as a "nationalist revisionist" faction.[30]

In the long term, the party's disregard for the criticisms of its own members demoralized the youngest members and undercut the effective dissemination of socialist ideas to the Iranian public. The initial recruits to the party were young and enthusiastic intellectuals; they had experienced both the autocracy and modernism of the Reza Shah years, and the kind of socialism the Tudeh Party offered resembled too closely the old practice of submission to authority, now simply rephrased as party discipline and "democratic centralism." Among the general public, the party's passive subservience to the Soviets created the impression that being a communist was synonymous, not only with being an atheist, but also with being subservient to Russia and the Soviet Union. However, not every member of the Tudeh Party was a "stooge" of the Soviet Union; their Russophilia was more a result of memories that had grown sweeter with the passage of time. For many who had become Tudeh supporters in their youth, pro-Tudeh sentiments, even after they had been discredited, remained too important to relinquish. Regardless of their profound intellectual disillusionment, a diehard loyalty continued among the older Tudeh supporters and was sometimes passed on to younger family members or to junior associates.

Another significant venue for politically active intellectuals in the 1940s and early 1950s was the Jebhe-ye Melli (National Front), a coalition of several parties and parliamentary groups, whose mission, broadly speaking, was to curb the power of the oligarchy of old families, and to support Mosaddeq in his fight against colonial influence, especially regarding the oil industry and interests. The most important components of the National Front were the Iran Party, the Toilers Party, the National Party of Iran, and the Fadâ'iân-e Islam.

The Iran Party (Hezb-e Iran), whose origins can be traced to an engineers' association, was established in October 1941; its membership expanded to include other nationalist and social democratic intellectuals and professionals, in addition to engineers. The majority of its early leading figures, including Sâdeq Rezazâdeh Shafaq, Karim Sanjâbi, Mehdi Bâzargân, Allâhyâr Sâleh, Shams al-Din Amir-'Alâ'i, and Kâzem Hasibi, were middle-class men in their forties, most of whom had been educated in Europe.[31]

The Toilers Party (Hezb-e Zahmatkeshân) was jointly founded by Mozaffar Baqâ'i and Khalil Maleki, a few years after the latter had left the Tudeh Party. Under Baqâ'i's leadership, the party had tried, unsuccessfully, to establish a power base among the industrial workers. Maleki and his intellectual group handled the party's publications.[32] In addition to the official organ, *Shâhed* (Witness), these publications included the party's youth paper, *Nirouy-e Sevvom* (the Third Force), and the intellectual journal *'Elm va Zendegi* (Science and Life), which was favored mostly by university students and the intelligentsia.

The National Party of Iran (Hezb-e Mellat-e Iran) was founded by Dâryoush Forouhar, who had started his political activities as a high school student, organizing school demonstrations in support of Mosaddeq. In 1941 at Tehran University, he and fellow student Mohsen Pezeshkpour collaborated to form a nationalist organization called the Pan-Iranist Party (Hezb-e Pân-Iranist). In 1952, Forouhar parted company with Pezeshkpour, whose loyalty to Mossadeq he had doubted, and formed his own National Party. Under Forouhar's leadership, the party opposed both capitalism and communism, the monarchy, and the influence of various religious groups, such as the Jews, the Baha'is, and the reactionaries among the mullahs. The party was fervently in favor of restoring both the territorial and spiritual integrity of Iran; it proposed regaining lost territories in the Caucasus, Afghanistan, and the island of Bahrein in the Persian Gulf. The National Party was popular mainly among high school students in Tehran. Its membership never exceeded a few hundred people, and the leadership of the National Front did not consider it significant.[33]

The last group, the Fadâ'iân-e Islam (Devotees of Islam), was close to Ayatollah Abul-Qâsem Kâshâni and was financed by a group of bazaar merchants. Kâshâni's followers consisted mainly of Shi'i zealots with strong anti-Western sentiments.[34] Although they initially supported Mosaddeq in his campaign to nationalize the oil industry, they later withdrew their support, thus contributing to his eventual fall.[35] On his part, however, Mosaddeq, by misreading the lessons of the mass demonstrations of 30 Tir 1331/21 July 1952, which restored him back to power,[36] failed to see that mere reliance on *"afkâr-e 'omoumi"* (public opinion) with no organization was not effective enough against an urban situation where a small army could topple a regime by grabbing the radio station and arresting a handful of individual politicians. He also displayed an inability to compromise and make necessary alliances. The same kind of illusion has often dominated the Iranian intellectuals, who have always craved ready-made blueprints yet failed to organize.

The Intellectual Element

One of the main factors in the ideological repertoire of the Iranian intelligentsia is what they call the "intellectual element" (*'onsor-e rowshan-fekri*), referring to the perspective, or the ideological attribute, through which the intelligentsia view the world and view themselves as a distinct social type. This self-image rests on certain a priori methodological and theoretical premises, which were not quite clearly spelled out; only a self-avowed intellectual could presume what was meant by this demarcation. For instance, in modern intellectual literary texts, reception of the intellectual element depended on the reader's typology and a shared vision with the author. Even in the extreme cases of propaganda literature, ideological statements were made from a position of taken-for-granted certainty, lest the text become less effective and less persuasive. Here, another aspect of the intellectual attribute can be seen in the production and reproduction of a tacit criterion of trust and the building of a mental bridge between the author and the reader. Readers of a different mentality and typology found it increasingly difficult to maintain a fully intelligible link with an intellectual text or argument that inclined to pre-suppose its ideal audience and was therefore inattentive or indifferent to readers who did not understand, mistrusted, or disagreed with its under-lying classifications and criteria. These readers often tended to regard such texts as either impenetrable or irrelevant, or both.

Intellectual texts frequently reflected the assumption that both the au-thor and the reader subscribed to particular notions of rationality that were taken in an erratic manner from modern European ideas. In any given case, such subscription was viewed as an indispensable compon-ent of modernity, though these notions and ideas varied in different phases of modernism. Earlier generations of reformists during the second half of the nineteenth century and during the Constitutional period were inspired by the Enlightenment and, in more radical cases, by Jaco-binic ideas; later modernists, especially during the Reza Shah period, were inspired by humanist ideas and in many cases by romantic national-ism; and Marxism and socialism, in one version or another, were domi-nant among the left between the 1940s and 1970s and almost monopo-lized the axiology of the "intellectual element."

These ideas were also influenced by certain traits of Iranian culture, whether those influences were acknowledged (e.g., by the humanists) or played down (e.g., by the Marxists). In the latter perspective the "intel-lectual element" often called for a holistic or, in effect, totalizing view of the world rather than a particularistic or individualistic approach. It tended to view the individual as belonging to general categories of cul-ture or class. This ideological credo equipped its followers with an iden-tity theory through which they saw the past and present in terms of a dialectic of historical exigencies, regarded the future as an inevitable out-come of a grand historical plan, and portrayed that future exclusively as the negation of both past and present. Marxists claimed to be the only representatives of a movement for radical social change and, like their counterparts elsewhere, they held their historical conceptualization as a universal and indisputable truth. They perceived themselves as the custo-dians of a scientific messianism, whose tasks were both theoretical (i.e., to engage in analysis and consciousness-raising) and organizational (i.e., to organize what they regarded as progressive political parties).

To articulate its ideas, the intelligentsia had to overcome particular problems and challenges posed by the Persian language. The semantic repertoire of the intellectuals in the 1940s, as in other periods in the twentieth century, included bureaucratic, religious, mystic, Western (es-pecially for technical, philosophical, and artistic terms), military, and so-called "pure" Persian terminologies.[37] But modern intellectual discourse also suffered from an aura of superficiality, though it professed and pre-supposed an adherence to objective rationality and causal explanation combined with a Promethean spirit. The crisis of syntax in this language was indicative of an innate insecurity regarding cultural identity. Al-though intellectuals were adamant in identifying themselves with their own style, in their broader social interactions they had to correspond with and relate to the common linguistic repertoire of the society. Nev-ertheless, the intellectual style left its mark on contemporary discourse by appearing as politically progressive. Many aspiring writers with a dif-ferent vision felt the need to adopt it as best they could. A case in point is the Maktabi (Doctrinaire) literature that has appeared since the revolu-tion of 1979, in which young, enthusiastic Muslim writers express their zeal in both poetry and prose using modern forms, even while they ex-plicitly reject the self-avowed secularism and modernism of the intellec-tuals who initiated them.[38]

It is not surprising that modern Iranian intellectuals who used this lan-guage did not succeed in reaching a literary self-confidence equal to their convictions in the realm of ideology and political criticism. Al-though among the writers and poets, especially, it would be inaccurate to link literary style with ideology, a notable degree of stylistic and termi-nological similarity existed across the ideological spectrum. Regardless of their ideological tendencies, intellectuals still needed to communicate with people if they were to develop an audience for their work. This was not a new dilemma, nor one the generation of the 1940s found easy to overcome. A common solution for those who were radical in their po-litical persuasion was to alter the content of their work but maintain the traditional and familiar form of the genre. Others experimented in both areas.

The First (and Last) Congress of Iranian Writers

The diversity of intellectual production was evident in the First Congress of Iranian Writers, held in the summer of 1325/1946 in Tehran. In all, seventy-eight poets and writers were invited to attend by the sponsors, the Iran-Soviet Cultural Society.[39] The congress was chaired by Moham-mad-Taqi Bahâr, who was then the minister of culture, and was presided over by Karim Keshâvarz (a pro-Tudeh writer and translator), Sâdeq Hedâyat (a pioneer of modern Persian prose), Ali-Akbar Dehkhodâ (known for his political satires during the Constitutional period, and for his later scholarship in Persian lexicography), Badi' al-Zamân Forouzân-far (an authority on classical Persian literature), and Ali-Asghar Hekmat (a scholar and politician), among others. At the main sessions of the congress several poets and writers read excerpts from their works. There were also longer papers, starting with a discussion by Ali-Asghar Hekmat on the state of Persian poetry during the fifty years following the assassination of Nâser al-Din Shah in 1896.[40] Ehsân Tabari, a Marxist writer and critic and a member of the Tudeh Party, Parviz Nâtel-Khânlari, a literary scholar and translator, and 'Abdol-Hosein Noushin, a writer and a member of the Tudeh Party, responded to Hekmat's speech. All of them mentioned the negative effects that Reza Shah's censorship had on literature. Tabari and Noushin gave a Marxist interpretation of the nature of poetry and its possible taxonomy.

Tabari said that the congress was not just another literary meeting: "Our purpose was to discuss, confer, and draw conclusions. We would like to see that at the end of the Congress every participant would have a clear conception about art and its future course."[41] Khânlari spoke on recent developments in Persian prose, giving a historical account of various styles and genres including travel books, journalism, translations, novels, and drama, as well as on recent trends in scholarship.[42] Noting what he regarded as the negative effects of both internal despotism and foreign exploitation on literary development in Iran, he welcomed the recent upsurge in literary activity and concluded that contemporary writers must try to attune their writing to the modern world.[43]

Respondents to Khânlari's paper included the literary critic and author Fâtemeh Sayyâh[44] and writers Parviz Khatibi and Bozorg 'Alavi, who also called for guidelines for future poetry and prose.[45] Sayyâh and Tabari presented more theoretical essays on the tasks of literary criticism[46] and on criticism and the nature of art and aesthetics,[47] respectively. They both elaborated on these arguments with reference to the ideas of nineteenth-century Russian literary critics such as V. G. Belinsky and N. G. Chernyshevsky,[48] perhaps the first time in Iran that such views and theories had been openly discussed.[49] Art is a social product, said Tabari, and like science, religion, and politics, it is an instrument of class struggle; its highest purpose is to speed up social evolution.[50] He recommended that contemporary Iranian writers should read the works of "foreign masters" (by which he presumably meant the classics of Marxism, the socialist realists, and Soviet-approved authors) and translate them into good Persian.[51] Sayyâh praised socialist realism as the most progressive perspective in both literary production and criticism. She further stated that the most fundamental task of criticism was to promote genuine realism as the dominant form of literary style, especially prose style, in Iran.[52]

Socialist realism was also a favorite subject among many of the congress's young participants. The congress offered an occasion at which the modernist trend in Persian literature, and especially the new poetry, was openly, if somewhat belatedly, introduced. In retrospect one must say that the congress also displayed a remarkable willingness to consider, or at least listen to, opposing ideologies and tastes. Literary and political conservatives like Mohammad-Taqi Bahâr, Badiʿ al-Zamân Forouzânfar, and Ali-Asghar Hekmat politely sat through lectures by young Marxists like Tabari, displaying a tolerance that disappeared in later years as literary occasions and associations of intellectuals became increasingly doctrinaire in their political outlook.[53] In fact, later in life, some of the main actors, like Khânlari and Tabari, opted for different roads, each of which showed the twists and turns of Persian history and the intellectuals' manifold reactions to them. The congress was one of those rare moments that not only encapsulates a period, but also hints at what is to come.

– 5 –

Critique of Westernism and Debates over Modernity

THE COUP D'ÉTAT IN THE SUMMER OF 1953 THAT OVERTHREW
the government of Mosaddeq was a turning point in the political history
of contemporary Iran. However, the same thing cannot be said for the
country's intellectual and cultural history, for which the coming of a
new era seems delayed by almost one decade. Most people, especially in
the cities, had grown weary of political confusion and economic austerity and were eager to return to a normal life. Some even approved of the
coup: although Mosaddeq's anti-imperialist policy had been a source of
popular support and, perhaps, international prestige, for the majority of
those who were not directly involved in politics the episode seemed like
a passing event.

In the years that followed, Mohammad-Reza Shah gradually succeeded in establishing his personal rule over the country. In 1957 the secret police or Sâzmân-e Ettelâ'ât va Amniyat-e Keshvar (National Information and Security Organization), better known by its acronym
SAVAK, was established to curb political opposition.[1] Their crackdown
shattered the Tudeh Party, and several of its leaders fled to the Soviet
Union and Eastern Europe. Many of those who remained were arrested
and tried; the military among them were given the harshest sentences.[2]
The disintegration of the National Front and the political parties attached to it was another consequence of the coup. Mosaddeq was tried
in a military court.[3] Most of his cabinet members and figures loyal to
him were arrested; Hosein Fâtemi, his foreign minister, was later executed. A month after the coup, in September 1953, a small group of vet-
erans of the National Front founded the National Resistance Movement

(Nehzat-e Moqâvemat-e Melli), but it was suppressed by the authorities in less than three years. In spring 1961, they tried again: a faction of the National Resistance Movement, consisting mainly of Muslim nationalists, formed the Liberation Movement of Iran (Nehzat-e Âzâdi-ye Iran).[4]

The Shah acted more cautiously in dealing with the ulama, the bazaaris, and the landlords. He tolerated the increased influence of the last group in the eighteenth and nineteenth sessions of the Majles and only gradually began to challenge its authority with the land reform he implemented in the early 1960s.[5] The government interfered even less in the affairs of the bazaar, which retained much of its economic independence. This situation also began to change after the land reform as the state exerted more control over the private sector.[6] The shah had little difficulty in isolating critical clerical opinion from daily political affairs. The government's main attention was given to the more moderate ulama, such as Ayatollah Behbahâni and Ayatollah Boroujerdi. Ayatollah Kâshâni and one of his associates, Shams Qanâtâbâdi, were briefly imprisoned, but they were released soon after they publicly dissociated themselves from the extremist group Fadâ'iân-e Islam.[7] In January 1956 some of the group's major figures, such as Mojtabâ Navvâb-Safavi, were executed on assassination and conspiracy charges. In order to please the ulama, in 1955 the government launched a campaign against the Bahâ'is, and the army occupied their central temple in Tehran. This move dampened the opposition among the ulama to the negotiations with the consortium of oil companies and to Iran's partnership in the Baghdad Pact.[8]

Throughout this period university campuses were among the main centers of opposition to the shah. On 7 December 1953, in protest against American vice president Richard Nixon's impending visit to Iran, students held a demonstration at Tehran University, despite the presence of martial law forces. When soldiers fired into the crowd, three students were killed. There was a strong feeling at the time that the incident had been staged to allow the use of violence to deter further protest.[9] If so, it was not a successful strategy in the end, because it merely generated more opposition to the government among students, both inside the country and abroad, which became more radicalized and took ever more militant forms as the years passed.

From the mid-1960s on, the younger generation of activists, disillusioned by the ambivalent response of the old opposition to such developments as the plan for land reform and the shah's White Revolution, increasingly favored armed resistance.[10] In the early 1970s, some of them began to carry out a series of attacks against state institutions. The static

Iranian government was also a factor contributing to resistance. In contrast to the 1940s and early 1950s, when prime ministers changed frequently, Amir 'Abbâs Hoveydâ remained at his post as prime minister for almost thirteen years (1965–1977), leading some intellectuals to believe that the government was becoming entrenched and impervious to reform. Finally, the popularity of an ideology of armed struggle owed much to the expansion of the educational system. During the 1960s and 1970s, those who sympathized most with this ideology were mainly university students and intelligentsia with middle-class backgrounds.

The Intelligentsia and the University

Relative political stability and the growth of a salaried middle class were among the factors needed to develop the country's educational system.[11] From the mid-1950s onward, the urban middle class expanded both in numbers and in prominence, as many were absorbed into the growing state bureaucracy.[12] The number of primary and high schools rose considerably from the early 1960s onward,[13] and demand for higher education soon increased to such an extent that the existing universities could not absorb all the applicants. In 1977, for example, out of 290,000 applicants who took part in the nationwide entrance examination to the universities, only 60,000 were accepted.[14] As a result, many went abroad for higher education, supported either by their families or by government grants.[15]

Throughout the period between the coup d'état of 1953 and the revolution of 1979, the universities continued to be the scene of student demonstrations and strikes, often with police intervention and, particularly in the 1970s, the arrest of student activists by SAVAK and a temporary closure of the campus. In 1970, special police units were stationed permanently on the more politically active campuses, most notably at Tehran University, Tehran Polytechnic, and the Âriâmehr University of Technology.[16] Most of the supporters of opposition groups such as the Tudeh Party, the National Front, and the Liberation Movement of Iran were associated with the universities, either as faculty or students. From the state's perspective, it was even more alarming that the majority of the founders, early cadres, and sympathizers of the underground guerrilla groups, notably the Mojâhedin and the Fadâ'iân, were university students or employees.[17] Security intelligence, as a result of its own assessment and advice from its foreign counterparts, became increasingly paranoid, convinced that a rising tide of socialism or "Islamic Marxism" (the shah's name for the ideology of young Muslim militants) would spill out over the walls of the universities into the country at large.[18] One excessive measure taken by SAVAK at Tehran University and reported in the personal diaries of Asadollah Alam, who was then the Minister of the Royal Court, even infuriated the shah:

> *Sunday, 7 April* [1974].
> *Reported that Savak have impounded the libraries of several student unions within Tehran University. They claim that all the books are subversive. "No book can be deemed subversive at a university", I said. "In any event, Your Majesty [the shah] left specific instructions that students should be free to read whatever they like, to study a problem from every possible angle." "Make sure that the books are returned", he replied, "and tell the parties responsible that such stupidity will not go unpunished in the future".*[19]

Another account, also by Alam, further illustrates the ambivalence of the shah toward the political demands of the student opposition movement.

> *Friday, 8 March* [1974].
> *Audience . . . Discussed the unrest in the universities. "It puzzles me", HIM [the shah] declared. "Most of our problems are behind us and our soldiers have shown they can fight like lions. Yet still we're plagued by the fuss generated by a tiny minority of students." "Some of them are keen to become martyrs", I said, "and others draw unfavourable comparisons between our political system and that of the European democracies." "But what has democracy ever done for Europe?", he retorted . . . adding, "Many of these subversives are in the pay of foreign powers." I pointed out that they were bound to appear so if we maintain that with so much material progress people are not entitled to express any sort of complaint. On the other hand, if we honestly admitted that our regime has its shortcomings, then we'd learn to regard these so-called subversives in a very different light. "Tell the President of Tehran University that I expect his students to display their dedication to this country. The same goes for our students everywhere", he replied.*[20]

Students studying abroad were openly critical of the Pahlavi regime.[21] This opposition was politically and ideologically diverse, but it tended to reflect the personalities of individual activists and the exigencies of host societies rather than the realities in Iran itself, especially among the left-ist groups.[22] Associations of Iranian students were among the most active foreign student groups in Western Europe and North America,[23] and their activities embarrassed a publicity-conscious regime sensitive to its international image[24] and undermined the state's claims of legitimacy. On 8 March 1974, Alam reports: "A few Iranian students have occupied our embassies in Stockholm, Brussels and The Hague and are demanding greater political freedom here in Iran. Thanks to the BBC, the incident has been blown up out of all proportion. Ridiculous!"[25]

The role of these students was particularly significant when one considers that many of them returned to Iran to take jobs in business, government administration, and public service, with their sense of personal loyalty to the state still weak or nonexistent, in part an extension of the global trend of student militancy in the 1960s. They had been impressed by the Paris riots in 1968 and the anti–Vietnam War activities in the United States around the same time, and following these models, they drew a sharp distinction between patriotic sentiments and allegiance to the ruling regime. It was not surprising, therefore, that the collapse of the shah's regime was greatly accelerated by the overwhelming participation of the skilled and professional classes through strikes and other forms of civil disobedience. As political dissent was shared between students at home and those who were protesting abroad, the state propaganda could not use one group to discount or discredit the other. Although SAVAK could not put the same degree of pressure and control on the Iranian students in foreign countries as on the students at home, they kept a close watch on them.[26]

Intellectual Expression in Periodicals

Periodicals were a major channel for the intelligentsia to disseminate their ideas in the post-1953 period; they included literary miscellanies and anthologies (frequently referred to as *jong*) that often contained essays on social and political issues, as well as the more usual public interest journals. The financial and political obstacles such periodicals had to overcome depended largely on the personal and political standing of their editors and patrons.[27] Some of these journals, such as *Sokhan* (Speech) and *Râhnamâ-ye Ketâb* (Review of Books), had a scholarly orientation and their editors and regular contributors consisted mostly of academics. Others, such as *Negin* (Gem), a monthly journal on politics, arts, and literature edited by Mahmoud Enâyat, and the weekly *Ferdowsi*, edited by ʿAbbâs Pahlevân, offered more variety in their content and therefore enjoyed a wider audience.[28] Still others, mainly the *jong*s, were more congenial to younger and less-established authors, and their editors were less concerned about complying with conventional academic norms.

The *jong*s played a significant role in the advancement of modern literature (especially the new poetry). In the pages of such *jong*s as *Khousheh* (Bunch), *Sadaf* (Shell), *Daftarhâ-ye Zamâneh* (Notebooks), and *Alefbâ* (Alphabet), works by younger writers began to appear alongside the contributions of better-known authors. One of the main objectives of the *jong*s was to introduce new Persian literature to a broader and younger audience. Although the *jong*s challenged the literary establishment, it was the political establishment that gave them trouble. They often were subjected to state censorship, were banned, or had their publication suspended for a while, and some never got off the ground; they were closed down after the first issue. No amount of state harassment succeeded in suppressing them completely, however, because they sprouted up continually all over the country.[29]

They published translations of poetry, prose, drama, and criticism from European, Russian, American, Asian, and African writers.[30] Among the younger generation of university students and intellectuals, they were regarded as reliable supplements[31] to, if not substitutes for, the arid and fossilized information contained in faculty journals and the more established periodicals, where current issues were given scant coverage, or in their course packages.[32] Various journals and *jong*s ran the gamut in ideology from conservative, to moderate, to "progressive" (radical or avant-garde). Periodicals such as *Mehr* (the Sun, also meaning Affection), *Yâdegâr* (Memento), *Armaghân* (Gift), *Bâgh-e Sâʾeb* (The Garden of Sâʾeb), *Vahid*, and *Yaghmâ* fell into the first category.[33] They were produced by literary conservatives and included regular contributions from established academics. They dismissed the new literature, especially new poetry, and continued an earlier tradition of scholarship that had developed during the Reza Shah period and was inspired by European Orientalism. Of special importance in this latter context is the literary and historical journal *Yâdegâr*, which was published by the prolific historian ʿAbbâs Eqbâl Âshtiâni.[34] The journal began to appear in 1324/1945 and lasted through five volumes. On the whole it displays some pioneering efforts by contemporary Iranian historians to employ a critical and scholarly approach to historiography, both in methodology and in substantive research on Iranian history.

A representative monthly journal of literary and social issues was *Mehr*, founded by Majid Movaqqar in Tehran in Khordâd 1312/June 1933. The last issue of the journal appeared in Âbân 1346/November 1967, with one interruption by the censor in 1940.[35] After the abdication of Reza Shah, Movaqqar entered politics and became a Majles deputy, but he continued to express his disillusionment with politics and his disapproval of political activity, considering his journal both a more valuable service and a more personally rewarding occupation.[36] The purpose of *Mehr* was to promote the idea of social development and cultural progress. It ran articles on diverse topics; there were passages from classical studies side by side with articles on popular science.[37] Later issues, however, emphasized literary and historical topics and therefore seem less diverse and random. In a series of articles entitled "Iran bar Lab-e Partgâh" (Iran on the Verge of a Precipice), written in 1952 just before the coup d'état, Movaqqar was uncharacteristically political in expressing his grave concern about the critical situation in Iran and his loyalty to the "young King," who, as Movaqqar saw it, "cared for [his] subject(s)" (*timâr-e ra'yat*),[38] but almost immediately the journal returned to its earlier pattern of random articles.[39]

Another group of periodicals combined an academic and scholarly approach with a more up-to-date selection of topics and material. They included historical and literary contributions by Iranian authors and/or translations of foreign works. The best of these is the monthly journal *Sokhan* (Speech),[40] founded in Tehran in the summer of 1943 by Parviz Nâtel Khânlari, who remained its editor throughout its existence and was responsible for the journal's high reputation as a lucid, literary publication.[41] Khânlari also succeeded in safeguarding the integrity of the journal during the politicized years of the 1940s and the post-1953 period. However, in his later life, Khânlari was unfairly cast as an Iranian Malraux[42] by the more radical intellectuals. After the revolution of 1979 and in view of his fame and high profile during the previous regime, Khânlari was detained for a short period and then released. *Sokhan* covered a wide range of topics from literature, arts, and history to sociology, psychology, and politics. A typical issue contained essays ranging in topic from the demography of Tehran to the Italian Renaissance to the poetry of T. S. Eliot and the politics of India. It provided writers, poets, and translators with a much-needed forum for expression.[43]

In each of its issues the journal tried to maintain a diversity of topics, which included, for example, new writings in poetry and prose as well as

Persian translations of modern and contemporary literary works in other languages, literary criticism, arts, social studies, history and historiography, philosophy, economics, and book reviews.[44] Although the publication of *Sokhan*, which in its later years had become slightly passé, came to an end after the revolution of 1979, it left a considerable impact on Iranian intellectual life.[45]

A third class of periodicals, the "progressive journals," can be exemplified by *Andisheh va Honar* (Ideas and Arts), a leftist journal founded by Nâser Vosouqi in Tehran in April 1954.[46] Vosouqi was both the owner and the editor-in-chief of *Andisheh va Honar*, though occasionally, for special volumes, he would call in guest editors such as Javâd Pour-Vakil, who was also later editor of the literary journal *Ârash*, and Shamin Bahâr. The journal was to be a monthly but seldom appeared regularly, owing to government bans.[47] It distanced itself from the government to retain its reputation as an independent, left-oriented, critical forum, but since most of the material it published was irrelevant to politics, the government's censorship was baseless and, because it led to the further alienation of its readership, which consisted mostly of intellectuals, counterproductive as well. Like *Sokhan*, *Andisheh va Honar* covered a wide range of topics—political economy, urban and rural sociology, politics, literature, arts, literary criticism, and linguistics, as well as translations, mainly from English, on a variety of contemporary and trendy topics. But it differed from *Sokhan* in its ideological orientation, themes, and style.

Andisheh va Honar was socialist rather than communist in orientation and steered clear of both the Tudeh Party and Soviet Marxism in general. Although it never directly criticized the traditional Iranian left, it regularly published translations of articles on the theory and practice of socialism that were in line with the ideas of "Western Marxists,"[48] and the writings of "ex-communists" and critics of Stalinism such as Arthur Koestler[49] and Isaac Deutscher.[50] *Andisheh va Honar* covered themes and topics in the social sciences that either were current or had previously been monopolized, if not manipulated, by the Tudeh Party,[51] as well as linguistics, sociology, and economics.[52] Its avant-garde themes and topics gave it an elitist cast that was heightened by affectations such as printing English terms, titles, and names in the Latin alphabet. That practice seemed particularly eccentric in later years, when the number of translations from English had increased and many European terms had well-established equivalents in Persian. Another editorial aim, to write in so-called "pure Persian" and to reduce the use of Arabic terms, was not unprecedented, but *Andisheh va Honar* went further. In certain cases, it followed a phonetic diction rather than observing conventional and grammatically correct forms.[53] An editorial note usually appeared at the beginning of each issue of the journal, restating its overall policy. A typical one reads:

> Andisheh va Honar *is in no one's pocket* (toyoul).[54] *It is a place to breathe freely for those who genuinely need unpolluted air; our standards for judging the works of poetry, prose, drama, and scholarship submitted to us are based neither on popular taste nor on adulation: we consider the work itself and its original and inherent values. Therefore if we cannot, or if they do not let us, publish a text [because of censorship], we shall return the original to the sender with a clarifying note, provided a self-addressed and pre-stamped envelope have already been supplied.*[55]

On another occasion, Vosouqi reminded his readers: "The style of life that we approve for ourselves must take its inspirations from this country. Commodities of democracy, exported from the West, and freedom, assigned by the East, regardless of all their beauties and advantages (and we do look at them with respect), are not suitable for this people unconditionally."[56]

All progressive or leftist intellectual journals emphasized contemporary issues in literature and art, society, politics, and culture. Since they considered themselves ideologically progressive, they published little by contemporary authors who were traditional in their literary taste and style, though occasionally a few pieces by modern classicist poets like Mohammad-Taqi Bahâr or Mohammad-Hosein Shahriâr might appear if they involved social criticism. Nothing was printed in these periodicals from such conservative figures as Ebrâhim Sahbâ, Gholâm-Ali Ra'di Âzarakhshi, and Jamshid Amir-Bakhtiâri.[57]

Culture as Ideology

To avoid censorship and suspended publication, intellectuals in Iran tried to write, as well as speak and act, as obliquely as possible, making frequent use of metaphors and arcane references. In addition to state censorship, a reason for this was the dichotomy between *mellat* (the people) and *dowlat* (the state), which led intellectuals to preserve their integrity by absolving themselves of responsibility for the despotic deeds of their rulers. Both aloofness toward the state and indirect criticism of it increased in the 1960s and 1970s with the growth of a new generation of intellectuals, many of whom were transplanted provincials who soon found themselves entangled in a love-hate relationship with the big cities, especially Tehran. Also, since they were not readily accepted by any established clique, they often felt marginalized, which in itself encouraged them to craft a counterdiscourse with which they could identify.

A wider implication of this symbolic and metaphorical tendency among the new generation of intellectuals was the reduction of different levels of sociopolitical criticism to a quasi-Marxist teleological notion of "last analysis," by which was meant a radical transformation of the status quo. This kind of conceptual polarization and moral detachment provided the necessary preconditions for the development of an ideology of armed struggle among the young generation of political activists from the mid-1960s onward. Throughout the 1960s, intellectuals addressed topics such as the conflict between generations, the brain drain, the woes of consumer society, the political economy of the Third World, the theory of Asiatic society, and the nature of Iranian precapitalist and capitalist modes of production.

The question of the Iranian encounter with the West and the issue of modernity as a whole were other typical themes. Western influence on Iranian culture had been of special concern since the 1920s, but in the immediate post-Constitutional period it had been somewhat overshadowed by more urgent political events. It took up considerable space in periodicals like *Kâveh* and in many of the literary works of new young writers such as Mohammad-Ali Jamâlzâdeh and Sâdeq Hedâyat. The debate increased in intensity as time went on and Western influence permeated the Iranian society ever more deeply. A characteristic treatment of the topics of social and literary modernism and the possibility of a synthesis between European progress and Iranian identity was written in the 1940s by Seyyed Fakhr al-Din Shâdmân and published under the title *Taskhir-e Tamaddon-e Farangi* (The Capturing of Western Civilization). Later, in the 1960s and 1970s, Jalâl Âl-Ahmad, Ehsân Narâqi, and Ali Shari'ati grappled with these same issues. Many of these authors, notwithstanding differences in career and perspective, shared certain values and sometimes arrived at similar conclusions. But among their respective audiences, there was considerable discord and ambivalence concerning the prospects of modernity in Iran.

Shâdmân and the Primacy of Language

Seyyed Fakhr al-Din Shâdmân (b. Tehran 1286/1907, d. London 1346/1967) began his studies with a traditional curriculum and then continued at Tehran's Dâr al-Fonoun, Dâr al-Moʿallemin-e ʿÂli (Teachers' Training College), and, later, Tehran University's School of Law. In 1928 he briefly collaborated with the socialist and radical poet Mohammad Farrokhi Yazdi in the publication of the literary and historical journal *Toufân-e Haftegi* (Toufân Weekly), to which Mohammad-Taqi Bahâr, Seyyed ʿAbdol-Rahim Khalkhâli, and Ahmad Kasravi also contributed.[58] Shâdmân moved on to the Sorbonne and London University, where he received a doctorate; he then spent two years at Harvard University and later taught Persian at London University's School of Oriental and African Studies. At Tehran University, he taught courses on the philosophy of history and Islamic civilization. His official appointments included membership in the Iranian Academy (Farhangestân), the Royal Cultural Council, and the Supreme Cultural Council (Showrâ-ye ʿÂli-e Farhangi). As an executive, he served as the head of Iran's Insurance Company; the minister of agriculture; the head of the Plan Organization's Supreme Council, where he was in charge of administering the United Nations technical aid to Iran; the Iranian head of a joint Iran–United States Fund; the minister of justice, in charge of the Holy Endowments Trust in Mashhad; and, finally, governor of Khorâsân.[59]

The central problem that interested Shâdmân in *Taskhir-e Tammadon-e Farangi* was the relationship of language to thought, and its significance in any meaningful attempt toward modernization.[60] The work is dedicated to "the great Iranian nation," which the author sees as suffering from cultural alienation.[61] It is important, he writes, to say candidly that the nation is "imprisoned in a fort of calamity,"[62] and it should take heed because no territory belongs unequivocally to the people who happen to live there—"Loss of nationhood and homeland is not unprecedented in history." The land of Iran is older than Iranians and can easily outlive the nation. If this happens future historians will explain it in terms of "social sciences and historical principles," and "no one will even shed a tear over our destruction."[63] The time to deal with the multitude of problems facing the Iranians is running out. Priority should be given to problems that can be tackled and solved immediately. Accordingly, "there are two kinds of ailments in this world: the curable and the incurable, and unfortunate is the nation which does not distinguish between the two and becomes lost in illusions."[64]

The author refers to a group of Iranians who "have neither the patience to remain silent, nor the stamina to study, nor the courage to speak and hear the truth."[65] These "dishonest" people are exploiting the prevailing "confusion of the Iranian mind."[66] Their ignorance, lack of critical foundation, and short-sighted opportunism complement one another, and in order not to offend anyone, they adhere to a naive idea of "relativity," according to which everything is tolerated. In poetry, for instance, they approve both the lifeless compositions of conservative reactionaries and the nonsensical utterances of pseudomodernists.[67]

To deal with these contemporary problems, simply resorting to endless references to the national heritage is more harmful than honestly facing the causes of poverty and ignorance. They are the "curable problems," however unpleasant, that Iranians need to learn to address.[68] Shâdmân calls on Iranians to gain intellectual independence (*esteqlâl-e fekri*) and self-confidence, so they can learn to distinguish between "groundless adulation" of everything European and "sensible criticism."[69]

The author identifies as his ideal audience the younger generation and those who grasp the value of Iranian civilization, both pre-Islamic and Islamic, and are committed to building a new and prosperous country.[70] Shâdmân then launches a bitter attack on those he calls pseudomodernists, whom he refers to as *fokolis*;[71] he classifies the *fokoli* as a "dirty enemy" from within.[72] The passion of the author's denunciation stems from what he believes is the harm done by their assuming the role of interpreter and introducer of modern Western civilization. "[A] *fokoli* is a shameless Iranian who knows a little of some European language and even less Persian, yet claims that he can describe to us the European civilization of which he has no knowledge and through a language he does not know."[73]

For Shâdmân, the *fokoli* could be found even among the clerical groups; he depicts this "dirty enemy" as "well-dressed" with a "trimmed beard," but shallow in learning. A *fokoli's* major source of knowledge would be "thirty or forty books" by recent "Egyptian and Syrian authors" who were prolific in writing but limited in thought.[74] These pseudomodernists, whether secular or religious, are linked through their assumption that merely imitating Europeans will guarantee progress and lead to modern civilization. An indication of the shallowness of the *fokolis* is their ignorance of language. Predictably, he is vehemently against such earlier examples of pseudomodernism in the Qajar period as Hosein-Qoli Âqâ[75] and Mirzâ Reza Afshâr,[76] or works such as *Dâstân-e Torktâzân-e Hend* (The Story of Indian Ramblers) that are written in allegedly pure Persian.[77] It is absurd to think that the spirit of modern Western civilization could be captured through such vague and inadequate measures as purifying the language. Modern civilization must be approached on its own terms, using "rational, scientific, and practical methods."[78] Anyone wishing to lead the way must, first and foremost, "know Persian well."[79]

Shâdmân finds Western civilization difficult to define and admits that it is not limited to a particular place or historical period. Ancient Greece, contemporary America, the Portugal of four hundred years ago, and even Japan are all admitted into this category; contemporary Greeks and the Balkan peoples are excluded.[80] The cycle of civilization depends on the vitality of the sciences and arts and can shift from one nation to another. Today is the era of Western (*farangi*[81]) civilization:[82] "We are among those great nations who have suffered major defeats yet survived. But Western civilization is altogether a different kind of foe equipped with a different kind of armour. In my opinion, however, the victory of Western civilization in Iran will be our last defeat, for there will be no more Iranian nation left to endure [another] loss from another enemy."[83]

There are only two options left for those nations that encounter modern Western civilization: to capture it voluntarily with the "guidance of reason" and with "prudence" or to surrender unconditionally to the victorious flood of Western influence.[84] Although many aspects of life, from "sewing garments to printing [such popular classics as] the *Golestân* and the *Shahnâmeh*," depend on Western technology, "neither our defeat nor its victory is yet certain. The only solution is to capture it before it captures us."[85] But this cannot happen so long as modernism is represented solely by *fokoli*s whose misperceptions and misleading conduct have made many Iranians suspicious of the actual merits of Western civilization.[86]

Shâdmân says that in Iran there has always been a tradition of resistance to rigid conservatives who had a dogmatic approach to religion and culture (all of whom he refers to by the name "Sheikh Wahab Roufaʿi"), but no such tradition has been established with respect to pseudomodernists (to whom he gives the name "Houshang Hanâvid" and identifies with *fokoli*s): "Today," he says, "in spite of all his demagoguery, ignorance, and negligence, Sheikh Wahab Roufaʿi has less power, and therefore can do less harm, than Houshang Hanâvid. Today the *fokoli* is Iran's greatest enemy from within."[87] And again,

In this treatise greater attention is given to the Persian [language] and the fokoli, for Persian is the only means of capturing Western civilization, and the fokoli *is the biggest enemy of Persian and therefore the obstacle in the way of true progress. He will never [be able to] lead us to European civilization, because the wretched man is himself lost in perplexity and darkness. [On the other hand,] expecting honest guidance from a Westerner stems from stupidity and lack of experience, and is a symptom of not knowing the Westerner. Therefore we must capture Western civilization without the mediation of either one: one is an ignorant wrongdoer and the other a wise ill-wisher. Only through the Persian language and the guidance of reason [can we begin] to understand this great apparatus which is the fruit of several thousand years of human thought and effort.*[88]

Shâdmân considers books to be the "complete manifestation of all European knowledge," through which Iranians can be introduced to the "fundamentals of Western civilization." He proposes the adoption of a systematic policy for translating into Persian "brief and very simple modern books" and classical works from Greek and Latin. Translation of the first group would enrich the contemporary Persian language in areas of modern scientific and technological expression and would be a prelude to the translation and possibly even the writing of more substantial and sophisticated works.[89] He even suggests legislation that would require "every graduating Iranian to write and publish a book in correct Persian."[90]

Overall, Shâdmân's tract is repetitious and lacks a coherent structure, in part perhaps because it first appeared in installments in a journal. Shâdmân belonged to a time when ideas of "purifying" the language were popular, but although he was a nationalist, he was not anti-Arab, and certainly not anti-Islamic. Unlike the chauvinists who championed ancient times, Shâdmân valued both the pre-Islamic and Islamic heritages.[91] Despite his many attacks on the so-called *fokolis*, the author does not discuss them in any detail, and he makes no effort to locate or explain their social, cultural, and psychological characteristics. It is at times evident from the text, however, that he equates the *fokoli* with the *rowshan-fekr* (intellectual),[92] though, aside from the scholar and politician Foroughi, he mentions no one by name.[93]

Shâdmân is critical of both pseudomodernists and reactionary conservatives, but he never substantiates his criticism of them by referring to either particular individuals or identifiable themes. It would be very useful to know, for instance, what Shâdmân thought of Ahmad Kasravi. Presumably, he would have been opposed to Kasravi's efforts to purify the language and his extremely critical ideas about the mystic heritage of classical Persian literature; on the other hand, Shâdmân would likely have approved of Kasravi's insistence on the necessity of embracing modern civilization and of a national awakening, his systematic approach to learning, and his recognition of the Islamic foundations of Iranian culture. In addition to his criticism of the pseudomodernists and those who, without having a full command of the language themselves, insist on "language purification," Shâdmân also pleads for a methodical and systematic approach to education and research, a theme echoed by other writers.[94]

Âl-Ahmad and the Notion of *Gharbzadegi*

Perhaps the most famous critic of Westernism among the Iranian intellectuals was the writer and critic Jalâl Âl-Ahmad (1923–1970), a veteran of socialist and nationalist activities of the 1940s and early 1950s. He was born to a respected clerical (*rowhâni*) family that had originally come to Tehran from Tâleqân. After completing his primary education, he enrolled in the Dâr al-Fonoun, from which he graduated in 1943; by then, he had already made it clear that he would not follow the family vocation of becoming a cleric. He left school just as Reza Shah abdicated and the period of relative political freedom began.[95]

Âl-Ahmad found the source of many contemporary social and cultural maladies to be the abandonment of the traditional heritage and submission to, and superficial imitation of, Western ways, combined with a lack of any real knowledge of the roots of Western progress. He termed the condition as a whole *gharbzadegi* (the state of being struck by the West) and first described it in a short booklet with the same title. The book had originally been prepared as a report given at meetings on the problems of contemporary Iranian culture (Showrây-e Hadaf-e Farhang-e Iran) sponsored by the Ministry of Culture, in November 1961 and January 1962, but owing to its controversial content and critical tone, it was not included in the seminar proceedings. Instead typescripts of the text were subsequently circulated among fellow intellectuals. Early chapters of *Gharbzadegi* appeared in spring of 1962 in the ill-fated *Ketâb-e Mâh* (Book of the Month), a literary journal published by the daily *Keyhân*.[96] Âl-Ahmad made further minor revisions but was never able to openly publish the work in his lifetime.[97]

In *Gharbzadegi*, Âl-Almad summarizes his critical observations in terms of the evil function of modern Western technology, for which he preferred to use the French term *machinisme*.[98] At times, his argument resembles a Marcusian criticism of positive science,[99] but then he introduces the mysterious and nebulous external agent devised as part of a grand colonial plan and attributes to it all historical manipulations since the medieval period, if not earlier. The term *gharbzadegi*, originally coined by a contemporary Iranian philosopher, Ahmad Fardid (1912–1994), though literally the state of being afflicted or struck by the West, has been variously translated into English as "plagued by the West," "Weststruckness," "Westoxication," "Occidentitis" (playing on the Persian suffix *-zadegi*, which in medicine refers to the state of being struck by an ailment or an infection), "Westamination," and "Euromania."[100] In any case, most connotations of *gharbzadegi* include the image of the nation or state as an organism, which is in itself an old metaphor, as are the medical and anatomical images of disease and plague. Fardid himself explained *gharbzadegi* by using the word "dysiplexia," a Greek neologism that he invented by joining *dysis*, which means the West, with *plexia*, meaning to be afflicted (as in, for example, "apoplexy").

Fardid's main complaint was not with modern Western technology, but with the very structure of the worldview (*Weltanschauung*) of Occidental epistemology, as it originated in ancient Greece, which posits an existential separation between the human mind as the knowing subject and the external world as the object of study. The emergence of that kind of perspective, as opposed to the totalizing, harmonious, and illuminative qualities of Oriental thought, began a period of universal darkness that has since concealed the original unity and totality of Being.[101]

If, in Fardid's thinking, any possibility for redemption was suspended until the eventual configuration (*Gestalt*) of the historical *Zeitgeist*, for Âl-Ahmad the question was less philosophical and more political: Iranians as a Muslim community must begin from the point where they lost their cultural integrity and self-confidence. He believed that the nineteenth-century liberal intellectual break with society's popular, mainly Islamic, traditions was a grave mistake. Âl-Ahmad regards the Constitutionalists as having the fatal flaw of dependence on Western sources, not only for the actual text of their Constitution, but also for their approach. He proposes a new and more genuinely indigenous movement of self-assertion to deal with all contemporary problems, from economic and political dependency to urban anomie.[102]

Although at this stage Âl-Ahmad did not articulate a definite plan, he gradually reduced his distance from Islam, which he thought still had great cultural and political potential. His rapprochement with Islam became particularly strong after he went on a pilgrimage to Mecca in the spring of 1964; a skillful and stylish writer, he gave a detailed and effective account of this journey in one of his last works.[103]

In *Dar Khedmat va Khiânat-e Rowshanfekrân* (The Intellectuals: How They Serve or Betray Their Country),[104] Âl-Ahmad begins by defining intellectualism as dealing with questions of thought and ideas and as involving a particular approach to reality[105] that uses the power of both written and spoken words (*kalâm*)[106] to guide and motivate people.[107] He traces the origins of Iranian intellectualism to the Constitutional movement. He does not like the word *rowshanfekr* for intellectual.[108] Of the earlier term *monavver al-fekr*, he says:

> *In the period when the children of the aristocracy who had just returned from Europe* (farang) *were busy translating the Belgian Constitution to serve as the Iranian Constitution,*[109] *the ordinary people in the street who followed the clergy referred to them as* fokoli, mostafrang *(Europeanized), [and] motajadded (modernist). . . . At that same time, these gentlemen [i.e., the intellectuals] referred to themselves as monavver al-fekr, a translation of the French les Éclairés, meaning, the Enlightened.*[110]

However, what word Âl-Ahmad does approve for use remains unclear. He echoes the standard definition of the intellectual as one who is "free from prejudice and [blind] imitation, is usually engaged in mental, and not manual, labor, and who puts the result of his work at the service of the populace. The result of his work is often oriented towards solving a social problem rather than promoting personal and material gain."[111]

In Iran ordinary people often regard the *rowshanfekr* as "*fokoli*, modernist, Europeanized, *dezanfekteh*" (French *désinfecté*, i.e., sanitized), and, to some extent, "show–offy and vain,"[112] with "European mannerisms, atheist or at least feigning it, and educated."[113] For Âl-Ahmad, these attributes in fact epitomize some broader ideological attitudes of the intellectuals that include alienation from their native, traditional environment[114] and having a "scientific worldview."[115] In *Dar Khedmat va Khiânat-e Rowshanfekrân*, Âl-Ahmad discusses the separation of modern education from traditional centers of learning:

> *If intellectualism is seriously related to modern science (that is, if it only flourishes in a society where modern science has already been firmly established and modern educational and research establishments constitute the living organs of that society), then why, since the early days [of Iranian modernism] in the time of the early Qajars, instead of introducing modern*

science into our old schools, did we build new, separate schools for the sciences? By doing this we undermined all the institutions of traditional culture.[116]

He contends that in Iran, new schools and universities have not so far made any significant contribution to knowledge because a genuine scientific spirit is generally absent in them. To show the detrimental effect of the split between old and new schools, he mentions that while an old seminary (madrasa) in Isfahan has been turned into a museum, the newly opened Isfahan University confers meaningless degrees on a generation alienated from both tradition and modernity.[117] Although he makes the obscurantist position of the ulama toward modern education during the Qajar period partly responsible for this situation, he adds that it was not the only cause.[118]

Âl-Ahmad then asks why institutions of modern education in Iran did not develop in traditional schools, in a way comparable to the transformations that allowed schools in Europe to lose their religious base and become modern centers of learning and research. In Iran, however, "we built the Dâr al-Fonoun in opposition to tradition."[119] He recalls times in Iranian history when sciences and arts were pursued in traditional establishments, such as "the Nezâmiyeh schools in Baghdad and Nishapur, and the Rab'-e Rashidi in Tabriz, which was a kind of university as well as living quarters for artists, and the Jondi-Shâpour, which was a centre of both Zoroastrian teaching and Greek medicine and philosophy."[120]

Here, he agrees with Shâdmân, who several years earlier had claimed that allowing the traditional schools to decay had been a mistake.[121] However, they both failed to note the underlying dangers of rigidity inherent in such settings. For example, the fate of the allegedly heretical movements both before and after Islam who were persecuted because of their unconventional ideas should have reminded them that traditional establishments seldom tolerate opposition to the ruling order. Âl-Ahmad was of course referring mainly to scientific knowledge, but even scientific communities that deal exclusively in applied sciences with industrial and commercial objectives always have close ties to the political establishment, as, for instance, the numerous contemporary American science parks demonstrate. In the modern world of the arts and humanities, however, such a unified design, no matter how desirable, would be obsolete; some have even argued that modern and traditional schools are methodologically incompatible.[122] On the other hand, had institutions of modern learning in Iran emerged from within traditional madrasas, it is debatable whether the fate of scientific practice and the arts would have been very different.

Like Shâdmân before him and many of his contemporaries such as Shari'ati and Narâqi, Âl-Ahmad limited his discussion of the intelligentsia and the social role and functions of modern education to a national perspective. The dichotomy between "them" (the West) and "us" (Iran) was at the center of all his explanations and analytical criteria. In almost every modern social problem, he finds the hidden hand of Western colonialism, acting independently or through its predictable local agents, such as the pseudomodernists and secular intelligentsia, or through an unholy alliance with native despots.

The assertion of genuine elements of selfhood or the rhetoric of authenticity in Âl-Ahmad overlays a series of allegorical assumptions. He did not engage in any systematic evaluation of traditional institutions, knowledge, or value judgments, and his analysis barely went beyond the level of introducing historical arguments into a political controversy. Yet, in spite of this, Âl-Ahmad enjoyed significant influence and personal charisma among Iranian intellectuals in the 1960s, and his views reflected much of the ideological rhetoric of the revolution of 1979.[123]

Narâqi on Spiritual Rehabilitation

Another writer who criticized Westernism in Iran and urged his readers to resist Western influence was Ehsân Narâqi (b. 1926). Like Âl-Ahmad, Narâqi came from a religious family background.[124] He first studied in his native town of Kâshân and then at the Dâr al-Fonoun in Tehran. He was a Tudeh Party member before leaving Iran to study sociology in Europe. In 1951, Narâqi graduated from Geneva University, and in 1956 he received his doctorate from the Sorbonne. From early in his career, Narâqi held various administrative appointments—with international organizations, mainly the United Nations Educational, Scientific, and Cultural Organization (UNESCO), and with state institutions, for example, as director of Tehran University's Institute of Social Research.[125] This interest in administration separates him from intellectuals like Âl-Ahmad or Shari'ati, who avoided holding official posts. As a result they were both far more popular and trusted by the intelligentsia than Narâqi was; he was considered an "establishment intellectual." On the question of Iran's encounter with the West, however, his views and terminology had many similarities to those of Âl-Ahmad and Shari'ati.

Most of Narâqi's published works are collections of essays, lectures, and interviews on youth culture and university education, the economic and demographic problems of Third World countries, the cultural impact of science and technology, and aspects of cultural identity.[126] The collection *Âncheh Khud Dâsht* (One's Own Treasures), a title borrowed from Hâfez that implies "the spiritual power within," is clearly influenced by the terminology current in the 1960s in Western, and particularly French, intellectual circles. According to Narâqi, in *Âncheh Khud Dâsht* he set out to answer a question already raised in a previous book called *Ghorbat-e Gharb* (Estrangement of the West), where he had critically examined contemporary Western societies and had pointed to some fundamental social and cultural crises that these societies had encountered in the course of their technological and administrative progress. This question was:

> [I]n the face of contemporary conditions in the West, what direction should the Oriental countries in general and Iran in particular pursue so that they will be able to regain their appropriate status vis-à-vis the West and at the same time protect themselves from the crises and mistakes with which Westerners, on their own road to progress in their own civilization, have become entangled? In other words, what should be done to allow the Oriental countries, and Iran especially, to become conscious of their national and cultural existence and be "for-themselves", without falling either into blind imitation of Western patterns or into extremist reactions to such patterns?[127]

Based on his "several years of residence in Western Europe" and "six years of service in a global organization [UNESCO]," Narâqi proposes this answer: "In this chaotic and disorderly world, the only thing which could lead us to the shores of salvation is serious and sincere attention to our own cultural life, national spirit, and historical heritage."[128] He admits that the West has made spectacular progress in the sciences, and he cautions that this is a reality that Easterners should neither want nor try to ignore. At the same time, recognizing the progress that the West had made should not be allowed to undermine the spiritual merits of the East. In the course of its history, the Orient has acquired an insight (*binesh*) that even the West admires.[129] He holds that the power of Western civilization is derived from its obsession with objective reality (*vâqe'iyat*), whereas "the glory of Oriental history stems from the eternal brilliance of 'truth' (*haqiqat*)." He concludes: "Now we are compelled to blend Western reality with Oriental truth and make them one. This is a difficult task but, at the same time, very enchanting and exciting.[130]

In the final chapter, Narâqi begins with a passage from Oswald Spengler's *Decline of the West* to the effect that all the theses proposed by Western civilization regarding time, space, motion, will, property, marriage, and science have limited scope and are problematic, because Western civilization has always tended to put forward a universal solution for everything. Narâqi argues that although the universal validity of Western civilization has been challenged by the awakening Third World countries and has even been questioned by Western intellectuals themselves, there are still some intellectuals in Iran who, in the name of modernity, sincerely think that their country's situation is too precarious to allow an exposition of this issue. Some "firmly believe in all the fundamental principles and values upon which the Western civilization is built. They hold that the remedy for all problems is an uncritical adoption of Western solutions."[131] With an almost superstitious belief in the superiority of Western civilization, they assume that the historical and cultural heritage of their country is of no use in the contemporary world.[132]

Narâqi links the mentality of this group to the earlier intellectual (*monavver al-fekr*) generation of the Constitutional period, who had supported a total and unconditional Westernism.[133] A second group, comprised mainly of younger intellectuals, did not share the same degree of enchantment with Western civilization as their elders, though they admitted that "the secrets of progress, development, freedom, justice, and democracy must be learned from the Westerners,"[134] and since Western civilization and democracy were inseparable, criticizing the West would "weaken the supporters of democracy and the libertarian spirit in general and that of popular democracy (*demokrâsi-ye khalqi*) in particular."[135]

Narâqi too regarded freedom and democracy as among the blessings of civilization and believed that they had been developed in the West in a specifically Western form, but he did not regard them as necessarily contingent upon or an inherent part of Western civilization,[136] for if they were, that civilization would not have interpreted them in one way for its own regard and differently with respect to others. Witness, for example, the colonial period and occasions in the twentieth century, such as the two world wars, when the justice and equality allegedly fostered by the West were repeatedly compromised.[137] At the same time, the author acknowledges that the encounter with modern Western ideas was instrumental in the Iranian awakening, but disagrees with those who believe that the Constitutional movement was entirely a by-product of Western influence. The readiness to accept liberal ideas was latent in Iran's own "spiritual background" and merely awaited an appropriate moment to be unveiled.[138] As examples from that period, he refers to Hasan Pirniâ (Moshir al-Dowleh) and the political satirist Ali-Akbar Dehkhodâ and claims that when the revolutionary episode subsided, these men turned to scholarship about Iranian history and literature because they were convinced by their "political experiences that their own culture was richer than that of the West."[139]

In his assessment of "freedom and democracy,"[140] Narâqi concludes by criticizing historical determinism as a notion imposed by the West on other peoples and as a mistaken interpretation that excludes the role of human will in history and society. He holds that liberal—or, in a more contemporary form, technocratic—ideas and Marxism both share the same point of departure, namely an egocentric opinion of a universally valid process of social development identical with the pattern experienced by the West. Such a world outlook holds Western history as standard and ignores national and cultural specificities. Their reliance on the notion of historical determinism had led many Western thinkers, from early Greek philosophers and medieval theologians to Karl Marx and Auguste Comte, to regard the linear and evolutionary process of history as a necessary order governing all world civilizations.[141]

Darwin's ideas have enabled Western thinkers to generalize the concept of evolution to all societies and cultures, and to regard Westerners as the most advanced of all people and Western civilization as the most complete of all civilizations.[142] Noting Nietzsche's rejection of the linear concept of history and Spengler's criticism of Western civilization, Narâqi recommends that his compatriots not sacrifice the spiritual and cultural qualities inherited from their ancestors to import capitalism and the rule of money from the West: "There is no reason to justify that, for the sake of elite prosperity, we should place capitalism at the pivot of our society and in return give rise to antagonistic and despondent groups and [therefore] worsen the situation to such an extent that in order to free ourselves from class differences we resort to Marxism and build hopes on this illusion that social classes will [ultimately] disappear."[143]

Neither liberals nor Marxists are interested in noneconomic issues, such as cultural history, psychology, and religious and spiritual beliefs, he claims, because in practice, both groups believe their own version of historical determinism and act according to the "principle of evolution"—liberals aiming for more accumulation of capital and Marxists anticipating a drastic social revolution irrespective of its future consequences.[144] As an alternative to modern political and administrative ideologies, as typical standards of any *Gesellschaft*, or society dominated by instrumental reasons, Narâqi refers rather vaguely to an ideal harmonious community, a *Gemeinschaft*, capable of benefiting from features of traditional society:

> *During centuries of social living, in either town or village, and through [institutions such as] religion, science, art, technology, as well as family, our fathers have developed certain norms and relationships which can automatically solve many [of our] problems from cradle to grave. For what reason should we carelessly abandon all these relationships? [Do we] hope to replace them with an immortal power called the state? This [solution] is the result of assuming the simplicity of the process of social evolution and regarding social affairs as one-dimensional.*[145]

Even though he was a trained sociologist, Narâqi did not produce a coherent or systematic analysis of contemporary Iran. His collections of essays and lectures do not go beyond generalities. In his emphasis on cultural identity, there is no reference to such fundamental issues as the existing structure of power and political legitimacy. Although he had claimed to be examining the impact of contemporary Western civilization on other societies, unlike Âl-Ahmad, whose opposition to the West stemmed primarily from his opposition to the internal political regime and to the West's support of the shah, Narâqi criticized the West on its own terms and then simply drew the conclusion that Third World countries, and Iran in particular, should not make the same mistakes when dealing with the problems of industrialization, such as nuclear weapons and pollution. In order to avoid the inevitable radical reactions (i.e., revolutionary movements), these countries must not pursue a line of development like that of the West.[146] In fact, a crude historical determinism can be noted here, notwithstanding Narâqi's own criticism in this regard, for there is no reason to believe that by pursuing much-delayed measures of social justice and structural political reform, Third World countries would automatically undergo forms of sociocultural crises similar to those that have occurred in the advanced industrial societies. Narâqi's self-assertion plan remains somewhat problematic. Although he offered specific recommendations, for instance, on questions such as academic cooperation or curbing elitism,[147] his references to national recovery based on indigenous cultural values lacked analytical verve and did not point to any tangible program.[148]

Narâqi's strength lay in his managerial abilities; he was probably a better administrator than scholar. As director of Tehran University's Institute of Social Research, he succeeded in securing government grants, recruiting many young faculty members, and publishing a series on Iranian rural and urban societies. During this period, people such as Gholâm-Hosein Sadiqi, a veteran of Mosaddeq's administration and a learned scholar; Nâder Afshâr-Nâderi, Houshang Keshâvarz, Khosrow Khosravi, and Javâd Safi-Nezhâd, experts on rural Iran; Mahmoud Rouh al-Amini, anthropologist; and sociologists Ahmad Ashraf and Jamshid Behnam, among others, enhanced the intellectual life of the institute.[149] But it was largely owing to Narâqi's good relations with the government that the institute flourished.

Shariʿati and the Idea of Return

At about the same time as Âl-Ahmad and Narâqi were tackling the question of Iran and the West, Ali Shariʿati turned to the same subject and, from a new revivalist standpoint, viewed Islamic identity as the authentic source of Iranian culture. Like Âl-Ahmad and Narâqi, he did not articulate a specific program; he envisioned a radical, mainly political, revival of Islamic culture rather than a relapse to the ancient past and traditional structures.

The kind of Islam Shariʿati had in mind was removed from customary or conventional understanding. First, by Islam he meant Shiʿism[150] combined with an eclectic synthesis of non-Muslim and non-Iranian ideas, including socialism, Marxism, existentialism, the writings of certain Third World theorists,[151] and esoteric themes and metaphors from the Perso-Islamic mystic tradition of Sufis. Shariʿati viewed Shiʿism as a religion of protest that called for the overthrow of repressive governments.[152] Later authors characterized him as "the most popular mentor of Islamic radicalism in modern Iran."[153]

Ali Shariʿati (1933–1977) was born in Mazinân, a village in Khorâsân, but his family soon settled in Mashhad, where he spent most of his formative years.[154] He first studied with his father, Mohammad-Taqi Shariʿati, an expert on Koranic interpretation (*tafsir*), whose political views were pro-Mosaddeq with socialist leanings. He went to a high school, and then on to the Faculty of Letters at Mashhad's Ferdowsi University. He later won a state scholarship to continue his studies at the Sorbonne.[155] During his stay in Paris (1960–1964), Shari'ati was involved in the Algerian liberation movement as well as in the political activities of the Iranian opposition, which resulted in his imprisonment for several months when he returned to Iran.[156] After his release, he taught at schools in his home province of Khorâsân; later, he was a popular lecturer at the university at Mashhad. His reputation as an effective speaker grew when he moved on to Tehran and began to lecture, in 1967, at the Hoseiniyeh Ershâd,[157] which he continued to do until the center was closed by SAVAK in late 1973 and Shari'ati was again arrested. This time he was imprisoned for eighteen months, after which he returned to his native village and was put under police watch. In the spring of 1977, he was given a passport with an exit permit and left Iran.

Before Shari'ati, Mehdi Bâzargân, among others, had attempted to produce scientific justifications of Islam,[158] partly on the assumption that scientific reasoning had a universal validity and should be incorporated into all arguments, and partly out of conviction that the achievements of the modern world (whether scientific and technological or administrative and institutional) should be adopted, provided the element of faith could be salvaged. Many who took this position, including Bâzargân himself, were, in terms of their politics, Constitutionalists. Shari'ati differed radically from this group, whom he regarded as old-fashioned apologists. Though he too tried to incorporate a social scientific perspective into his analysis, he was concerned primarily with the critical situation of the Third World countries, and Muslim societies in particular, in their encounter with the West. He freely used a wide variety of arguments, concepts, and terminologies from both the Islamic tradition and Western philosophies and social theories (notably Marxism and existentialism) for the purpose.

Shari'ati was evidently aware of the social function of ideology; he knew that if, to borrow the expression from Marx, ideas were to become a material force, they had to correspond to contemporary conditions and be advanced in a language with which as many people as possible could identify. He wrote and lectured on topics ranging from history and the sociology of religion to politics, psychology, philosophy, and literature. His works, most of them published posthumously, consist mainly of his personal notes and transcribed lectures,[159] some of which have been translated and published in European languages.[160] His appeal was primarily among the younger generation of Muslim activists, though he addressed problems of interest to many groups, especially the urban population. From the left, he received a more negative or, at best, cynical reception.[161] His detachment also contributed to his popularity. The state did not provide easy access to the public for its known opponents, and Shari'ati lacked the necessary credentials to enter the higher circles of the religious elite, but he used this isolation to his own advantage, by underscoring his detachment from both the political and religious establishments. In order to provide a summary of Shari'ati's works, three major aspects of his writings will be discussed: his analysis of modern Iranian society and culture, his views on the intelligentsia, and his radical interpretation of Islam.

For Iranians to find their true identity, Shari'ati argued, they must first recognize what caused their historical discontinuities and the suppression of the more positive aspects of their national culture.[162] Throughout its history, Iran has been at the crossroads of "civilized, semi-civilized, and barbaric nations" that have repeatedly interrupted its "historical and cultural continuity."[163] This "stormy sea of religions, ideas, ethnicities, and great civilizations," all of which influenced it and were influenced by it, provided a situation for enriching and expanding the Iranian worldview, but Shari'ati contends that, under deteriorating social circumstances, these same factors made it more vulnerable.[164] Class differences that developed in the late Sassanid era constituted the basis for the type of Iranian feudalism that developed during the Islamic period and this, in turn, destroyed national harmony and the "unity of language, culture, thought, and spirit."[165]

Alien rule—by Greeks, Arabs, Turks, and Mongols—further contributed to the weakness of the Iranian collective spirit by disrupting the continuity of Iranian history.[166] A misrepresentation of Islam also played a role in creating Iranian estrangement. Shari'ati argues that during the Islamic period, in order to secure their rule, various invading forces interpreted Islam as a culture distinct from other cultures and ethnicities, including that of Iran, which had converted to Islam. Such a misrepresentation weakened Iran's links with its pre-Islamic heritage and generated a kind of historical amnesia.[167] Finally, modern Western colonialism, with its assumption that Western progress was linear and universally valid and that "primitive" and "ahistorical" societies and cultures were therefore destined to follow the same path, joined forces with Christianity to overcome resistance to Western domination in other societies and to make them adopt Western ways, leading to the "assimilation" of non-

Western societies, especially in Asia and Africa.[168] This process destroyed their *taʿassob* (sense of belonging)[169] and thus opened the way to both Western influence and the "destruction of the historical, traditional, and moral values of Oriental countries."[170] Shariʿati further holds that in this historical transformation, the Iranian people were defenseless because the pioneers of the Western cultural "offensive" in Iran were native Iranian "modernist intellectuals" who promoted deceptively attractive new slogans like "cosmopolitanism," "humanism," "internationalism," "liberalism," and "modernism."[171]

In his diagnosis of Iranian sociocultural alienation, Shariʿati turns, finally, to the effect of modern ideologies. He writes, "Colonial imperialism with reliance on the [concept of] 'world market,' occidentalism with reliance on the [concept of] 'world culture,' and Marxism . . . with reliance on the [concept of] 'world class,' have completed the task of the 'religious missions of the church' in establishing a world order based on the power of the pope, albeit in other guises and through different and even contradictory ways, and have expanded [the same project of global domination] with new strength and speed."[172]

Modernism and Marxism are viewed by Shariʿati as different aspects of the same attack on the indigenous character and "historical selfhood" of non-Western nations.[173] Modernism operates and commands "unconsciously and indirectly," altering the identity of non-Western nations in such a way that an Iranian or Muslim modernist would feel as if he had closer ties to Western culture than to his own.[174] Marxism, by stressing class culture as opposed to national culture, and by supporting a universal world class over particular nationalities, poses an explicit and rigorous challenge to national identity. Shariʿati compares the role of Marxist ideology in the expansionist actions of Soviet Russia in Eastern Europe after the Second World War with the ideas of the Catholic church during the earlier advances of Western colonialism. He concludes that both modernism and Marxism are destructive of other religions and cultures.[175]

Shariʿati maintains that all of the factors outlined above have undermined Iranian historical continuity and that contemporary Iranians possess almost no sense of national identity.[176] He then turns to the role of the intellectual in remedying these problems.[177] Like Âl-Ahmad, he argues that the Persian term *rowshanfekr* for "intellectual" does not convey the idea of what an intellectual is. The Western intellectual is engaged in mental labor, whereas the Persian word *rowshanfekr*, like the French *clairvoyant*, conveys the idea of a special quality of mind. A person who may not even be formally educated but who grasps the social problems of contemporary society can be *rowshanfekr*. For skilled and institutionally integrated intellectuals, Shariʻati suggests instead the word *tahsil-kardeh* (educated) or *tasdiq-dâr* (licentiate).[178]

In the West the growth of an intellectual class was a logical development of the Renaissance and the Enlightenment and the rise of the middle class.[179] Islamic societies, after they began to have more regular contacts with the West, in contrast, simply formed a *rowshanfekr* class by imitating the characteristics of its Western counterpart, without going through the same historical process. When these newly minted intellectuals began to challenge religion, they failed to note that reaction to Christianity had been a cause of the emergence of the Western intellectual class, and that Christianity was not the same as Islam.[180] Shariʻati concludes that while criticism of religion in the West produced freedom of thought and led to the growth of science, in Islamic societies the only "barrier against imperialism, economic colonialism, consumerism, and intellectual decline" was Islam.[181] Religious identity is an integral part of national culture in non-Western societies and its recovery is the necessary first step in an overall movement toward self-assertion.

The essence of Shariʻati's interpretation of Islam is that contemporary Muslim societies, in their political struggle to free themselves from internal corruption and stagnation and from Western economic domination and cultural influence, need only recover their Islamic identity. Without this reassertion of identity, these societies cannot liberate themselves, since ideological dependency would only prolong material dependency. Islam contains all the theoretical qualifications necessary for a radical doctrine, while simultaneously offering a sense of spiritual salvation that is nonexistent in modern materialist ideologies.[182]

Shariʻati holds that Islam, theoretically and through its various institutions, serves both as a practical political ideology and as a universal philosophy of life. He favors Shiʻism as representing the original spirit of Islamic teachings and every characteristic attributed to the Party of God (hezbollâh) in the Koran.[183] He assures intellectuals that Shiʻism provides all the necessary components of an up-to-date radical ideology. Shiʻism, he explains, has a specific "worldview, ideological foundation, philosophy of history, mission, agenda, class base, political strategy, system of leadership, tradition of party campaign and organization,"[184] all rooted in the early history of Shiʻi Imams and preserved through the relentless efforts of the "ulama, mojâhedin [Islamic warriors], orators, poets, and even by the *zâkerin* [professional rememberers and praisers of God] and the *maddâhin* [professional encomiasts of the Prophet and of the Imams]," [185] although it waned and was almost completely subdued under the Safavids. [186]

Shari'ati regarded certain aspects of Shi'i teachings as capable of performing ideological functions and of freeing Iranians from the need to import Western ideology. One was the notion of "*maktab*," which Shari'ati defines as a harmonious totality and system of ideas, manners, and judgments that, unlike technical skills and science, gives not only meaning and direction but also responsibility and mission (*resâlat*) to the person who is influenced by it. [187] *Maktab* is therefore the equivalent of a system of beliefs and ideological conviction. [188] In connecting practical imports to subjective components, it is the conceptual overture to grasping Shi'ism as an ideology. Shari'ati's references to ideology are thus broad and often ambiguous. For him, ideology is the extension of *maktab* (in the sense of doctrine) and determines the individual's mode of conduct. It is valid only if it includes two fundamental notions, *madineh-ye fâzeleh* (an ideal polity or perfect city) and *ensân-e kamel* (perfect human being). On the other hand, a major characteristic of *mellat* (a collective body of people) is that its members share the same *maktab* (common belief system), as in the Koranic *mellat-e Ebrâhim* (the people of Abraham), who all believed in *tawhid* (the absolute oneness of God). In this sense, it is also possible to identify *maktab* with "ideology" and to regard *tawhid* as "*eide'uluzhi-ye Ebrâhimi*" (Abrahamic ideology). [189]

At this point, however, Shari'ati diverges from his earlier identification of *maktab* with ideology and argues that ideology has a specific social function that, through political mobilization of the people toward an ideal goal, tends to change the society. *Maktab* is mainly the accumulation of knowledge and skills for the sake of interpreting the world; it is more in line with a school of thought in intellectual history or a style in the history of art, and its most accomplished members would therefore be scientists, professional artists, philosophers, and so on. Ideology, because of its value judgments, exclusive claims to the truth, and required commitment, would produce *rowshanfekr-e mojâhed* (partisan intellectuals). Thus ideology is identical with religion, and the truest of all contemporary ideologies share essentially similar features with the truest of all religions, Islam. [190] Here Shari'ati gives a selective long list of parallel conceptual premises, axioms, and terms juxtaposing properties of Islam and ideology in order to infer the former's superiority; examples are:

Ideology: *Payâm* [message]—*resâlat* [calling, or mission]—*ta'ah-hod* [commitment]—*mas'ouliyat* [responsibility]—*mob-ârezeh* [campaign]—*mardom* [the people]!

Islam: *Da'vat* [invitation, call]—*resâlat* [mission]—*taklif* [duty]—*mas'ouliyat* [responsibility]—*jihâd* [holy war]—*nâs* [the people]!

Ideology: *Barâbari* [equality]—*'adl* [justice]—rejection of class differences—humanism—human being as the lord of nature.

Islam: *Qest* [implementation of justice]—*'adl* [divine justice]—*enfâq* [disbursing one's wealth among the poor]—*tafviz* [deferring one's own interests in favor of others'] or *hobout* [the Descent from the Heavens to Earth]—human being as God's successor in nature.

Ideology: *Pârsâ'i-ye enqelâbi* [revolutionary puritanism]—rejection of private property—collective ownership—leadership—[rejection of] capitalism—profit does not belong to capital.

Islam: *Zohd* [continence]—rejection of private property—God's [overall] ownership; Imamate—*kanz* [the practice of hoarding]—*rebâ* [usury] is fighting with God.[191]

Ideology: Rule of the people—*showr* [consultation] and *ra'y* [vote]—leadership from the above during the period of revolution—*râz-dâri* [concealment and secrecy].

Islam: *Hokoumat-e ijmâ'* [rule by unanimous consent]—*showr* [consultation] and *bey'at* [allegiance or acclamation]—*vesâyat* [mandate]—*taqiyya* [caution or tactical prudence].

Ideology: *Etâ'at-e tashkilati* [organizational obedience].
Islam: *Taqlid* [emulation].[192]

The majority of these points are identical to the preoccupations of the Iranian intellectuals, especially the Marxists, during the 1960s and 1970s. Shari'ati's main objective is to demonstrate that Islamic teachings, if interpreted radically, are capable of accommodating modern questions. He cautions that intellectuals in all Muslim societies can transcend the cleavage between themselves and the popular culture only if they realize that fact and sincerely adopt as their ideology and philosophy of life a revived, radicalized, and ideologized Islam. Shari'ati concludes that, despite their many similarities, Islamic ideology supersedes humanist ideology by offering additional dimensions, such as a belief in "the realm of Divine invisibility (*qayb*), morality, love, worship, redemption, reward, punishment, resurrection (*ma'âd*), and eternity (*baqâ'*)."[193]

Shari'ati often stresses that great individuals have an eternal life force in history and their memory should be cherished by new generations.[194] Accordingly, Islam has a rich reserve of such examples, in the personas of Ali, Hosein, Fatima, and Abouzar.[195] For instance, by commemorating the martyrdom of Hosein, people remain aware that "every day is Âshourâ, and every place is Karbalâ."[196] These exemplars will induce ideological motivation. Furthermore, in Shi'ism every individual is potentially both able to and entitled to lead his or her own life and is also urged to encourage others toward the right way. This, accordingly, leads to the idea of independent judgment (*ijtihâd*). In a narrow sense, *ijtihâd* refers only to the practice of deliberating on legal questions by a mujtahid, an expert on jurisprudence (*fiqh*). In a more general sense, however, *ijtihâd* can be interpreted as the ability of every individual to exert independent judgment on issues relating to personal and social life and to encourage others to do the same, provided that the meaning and the extent of Islamic teachings have been adequately grasped. Shari'ati thinks that the mujtahids should broaden their knowledge and modify their methods of reasoning in accordance with the exigencies of the modern world; at the same time, he also stresses that people have a duty to do the right thing in life.[197]

The "revolutionary reconstruction of the self" ("*khud-sâzi-e enqelâbi*") is a theme that links the theoretical qualities of Shi'ism with individual action. Shari'ati argues that *khud-sâzi* (self-cultivation) differs from seclusion (pursued by the yogis and the Christian anchorites), romantic nationalism, and Marxist commitment to participation in a temporal political movement. It includes all the dimensions of human existence—"freedom, equality, and gnostic knowledge (*'erfân*)." This in turn must be supported by "adoration (*'ebâdat*), exertion, and social struggle."[198]

The idea of human being as mediation of teleology occupies a special place in Shari'ati's ideas. Traces of this idea can indeed be found in Manichaeist as well as Islamic gnostic teachings. It was also a current theme in Marxist humanism and existentialism of the 1960s, which were popular among European intellectuals.[199] But whereas both Manichaeist doctrine and Islamic philosophy pose the issue in an ultimately metahistorical context and axiology, for Marxism and existentialism the question of mediation of human agency is an exclusively historical project. Yet with an almost complete disregard of this basic conceptual and theoretical difference, Shari'ati blends them together. In fact, those who want to charge him with eclecticism need not go any further.

Shari'ati defines the human being (*ensân*) in various terms, such as a "utopian, political, rebellious, and expectant (*montazer*)" creature.[200] Originally, Adam was the ideal *ensân*. The entire historical process has been the story of the conflict between Abel and Cain, i.e., the conflict between two opposing types of humanity. Opposing forces are in continuous battle in an *ensân*, who is also viewed as a "god-like émigré," a "dialectical phenomenon," and a "free will," whose philosophy of being is to overcome forces of darkness and evil in himself and, bearing the burden of God's trust, to shape his own destiny and create a "human heaven" on earth.[201] The existential responsibility of *ensân* lies in his effort to leave behind the evil aspects of his nature and move closer to his *khishtan-e khodâ'i* (godlike self). Shari'ati portrays this effort as a permanent process of mental and spiritual departure (*hijra*) from the lower states of the self to higher ones.[202] This notion is yet another preparatory subjective device to mobilize individuals and equip them with an Islamic ideology. But unlike the practical imports and subjective components described earlier, the notion of *hijra* entails a high degree of individual involvement and volition.

An important theme in the biblical tradition is remembrance, which also has a particular status in modern utopian ideologies such as Marxism.[203] Remembrance is viewed by Shari'ati as a significant practice through which individuals can reconstruct their identity in accordance with their beliefs. In this context remembrance is an act in the present tense and is directly involved in the construction of identity and self-image. In the words of a contemporary sociologist, "[W]e are what we remember we were."[204] Through remembrance, *ensân* retains a link between himself and the entire background of his faith; thus, he acquires a vision of history in which he is also a participant.[205]

Shari'ati identifies the act of divine worship (*'ebâdat*) as a technique for preserving and increasing self-consciousness. Coming from the Arabic root *'abd*, meaning a servant as well as the act of leveling and paving the way, *'ebâdat* (or *'ibâda* in Arabic pronunciation) is, according to Shari'ati, the removal of barriers within oneself to prepare for the manifestation of God's will.[206] In the contemporary world, *'ebâdat* as an act of self-purification has both mystic and political functions, because it is "the only practice which can protect man from his existential metamorphosis, from his human banality and from forgetting human values, and [it thus] re-establishes our link with the origin of being and saves us in a world where *mâshinizm* [Fr. *machinisme*, referring here to the cultural prevalence of the modern industrial and mechanical ethos], capitalism, and politics are exerting tremendous pressures [on humanity], and it gives us a reliable support."[207]

Finally, Shari'ati's teleological and utopian tendency is clear in his interpretation of *entezâr* (divine anticipation).[208] As a precept, *entezâr* has a special significance in Islam because of the belief in the Day of Judgment (*ma'âd*), and particularly in Shi'ism, because of the expectation of the return of the Hidden Imam, but Shari'ati reads into it an interpretation that encourages nonsubmission to the status quo.[209]

Shari'ati's version of politicized Islam had a significant impact on the emergence of Islamic revivalism in Iran.[210] His language had particular appeal for the young Muslim intellectuals who could not relate as easily to the traditional version used by the ulama. Like Bizhan Jazani (1937–1975), a figurehead of the young generation of Iranian Marxists, Shari'ati became a charismatic figure for the new wave of Islamic revivalism in the late 1960s and 1970s.[211] They both had direct experience and links with the political life of the older generation as well. Jazani had been a member of the Tudeh Party and was active in Tehran University's student organization, which during the early 1960s was controlled by the Second National Front; Shari'ati, together with his father, was involved in the Islamic faction of the National Front after 1953. From 1956 to 1958, Shari'ati was associated with the Nehzat-e Moqâvemat-e Melli (National Resistance Movement); he later joined the Nehzat-e Âzâdi-e Iran (Liberation Movement of Iran).[212] Both Jazani and Shari'ati soon broke with the older generation, however, on ideological and political grounds and went on to advance their own more radical approach.

Shari'ati's work provides a good example of a tendency, shared by many intellectuals of the period, to stress the importance of self-assertion in a time of social and cultural alienation. To achieve this, they felt that a critical stance, detached from official norms and symbols, was essential. Intellectuals who criticized the government were not only opposing the regime but also, and at a more personal level, trying to comprehend the new developments that were taking place in Iranian society. Shari'ati's expression, "*bâzgasht-e beh khish*" (return to one's [original and authentic] self), makes sense in the context of that mentality. His ideas politicized a considerable segment of urban youth, mainly those who came from traditional backgrounds and whose ideal vision was not to isolate themselves from society but to challenge its pervasive sense of cultural alienation and its political and economic dependency.

The Crisis of Legitimacy: Armed Struggle as Ethics and Politics

In the 1960s and 1970s, the gap between the Iranian intellectuals and the state widened to the point where an intellectual was almost automatically identified as belonging to the opposition. Discourse among the opposition expressed a nonconformist, even outright rejectionist, attitude toward the state. The idea of armed struggle with the regime was upheld by many intellectuals as the only justifiable stand under the circumstances. Those who adhered to this idea were not necessarily members of secret opposition organizations, though a few did join them or created organizations of their own.

Most of the groups that subscribed to the idea of armed struggle were either Marxist-Leninist or militant Islamists. The impact of both went far beyond the active membership to permeate the society at large. Among the Marxist organizations, the most important was the Sâzmân-e Cherikhâ-ye Fadâ'i-ye Khalq-e Iran (Organization of the Iranian People's Devotee Guerrillas). Other leftist units included two pro-Chinese groups, Setâreh-ye Sorkh (The Red Star) and Beh Sou-ye Enqelâb (Toward the Revolution), both of which SAVAK suppressed in 1971; Ârmân-e Khalq (People's Ideal [or Cause]);[213] Sâzmân-e Marxisti-Leninisti-e Toufân (Marxist-Leninist Storm Organization); and Gorouh-e Felestin (Palestine Group).[214]

Among the Islamic groups, the most important organization was the Sâzmân-e Mojâhedin-e Khalq-e Iran (Organization of the Iranian People's Warriors), which promulgated a militant interpretation of Shi'i Islam. Other Islamic units included Gorouh-e Abouzar (Abouzar Group); Hezb-e Melal-e Islami (Party of the Islamic Nations), and Fadâi'ân-e Islam (Devotees of Islam).[215] *Fadâ'i* literally means a "devotee," and *mojâhed*, a "holy warrior," both terms suggesting that individuals are prepared to sacrifice themselves for the cause of the oppressed. The term *mojâhedin* was borrowed from the Koran, where it is used to refer to those who rise and fight for the holy cause and who are praised and promised great rewards (e.g., surahs 4:97 and 29:69). Both terms were used during the Constitutional period, when a member of a revolutionary militia connected to a political society with a Constitutional agenda was known as a *mojâhed* or *fadâ'i*. In adopting these terms, the new clandestine guerrilla groups sought to identify themselves with this precedent.[216]

As a reaction against the official nationalism of the Pahlavi state, many intellectuals, particularly the radicals, often feigned an internationalism they did not really feel.[217] Although their attitude did not altogether succeed in submerging their inner feelings of national identity and patriotism, the attempt weakened their commitment to the official nationalist rhetoric. During the 1960s and 1970s, these intellectuals, in order to distance themselves from state propaganda and thwart any claims the state might have wished to make on their nationalistic spirit, turned these feelings inward. This kind of mental strategy, while effective in the apparent, if narrow, sense of restraining the individual's show of loyalty to the state, did not nurture a pragmatic approach to reality. Under such circumstances, supporting a usurping authority and abiding by its claims to legitimacy would be unacceptable[218] and the individual would either retreat from participation or postpone it until an ideal order could be achieved.

This all-or-nothing perspective prevented the individual from attaining the practical training in the political culture needed to institutionalize the normative structures of modern society. From the intellectuals' point of view, however, this reaction was both unavoidable and commendable, because they saw no hope for a gradual, reform-oriented compromise under a dictatorship and because they were limited by their own rhetoric, which held that the individual should never bargain for piecemeal gains with a usurping authority, but instead should undermine it altogether—a rhetoric that itself was magnified, if not caused, by the intellectuals' feeling of being marginalized by the state and of being barred from any meaningful political participation. In fact, the making of the Iranian revolution of 1979 and many of its subsequent manifestations were largely influenced by this attitude.

– 6 –

Epilogue

IN OCTOBER 1977 THE IRANIAN WRITERS' ASSOCIATION HELD a series of poetry readings and speeches at Tehran's Goethe Institute for ten consecutive evenings. These meetings contained a summary statement of the political and artistic position of the intellectuals on the eve of the revolution. The proceedings of these nights, with attendance by close to ten thousand people every evening, were recorded on tape and distributed both in Iran and abroad; the tapes were later transcribed and published as a book.[1] This volume is representative of the attitudes and beliefs held by Iranian intellectuals in that period. It is therefore a good starting point to review postrevolutionary intellectual literature.[2]

In all, fifty-nine members of the Writers' Association spoke or read excerpts from their works. A central theme of the lectures and recitations was the lack of political freedom in Iran and its corollaries, such as censorship, repression, and the arbitrary intervention of the state into the activities of writers. The speakers had a range of ideological sympathies. Some, like the poet Siâvash Kasrâ'i and the critic Fereydoun Tonekâboni, supported the newly revived Tudeh Party, and some, like the poet and critic Sa'id Soltânpour, supported guerrilla organizations. Others, like the eminent writer Simin Dâneshvar and the lawyer and writer Rahmatollâh Moqaddam-Marâgheh'i, adhered to more moderate political views. They held in common opposition to the shah, however, and for the time being removal of the monarchy took precedence over ideological differences.[3]

At the beginning of the revolution, many intellectuals believed that the clerical leaders who had seized power would prove to be figureheads and certainly temporary. They viewed the situation as an instance of the "ideological hegemony" of religion that, owing to the absence of freedom in politics, had become the popular channel for expressing political dissent. They assumed that it would be possible to contain this clerical composition and ultimately replace it with a more "rational" and "historical," or at least less anachronistic, alternative.

The shah's departure from the country in January 1979 was celebrated in Tehran and other cities. These celebrations reached their climax in February, when Ayatollah Khomeini triumphantly returned from his fifteen years of exile. In addition to conveying this news in extra-large type, *Keyhân*, a major Tehran daily newspaper, printed a poem on its front page by Houshang Ebtehâj (also known by his pen name, Sâyeh, meaning Shadow), a well-known contemporary poet and member of the Writers' Association, that was composed for the occasion:

> *Open the door,*
> *Bring the candle,*
> *Burn incense,*[4]
> *Unveil the moon's face,*
> *Perhaps this, who has emerged amid the road's dust,*
> *Is that missing dear traveler.*[5]

For the majority the celebration soon ended. It was not long before the Islamic Revolutionary Committees had tightened their grip in the cities and particularly in certain streets and suburbs where the most "Westernized" citizens lived. As early as July 1979, another prominent poet, Ahmad Shâmlou, expressed the general sense of betrayal among the intelligentsia in a poem entitled "Dar in Bonbast" (In This Blind Alley):

> *They smell your mouth*
> *lest you might have said: I love . . .*
> *they smell your heart.*
> > *Strange times, my dear!*
> *And they flog love*
> *by the roadblock.*
> > *We should hide love in the larder.*
> *In this crooked blind alley, at the turn of the chill*
> *they feed the fire*
> *with logs of songs and poetry*
> *hazard not a thought.*
> > *Strange times, my dear!*
> *He who knocks at your door in the noon of the night*

has come to kill the light.
> *We should hide light in the larder.*

There, butchers
posted in passageways
with bloody chopping blocks and cleavers.
> *Strange times, my dear!*

And they chop smiles off lips
songs off the mouth.
> *We should hide joy in the larder.*

Canaries barbecued
on a fire of lilies and jasmines
> *Strange times, my dear!*

Satan, drunk with victory
squats at the feast of our undoing.
> *We should hide God in the larder.*[6]

Gradually, disputes among the intellectuals began to surface over attitudes toward the new regime. A split within the Writers' Association mirrored this erosion of the earlier consensus. In a general meeting in January 1980, the executive committee voted to expel five pro–Tudeh Party members because of the party's collaboration with the more zealous and increasingly dominant faction within the clerical circles.[7] Soon after, the expelled writers, together with a number of lesser-known younger writers and artists of similar persuasion, founded the Council of the Iranian Writers and Artists, with the support of the Tudeh Party.[8]

The revolution also generated considerable activity in literary journals and miscellanies, a literature always popular among intellectuals.[9] Much of the intellectual literature of the 1980s continued to rail against the abrogation of individual rights and cultural suppression by the state and by various pressure groups whose activities the authorities were unable or unwilling to contain, but added to it was a new and deeper feeling of disillusionment stemming from the revolution's outcome. Then, after a pause, new works began to appear, some of which dealt exclusively with postrevolutionary topics.[10] Among these topics were the debilitating effects of obscurantist traditionalism, a topic treated either satirically or in blunt denunciation; the psychological crisis and decadence of the Iranian aristocracy of the late nineteenth and early twentieth centuries, along with its surviving vestiges and memories; and the relationship between Iranian national identity and Islam.[11]

This literature also reflects the continued preoccupation with questions of technique and style that have come to characterize modernist prose and poetry and to differentiate this literature from the more accessible popular versions. Postrevolutionary writings, despite their revisionism, have not compromised the literary merits of a work for the sake of a populist appeal. The importance of technique is clear, for example, in some of the works of Simin Dâneshvar, Houshang Golshiri, Parviz Owsiâ', and, to a lesser extent, Reza Barâheni.[12]

Less poetry than prose has been published in Iran since the revolution. Although poets continue to be concerned with style and technique, post-1979 critical poetry finds traditional forms more suitable than the "free" form of modernist verse, which has an essentially personal and confessional structure. For example, for writing political invectives, the *mashruteh* tradition of satire is again in favor, though the blunt language of their criticism means that most such poems are published outside Iran.[13] Traditional forms are often also used as an antielitist gesture to reach a wider audience.

Along with the mainstream intellectual literature a new variety, the so-called *maktabi* (doctrinaire) literature, has appeared to further the cause of political Islam. The word *maktab* means a place of writing, a school, or a school of thought, but it can also mean something like path, as in, for example, the mystic path. In its most recent usage, *maktab* has acquired a particular ideological connotation, as evidenced in, for example, Shari'ati's writings. After the revolution, the fervent supporters of the Islamic regime began to use it to express their ideological militancy and populism, and to dissociate themselves both from the secularists (and secular intellectuals in general) and from the moderate—or, as they put it, "liberal"—Muslims.

What is significant, however, is that *maktabi* writings are in many ways an imitation of the engagé intellectual literature. There are many *maktabi* poems written in the manner of New Poetry or even free verse, forms originally associated exclusively with modernist writers.[14] The influence of intellectual literature has extended beyond the confines of literary works. The terminology inherited from the pre-1979 period (from the intellectual language, the press, and even the bureaucracy) has left its mark on postrevolutionary discourse, both in *maktabi* literary writings and in the official language.[15]

There are numerous *maktabi* plays and short stories, many of which originally appeared in *Soureh*, a *maktabi* literary journal published regularly in Tehran by Howzeh-ye Honari-e Sâzmâm-e Tabliqât-e Islami (the arts department of the Organization for Islamic Communications). The Ministry of Islamic Guidance also published a series of short plays written by young and previously unknown *maktabi* writers to commemorate the fifth anniversary of the revolution.[16] Overall, the state has taken an active role in the publication and distribution of *maktabi* literature, for example, by subsidizing regular journals and publishing houses. In addition to the journal *Soureh*, *Fasl-nâmeh-ye Honar* (a quarterly on the arts published in Tehran by the Ministry of Islamic Guidance) and *Keyhân-e Farhangi* (a monthly cultural and literary supplement to the newspaper *Keyhân*), among others, are also funded by the state.[17] The general format of these publications reflects the influence of the literary journals and miscellanies initiated years earlier by modernist intellectuals.[18]

The *maktabi* literature, while impressive in the volume of its published material, leaves much to be desired in quality. The majority of those who contribute to it are young, with no previous publication record; some of them are from the ranks of the Revolutionary Guards and often identify themselves as "Hezbollâhis" (members of the Party of God). Their work, though often of poor literary and artistic quality, is highly ideological, a characteristic that the *maktabi* literary theoreticians approve and advocate.[19] The urge to write and publish in modern genres is in itself worthy of attention. At the same time, *maktabi* authors display a deliberate disregard for technical refinement and finish, an attitude that is often expressed in terms of an ideological preference for *taʿahhod* (commitment) over *takhassos* (professionalism). Whereas the prevailing conception of self in the intellectual literature often embodies existentialist, elitist, and nontraditionalist dimensions, *maktabi* works make populist and traditionalist claims. For all its populist claims, however, *maktabi* literature has not proved popular with its intended audience.

Maktabi ideology intends to help the individual to familiarize and privatize the social world through a supposedly traditionalist self-image. Although its declared utopianism is rooted in early Islam, it also has sources in popular culture, and it tends to reconstruct Islam according to the specific images and properties of that background. References to early Islam are important, however, since it is through them that the *maktabi* ideology establishes its precedents. Early Islam (*sadr-e Islam*), as a period that witnessed the lives and deeds of the Prophet, his companions, and, in the case of Shiʿis, the Imams, constitutes a significant point of reference in the Muslim conception of historical time. The maxim "every day is ʿÂshourâ, and every place is Karbalâ" reflects a figural interpretation of history in which certain periods are believed, through divine intervention or plan, to have particular importance for all time. ʿÂshourâ, for example, is presented as a paradigmatic time for concentrating the mind and purifying the soul.[20] Given its dominant political position in the 1980s, the *maktabi* ideology used the opportunity to impose its precepts on the society at large.

At the same time, the relationship of the *maktabi* ideology to political power has been problematic. This ideology derives much of its mobilizing force from its own adherents' prior experience with suffering and suppression. A rhetoric rooted in such a history loses much of its rigor once the *maktabi* ideology itself has the upper hand. The traditional complaint about being victimized by a usurper now becomes a temporary theme; hence it constitutes a historical challenge and can no longer remain an eternal philosophy of history. Yet the political regime and the people adhering to this ideology and its corresponding discourse seem not to be able to maintain their self-image without expressions of lamentation and grief.

In *maktabi* literature, as in the ideology that supports it, there is an explicit and deliberately displayed disapproval of positive or assertive modes of aesthetic experience such as a show of interest in comfort and leisure or the tendency to self-presentation and exhibition of luxury. Instead, in the public sphere and before the public eye, expressions of grief and a somber look are upheld as signifiers of an appropriate aesthetic style or as signs of moral virtue and, more generally, as indicators of a correct methodology of experience. As Ayatollah Khomeini once put it, "It is the tradition of lament which keeps us alive" (*Mâ bâ rowzeh zendeh hastim*). Failing to observe such codes of conduct or failing to comply with their objective spirit would, at best, be interpreted as emblematic of a person's cultural amnesia, and such a person would be regarded as a renegade of the society's collective memory. Consequently, the search for potential or actual threats to the Islamic state became a preoccupation. Foreign conspiracies and counterrevolution are among the most frequently cited threats.[21] Since the *maktabi* vision includes all Muslims and recognizes no purely national borders, and the commitment to protect Islam is a global one, instances in which Islam may be said to be "in danger" are also legion.[22]

The revolution drew a large number of social groups into politics.[23] Another widely publicized quotation from Ayatollah Khomeini in the early days of the revolution, speaking to the "*mostazʿafin*" (the downtrodden), proclaimed that "Islam has taken you out of the *Zavâyâ* (corners)," i.e., out from the margins of the society and isolation. "Do not let them push you back there again!" During the 1980s, the young generation of *maktabi* intellectuals and the followers of *maktabi* ideology viewed the entire society as their own social space and their ideology as the definitive discourse. One of the reasons young Muslim intellectuals who identified with the cause of the *mostaz'afin* came to support the new order was that its objective spirit and codes of conduct allowed them, for the first time in their collective memory, to feel at home in their own society—a clear departure from the cultural dualism and typological tension so prevalent under the Pahlavis. They were able to identify themselves with the officially endorsed populist culture, through which they also tried to insulate themselves from those who, in their eyes, still represented the prerevolutionary "arrogance" (*estekbâr*). At the same time, the process of acquiring, or at least experimenting with, the modernist idiom, from genre to terminology and technique, has been pursued uninterruptedly and willingly.[24]

Intellectual Formalism

In the preceding chapters, Iranian intellectuals were by and large portrayed not simply as representatives of a particular class, ideology, or interest, but also as social actors of an emerging type who construct their distinctive discourse while sharing a cultural milieu with other social types. In nineteenth-century Iran a new intellectual vision gradually took shape and soon found a number of significant institutional and objective means of representation. The Dâr al-Fonoun school, the press, an increase in foreign travel, and literary and political societies were among its early manifestations. Intellectual discourse flourished in the period of the Constitutional movement during the first decade of the twentieth century. Intellectuals now began to assume an active role in literary production and in developing the language into new directions, a factor that distinguished them from the traditional clergy and the government secretaries.[25] There was also a gradual distance between the basic educational foundations of different types. For instance, modern intellectuals dealt little with Arabic and the canon of literary Persian, especially in the 1960s and 1970s.

Nevertheless, intellectual discourse became the given medium for modern political language and, more so, political criticism. A methodological implication of this fact is the way different discourses can be used by different typologies without any necessary paradigmatic commitment toward their contents and intents.[26] It may also shed light on one of the more pervasive questions of intellectual activity in modern Iran, namely, the question of formalism, manifestations of which can often be noted in epistemological contraction of politics, i.e., an overriding concern with immediate politics and with formal, in the sense accidental, political attributes. The infatuation with politics meant that concern with immediate political issues and interests dominated the substance and inner logic of ideas and thought and, as a result, of the formation of concepts.[27] Philosophical engagement was deferred in favor of recourse to politics to comply with imagined moral and practical duties or to maintain a popular image. That is why encounters with modern Western ideas in Iran, within the last 150 years or so, have remained intellectually and philosophically so haphazard. The good majority of ideas in circulation have been developed in reaction to the political implications of Western ideas and have tried to propose political remedies.

This preoccupation with politics has affected the process of intellectual production, both epistemologically and ontologically. At both levels, direct intellectual or theoretical involvement with the subject matter (which can also be regarded as the object of study, or *Gegenstand*) has been deferred. Instead people have often developed the mental attitude that sheer compliance with the formal, i.e., objective, exigencies of the politics of the given situation would inevitably be sufficient to transcend the present moment, or the status quo, and pass on to an ideal state of affairs in which there would be no further need to engage in mundane politics. Consequently they have tended to engage in the political dimensions of the reality without recognizing the need to also engage in its intellectual composition. Yet such a formalistic attitude would soon be confronted with social and political implications that it could neither conceptualize nor evade. The result has often been to blame adversity on metalogical and metapolitical causes such as bad luck, conspiracy, and the like.

The shortcoming of a predominantly politicized perspective is that it regards the intellectual as well as the practical questions of modernity as essentially political. It sees modernity as an external phenomenon and concludes that the grapple with modernity is only a political project. Thus on both the intellectual and practical levels, a direct philosophical and theoretical involvement is avoided and is replaced by a formalistic approach (whether positively or negatively) that reifies the meaning and dynamics of modernity.

Political Motivation and Knowledge

We can now turn to the impact of political motivation on the construction of intellectual discourse and the overall formation of basic knowledge. It can be argued that a politically motivated standpoint can be the catalyst for the formation of knowledge. In the case of modern intellectuals, politics constituted the primary criterion for making typological, educational, and communicative distinctions.[28] The quest for knowledge, moral conscience, and a sense of responsibility and commitment toward the realization of a better society or, at least, toward opposing a bad existing one, lay at the foundation of the political orientation and motivation of modern intellectuals. This political motivation in turn determined the subsequent intellectual discourse and the way subjects were chosen and articulated. As a result, a canon or repertoire of literature gradually developed that was shared among members of a cultural generation.[29]

The twentieth century has seen significant changes in the institutions, methodology, and substance of learning. As a result, there is institutional diversity and multiplicity of discourse in the production of knowledge. Different types of education offered not only specific theoretical paradigms but also, at a more concrete level, the necessary interest both to attract young pupils and to present them with a given body of material as standard educational topics. Gradually different styles of representation and education defined their specific discourse, topics, and body of texts. Intellectual discourse shared a "technical interest" in its pursuit of knowledge with others who were specifically aiming at this pursuit, but it was also interested in, and motivated by, the "emancipatory interest" of knowledge, which was articulated, selected, defined, and represented through political motivations.[30]

Therefore, as the nonmodern discourses in the production of knowledge (such as clerical [*dini*], scribal [*divâni*], and mystic or gnostic [*'erfâni*] discourses) underwent institutional changes in the twentieth century, intellectual discourse soon established itself as a viable means of representation of modernity. It accommodated the project and the discourse of modernity and at the same time tried to transcend them. Whereas modern bureaucratic or military discourse was primarily interested in advocating social participation, a homogeneous national agenda, and secularism—all within a set political program and in order to safeguard political continuity—intellectual discourse maintained its practical detachment from the immediate political interests of the status quo by expressing its ideal political interests and its moral obligation in terms of structural transformation, a characteristic that, more often than not, was a utopian quest.[31]

As a result, while other forms of discourse either were defused by isolation or, by maintaining an official position, developed a vested interest in the preservation of the status quo, intellectual discourse assumed a self-avowed transcendental standpoint by combining knowledge with emancipatory interest. Therefore, intellectual discourse, in spite of all its theoretical shortcomings, provided a venue through which the younger generations of modern intellectuals were trained and received their readings and gradually became acquainted with a relatively shared body of information, topics, and values. Any assessment of modern intellectuals in Iran should give due attention to this twofold situation.

Intellectual Discourse and Moral Responsibility

In the formation and development of the intellectual paradigm, there are some values about ethical correctness that are based primarily on political standards and classifications. Commitment to partisan ethics, as a major characteristic of intellectuals, has influenced their personal style and the objective spirit of their discourse.[32] Motivated by this value judgment, the intellectual discourse sought to articulate its axiology of truth and morality. A similar classification can also be seen in Marxist writings, where truth, rights, and ethics were defined in historically and culturally relativized terms.[33] Also, by assuming a dogmatic and self-righteous claim to ethics and politics, the intellectual discourse found itself in a position in which both ethics and politics became its responsibility, and sometimes even a liability. For instance, as far as ethics were concerned, issues were lodged post hoc; i.e., they were to be postponed until *after* the realization of the proposed political solution and ideal situation. Abstract ethical considerations were abundant in both analysis and criticism.

Intellectual discourse often maintained a basic teleology through which it tended to postulate an inexhaustible source of truth (or, in a Kantian sense, intuitive certainty[34]) that in moments of despair would inspire the individual to keep the element of hope alive, like a guardian angel who intervenes at the eleventh hour. The reality was thus conceptualized in terms of a fundamental dialectic between contingent opposite forces such as good and evil, freedom and bondage, friendship and animosity, benevolence and banality, authenticity and alienation, elegance and mediocrity, felicity and anguish, and so on. In this regard teleological vision itself was also based on transitory grounds. Although the idea of everlasting harmony rests purely on religious convictions, in the realm of contingent imagination theses and antitheses rotate, and syntheses are only momentary—i.e., at best they have periodic, and therefore transitory, duration. In this context, maxims of practical reason too would only be effective from one moment to another. Therefore, the next moment, or station, would not necessarily be viewed as a historical continuation, extension, or development of the present stage, nor would it be part of a general rational plan. It would, however, be identified as an instant among many—a coincidence in the uncertain and ephemeral field of all other possible moments.

The odyssey of the Iranian intellectuals in the twentieth century began by searching for ways to remedy autocracy and to best incorporate modernity; in the closing years of the century intellectuals seem to be confronting the same set of questions. Whatever the result, it will affect both their style and their destiny. By basing itself on the modern Western paradigm of rational politics without sharing its philosophical underpinnings, intellectual discourse assumed responsibility in an area in which it could not fulfill its promises and the obligations expected of it, expectations that were once within the domain of religion.

~ NOTES ~

Chapter 1

1 Closing line of a letter from New York to the poet Ahmad-Reza Ahmadi, dated "Third of Ramadan," n. yr. (1390 A.H./1970?), reprinted in Lili Golestân, ed., *Sohrâb Sepehri: Shâʿer, Naqqâsh* (Sohrâb Sepehri: Poet, Painter) (Tehran: Amir-Kabir, 1359/1980), p. 18. Although it may be of marginal relevance here, in order to ascertain the full date of Sepehri's seemingly jocular reference to the lunar "Ramadan" instead of the Gregorian or the still more familiar Persian solar (*shamsi*) calendar, it can be noted that Sepehri twice visited New York, once in 1349/1970 for seven months, and a second time for a short visit in 1350/1971. Judging by the overall tone and length of his letter, it is very likely that Sepehri wrote it during his first visit to New York, for which the "Third of Ramadan" (1390 A.H.) coincides with 12 Âbân 1349/3 November 1970. For a biographical profile of Sepehri, see "Sâlshomâr-e Zendegi-ye Sohrâb Sepehri" (A Chronology of Sohrab Sepehri's Life), in Dâriush Âshouri, Karim Emâmi, and Hosein Maʿsoumi-Hamedâni, eds., *Payâmi dar Râh: Nazari be Sheʿr va Naqqâshi-ye Sohrâb Sepehri* (A Message in the Way: Glancing at Sepehri's Poetry and Paintings) (Tehran: Tahouri, Winter 1359/1982), pp. 9–14, note in particular p. 13. I am further grateful to Karim Emâmi for his inquiries to verify the above date.

2 Hence the popularity of the book *Gozashteh, Cherâgh-e Râh-e Âyandeh Ast: Târikh-e Iran dar Fâseleh-ye Du Koudetâ* (The Past Shows the Road to the Future: A History of Iran between the Two Coups d'État), in the first few years after the revolution; the book was published by JÂMI (Jebhe-ye Âzâdi-e Mardom-e Iran) (Front for the Liberation of the Iranian People) (n.p., n.d. [1st edition, n.p., 1355/1976; reprinted, Tehran, 1357/1978–1979]).

3 The category of the self is of particular relevance to the study of ideology and false-consciousness and to the interpretation of culture, including the historical sociology of culture and culture in the immediate, everyday context of the life-world. For further discussions, see, for example, M. Carrithes, S. Collins, and S. Lukes, eds., *The Category of the Person* (Cambridge, 1985). For a philosophical exposition of this topic with particular reference to the constitution of modern subjectivity and morality in Western culture, see Charles Taylor, *Sources*

of the Self: The Making of the Modern Identity (Cambridge, Mass.: Harvard University Press, 1989).

4 In this context, note the criticism made by the writer and critic Houshang Golshiri of Mahmoud Dowlatâbâdi's long novel *Kleydar*, where the individual is portrayed as a mere type whose actions are somewhat predictable within a pre-set picture of social relations. See Houshang Golshiri, "Hâshiyeh'i bar Român-hâ-ye Mo'âser: Hâshiyeh'i bar Kleydar" (A Commentary on Contemporary Novels: A Commentary on Kleydar), in *Naqd-e Âgâh* (No. 1) (Tehran: Erteshârât-e Âgâh, 1361/1982), pp. 38–62.

5 On the quest for the self, e.g., "country as self, people as self, history as self," in a parallel context of the Arab world, see Jacques Berque, *Cultural Expression in Arab Society Today*, translated by Robert W. Stookey (Austin and London: University of Texas Press, 1978, Chap. 13, pp. 237–258, note in particular p. 238).

6 For references, see Chapter Two, note 2.

7 See *S/N*, Vol. 1. See also E. G. Browne, *A Literary History of Persia*, Vol. 4 (reprinted, Cambridge: Cambridge University Press, 1959).

8 See Mohammad-Taqi Bahâr (Malek al-Sho'arâ), *Sabk-Shenâsi* (Stylistics), Vol. 3, 4th edition (Tehran, 2535 [1335]/1976).

9 See Nikki R. Keddie, "The Origins of the Religious-Radical Alliance in Iran," *Past and Present*, Vol. 34 (1966), pp. 70–80.

10 See Chap. 2.

11 Max Weber, "Politics as a Vocation," in *From Max Weber: Essays in Sociology*, translated, edited, and with an introduction by H. H. Gerth and C. Wright Mills (London and Boston: Routledge and Kegan Paul, 1948; reprinted, 1974, pp. 77–128). A similar point was also evoked recently by Edward Said, who argued that intellectuals on the whole have a vocation for the "art of representing." Accordingly,

> *There is no such thing as a private intellectual, since the moment you set down words and then publish them you have entered the public world. Nor is there* only *a public intellectual, someone who exists just as a figurehead or spokesperson or symbol of a cause, movement, or position. There is always the personal inflection and the private sensibility, and those give meaning to what is being said or written. . . .*
>
> *So in the end it is the intellectual as a representative figure that matters — someone who visibly represents a standpoint of some kind, and someone who makes articulate representations to his or her public despite all sorts of barriers. My argument is that intellectuals are individuals with a vocation for the art of representing, whether that is talking, writing, teaching, [or] appearing on television. And the vocation is important to the extent that it is publicly recognizable and involves both commitment and risk, boldness and vulnerability. (Edward W. Said,* Representations of the Intellectuals: The 1993 Reith Lectures [*New York: Pantheon House, 1994*], pp. 12–13)

Said further refers to intellectuals as "those individuals whose capacity for thought and judgment made them suitable for representing the best thought—culture itself—and making it prevail" (Ibid., p. 29).

Chapter 2

1 See Javâd Tabâtabâ'i, *Darâmadi Falsafi bar Târikh-e Andisheh-ye Siâsi dar Iran* (A Philosophical Prologue to the History of Political Thought in Iran) (Tehran, 1367/1988).

2 See Hamid Enayat, *Modern Islamic Political Thought: The Response of the Shi'i and Sunni Muslims to the Twentieth Century* (London, 1982), pp. 161–169. For further background information, see Ann K. S. Lambton, "Some New Trends in Islamic Political Thought in Late Eighteenth and Early Nineteenth Century Persia," *Studia Islamica*, Vol. 32 (1974), pp. 95–128; and Mangol Bayat, *Mysticism and Dissent: Socioreligious Thought in Qajar Iran* (Syracuse, N.Y.: Syracuse University Press, 1982). See also Said Amir Arjomand, *The Shadow of God and the Hidden Imam: Religion, Political Order, and Societal Change in Shi'ite Iran from the Beginning to 1890* (Chicago: University of Chicago Press, 1984), pp. 144–149; Juan R. I. Cole, "Shi'i Clerics in Iraq and Iran, 1722–1780: The Akhbari-Usuli Conflict Reconsidered," *IS*, Vol. 18, No. 1 (1985), pp. 3–34; and, also by the same author, "Ideology, Ethics, and Philosophical Discourses in Eighteenth Century Iran," *IS*, Vol. 22, No. 1 (1989), pp. 7–34. For Sheikhi ideas, see Henri Corbin, *L'École Shaykhie en Théologie Shi'ite* (Paris: Annuaire de l'École Pratique des Hautes Études, Section des Sciences Religieuses, 1960–1961); reprinted with Persian translation by Ferydoun Bahmanyâr, Tehran: Tâbân, 1964. On the rise of the Babi movement, see Abbas Amanat, *Resurrection and Renewal: The Making of the Babi Movement in Iran, 1844–1850* (Ithaca, N.Y.: Cornell University Press, 1989).

3 *Monavvar* is the Arabic equivalent of *rowshan*, meaning enlightened. During Reza Shah's period, the newly formed Iranian Academy, in its task of "purifying" the Persian language from foreign words, changed *monavvar al-fekr* to *rowshanfekr*. See Ervand Abrahamian, *Iran between Two Revolutions* (Princeton, N.J.: Princeton University Press, 1982), pp. 142–143; see also Farhangestân-e Iran (Iranian Academy), *Vâzhehâ-ye Now* (New Words), Vols. 6 and 7 (Tehran, n.d.).

4 See Fereydoun Âdamiyat, *Andishehâ-ye Mirzâ Âqâ Khân-e Kermâni* (The Ideas of Mirzâ Âqâ Khân Kermâni) (Tehran, 1346/1967), p. 241. Âdamiyat points out that in the term *monavvar al-'oqoul*, Mirzâ Âqâ Khân had captured the meaning of both the Age of Reason and the Enlightenment.

5 Ibid., p. 241. Quoted from one of Kermâni's works entitled *Ketâb-e Reyhân-e Boustân Afrouz bar Tarz va Tarbiyat-e Adabiyât-e Farangestân-e Emrouz* (The Book of Garden-Dazzling Herbs on the Manners and Formation of Modern Western Culture) (1st edition, 1313 A.H./1894).

6   Mirzâ Âqâ Khân, by employing the terms *rowshan* (enlighten, lighted) and *nour* (light) as prefixes had coined certain new compounds, such as *rowshan-sarâ* (the enlightened house), *rowshanestân* (the enlightened place), and *nour-e khwishtâb* (the self-reflecting light), expressions inspired by the general spirit of the Enlightenment, a spirit shared by many secular reformists.

7   Asadollâh Mamaqâni, *Maslak al-Imam fi Salâmat al-Islam* (The Doctrine of Imam for the Well-Being of Islam) (Istanbul: Matba'eh-ye Shams, 1328 A.H./1910, pp. 59–60; reprinted, Tabriz, 1329 A.H./1911; new edition, Tehran: Nashr-e Târikh-e Iran, 1363/1984), pp. 57–58. Among other early references to the "intellectual" ulama, mention can be made of Mollâ Hosein Fâzel Ardakâni, a resident of Karbala and teacher of *fiqh* in the late nineteenth century, who was referred to by Yahyâ Dowlat-Âbâdi as the "head of intellectuals" (*sarhalqeh-ye monavvar al-afkârân*). See Yahyâ Dowlatâbâdi, *Hayât-e Yahyâ* (Yahyâ's Life), 4 Vols. (2nd edition, Tehran, 1361/1982), here Vol. 1, p. 26. Hâj Mirzâ Ali Saqat al-Islam, a Constitutionalist activist among the ulama of Tabriz, who was hanged by the Russians on 10 Muharram 1330 A.H./31 December 1911, was later classified by a native historian as belonging to the intellectual ulama (*ulama-ye monavvar al-fekr*). See Hosein Farzâd, *Târikh-e Enqelâb va Tahavvul-e Âzarbâyjân dar Dowreh-ye Mashrutiyat yâ Târikh-e Sattâr Khân Sardâr-e Melli* (A History of Revolution in Âzarbâyjân during the Constitutional Period or a History of Sattar Khan the National Commander) (Tabriz, 1324/1945), p. 84. The author also lists the "intellectuals" (*rowshanfekrân*) among the pro-Constitutionalist camp. Ibid., p. 58.

8   Mohammad-Taqi Bahâr (Malek al-Sho'arâ), *Sabk-Shenâsi*, pp. 403–405. Among other examples of the use of *monavvar al-fekr* was by Farrokh-Din Pârsây, the proprietor of the economic journal *'Asr-e Hadid* (The Age of Steel). Commenting on his earlier collaborations with the Chamber of Commerce in an editorial (dated Âzar 1308/December 1929), he referred to some of the Chamber's members as "intellectual" (*monavvar al-fekr*). See *Jarâ'ed*, Vol. 4, p. 32. In a brief autobiographical note, he recalled a young intellectual (*rowshan-fekr*) and learned theology student (*talabeh*) who in 1325 A.H./1907 was the principal of a primary school in Tehran and was a Constitutionalist. Ibid., p. 34. Further, Sadr Hâshemi refers to Fakhr-Âfâq Pârsâ, the editor of the reformist women's magazine *Jahân-e Zanân* (Women's World), published in 1921, and wife of Farrokh-Din, as an intellectual (*rowshan-fekr*). See *Jarâ'ed*, Vol. 2, p. 184.

9   For a brief discussion of this topic, see Shahrokh Meskoob, *Melliyat va Zabân: Naqsh-e Divân, Din, va 'Erfân dar Nasr-e Farsi* (Nationality and Language: The Role of the Court, Religion, and Mysticism in the Development of Persian Prose) (Paris: Ferdowsi, n.d. [1360/1981]); English edition as: Shahrokh Meskoob, *Iranian Nationality and the Persian Language* (Washington, D.C.: Mage, 1992). Government secretaries (*ahl-e divân*) were no longer members of the royal court but had become state employees and had no immediate urge for literary or linguistic competence. Similarly, mystic and Sufi authors (*ahl-e 'erfân*) had al-

ready lost their traditional vitality as a "culture-generating" force to the state of mental stagnation that has been so characteristic of recent centuries. Meskoob concludes that following the Constitutional movement, the Iranian intelligentsia became directly involved in developing the language. Meskoob, *Melliyat va Zabân*, pp. 216–217. Such a classification was largely subjective. Although many intellectuals *were* state employees, they did not define themselves as such; witness Meskoob's own employment in the Plan Organization before the recent revolution, while he was largely known for his translation of Sophocles, works on the *Shahnâmeh*, etc.

10 Even in the post-Constitutional period, most poetry followed the traditional patterns of Persian metrics (*'arouz*). For a study of post-Constitutional poetry, see M. Rahman, *Post-revolution Persian Verse, with Special Reference to the Poetry of Lahuti, Bahar, 'Arif, Iraj, 'Ishqi and Parvin* (Ph.D. thesis, School of Oriental and African Studies, University of London, 1953–1954); and Mohammad Ishaque, *Modern Persian Poetry* (Calcutta, 1943). See further Mohammad-Reza Shafi'i Kadkani, *Advâr-e She'r-e Farsi az Mashrutiyat tâ Soqout-e Saltanat* (Periods of Persian Poetry from the Constitutional Movement to the Fall of the Monarchy) (Tehran, 1359/1980); and Ali Gheissari, "The Poetry and Politics of Farrokhi Yazdi," *IS*, Vol. 26, Nos. 1–2, Winter–Spring 1993, pp. 33–50. For a general survey of the literature of the Constitutionalist period, see Mohammad-Reza Shafi'i Kadkani, "Persian Literature (Belles-Lettres) from the Time of Jâmi to the Present Day," in G. Morrison, ed., *History of Persian Literature from the Beginnings of the Islamic Period to the Present Day* (Leiden: E. J. Brill, 1981), pp. 135–206, note "The Constitutional Period," pp. 175–206.

11 The journal *Akhtar* is a good case in point. See Orhan Kologlu, "*Akhtar*, journal persan d'Istanbul," and Anja Pistor-Hatam, "The Persian Newspaper *Akhtar* as a Transmitter of Ottoman Political Ideas," both in Thierry Zarcone and Fariba Zarinebaf-Shahr, eds., *Les Iraniens d'Istanbul* (Paris and Tehran, 1993).

12 For this observation, I am particularly indebted to Anna Enayat. Several recent studies on different aspects of the Iranian community in Istanbul in the nineteenth and early twentieth centuries can be found in Zarcone and Zarinebaf-Shahr, eds., *Les Iraniens d'Istanbul*, among them Fariba Zarinebaf-Shahr, "The Iranian Merchant Community in the Ottoman Empire and the Constitutional Revolution," and Djamshid Behnam, "Le rôle de la communauté iranienne d'Istanbul dans le processus de modernisation de l'Iran." For a Persian version of the latter article, see Jamshid Behnam, "Manzelgâhi dar-Râh-e Tajaddod-e Iran: Istanbul" (Istanbul: A "Way Station" to the Modernization of Iran), *Iran Nameh*, Vol. 11, No. 2 (Spring 1993), pp. 271–282. For the influence of the Ottoman reformist ideas in Iran, see Anja Pistor-Hatem, *Iran und die Reformbewegung im Osmanischen Reich* (Berlin, 1992).

13 For a recent study of the Iranian community in the Caucasus, see Mangol Bayat, *Iran's First Revolution: Shi'ism and the Constitutional Revolution of 1905–1909* (New York and Oxford, 1991). See also Ali Forouhi, "Arâmaneh-ye

Gilân va Nehzat-e Mashrutiyat" (The Armenians of Gilân and the Constitutional Movement), *Âyandeh*, Vol. 19, Nos. 7–9 (Mehr-Âzar 1372/October–December 1993), pp. 695–711.

14 Abd al-Rahim Tâlebuf and Mirzâ Hasan Roshdiyeh are good examples. See Fereydoun Âdamiyat, *Andishehâ-ye Tâlebuf-e Tabrizi* (The Ideas of Tâlebuf Tabrizi) (2nd edition, Tehran, 1363/1984); and Shams al-Din Roshdiyeh, *Savâneh-e ʿOmr* (Life's Events: The Life and Works of Mirzâ Hasan Roshdiyeh) (1st edition, Tehran, 1364/1985).

15 Though of Arabic origin, *enqelâb* should be differentiated from *thawra*, the term for revolution current in Arabic.

16 For instance, the pro-Constitutionalist Mollâ ʿAbdol-Rasoul Kâshâni, in his well-argued *Resâleh-ye Ensâfiyeh* (Treatise on Impartiality and Justice) (Kâshân, 1328 A.H./1910), stresses the importance of the implementation of laws and the spread of social justice, or else, he says, "there will be fear of revolution" (p. 48). In an earlier and more provocative tract, *Haqq-e Dafʿ-e az Sharr va Qiâm bar Zedd-e Zolm* (The Right to Repulse Evil and Rise against Injustice) (n.n., Istanbul, 1326 A.H./1908), the anonymous author uses the term in both its old and new senses. On the one hand (for example, on p. 22), *enqelâb* is identified with *revolution* and is strongly recommended under tyranny, and on the other (p. 36), its contemporary period, which was marked by Mohammad-Ali Shah's attacks against the Constitutional movement, is described as involving days of "increased crisis and intense revolution" (*sheddat-e bohrân va heddat-e enqelâb*). The subtitle of the latter tract is "When Will Mutiny and Rebellion Become Sacred?" Judging by today's standards, this work can be classified as subversive literature.

17 As used by, for example, Mirzâ Âqâ Khân Kermâni in both *Ketâb-e Rezvân* (The Book of Paradise) (ca. 1304 A.H./1886–1887), and *Seh Maktoub* (Three Tracts) (transcribed 1326 A.H./1908); see Âdamiyat, *Andishehâ-ye Mirzâ Âqâ Khân-e Kermâni*, pp. 268 and 271.

18 See *Jarâʾed*, Vol. 4, pp. 341–343; and *Press and Poetry*, pp. 152–153.

19 See Mohammad Farrokhi Yazdi, *Divân-e Farrokhi Yazdi*, edited with an introduction by Hosein Makki (7th edition, Tehran, 1363/1984), pp. 92, 93, 106, and 245. In a lyric (*ghazal*), Farrokhi made an implicit reference to the Constitutional movement as an "unfinished revolution" (*enqelâb-e nâqes*). Ibid., p. 93.

20 Many examples have been collected by Mohammad Moʿin in his *Mazdiasnâ va Adab-e Pârsi* (Mazdiasnâ and Persian Literature) (3rd edition, Tehran, 2535 [1355]/1976). Or Sâdeq Hedâyat's interpretation of Omar Khayyâm's nostalgic sentiments about ancient Iran, expressed in Hedâyat's introduction to the *Rubâʿiyât*, also can be regarded as an indication of continuity in literary consciousness. See Sâdeq Hedâyat, ed., *Tarânehâ-ye Khayyâm* (Khayyâm's Poems), with an Introduction by Sâdeq Hedâyat (6th edition, Tehran, 1353/1974), pp. 9–64. See further A. S. Melikian-Chirvani, "Le Royaume de Salomon les

inscriptions persanes de sites achéménides," *Le Monde iranien et Islam*, Vol. 1, Geneva and Paris (1971), pp. 1–41; and Mohammad Mohammadi-Malâyeri, "Negâhi beh darbâr-e Sâsâni az Khelâl-e Ma'âkhez-e Islami" (A View of the Sassanian Court in Islamic Historical Sources), article in three parts in *Iranshenasi*, Vols. 3 and 4 (1991–1992). For a general observation on the uses of history and language in the modern articulation of the Iranian national identity, see Mostafa Vaziri, *Iran as Imagined Nation: The Construction of National Identity* (New York: Paragon House, 1993).

21   See Abd al-Hosein Zarrinkoub, *Naqd-e Adabi* (Literary Criticism), Vol. 2 (3rd edition, Tehran, 1361/1982), p. 636; see also Sir Denis Wright, *The English Amongst the Persians: During the Qajar Period 1787–1921* (London, 1977), pp. 155–157. Rawlinson had begun to copy the inscriptions in 1835. The full copy and its translation were not completed until 1846, however. He sent them to London where, together with his notes, they were published as "The Persian Cuneiform Inscription at Behistun" in *The Journal of the Royal Asiatic Society*, in 2 Vols., 1846 (Appendices, 1850 and 1853). Rawlinson was a recipient of the Persian order of the Lion and Sun (c. 1844). See Stanley Lane-Poole, "Rawlinson, Sir Henry Creswicke," in Sir Leslie Stephen and Sir Sidney Lee, eds., *The Dictionary of National Biography*, Vol. 16 (Oxford, 1959–1960, pp. 771–774. For further details on Rawlinson and his travels, see George Rawlinson, *A Memoir of Major-General Sir Henry Creswicke Rawlinson* (London, 1898). Rawlinson had been anticipated by others who had produced earlier transcriptions of Persian cuneiform inscriptions. Sir Robert Ker Porter (b. Durham 1777, d. St. Petersburg 1842) traveled to southern and western Iran in 1817 and copied many inscriptions, which he later published in his *Travels in Georgia, Persia, Armenia, Ancient Babylonia, &c. &c. During the Years 1817, 1818, 1819, and 1820*, 2 Vols. (London, 1821–1822). While at Tehran, Ker Porter had an audience with Fath-Ali Shah (ibid., Vol. 1, pp. 323–329), whose portrait he later drew and delivered on his second visit to Tehran in 1819. This won him the insignia of the Lion and Sun (ibid., Vol. 2, p. 523). For Ker Porter, see Thomas Seccombe, "Porter, Sir Robert Ker," in Stephen and Lee, eds., *Dictionary of National Biography*, pp. 190–192.

22   For instance, Fath-Ali Shah's title and pen name was *Khâqân*, the title of the Turkic and Mongol rulers and the Chinese Tartary. In an elegy (*qasidah*) that he composed in praise of his "crowned uncle" while being the crown prince himself, Fath-Ali compared Âqâ Mohammad Khân (r. 1779–1797) in monarchy with Mohammad in prophecy. He wrote that "two Mohammads emerged in the world, one Turk, the other Arab." See Zarrinkoub, *Naqd-e Adabi*, p. 619.

23   The names thus given were primarily Turkish and Arabic up to the twentieth son, and predominantly Persian afterward. For example, Abbas Mirzâ, Mohammad-Ali Mirzâ Dowlatshâh, Mohammad-Qoli Mirzâ Molkârâ, Hosein-Ali Mirzâ Farmânfarmâ, Hasan-Ali Mirzâ Shojâ' al-Saltaneh, Mohammad-Taqi Mirzâ Hesâm al-Saltaneh, Ali-Naqi Mirzâ Rokn al-Dowleh, and Imamverdi

Mirzâ Ilkhâni fit in the first group, while Keyqobâd Mirzâ, Bahrâm Mirzâ, Shâpour Mirzâ, Manouchehr Mirzâ, Hormoz Mirzâ, Iraj Mirzâ, Keykâvous Mirzâ, Keykhosrow Mirzâ, Keyoumars Mirzâ Ilkhâni Ab al-Molouk, Jahânshah Mirzâ, Bahman Mirzâ Bahâ' al-Dowleh, Farrokh-siar Mirzâ, Tahmoures Mirzâ, Parviz Mirzâ, and Kâmrân Mirzâ belong to the second. I owe this observation to Abbas Amanat. See Mirzâ Mohammad-Taqi Lesân al-Molk (Sepehr), *Nâsekh al-Tawârikh: Salâtin-e Qâjâriyeh* (The Conclusion of All Histories: On Qajar Rulers), 4 Books in 2 Vols., edited by Mohammad-Bâqer Behboudi (Tehran, 1353/1974–1975), here Book 2, pp. 140–155. For Fath-Ali Shah's wives and children, see further Ahmad Mirzâ Azod al-Dowleh, *Târikh-e Azodi* (The Azodi History), written originally in 1304 A.H./1886–1887 and subsequently published in Bombay in Sha'bân 1306 A.H./April 1888; edited and reprinted by H. Kouhi Kermâni (Tehran, 1328/1949, reprinted, Karaj, 1362/1984); new edition edited by Abd al-Hosein Navâ'i (Tehran, 1355/1976).

24   See Lesân al-Molk (Sepehr), *Nâsekh al-Tawârikh*, Book 1, p. 79.

25   See, for example, a series of fifty-two nineteenth-century plates (21 × 35 cm) that show different scenes from Ferdowsi's *Shahnâmeh*, where portraits of the legendary kings, their courtiers, and their costumes bear a striking resemblance to those of the Qajar rulers (especially Fath-Ali Shah and his court). See *Majâles-e Shahnâmeh* (Shahnameh Album) (Tehran, Kolâleh-ye Khâvar, 1354/1975). For earlier periods, see C. E. Bosworth, "The Heritage of Rulership in Early Islamic Iran and the Search for Dynastic Connections with the Past," *Iran*, Vol. 11 (1973), pp. 51–62; see also H. Busse, "The Revival of Persian Heritage under the Bûyids," in D. H. Richards, ed., *Islamic Civilisation 950–1150* (Oxford, 1975), pp. 47–70. For discussions of ceremonies as sources of legitimization of power, see David Cannadine and Simon Price, eds., *Rituals of Royalty: Power and Ceremonies in Traditional Societies* (Cambridge: Cambridge University Press, 1987); and Steven Lukes, "Political Rituals and Social Integration," in *Essays in Social Theory* (London, 1977).

26   Homâ Nâteq, *Mosibat-e Vabâ va Balâ-ye Hokoumat: Majmou'eh-ye Maqâlât* (The Tragedy of Cholera and the Calamity of Government: A Collection of Essays) (Tehran, 1358/1979), p. 153. For Badâye'-Negâr see, for example, Bahâr, *Sabk-Shenâsi*, pp. 364–365; *S/N*, Vol. 1, pp. 145–149; and Nâteq, *Mosibat-e Vabâ*, pp. 133–134. Badâye'-Negâr also translated a biography of Imam Hosein to eloquent Persian: see Mirzâ Mohammad-Ebrâhim Navvâb Tehrâni (Badâye'-Negâr), Persian translation of Seyyed ibn Tâvous, *Faiz al-Domou'* (Munificence of Tears) (Tehran: lithograph edition, 1286 A.H./1869; new edition, edited by Akbar Irani, Tehran: forthcoming). For bibliographic reference, see Daftar-e Nashr-e Mirâs-e Maktoub (Written Heritage Press), *Kârnâmeh-ye Mirâs: Fehrest-e Âsâr va Motoun-e Dar Dast-e Tas-hih va Enteshâr* (The Heritage Records: A List of Works and Manuscripts in Editorial Preparation for Publication) (Tehran, Fall 1374/1995), p. 110.

27 See Homa Katouzian, *The Political Economy of Modern Iran: Despotism and Pseudo-Modernism, 1926–1979* (London, 1981), p. 16; and "The Aridosoladic Society: A Model of Long-Term Social and Economic Development in Iran," *IJMES*, Vol. 15 (1983), pp. 259–281. See further Mohammad-Ali Homâyoun Kâtouziân and Amir Pishdâd, *Melli Kist va Nehzat-e Melli Chist?* (Who Is Nationalist and What Is the National Movement?) (Europe [Paris?], January 1981); and Mohammad-Ali Homâyoun Kâtouziân, "Yâd-dâshti dar bâreh-ye Mellat, Melli, Melli-gerâ'i va Nâsiounâlism" (A Note on Nation, National, Nationalist, and Nationalism), *Fasl-e Ketâb*, London, Nos. 2 and 3 (Summer and Fall 1367/1988); reprinted in Mohammad-Ali Homâyoun Kâtouziân, *Estebdâd, Demukrâsi va Nehzat-e Melli* (Democracy, Arbitrary Rule, and the Popular Movement of Iran) (Washington, D.C.: Mehregan, 1372/1993), pp. 38–51.

28 In his book, *An Historical and Descriptive Account of Persia from the Earliest Ages to the Present Time* (Edinburgh: Oliver & Boyd, 1834), James B. Fraser, a European visitor to Iran during the early Qajar period, started his chapter, "Description and Character of the Persian People," with the following observation: "The character and manners of a people are ever greatly influenced by their government. When that is well regulated, a corresponding consistency and order pervade their habits; but under despotic sway, where they only reflect the qualities of the ruler, their dispositions vary with that of the reigning prince." He further commented about Iranians, "Capriciously, haughtily, and cruelly dealt with themselves, they become capricious, haughty, and cruel to their inferiors; and thus the court and all who are attached to it are rendered, to the poor man, objects of terror and disgust" (pp. 342–343).

29 See S. M. Stern, "Ya'qûb the Coppersmith and Persian National Sentiment," in C. E. Bosworth, ed., *Iran and Islam* (Edinburgh, 1971), pp. 535–555; and R. P. Mottahedeh, "The Shu'ûbîyah Controversy and the Social History of Early Islamic Iran," *IJMES*, Vol. 7 (1976), pp. 161–182. Several references to *vatan* in Persian literature can be found in Ali-Akbar Dehkhodâ, *Loghat-Nâmeh* (Persian Lexicon), No. 179 (Tehran, 1351/1972), pp. 214–216. For further discussion of this topic, see Mohammad-Reza Shafi'i Kadkani, "Talaqqi-e Qodamâ az Vatan" (Predecessors' View of Nation), *Alif-Bâ*, Vol. 2 (Tehran, 1352/1973), pp. 1–26. Likewise, the word *dowlat* in classical literature had several meanings, of which "state" was only one. It also meant good fortune, felicity, wealth, victory, power, and reign, most of which still hold. For a discussion of *dowlat* in classical literature, see Wojciech Skalmowski, "Remarks on Daulat in Hafiz," *Folia Orientalia*, Vol. 22 (1981–1984), 1985, pp. 131–137.

30 Even Ahmad Kasravi, who was normally critical of the "mortifying effects" of poetry on the Iranian mind, acknowledged that on the eve of the Constitutional movement, certain "harmless" poems were composed that contributed to the national awakening. See Ahmad Kasravi, *Târikh-e Mashruteh-ye Iran* (A History of the Iranian Constitutional Movement), 13th edition (Tehran,

2536 [1356]/1978), pp. 46–47. Kasravi (b. Tabriz 14 Safar 1308 A.H./31 September 1890, assassinated in Tehran 20 Esfand 1324/11 March 1946) was a prolific and controversial linguist, historian, and reformist. See Ervand Abrahamian, "Kasravi: The Integrative Nationalist of Iran," *MES*, Vol. 9, No. 3 (October 1973), pp. 271–295.

31   See A. de Gardanne, *Mission du Général Gardanne en Perse sous le premier empire* (London, 1865).

32   See Gurney and Nabavi, "Dâr al-Fonûn," *EIr*, Vol. 6, 1993, pp. 662– 668. See further Maryam D. Ekhtiar, "The Dar al-Funun: Educational Reform and Cultural Development in Qajar Iran," Ph.D. Dissertation, New York University, 1994.

33   See Fereydoun Âdamiyat, *Amir Kabir va Iran* (Amir Kabir and Iran), 4th edition (Tehran, 1354/1975); and Fereydoun Âdamiyat, *Andisheh-ye Taraqqi va Hokoumat-e Qânoun: ʿAsr-e Sepahsâlâr* (The Idea of Progress and the Rule of Law: The Period of Sepahsâlâr), Tehran, 1351/1972. See also J. H. Lorentz, "Iran's Greatest Reformer of the Nineteenth Century: An Analysis of Amir Kabir's Reforms," *IS*, Vol. 4 (1971), pp. 85–103; and A. Karny, "The Premiership of Mirza Hosein Khan and His Reforms in Iran," *Asian and African Studies*, Vol. 10 (1974), pp. 127–158.

34   See Âdamiyat, *Amir Kabir va Iran*, Chap. 7.

35   For an early study of the different stages of contact between Iran and the West, see Ali Akbar Siassi, *La Perse au contact de l'Occident: Étude historique et sociale* (Paris, 1931).

36   It is estimated that the Iranian population in 1900 was about 9.86 million, with the rate of distribution in urban and rural areas being 2.07 and 7.79 million, respectively. See also Julian Bharier, *Economic Development in Iran, 1900– 1970* (London: Oxford University Press, 1971), pp. 26–27, Tables 1 and 2; "A Note on the Population of Iran 1900–66," *Population Studies*, Vol. 22, No. 2 (July 1968), pp. 273–279, note in particular p. 275; and "The Growth of Towns and Villages in Iran, 1900–66," *MES*, Vol. 8, No. 1 (January 1972), pp. 51–61.

37   For instance, over the course of the nineteenth century in Egypt, Syria, and Iraq, there was a continuous rise in urban population, whereas in Iran the population declined from its mid-seventeenth-century level. See Charles Issawi, "Economic Change and Urbanization in the Middle East," in Ira M. Lapidus, ed., *Middle Eastern Cities: A Symposium on Ancient, Islamic, and Contemporary Middle Eastern Urbanism* (Berkeley: University of California Press, 1969), pp. 102–121, note pp. 103–104 and 109.

38   For instance, in 1907 some 25 percent of the population of Alexandria and 28 percent of the population of Port Said were foreigners, mostly French, Spanish, and Italian. Ibid., pp. 108–109.

39   For more information on the ethnic and religious diversity of nineteenth-century Ottoman society, see Albert Hourani, "The Ottoman Background of the Modern Middle East" and "Ottoman Reform and the Politics of

Notables," reprinted in Albert Hourani, *The Emergence of the Modern Middle East* (London, 1981), pp. 1–18 and 36–66, respectively. See also Albert Hourani, *Minorities in the Arab World* (London, 1947).

40 For information on Christian and Jewish communities in Iran, see Robin E. Waterfield, *Christians in Persia: Assyrians, Armenians, Roman Catholics and Protestants* (London: George Allen and Unwin, 1973); Walter J. Fischel, "The Jews of Persia, 1795–1940," *Jewish Social Studies*, Vol. 12, No. 2 (April 1950), pp. 119–160; and Henry Field, *Contributions to the Anthropology of Iran*, Anthropological Series, Vol. 29, Nos. 1 and 2 (Chicago: Field Museum of Natural History, December 15, 1939), Publication 458, No. 1, "Jews of Isfahan" and "Comparative Data on Jews from Southwestern Asia and the Caucasus," pp. 290–315 and 316–330, respectively.

41 Sir Robert Ker Porter, *Travels in Georgia, Persia, Armenia, Ancient Babylonia, &c. &c. During the Years 1817, 1818, 1819, and 1820*, 2 Vols. (London, 1821–1822), Vol. 1, p. 687.

42 See Abd al-Hâdi Hâʾeri, *Nakhostin Rouyârouʾihâ-ye Andisheh-garân-e Iran bâ Du Rouyeh-ye Tamaddon-e Bourzhovâzi-e Gharb* (Early Encounters of Iranian Thinkers with the Two Faces of Modern Western Civilization) (Tehran, 1367/1988), Chap. 12 on Henry Martyn, pp. 507–545.

43 Persian manuscript, transcribed in 1229 A.H./1814 by Mohammad-Hosein al-Mâzandarâni. Ibid., p. 534, n. 75.

44 See Nour al-Din Modarresi Chahârdehi, *Seyri dar Tasavvof* (A Study in Persian Sufism), 2nd edition (Tehran, 1361/1982), p. 265. For Henry Martyn see further, Waterfield, *Christians in Persia*, pp. 89–95. Kowsar-Alishâh (d. Jamâdi I 1247 A.H./October 1831) wrote another book, also requested by Fath-Ali Shah, in defense of Islam and the prophecy of Mohammad, entitled *Meftâh al-Nobuwwat* (The Opening of Prophecy), with an introduction by Mirzâ Abu al-Qâsem Qâʾem-Maqâm Farâhâni. See Kowsar-Alishâh, *Meftâh al-Nobuwwat* (Tehran, 1240 A.H./1824–1825; reprinted, Tehran 1340 A.H.?/1921–1922?), Qâʾem-Maqâm's introduction on pp. 2–5; also reprinted in Mirzâ Abu al-Qâsem Qâʾem-Maqâm Farâhâni, *Monshaʾât* (Writings), edited by Mohammad ʿAbbâsi (Tehran, 1356/1977–1978), pp. 283–284. See Modarresi Chahârdehi, *Seyri dar Tasavvof*, p. 265; and Hâʾeri, *Nakhostin Rouyârouʾihâ*, p. 543, n. 72. Among further refutations of Henry Martyn written by the Iranian clergy, see Mollâ Ali Nouri, *Borhân al-Milla* (The Proof of Faith), edited by Gholâm-Hosein Ebrâhimi-Dinâni, associate editor Sahl-Ali Madadi (Tehran, forthcoming); for bibliographical reference, see Daftar-e Nashr-e Mirâs-e Maktoub, *Kârnâmeh-ye Mirâs*, p. 38.

45 For more information on these developments, see John F. Baddeley, *The Russian Conquests of the Caucasus* (London, 1908); Nâser Najmi, *Iran dar Miân-e Toufân yâ Sharh-e Zendegâni-ye ʿAbbâs Mirzâ Nâyeb al-Saltaneh va Janghâ-ye Iran va Rous* (Iran in the Storm, or the Biography of the Crown Prince Abbas Mirzâ and the Perso-Russian Wars) (Tehran: Kânoun-e Maʿrefat, 1336/1957); and Peter W.

Avery, "An Enquiry into the Outbreak of the Second Russo-Persian War, 1826–28," in C. E. Bosworth, ed., *Iran and Islam: In Memory of the Late Vladimir Minorsky*, pp. 17–45.

46 See, for example, "The Murder of Griboyedov in Tehran," *Central Asian Review*, Vol. 7, No. 4 (1959), pp. 382–386, based on four separate sources by G. M. Petrov, V. Minorskiy, M. N. Pokrovskiy, and V. O. Klyucheskiy. The date of the massacre, given in this article as 30 January, seems to have been based on the Julian calendar, reflecting a difference of twelve days with the Gregorian calendar. Aleksandr Sergeyevich Griboyedov, who was born in Moscow in 1795, is also a noted figure in Russian literature as a major playwright and satirist contemporary to Pushkin. For a dramatized account of this incident, see Yuri Tynianov, *Death and Diplomacy in Persia*, translated from the Russian by Alec Brown (first published, London: Boriswood, 1938; reprint edition, Westport, Conn.: Hyperion Press, 1975 [translation of *Smert' Vazir-Mukhtara*]).

47 See A. K. S. Lambton, "The Tobacco Régie: Prelude to Revolution," *Studia Islamica*, Vol. 22 (1965), pp. 119–157, and Vol. 23 (1966), pp. 71–90; also reprinted in A. K. S. Lambton, *Qajar Persia: Eleven Studies* (London, 1987), pp. 223–276. See also Fereydoun Âdamiyat, *Shouresh bar Emtiâz-Nâmeh-ye Rezhi: Tahlil-e Siâsi* (Protest against the Régie Concession: a Political Analysis) (Tehran, 1360/1981).

48 See *S/N*, Vol. 1, pp. 1–220.

49 See Fereydoun Âdamiyat, *Andishehâye Mirzâ Fath-Ali Âkhoundzâdeh* (The Ideas of Mirzâ Fath-Ali Âkhoundzâdeh) (Tehran, 1349/1970–1971), p. 109.

50 See Jalâl al-Din Mirzâ Qajar, *Nâmeh-ye Khosrovân* (The Book of Kings), 3 Vols. (Tehran, 1285–1288 A.H./1868–1871). Jalâl al-Din Mirzâ (b. Tehran 1242 A.H./1826–1827, d. Tehran 1287 A.H./1870–1871) was Fath-Ali Shah's fifty-eighth son, who, according to Malek Iraj Mirzâ's genealogy of the Qajar dynasty, was more interested in socializing with European teachers from the Dâr al-Fonoun than in preserving his adherence to Islam. It is reported in the same source that in preparing *Nâmeh-ye Khosrovân*, Jalâl al-Din Mirzâ benefited from the assistance of Imam-Qoli Khân Zand (d. 1280 A.H./1863–1864). See *Rejâl*, Vol. 6, pp. 69–71. Imam-Qoli Khân, whose pen name was Ghârat (Pillage), was a learned and well-versed, but apparently "unorderly," poet who was a contemporary of Jalâl al-Din Mirzâ. Ibid., pp. 50–51.

51 Yaghmâ was the pen name of a major literary figure during the first half of the Qajar period, Mirzâ Rahim (later Abu al-Hasan) Jandaqi (b. in the Khorâsân village of Khour near Jandaq in the central desert 1196 A.H./1781–1782, d. 16 Rabi' II 1276 A.H./13 November 1859 at the same place), known for his eloquent, sometimes invective, style. Many of his poems, which he was never interested in compiling for publication, were well circulated and widely remembered during his lifetime. He was also favored by some of the literary-minded sons of Fath-Ali Shah such as Sultan Mohammad Mirzâ Seyf al-Dowleh, the author of *Seyf al-Rasâ'el*, and, interestingly enough, became a model for Mohammad Shah's powerful prime minister, Hâj Mirzâ Âqâsi, who had Sufi leanings. This may be attributed to Yaghmâ's early recourse to mysticism under the influence of his teacher, a Sufi poet in the desert town of Khour named Lotf-Ali Mohtaram. However, Yaghmâ later became highly critical of dervishes and their life-style. See Abu al-Qâsem Yaghmâ'i (Toghrâ), "Soufiân-e Jandaq" (Sufis of Jandaq), *Âyandeh*, Vol. 15, Nos. 10–12 (Dey–Esfand 1368/1990), pp. 824–828, see p. 826, fn. 2. For Yaghmâ and his complete works, see Mirzâ Rahim Yaghmâ-ye Jandaqi, *Majmu'eh-ye Âsâr-e Yaghmâ-ye Jandaqi* (Collected Works of Yaghmâ of Jandaq), edited and with an introduction and commentary by Seyyed Ali Âl-Dâvoud, 2 Vols., Vol. 1: Poetry (Tehran, 1357/1978); Vol. 2: Prose (Tehran, 1362/1983). For Yaghmâ, see further *S/N*, Vol. 1, pp. 109–112; Browne, *Literary History of Persia*, Vol. 4, pp. 337–344. For literary trends during Fath-Ali Shah's period, see Bahâr, *Sabk-Shenâsi*, Part 4. See also *S/N*, Vol. 1, Book I.

52   See Mirzâ Reza Khân Afshâr Begeshlu Qazvini, *Parvaz-e Negâresh-e Pârsi* (The Principal Method of Writing Persian) (Istanbul: Akhtar, 1300 A.H./1883), 6 pp. errata. It is evident from the text that Mirzâ Reza was under the influence of *Dasâtir*. Written during the seventeenth century by the followers of Âzar Keyvân, a Zoroastrian leader in India, *Dasâtir* (or *Desâtir*, in the sense of Ordinances, the Arabic plural form of the Persian term *dastour*, originally *dastvar* in Pahlavi, with several meanings such as authority, official, vizier, permission, custom, formula, program, and grammar) consisted of some sixteen shorter books, or "letters," using allegedly pure, but mostly forged, Persian vocabulary. It was reportedly "written in Iran and brought to India in 1818 by Mollâ Firouz, a famous Kadmi priest who was born in India, but with strong Iranian connections." See Mary Boyce, *Zoroastrians: Their Religious Beliefs and Practices* (London: 1979), p. 197. For nearly three centuries, the terminology of *Dasâtir* appealed to many authors who intended to purify Persian from Arabic but who did not question the authenticity of its allegedly pure words. Apart from *Parvaz-e Negâresh-e Pârsi* and *Alif-Bâ-ye Behrouzi* (Alphabet of Happiness), another book by Mirzâ Reza Khân on the reform of the Persian alphabet, the influence of *Dasâtir* can also be traced in more important works such as the Persian dictionary *Borhân-e Qâte'* (Definite Proof), by Mohammad-Hosein ibn Khalaf Tabrizi, written in 1062 A.H./1652, edited by Mohammad Mo'in, 3rd edition (Tehran, 1357/1978). For a critical discussion of *Dasâtir*, see, for example, Ebrâhim Pourdâvoud, "Dasâtir," reprinted in the introduction to *Borhân-e Qâte'*, edited by Mohammad Mo'in, 3rd edition (Tehran, 1357/1978), pp. 52–59.

53   See Âdamiyat's *Andishehâye Mirzâ Fath-Ali Âkhoundzâdeh*, *Andishehâye Mirzâ Âqâ Khân Kermâni*, and *Andishehâye Tâlebuf Tabrizi*. For a critical note on the linguistic chauvinism of Mirzâ Reza Khân Afshâr and Mirzâ Âqâ Khân Ker-

mâni, see Seyyed Hasan Taqizâdeh, "Lozoum-e Hefz-e Farsi-e Fasih" (The Necessity of Preserving Eloquent Persian), *Yâdegâr*, Vol. 4, No. 6 (Esfand 1326/ February–March 1948), pp. 1–40, here p. 14.

54 See Abdul-Hadi Hairi, *Shi'ism and Constitutionalism in Iran: A Study of the Role Played by the Persian Residents of Iraq in Iranian Politics* (Leiden, 1977), pp. 182–189. Here Hairi refers to Shams-e Kâshmari, Mahallâti, and Adib al-Hokamâ as "examples of Persian authors who understood the term [*Mashruteh*] in the sense 'conditional.'" Ibid., p. 183.

55 Taqizâdeh and Rezazâdeh Shafaq were in favor of this idea. See Seyyed Hasan Taqizâdeh, *Khatâbeh: Moshtamel bar Shammeh'i az Târikh-e Avâ'el-e Enqelâb va Mashrutiyat-e Iran* (Lecture: Early Days of the Iranian Constitutional Revolution) (Tehran, 1338/1959), pp. 18 and 53; and Sâdeq Rezazâdeh Shafaq, *Khâterât-e Majles, va Demokrâsi Chist?* (Majles Memoirs, and What Is Democracy?) (Tehran, 1334/1955), p. 141.

56 Dehkhodâ, *Loghat-Nâmeh*, entry on *Mashrutiyat*.

57 For example, Javâd Khân Sa'd al-Dowleh, a Qajar statesman who had initially sided with the Constitutionalists before turning against them, had once argued that the term *Mashruteh* meant "conditional" and was therefore a wrong translation of *constitution*, for which he suggested the use of the French word itself. See Taqizâdeh, *Khatâbeh*, p. 53.

58 Ibid., pp. 53–54.

59 For further discussion of this topic, see 'Abd al-Hâdi Hâ'eri, "Sokhani Pirâmoun-e Vâzheh-ye Mashruteh" (A Note on the Term *Mashruteh*), *Vahid*, Vol. 12 (1353/1974), pp. 287–300. See also Mohammad Mohit Tabâtabâ'i, "Risheh-ye Mashruteh" (The Origin of *Mashruteh*), *Mohit*, 2nd Series, Vol. 1, No. 3 (1326/1947), p. 24; and Mohammad Mohit Tabâtabâ'i, "Farmân-e Mashruteh az Kist?" (Who Proclaimed *Mashruteh?*), *Mohit*, Vol. 1 (1321/1942), pp. 9–18; and 2nd Series, Vol. 1, No. 4 (1326/1947), pp. 18–20 and 23.

60 A clear indication of this theme can be found in the literature of that period. See, for example, A. H. Hairi, "The Idea of Constitutionalism in Persian Literature prior to the 1906 Revolution," in *Akten des VII Kongresses für Arabistik und Islamwissenschaft*, Götingen, August 15–22, 1974, edited by Albert Dietrich (Götingen: Vandenhoeck & Ruprecht, 1976), pp. 189–207.

61 See Fereydoun Âdamiyat, *Eide'uluzhi-ye Nehzat-e Mashrutiyat-e Iran* (The Ideology of the Iranian Constitutional Movement), Vol. 1 (Tehran, 2535 [1355]/1976), see in particular "The Failure of Reforms." See also Âdamiyat, *Shouresh bar Emtiâz-Nâmeh-ye Rezhi*; and Shaul Bakhash, "The Failure of Reform: The Prime Ministership of Amin al-Dawla, 1897–8," in Edmund Bosworth and Carole Hillenbrand, eds., *Qajar Iran* (Political, Social and Cultural Change 1800–1925), Edinburgh, 1983, pp. 14–33.

62 Works by Soviet Iranologists who were pioneers of this kind of analysis include M. Pavlovitch, V. Teria, and S. Iranski, *Seh Maqâleh Dar-bâreh-ye Enqelâb-e Mashruteh-ye Iran* (Three Essays on the Iranian Constitutional Revo-

lution), originally written in 1926, translated into Persian (1329/1951) by M. Houshyâr (1st edition, Tehran, 1339/1960; 2nd and 3rd editions, Tehran, 1357/1978); and M. S. Ivanov, *Enqelâb-e Mashrutiyat-e Iran* (Iranian Constitutional Revolution), Persian translation by Kâzem Ansâri (Tehran, n.d.). Among the works inspired by this type of analysis and produced by Iranian authors are: Ehsân Tabari, *Forou-pâshi-e Nezâm-e Sonnati va Zâyesh-e Sarmâyeh-dâri dar Iran: Az Âghâz-e Tamarkoz-e Qajar tâ Âstâneh-ye Enqelâb-e Mashrutiyat* (Disintegration of Traditional Society and the Birth of Capitalism in Iran: From the Beginnings of Qajar Centralization to the Eve of the Constitutional Revolution) (Stockholm: Tudeh Party, 1354/1975); Bâqer Mo'meni, *Iran dar Âstâneh-ye Enqelâb-e Mashrutiyat* (Iran at the Threshold of the Constitutional Revolution), 6th edition (Tehran, 1359/1980) (according to the author, this work was originally written in 1329/1950); Mahmoud Seyrafizâdeh (Javâd Sadiq [pseudonym]), *Melliyat va Enqelâb dar Iran* (Nationality and Revolution in Iran), 1st edition (New York, 1352/1973); 2nd edition (Tehran, 1358/1980).

63 Examples of works from this perspective include Ali Davâni, *Nehzat-e Rowhânioun-e Iran* (The Movement of the Iranian Clergy), 10 Vols. (Tehran, n.d. [1360/1981]); Ali-Mohammad Naqavi, *Jâmeʿeh-shenâsi-ye Gharb-gerâ'i* (The Sociology of Westernism), 2 Vols.: Vol. 1 (Tehran, 1361/1982); Vol. 2 (Tehran, 1363/1984); and Ali-Akbar Valâyati, *Moqaddameh-ye Fekri-ye Nehzat-e Mashrutiyat* (The Intellectual Background of the Constitutional Movement), 3rd edition (Tehran, 1365/1986). We can contrast the Mashruteh movement with the Islamic revolution in two contemporary and opposing accounts: the secular intellectuals maintain that the revolution of 1979 was started by them (or at least with a great contribution by them) and then highjacked by the mullahs. The mullahs argue that the Constitutional movement was started by them and corrupted by secular forces.

64 See Keddie, "The Origins of the Religious-Radical Alliance in Iran." See further Ann K. S. Lambton, "The Persian 'Ulamâ' and the Constitutional Reform," in T. Fahd, ed., *Le Shîʿsme imâmite* (Paris: Presses Universitaires de France, 1970), pp. 245–269; reprinted in Lambton, *Qajar Persia*, pp. 277–300.

65 For a critical evaluation of the role of the ulama, see Abdol Karim Lahidji, "Constitutionalism and Clerical Authority," in Said Amir Arjomand, ed., *Authority and Political Culture in Shiʿism* (Albany: State University of New York Press, 1988), pp. 133–158.

66 See Kasravi, *Târikh-e Mashruteh-ye Iran.*

67 Mehdi Malekzâdeh, *Târikh-e Enqelâb-e Mashrutiyat-e Iran* (A History of the Iranian Constitutional Revolution) (Tehran, 1351/1972–1973). For the role of political societies in the Constitutional period, see also Fereydoun Âdamiyat, *Fekr-e Demokrâsi-ye Ejtemâʿi dar Nehzat-e Mashrutiyat-e Iran* (The Idea of Social Democracy in the Iranian Constitutional Movement) (Tehran, 1355/1976); Ann K. S. Lambton, "Secret Societies and the Persian Revolution of 1905–1906," in *St. Antony's Papers*, No. 4, Middle Eastern Affairs: No. 1 (London, 1958),

pp. 43–60 (reprinted in Ann K. S. Lambton, *Qâjâr Persia: Eleven Studies* [London, 1987], pp. 301–318), and "Persian Political Societies 1906–11," in *St. Antony's Papers*, No. 16, Middle Eastern Affairs: No. 3 (London, 1963), pp. 41–89; and Homâ Nâteq, "Jang-e Ferqeh-hâ dar Enqelâb-e Mashrutiyat-e Iran" (Factional Disputes in the Iranian Constitutional Revolution), *Alif-Bâ*, New Series, No. 3 (Paris, Summer 1983), pp. 30–52, note p. 40.

68 Âdamiyat, *Fekr-e Demokrâsi-e Ejtemâ'i*, p. 3. For the impact of the French Revolution on the development of Constitutional discourse in Iran, see further Mohammad Tavakoli-Targhi, "Asar-e Âgâhi az Enqelâb-e Farânseh dar Shekl-giri-ye Engâreh-ye Mashrutiyat dar Iran" (Constitutionalist Imagery in Iran and the Ideals of the French Revolution), *Iran Nameh*, Vol. 8, No. 3 (Summer 1369/1990), pp. 411–439; also by the same author, "Refashioning Iran: Language and Culture during the Constitutional Revolution," *IS*, Vol. 23, Nos. 1–4 (1990), pp. 77–101.

69 In the words of a later observer, "The most potent weapon that the urban population had against the tyranny of government officials was the closing of the bazaar. This weapon was so frequently and successfully used that at times merely the threat of resorting to this device sufficed to achieve a specific goal" (Donald N. Wilber, *Riza Shah Pahlavi: The Resurrection and Reconstruction of Iran* [New York, 1975], p. 21). For the role of merchants in the Constitutional movement, see, for example, Gad G. Gilbar, "The Big Merchants (*tujjâr*) and the Persian Constitutional Revolution of 1906," *Asian and African Studies*, Vol. 11, No. 1 (Summer 1976), pp. 275–303.

70 Âdamiyat, *Fekr-e Demokrâsi*, p. 4.

71 Âdamiyat, *Fekr-e Demokrâsi*, p. 4.

72 The controversy between Osouli and Akhbâri ideas that was mentioned earlier is one of the best indications of that background.

73 See Mansoureh Ettehadieh Nezam-Mafi, "The Council for the Investigation of Grievances: A Case Study of Nineteenth Century Iranian Social History," *IS*, Vol. 22, No. 1 (1989), pp. 51–61.

74 See Tavakoli-Targhi, "Asar-e Âgâhi az Enqelâb-e Farânseh." For references to knowledge about the French Revolution among Iranians during the earlier periods, see, for example, A. Rouh-Bakhshân, "Nakhostin Âshnâ'i-hâ-ye Irâniân bâ Enqelâb-e Farânseh" (Early Iranian Encounters with the French Revolution), *Nashr-e Dânesh*, Vol. 9, No. 4 (Khordâd–Tir 1368/June–July 1989), pp. 4–11.

75 For studies on Malkam and the trend of thought he represented, see Fereydoun Âdamiyat, *Fekr-e Âzâdi va Moqaddameh-ye Nehzat-e Mashrutiyat-e Iran* (The Idea of Liberty and the Beginning of the Iranian Constitutional Movement) (Tehran, 1340/1961–1962); Esmâ'il Râ'in, *Mirzâ Malkam Khân: Zendegi va Koushesh-hâ-ye Siâsi-ye Ou* (Mirzâ Malkam Khan: His Life and Political Activities) (Tehran, 1350/1971); Fereshteh Nourâ'i, *Tahqiq dar Afkâr-e Mirzâ Malkam Khân Nâzem al-Dowleh* (Mirzâ Malkam Khan: An Intellectual Study) (Teh-

ran, 1352/1973); Shaul Bakhash, *Iran: Monarchy, Bureaucracy and Reform under the Qajars: 1858–1896* (London: Ithaca Press, 1978), especially Chap. 6, "The Qajar Reformers and Their Ideas: The Later Phase," pp. 305–374); Hamid Algar, *Mirza Malkum Khan: A Study in the History of Iranian Modernism* (Berkeley: University of California Press, 1973); Homâ Nâteq, "Mâ va Mirzâ Malkam Khân-hâ-ye Mâ" (Us and Our Mirzâ Malkam Khans), in Homâ Nâteq, *Az Mâst Keh Bar Mâst: Chand Maqâleh* (We Have Only Ourselves to Blame: Essays) (Tehran, 2537 [1357]/1978), pp. 163–199. For a brief but generally favorable account of Malkam written by an Âzari author in the ex–Soviet Union, see Mobârez Al-izâdeh, "Pirâmoun-e Jahânbini-e Mirzâ Malkam Khân" (On the World Outlook of Mirzâ Malkam Khan), in Hosein Mohammadzâdeh (H. Sadiq), ed. and trans., *Masâ'el-e Adabiyât-e Nuvin-e Iran* (Problems of Modern Persian Literature) (Tehran, 1354/1975), pp. 99–121, who argues that Malkam entered a second and more progressive phase of his life only after his encounters with Mirzâ Fath-Ali Âkhoundzâdeh.

76 Malkaum Khan, "Persian Civilization," *Contemporary Review*, Vol. 59 (February 1891), pp. 238–244. See further Abrahamian, *Iran between Two Revolutions*, pp. 65–69.

77 See Bakhash, *Iran: Monarchy, Bureaucracy, and Reform*, p. 326.

78 See *Press and Poetry*, p. 18. For *Qânoun* and other works by Malkam, see Mirzâ Malkam Khân, *Rouznâmeh-ye Qânoun* (London); collected and reprinted with an introduction by Homâ Nâteq (Tehran, 2535 [1355]/1976). See also Mirzâ Malkam Khân, *Kolliyât* (Collected Works), edited by Hâshem Rabi'zâdeh, Vol. 1 (Tehran, 1325/1946–1947) (only one volume was published); and Mirzâ Malkam Khân, *Majmou'eh-ye Âsâr-e Mirzâ Malkam Khân* (Collected Works), edited by Mohammad Mohit Tabâtabâ'i, Tehran, 1327/1948–49.

79 Among the most articulate of these tracts was *Tanbih al-Umma va Tanzih al-Milla* (Awakening the Community and Purifying the Nation), by Mirzâ Mo-hammad-Hosein Nâ'ini (3rd edition, Tehran, 1374/1955). For a discussion of this work, see Âdamiyat, *Eide'uluzhi-ye Nehzat-e Mashrutiyat-e Iran*, pp. 229–249; and Hairi, *Shi'ism and Constitutionalism in Iran*.

80 See Albert Hourani, *Arabic Thought in the Liberal Age: 1798–1939* (London and Oxford, 1962 and 1967); and Hamid Enâyat, *Seyri dar Andisheh-ye Siâsi-ye 'Arab: Az Hamleh-ye Nâpole'oun beh Mesr tâ Jang-e Jahâni-ye Dovvom* (A Survey of Arab Political Thought: From Napoleon's Incursion into Egypt to the Second World War) (1st edition, Tehran, 1356/1977; 2nd edition, Tehran: Amir Kabir, 1358/1979, note especially Chap. 3, pp. 77–192.

81 For al-Afghani (b. Sha'bân 1254 A.H./1838 in Asad-Âbâd near Ha-madân, Iran, d. 1314 A.H./October–November 1896–1897, poisoned in Istanbul), see Mirzâ Lotfollâh Khân Asad-Âbâdi, *Sharh-e Hâl va Âsâr-e Seyyed Jamâl al-Din Asad-Âbâdi* (The Life and Works of al-Afghani), Vol. 1 (Berlin, 1304/1926; reprinted, Tehran, 2536 [1356]/1977); Mirzâ Lotfollâh Khân Asad-Âbâdi, ed., *Maqâlât-e Jamâliyeh* (al-Afghani's Essays) (Tehran, 1312/1933); Mortezâ Modar-

resi-Chahârdehi, *Seyyed Jamâ al-Din va Andishehâ-ye Uo* (al-Afghani's Ideas), 6th edition (Tehran, 1360/1981); Asghar Mahdavi and Iraj Afshâr, eds., *Majmou'eh-ye Asnâd va Madârek-e Châp-Nashodeh dar bâreh-ye Seyyed Jamâl al-Din mashhour beh Afghani* (A Collection of Formerly Unpublished Material on al-Afghani) (Tehran, 1342/1963); Ali-Asghar Halabi, *Zendegi va Safarhâ-ye Seyyed Jamâl al-Din Asad-Âbâdi* (The Life and Travels of al-Afghani) (Tehran, 2536 [1356]/1977–1978); and Karim Mojtahedi, *Seyyed Jamâl al-Din Asad-Âbâdi va Tafakkor-e Jadid* (al-Afghani and Modern Thought) (Tehran, 1363/1984). See also E. G. Browne, *The Persian Revolution of 1905–1909* (1st edition, Cambridge, 1910; new impression, London, 1966), Chap. 1, "Sayyid Jamálu'd-Dín, the Protagonist of Pan-Islamism," pp. 1–30; Nikki R. Keddie, *An Islamic Response to Imperialism: Political and Religious Writings of Sayyid Jamâl ad-Dín "al-Afghâni,"* including a translation of "Refutation of the Materialists" from the original Persian by Nikki R. Keddie and Hamid Algar (Berkeley: University of California Press, 1968); and the comprehensive study by Nikki R. Keddie, *Sayyid Jamal al-Din "al-Afghani": A Political Biography* (Berkeley: University of California Press, 1972). See further Nikki R. Keddie, "Sayyid Jamal al-Din 'al-Afghani'," in Ali Rahnema, ed., *Pioneers of Islamic Revival* (London: Zed Books, 1994), pp. 11–29. For a recent study of al-Afghani's impact on ideological trends in Egypt, see Rudi Matthee, "Jamal al-Din al-Afghani and the Egyptian National Debate," *IJMES*, Vol. 21, 1989, pp. 151–169.

82   In an article entitled "Favâyed-e Falsafeh" (Fruits of Philosophy), published originally in India in the journal *Majalleh-ye Mo'allem-e Shafiq*, No. 10 (August 1881), al-Afghani stated that philosophy "is the movement of the living man towards the sacred rational life" (Asad-Âbâdi, ed., *Maqâlât-e Jamâliyeh*, p. 135, cited in Mojtahedi, *Seyyed Jamâl al-Din*, p. 24).

83   al-Afghani made these remarks in a speech delivered on 8 November 1872 in Calcutta's Albert Hall. See Asad-Âbâdi, ed., *Maqâlât-e Jamâliyeh*, pp. 92–93, cited in Mojtahedi, *Seyyed Jamâl al-Din*, p. 22.

84   See Hamid Enâyat, "Din va Donyâ" (Sacred and Secular), *Negin* (31 Mordâd 1347/22 August 1968); reprinted in Hamid Enâyat, *Jahâni Az Khud Bigâneh: Majmou'eh-ye Maqâlât* (An Alienated World: Collection of Essays) (Tehran, 1351/1972), pp. 75–102, here pp. 86–87. According to Enâyat, "[A]lthough Seyyed Jamâl views Islam as possessing all three conditions, he obviously regards Protestantism to be similar to Islam in respect to the last two conditions" (ibid., p. 87).

85   Cited in Keddie, *Sayyid Jamal al-Din*, p. 193.

86   Hamid Enayat, review of Nikki R. Keddie's *Sayyid Jamâl al-Dín "al-Afghani," A Political Biography*, in *IS*, Vol. 6, No. 4 (Autumn 1973), pp. 246–255, here p. 254.

87   See Hairi, *Shi'ism and Constitutionalism*. Religious figures like Najmâbâdi (b. 1250 A.H./1834–1835, d. 1320 A.H./1902–1903), though firm in their philanthropist, rationalist, and reformist stance, did not align themselves

with any narrow political view. Their overall attitude was to facilitate the improvement of sociopolitical conditions in favor of the populace with minimum hardship and violence. For further information on Hâj Sheikh Hâdi Najmâbâdi, see Sheikh Abd al-Ali (ibn Mohammad) Bidgoli Kâshâni (a pupil of Hâj Sheikh Hâdi whose pen name was "Sobhi" and who was also known as "Mu'bed"), *Majmou'eh-ye Mu'bed* (Tehran, 1320 A.H./1902–1903); see also Mirzâ Mohammad Qazvini's note in Browne, *The Persian Revolution*, pp. 406–407. For his published works, see Hâj Sheikh Hâdi Najmâbâdi Tehrani, *Tabaqeh-bandi-e Ers* (Classification of Inheritance), a work on laws of inheritance, lithograph edition (Tehran, 1308 A.H./1890–1891); see also Hâj Sheikh Hâdi (ibn Mehdi) Najmâbâdi Tehrani, *Tahrir al-'Oqalâ*, foreword by Mirzâ Mohammad-Hosein Foroughi (Zakâ' al-Molk), edited by Sheikh Mortezâ Najmâbâdi (Tehran, 1352 A.H./1933–1934), 295 pp. This volume also contains a refutation of the Bahâ'i sect by the author, entitled *Resâleh dar Radd-e Ferqeh-ye Bahâ'iyeh* (Refutation of the Bahâ'i Sect).

88   The first edition refers to the anonymous author as "A Grand Mujtahid of Najaf" Asadollâh Mamaqâni, *Maslak al-Imam*; here all references will be to a recent edition (Tehran, 1363/1984). The author also wrote another book on the idea of government in Shi'ism, entitled *Din va Sho'oun va Tarz-e Hokoumat dar Mazhab-e Shi'a* (Religion, Functions and the Method of Government in Shi'ism) (Istanbul, 1334 A.H./1916, 191 pp.; 2nd edition, Tehran: Majles, 1335/1956). Hâj Sheikh Asadollâh (son of Abd al-Karim) Mamaqâni (b. 1300–1301 A.H./1883–1884) studied first in Tabriz, then went to Najaf and studied with Âkhound Khorâsâni. In 1908–1909, his pro-Mashruteh activities took him, as a personal envoy of Âkhound Khorâsâni, to Anjoman-e Sa'âdat, a Constitutionalist society of Iranians in Istanbul; he became an active member of the society. See Hairi, *Shi'ism and Constitutionalism*, p. 91, based on Malekzâdeh, *Târikh-e Enqelâb-e Mashrutiyat*, pp. 105–109. For Anjoman-e Sa'âdat, see Hodjatollah Djoudaki, "L'*Anjoman-e Sa'âdat* des Iraniens d'Istanbul," in Thierry Zarcone and Fariba Zarinebaf-Shahr, eds., *Les Iraniens d'Istanbul* (Paris and Tehran, 1993). As a clergyman, Mamaqâni reportedly was at first conservative in his manners but later became a modernist and was acquainted with modernist Ottomans. See Yahyâ Dowlatâbâdi, *Hayât-e Yahyâ*, p. 33. For Mamâqin's close associations with the Ottomans, see also Khân Malak Sâsâni, *Yâd-boud-hâ-ye Sefârat-e Istanbul* (Memoirs of the Embassy in Istanbul) (Tehran, 1345/1965), p. 112. The poet Mirzâdeh 'Eshqi, who was also in Istanbul during the First World War, wrote (in 1336 A.H./1917–1918) a long, derisive piece on Mamaqâni. See Ali-Akbar Moshir-Salimi, ed., *Kolliyât-e Mosavvar-e Mirzâdeh Eshqi* (Collected Works of Mirzâdeh 'Eshqi), 7th edition (Tehran, 1357/1978), pp. 434–438. After the First World War, Mamaqâni returned to Tabriz and held sermons at the mosque of Hâj Seyyed al-Mohaqqeqin. During the Reza Shah period, he was somewhat transformed and was no longer a clergyman. In 1306/1937, he was an appointed member of the Supreme Court (Divân-e 'Âli-e Tamiz), and he later took part in founding the Âzarbâyjân Club (Kloub-e Âzarbâyjân) in Tehran. In the cabinet of Mohammad Sâ'ed (1323/1944), he was minister of justice and then an elected deputy from Tabriz in the Fifteenth Majles. For Asadollâh Mamaqâni, see further Mehdi Mojtahedi, *Rejâl-e Âzarbâyjân dar 'Asr-e Mashrutiyat* (Azarbâyjâni Figures in the Time of the Constitutional Movement) (Tehran, 1327/1948), p. 151; *Moshâr*, Vol. 1, pp. 558–559; and Zahrâ Shaji'i, *Namâyandegân-e Majles-e Showrâ-ye Melli dar Bist va Yek Dowreh-ye Qânoun-gozâri* (Majles Deputies during Its Twenty-One Sessions) (Tehran, 1344/1965), p. 360. For Mamaqâni's Constitutional phase and a discussion of his tracts, *Maslak al-Imam* and *Din va Sho'oun*, see also Said Amir Arjomand, "Ideological Revolution in Shi'ism," in Said Amir Arjomand, ed., *Authority and Political Culture in Shi'ism*, (Albany: State University of New York Press, 1988), pp. 178–209, note on pp. 183–184.

89 Construction of a railway system was a top priority for Iranian reformists, regardless of their ideological preference. Reportedly, Mirzâ Yousef Khân Mostashâr al-Dowleh, a prominent Qajar diplomat and a contemporary of Malkam's "was passionately devoted to two goals: the construction of trans-Persian railways and the establishment of a code of law under a national constitution. His ideas concerning the first were set down, in 1877, in a book called *Ketabche-ye Banafsh* (The Purple Notebook). His zeal for railways was due to his conviction that successful adoption of Western culture and all material progress heavily depended on their construction and operation." Hafez Farman Farmayan, "The Forces of Modernization in Nineteenth Century Iran: A Historical Survey," in William R. Polk and Richard L. Chambers, eds., *Beginnings of Modernization in the Middle East: The Nineteenth Century* (Chicago: University of Chicago Press, 1968), pp. 119–151, note on p. 139. Among earlier tracts advocating the necessity of a railroad, see Mohammad Kâshef, *Favâyed-e Râh-Âhan* (Benefits of the Railway), edited by Mohammad-Javâd Sâhebi (Tehran, 1374/1995); for a bibliographical reference, see Daftar-e Nashr-e Mirâs-e Maktoub, p. 101.

90 Mamaqâni, *Maslak al-Imam*, p. 40.

91 Ibid., pp. 46–47.

92 Mirzâ Mohammad Nâzem al-Islam Kermâni, *Târikh-e Bidâri-e Iranian* (History of the Iranian Awakening), edited by Ali-Akbar Sa'idi Sirjâni, Part 1, Vol. 1 (Tehran, 1349/1971), p. 4.

93 Nâzem al-Islam Kermâni, *Târikh-e Bidâri*, p. 4. On the subject of women in the era of the Constitutional movement, see further Parvin Paidar, *Women and the Political Process in Twentieth-Century Iran* (Cambridge: Cambridge University Press, 1995), pp. 50–77.

94 Mamaqâni, *Maslak al-Imam*, pp. 16–17.

95 Ibid., pp. 14–15.

96 Ibid., p. 15.

97 Ibid., p. 19.

98   See Nāʾini, *Tanbih al-Umma va Tanzih al-Milla*. Although in a real sense the Constitution was designed to replace the Shariʿa, Naʾini nevertheless dismissed an Akhbâri criticism that Constitutional legislation in Islamic countries would be a heretical innovation (*bidʿa*). Here, too, his line of argument is somewhat reminiscent of the social contract political philosophy. See Adamiyat, *Eideʾuluzhi-ye Nehzat-e Mashrutiyat-e Iran*, pp. 241–242. For further discussion of Nâʾini, see Fereshteh M. Nouraie, "The Constitutional Ideas of a Shiʿite Mujtahid: Muhammad Husayn Nāʾînî," *IS*, Vol. 8 (1975), pp. 234–247.

99   For further discussion, see A. H. Hairi, "Shaykh Fazl Allah Nuri's Refutation of the Idea of Constitutionalism," *MES*, Vol. 13, No. 3 (1977), pp. 327–339; Fereydoun Âdamiyat, "ʿAqâyed va Ârâ-ye Sheikh Fazlollâh Nouri" (The Ideas of Sheikh Fazlollâh Nouri), *Ketâb-e Jomʿeh*, Vol. 1, No. 31, Tehran (28 Farvardin 1359/17 April 1980), pp. 52–61; V. A. Martin, "The Anti-Constitutionalist Arguments of Shaikh Fazlallah Nuri," *MES*, Vol. 22, No. 2, April 1986, pp. 181–196. For a general analysis, see Said Amir Arjomand, "The ʿUlamâʾa Traditionalist Opposition to Parliamentarism: 1907–1909," *MES*, Vol. 17, No. 2 (1981), pp. 174–190. For a discussion on the broader social and political aspects of the controversy, see Bayat, *Iran's First Revolution*, Chap. 8, "The Mashruta-mashruʿa Battle," pp. 161–183. For further study on the ulama and the Constitutional movement, see Vanessa Martin, *Islam and Modernism: The Persian Revolution of 1906* (London, 1989).

100   See Abu al-Hasan Bozorg Omid, *Az Mâst keh Bar Mâst: Mohtavi-e Khâterât va Moshâhedât* (We Have Only Ourselves to Blame: Memoirs), 2nd edition (Tehran, 1363/1984), pp. 142–143.

101   See Hairi, *Shiʿism and Constitutionalism*, p. 114. For further discussion on Sheikh Fazlollâh Nouri, see Yann Richard, "Le Radicalisme islamique du Sheykh Fazlollâh Nuri et son impact dans l'histoire de l'Iran contemporain," *Laïcité*, n.s. 29, 2 (*Les Intégrismes*) (Brussels, 1986), pp. 60–86; and V. A. Martin, "Shaikh Fazlallah Nuri and the Iranian Revolution 1905–09," *MES*, Vol. 23, No. 1 (January 1987), pp. 39–53.

102   Hairi, *Shiʿism and Constitutionalism*, p. 240.

103   See Hâj Âqâ Mujtahid Shirâzi, *Vâqeʿât-e Du Sâleh yâ Târikh-e Badbakhti-e Iran* (Events of [the Last] Two Years, or a History of Iranian Misery) (Tehran, 1330 A.H./1912), pp. 6 and 8. Having a clerical status, the author was elected from Shiraz and Tehran to the Second and Third sessions of the Majles, respectively, where he joined the Eʿtedâli (moderate) faction. See *Rejâl*, Vol. 6, pp. 162–163; Shajiʿi, *Namâyandegân*, p. 337; and Seyyed Hasan Taqizâdeh, *Owrâq-e Tâzeh-yâb-e Mashrutiyat va Naqsh-e Taqizâdeh: 1325–1330 A.H.* (Newly Found Papers concerning the Constitutional Movement and the Role of Taqizâdeh: 1907–1912), edited by Iraj Afshâr (Tehran, 1359/1980), p. 336. In a letter (c. 1910) to Taqizâdeh, Sheikh Ebrâhim Zanjâni, who had been a famous Constitutionalist activist among the clergy and a prosecutor of Sheikh Fazlollâh

Nouri in the revolutionary tribunal of 1909, and who had subsequently kept his alliance with modernists, refers to Hâj Âqâ Mujtahid Shirâzi with contempt. Taqizâdeh, *Owrâq-e Tâzeh-yâb-e Mashrutiyat*, p. 336. For a brief political biography of Zanjâni, see *Rejâl*, Vol. 1, p. 15.

104 For additional primary sources both in defense of Constitutionalism and in opposition to it, see Gholâm-Hosein Zargari-nezhâd, ed., *Rasâ'el-e Mashrutiyat: 18 Resâleh va Lâyeheh dar-bâreh-ye Mashrutiyat* (Constitutional Treatises: Eighteen Treatises and Tracts about Constitutionalism) (Tehran: Enteshârât-e Kavir, 1374/1995).

105 For instance, from the Supplementary Fundamental Laws of 7 October 1907, the following articles, classified under "Rights of the Persian Nation," are relevant:

> *Art. 8. The people of the Persian Empire are to enjoy equal rights before the Law.*
> *Art. 9. All individuals are protected and safeguarded in respect to their lives, property, homes, and honour, from every kind of interference, and none shall molest them save in such case and in such way as the laws of the land shall determine.*
> *Art. 10. No one can be summarily arrested, save* flagrante delicto *in the commission of some crime or misdemeanour, except on the written authority of the President of the Tribunal of Justice, given in conformity with the Law. Even in such case the accused must immediately, or at latest in the course of the next twenty-four hours, be informed and notified of the nature of his offence. (Translated in E. G. Browne,* The Persian Revolution, *p. 374)*

Further, under "Powers of the Realm," it specifies:

> *Art. 26. The powers of the realm are all derived from the people; and the Fundamental law regulates the employment of these powers. (Ibid., p. 375)*

Also, the "Rights of the Persian Throne" were defined as:

> *Art. 35. The sovereignty is a trust confided (as a Divine gift) by the people to the person of the king. (Ibid., p. 377)*

106 Despite the difficulties of the times, the early sessions of the Majles did result in some noteworthy achievements. See Seyyed Hasan Taqizâdeh, "*Târikh-e Mokhtasar-e Majles-e Melli-ye Iran*" (A Short History of the Iranian National Assembly), *Kâveh* (Berlin, 1337 A.H./1918–1919), pp. 1–97; reprinted in Iraj Afshâr, ed., *Maqâlât-e Taqizâdeh* (Taqizâdeh's Essays), Vol. 5 (Tehran, 2535 [1355]/ 1976), pp. 241–337; Fereydoun Âdamiyat, "Barkhurd-e Afkâr va Takâmol-e Pârlemâni dar Majles-e Avval" (Exchange of Ideas and Parliamentary Development in the First Majles), in *Maqâlât-e Târikhi* (Historical Essays) (Tehran,

1352/1973), pp. 109–118; Mansoureh Ettehâdiyeh (Nezâm-Mâfi), *Peydâyesh va Tahavvol-e Ahzâb-e Siâsi-ye Mashrutiyat: Dowreh-ye Avval va Dovvom-e Majles-e Showrâ-ye Melli* (The Rise and Development of Political Parties in the Constitutional Movement during the First and Second Sessions of the Majles) (Tehran, 1361/1982), originally a Ph.D. thesis submitted to Edinburgh University as "The Origin and Development of Political Parties in Persia (1906–1911)" (1980); and Âdamiyat, *Eideʾulozhi-ye Nehzat-e Mashrutiyat-e Iran*, Vol. 2.

107 On the question of institutionalization, see, for example, Peter L. Berger and Thomas Luckmann, *The Social Construction of Reality: A Treatise in the Sociology of Knowledge* (London, 1967 and 1976), pp. 65–109.

108 See Golshiri's address, "Javânmargi dar Nasr-e Moʿâser-e Farsi" (Premature Death in Contemporary Persian Prose), to the large open-air audience during the Ten Nights of poetry readings and lectures organized by the Iranian Writers' Association, between 18 and 27 Mehr 1356/10 and 19 October 1977 at the compound of Tehran's Goethe Institute, transcribed in Nâser Moʾazzen, ed., *Dah Shab* (Ten Nights) (Tehran: Iranian Writers Association, 1357/1978), pp. 346–356, here pp. 352–353.

109 Mehrdâd Mândegâr (pseudonym), "Parirouyân-e Bitâb va Asâtir-e Motevarrem: Jorʾat-e ʿNaʾ Nagoftan" (Impatient Fairies and Inflated Myths: The Courage Not to Say "No"), *Iran va Jahân*, No. 93 (Paris, 24–31 Khordâd 1361/14–21 June 1982), pp. 15–19, here p. 15.

Chapter 3

1 Jamshid Mesbâhi-pour Iranian, *Vâqeʿiyat-e Ejtemâʿi va Jahân-e Dâstân* (Social Reality and the World of the Novel) (Tehran, 1358/1979–1980), 72.

2 *S/N*, Vol. 2, pp. 231–233. Taqizâdeh was later—for example, in a 1960 lecture in Tehran—to reject these ideas and became critical of them. Ibid., p. 232, n. 3. For a text of this lecture, see Hasan Taqizâdeh, "Akhz-e Tamaddon-e Khâreji" (Adoption of Foreign [i.e., Western] Civilization), *Yaghmâ*, Vol. 13, Nos. 9 and 10 (Âzar and Dey 1339/December 1960 and January 1961). For more on this topic, see G. Vatandoust, "Sayyed Hasan Taqizadeh and Kaveh: Modernism in Post-Constitutional Iran (1916–1921)" (Ph.D. dissertation, University of Washington, 1977).

3 Mirzâ Hasan Khân Esfandiâri (Mohtasham al-Saltaneh) was the son of Mirzâ Mohammad Raʾis (Sadiq al-Molk) Mâzandarâni. He was born in 1283 A.H./1866–1867 and died in Tehran on 6 Esfand 1323/25 February 1945. See *Rejâl*, Vol. 1, pp. 321–322. Further references to Mohtasham al-Saltaneh in *Rejâl* include: Vol. 2, p. 24; Vol. 3, pp. 180 and 243; and Vol. 5, p. 147. See also Ali-Akbar Tashayyod, "Hâji Mohtasham al-Saltaneh-ye Esfandiâri," *Khâterât-e Vahid*, No. 5 (1350/1971), pp. 73–76.

4 Hâj Mirzâ Hasan Khân Mohtasham al-Saltaneh Esfandiâri, ʿ*Elal-e Bad-*

bakhti-e Mâ va ʿAlâj-e Ân (Causes of Our Misery and Its Cure), lithograph edition in 105 pages, printed in Matbaʿeh-ye Ali ([Tehran], 1340 A.H./1921). Following references are to this edition. I am grateful to Abbas Amanat for providing me with a copy of this booklet.

5   Mohtasham al-Saltaneh, *ʿElal-e Badbakhti*, pp. 2–6. The term "*showravi*" later became the standard equivalent for the Soviet system. However, the term "consultative" is closer to the author's overall political vision and he uses it with reference to the Mashruteh (Constitutional) movement, in which consultation was a central principle; for instance, the Parliament was called Majles-e Showrâ-ye Melli (National Consultative Assembly).

6   Capitulation is an agreement by which foreign residents in a country have extraterritorial rights. Its origins in modern Iran can be traced back to the Turkmenchay Treaty with Russia in 1828. This treaty was cancelled only following the 1921 treaty between Iran and the Soviet Union. Later, in April 1927, during the premiership of Mostowfi al-Mamâlek, Reza Shah, in an official communiqué to the Cabinet, ordered the cancellation of all capitulations in Iran.

7   Mohtasham al-Saltaneh, *ʿElal-e Badbakhti*, pp. 8–10.

8   Ibid., pp. 10–12.

9   Ibid., p. 19.

10   Ibid., pp. 21–22.

11   Ibid., p. 24. Jules-François Simon (1814–1896) was a French philosopher and politician known for his strong belief in the freedom of speech, religion, and thought. His *La Politique radicale* (Paris, 1868) was a manifesto for the French Radical Party. In 1848, he was elected to the National Assembly; he was prime minister during 1876–1877, the critical phase of the Third Republic. The precise source of Mohtasham al-Saltaneh's reference is not clear.

12   Mohtasham al-Saltaneh, *ʿElal-e Badbakhti*, p. 32. An expression of the same point can be found in a letter by Abd al-Hosein Teymourtâsh (dated 12 ʿAqrab [Âbân] 1302/5 November 1923) written from Kermân to Taqizâdeh, who was then residing in Berlin. Here Teymourtâsh, after stating that "Iran is not yet ready for socialism," proposes the creation of a strong reformist faction that, instead of copying from the "unpractical" programs of "other countries," would lay the foundations of progress on the "basis of [a] bourgeois and capitalist regime." See Abd al-Hosein Teymourtâsh (Sardâr Moʿazzam-e Khorâsâni), "Nâmeh'i beh Seyyed Hasan Taqizâdeh" (A Letter to Taqizâdeh), with an introductory note by Iraj Afshâr, *Âyandeh*, Vol. 14, Nos. 9–12 (1367/1988–1989), pp. 657–660. In his note, Iraj Afshâr indicates that in that period Teymourtâsh was anxious about the growing power of Iranian socialists, whom he thought were being supported by the Soviets. He also thought that the socialists would soon succeed in recruiting Sardâr Sepah (Reza Khân). To counter such eventualities, he made the above proposition to Taqizâdeh, hoping that he would return to Iran and organize an alternative party. Teymourtâsh, "Nâmeh'i beh Seyyed Hasan Taqizâdeh," pp. 657–658. However, Teymourtâsh was later in-

strumental in Reza Shah's rise to total power, to which he himself subsequently
fell victim.

13 Mohtasham al-Saltaneh, *ʿElal-e Badbakhti*, pp. 35–38.

14 Ibid., pp. 39–40.

15 Ibid., p. 40.

16 Ibid., pp. 41–45.

17 Ibid., pp. 46–48.

18 Ibid., pp. 53–56.

19 Ibid., pp. 57–68.

20 Ibid., pp. 68–82.

21 Ibid., pp. 82–97.

22 Ibid., pp. 97–102.

23 Ibid., p. 68.

24 Ibid., pp. 51–52.

25 Ibid., p. 73.

26 Ibid., p. 74.

27 Ibid., p. 75.

28 Ibid., pp. 75–78.

29 Ibid., pp. 78–79. This was prior to the systematic secularization of the
ministries of Justice and the Interior that followed, and it was also before the expansion of the theological center at Qom.

30 Ibid., p. 79.

31 Ibid., p. 81.

32 Ibid., pp. 88–89.

33 Ibid., pp. 90–96.

34 Ibid., pp. 97–99.

35 Ibid., p. 100.

36 Ibid., pp. 100–102. The notion of "company" (referred to in Persian as
both *kompâni* and *sherkat*) used to be highly regarded in Iran during the period
under consideration and was invariably viewed as an efficient form of economic
conduct in modern society. It was also adopted as a surname, as in, for example,
Hâj [Mohammad-] Hasan Kompâni and Mashadi Mohammad Âqâ Kompâni,
who were among the well-established *sarrâfs* (private bankers) of Tehran and
who were originally from Tabriz. For an earlier reference to "company," see
Goftogouy-e Yek Mirzâ-ye bâ ʿElm bâ Yek ʿAvâm-e Mostahzar (Conversation between a Learned Scribe and an Intelligent Commoner), an incomplete critical
booklet in dialogue form written anonymously around 1298 A.H./1881, introduced in Fereydoun Âdamiyat and Homâ Nâteq, *Afkâr-e Ejtemâʿi va Siâsi va
Eqtesâdi dar Âsâr-e Montasher-Nashodeh-ye Dowrân-e Qajar* (Social and Political
and Economic Ideas in the Unpublished Sources of the Qajar Period) (Tehran,
2536 [1356]/1977), pp. 136–144, here p. 139.

37 Mohtasham al-Saltaneh, *ʿElal-e Badbakhti*, pp. 102–103.

38 Ibid., p. 104.

39   The bill was passed through the Majles with relative ease. However, Seyyed Hasan Modarres, a clerical member, loudly opposed the bill and left the chamber in protest. Also Seyyed Hasan Taqizâdeh, Hosein Alâ, Dr. Mohammad Mosaddeq, and Yahyâ Dowlatâbâdi spoke against the resolution. See Katouzian, *The Political Economy of Modern Iran*, p. 91.

40   For a detailed report on these developments, see Hosein Makki, *Târikh-e Bist Sâleh-ye Iran* (A Twenty-Year History of Iran), Vol. 3: *Enqerâz-e Qâjâriyeh va Tashkil-e Selseleh-ye Diktâturi-ye Pahlavi* (Termination of the Qajars and the Rise of Pahlavi Dictatorship), new edition (Tehran, 1357/1978), pp. 421 ff.

41   See Shahrough Akhavi, *Religion and Politics in Contemporary Iran: Clergy-State Relations in the Pahlavi Period* (Albany: State University of New York, 1980). See also Mohammad H. Faghfoory, "The Impact of Modernization on the Ulama in Iran, 1925–1941," *IS*, Vol. 26, Nos. 3–4 (Summer–Fall 1993), pp. 277–312.

42   See Mohammad H. Faghfoory, "The Ulama-State Relations in Iran: 1921–1941," *IJMES*, Vol. 19 (November 1987), pp. 413–432.

43   The Academy's first official meeting, with twenty-four principal members, was on 12 Khordâd 1314/3 June 1935; its charter, a full list of principal and affiliated members, as well as those who joined in subsequent years (until 1321/1942), can be found in Farhangestân, *Nâmeh-ye Farhangestân* (The [Iranian] Academy's Newsletter), Vol. 1, No. 1 (Tehran, Ordibehesht 1322/April–May 1943). For more information on different functions within the Farhangestân and some of its proposed terms, see Farhangestân, *Farhangestân-e Iran: Vâzheha-ye Now* (Iranian Academy: New Terms), Vols. 6 and 7 (Tehran, n.d.). See also *S/N*, Vol. 3, pp. 15–32, note, in particular, pp. 19–22. For Farhangestân and attempts to reform the language in Iran, see Ahmad Karimi-Hakkak, "Language Reform Movement and Its Language: The Case of Persian," in Björn H. Jernudd and Michael J. Shapiro, eds., *The Politics of Language Purism* (Berlin and New York, 1989), pp. 81–104; for further analysis of language purism, see Björn H. Jernudd, "The Texture of Language Purism: An Introduction," and Michael J. Shapiro, "A Political Approach to Language Purism," in the same volume, pp. 1–19 and 21–29, respectively. For a comparative study of language reform in Iran and Turkey, see John R. Perry, "Language Reform in Turkey and Iran," *IJMES*, Vol. 17 (1985), pp. 295–311.

44   For the reform measures of the Reza Shah's period, see Amin Banani, *The Modernization of Iran (1921–1941)* (Stanford, Conn., 1961); and Wilber, *Riza Shah Pahlavi*. A more detailed account of this period can be found in Makki, *Târikh-e Bist Sâleh*. For studies on modernization in Turkey, see Niyazi Berkes, *The Development of Secularism in Turkey* (Montreal, 1964); and Walter F. Weiker, *The Modernization of Turkey: From Ataturk to the Present Day* (New York and London), 1981.

45   Abrahamian, *Iran between Two Revolutions*, p. 149.

46   Note, for example, the reference to "Diktâtouri-ye Pahlavi" (The

Pahlavi Dictatorship) in Makki, *Târikh-e Bist Sâleh-ye Iran*, Vols. 3–7.

47 According to Lambton, "relationship[s] within the family, the guilds and the tribes were authoritarian, as also was the relationship of the *pir* and the *murid*, the religious leader or master and his disciple, which pervaded society. The government was absolute." Lambton, "Secret Societies and the Persian Revolution of 1905–1906," reprinted in Lambton, *Qajar Persia*, p. 302.

48 In the words of one observer, the "orientation of an Iranian is constantly upward where authority is found. Order and discipline are imposed from above." Richard W. Gable, "Culture and Administration in Iran," *MEJ*, Vol. 13, No. 4 (Autumn 1959), pp. 407–421. However, such cultural and personality traits can be found in any society and should not therefore be exaggerated. For a critical review, see Ali Banuazizi, "Iranian 'National Character': A Critique of Some Western Perspectives," in L. Carl Brown and Norman Itzkowitz, eds., *Psychological Dimensions of Near Eastern Studies* (Princeton, N.J.: Darwin Press, 1977), pp. 210–239.

49 This tendency had begun during the Constitutional movement. The military-style outfits were influenced by the vogue of dressing like Russian cossacks and Swedish gendarmerie. Similar moves toward Europeanization had also begun to take place in civilian dress.

50 See Banani, *The Modernization of Iran*; and Wilber, *Riza Shah Pahlavi*.

51 For some figures concerning this project, see Dharm Pal, *Campaign in Western Asia: Official History of the Indian Armed Forces in the Second World War 1939–45*, general editor Bisheshwar Prasad (Calcutta, 1957), p. 276. See further Patrick Clawson, "Knitting Iran Together: The Land Transport Revolution, 1920–1940," *IS*, Vol. 26, Nos. 3–4 (Summer–Fall 1993), pp. 235–250.

52 See Eckart Ehlers and Willem Floor, "Urban Change in Iran, 1920–1941," *IS*, Vol. 26, Nos. 3–4 (Summer–Fall 1993), pp. 251–275. See also Mina Marefat, "The Protagonists Who Shaped Modern Tehran," and Mohsen Habibi, "Réza Chah et le développement de Téhéran (1925–1941)," both in Chahryar Adle and Bernard Hourcade, eds., *Téhéran: Capitale bicentenaire* (Paris and Téhéran: Institut Français de Recherche en Iran, 1992), pp. 95–125 and 199–206, respectively; and Reza Moghtader, "Dowrân-e Sad-Sâleh-ye Tajaddod dar Shahr-sâzi va Meʿmâri-ye Iran" (A Hundred Years of Modernization in Iran's Architecture), *Iran Nameh*, Vol. 11, No. 2 (Spring 1993), pp. 259–282, note pp. 265–269.

53 For background information, see Issa Khan Sadiq, *Modern Persia and Her Educational System* (New York, 1931); and A. H. K. Sassani, "Higher Education in Iran," *College and University*, Vol. 24 (October 1948), pp. 78–96. For a more detailed study, see David Menashri, *Education and the Making of Modern Iran* (Ithaca, N.Y.: Cornell University Press, 1992), note Part 2, "Education under Reza Shah," pp. 91–154.

54 A law passed in 1928 established a procedure for sending students to foreign countries to pursue higher education.

55 See Houchang E. Chehabi, "Staging the Emperor's New Clothes: Dress Codes and Nation-Building under Reza Shah," *IS*, Vol. 26, Nos. 3–4 (Summer–Fall 1993), pp. 209–229, here pp. 213–214.

56 Attending the opening ceremonies at Tehran's Dâneshsarâ-ye Moqaddamâti (Teachers' Training College) on 17 Dey 1314/8 January 1936, Reza Shah was accompanied by his unveiled wife and daughters, showing his personal endorsement of the new measure. See Makki, *Târikh-e Bist-Sâleh*, Vol. 6, pp. 258–268. In the official calendar, that date was subsequently marked to commemorate "Iranian women's emancipation."

57 Sarah Graham-Brown, *Images of Women: The Portrayal of Women in Photography of the Middle East, 1860–1950* (London: Quartet Books, 1988), p. 131. A photograph reproduced in the same source, on p. 130, from London's *The Sphere* (25 September 1937), shows a group of Tehran residents in their newly acquired clothing. The obvious lack of self-confidence, evident especially in the faces of the women, contrasts sharply with the self-assured gesture of a couple of military officers in the same picture and with the paper's commentary, which declared, "Tehran Emerges from Its Medieval Languor: Iran's Modern Capital Thrives under the Enlightened Policy of Reza Shah." For more illustrations of the superficiality of the compulsory dress codes, see Wilber, *Riza Shah Pahlavi*, illustrations 21 and 22, between pp. 242 and 243.

58 See K. Sandjabi, *Essai sur l'économie rurale et le régime agraire de la Perse* (Paris, 1934), where the author argues that during this period many traditional practices were strengthened by the government. Cited in Nikki R. Keddie, *Roots of Revolution: An Interpretive History of Modern Iran* (New Haven: Yale University Press, 1981), p. 103. For additional information on the agrarian problems of Iran in this period, see A. K. S. Lambton, *Landlord and Peasant in Persia* (Oxford, 1953).

59 For some background information, see Hosein Mahboubi Ardakâni, *Târikh-e Muʾassesât-e Tamaddoni-e Jadid dar Iran* (A History of Modern Institutions in Iran), Vol. 2 (Tehran, 2537 [1357]/1978), pp. 168–181.

60 Among the few published studies on this genre, see, for example, H. Kamshad, *Modern Persian Prose Literature* (Cambridge, 1966), Chaps. 6–9; see also *S/N*, Vol. 2, pp. 235–277; and, more recently, Shahrokh Meskoob, "Qesseh-ye Ghosseh yâ Român-e Haqiqi" (A Tale of Grief or the True Story), *Iran Nameh*, Vol. 11, No. 3 (Summer 1993), pp. 451–480. I have elsewhere given a selective list of historical and social novels, short stories, and dramas: see Ali Gheissari, "The Ideological Formation of the Iranian Intelligentsia: From the Constitutional Movement to the Fall of the Monarchy" (D.Phil. thesis, Oxford University, 1989), Appendix 1, pp. 352–360.

61 *Kolliyât-e Mosayyeb-Nâmeh: Sâmel-e Behtarin Revâyât va Akhbâr va Janghâ-ye Vâqeʿi bâ Qataleh-ye Hazrat-e Seyyed al-Shohadâ va Koshteh-Shodan-e Ân-hâ be-dast-e Ân Nâmdâr-e Vafâdâr* (A Collection of Mosayyeb-Nâmeh: Including the Fullest Narrative of Campaigns with the Murderers of Imam Hosein and Their

Death in the Hands of the Acclaimed and Loyal Mosayyeb) (Tehran: Elmi, n.n., n.d.), 178 pp.

62   See below, note 76.

63   See *Shirouyeh Nâmdâr: Kolliyât-e Haft-Jeldi-ye Shahzâdeh Shirouyeh ibn Malekshah-e Rumi Barâdar-e Kâmkâr-e Shahzadeh Amir Arsalân-e Rumi va Malakeh-ye Simin-ʿOzâr va Ghoncheh-Lab va ʿEshqbâzihâ-ye Ânhâ* (Glorious Shirouyeh: A Complete Story in Seven Parts of Prince Shirouyeh ibn Malekshah-e Rumi the August Brother of the Prince Amir Arsalân-e Rumi, and His Amorous Affairs with the Silver Cheeks and Rose-bud Lips Queen) (Tehran, ʿElmi, n.n., n.d.), 288 pp.

64   For a comparison of the narrative in *naqqâli* with that in the modern novel, see Golshiri, "Hâshiyeh'i bar Român-hâ-ye Moʿâser," pp. 38–62, note pp. 39–44.

65   For popular reference to the *Divân* of Hâfez (i.e., the practice of *fâl*), see Mahmoud Rouh al-Amini, ed., *Bâvarhâ-ye ʿÂmiâneh dar-bâreh-ye Fâl-e Hâfez* (Popular Beliefs on Seeking Augury from Hâfez) (Tehran, 1369/1990).

66   For more information about taʿziyeh (passion play), minbar, and Friday prayer, see Peter J. Chelkowski, ed., *Taʿziyeh, Ritual and Drama in Iran* (New York, 1979); Asghar Fathi, *Menbar, Yek Rasâneh-ye ʿOmoumi dar Islam* (The Minbar as a Medium of Public Communication in Islam) (Tehran, 1358/1980); and S. D. Goitein, "The Origin and Nature of the Muslim Friday Worship," *Studies in Islamic History and Institutions* (Leiden, 1966), pp. 111–126.

67   An ideological "revolution," as it were, to revive the existential and political potentialities of religion, as would have been advocated by someone like Ali Shariʿati, had to wait for several more decades before being contemplated. Even the ideas of al-Afghani were largely overshadowed by the general tide of modernism and did not inspire much literary activity. A contemporary example of Islamic militancy during the period under discussion was the Jangali movement in Gilân led by Mirzâ Kouchek Khân. Several writers, such as Ebrâhim Fakhrâ'i and Mahmoud-Reza Tolouʿ, were collaborating with the movement, and its ideological composition, reflected in its organ *Jangal*, was a mixture of pan-Islamism (a remote influence of al-Afghani's teachings) and socialism (a direct influence of radical ideas circulating in Russia at that time that had also reached northern Iran). But this movement too did not contribute to the assertion of the religious element in literary practice, not least because of its localism, short life, and exclusively political reputation.

68   For studies on privacy, see J. Roland Pennock and John W. Chapman, eds., *Privacy*, Vol. 8 of *Nomos* (Yearbook of the American Society for Political and Legal Philosophy) (New York: Atherton Press, 1971); Paul Weiss, *Privacy* (Carbondale: Southern Illinois University Press, 1983); and Barrington Moore, Jr., *Privacy: Studies in Social and Cultural History* (New York and London: M. E. Sharpe, 1984).

69   For references on leisure time in Iran, see Noushin Omrâni, ed., *Ketâb-*

Shenasi-ye Owqât-e Farâghat (A Bibliography of Leisure Time) (Tehran, 1368/1989).

70   New notions of privacy were reflected in the spatial arrangements in household interiors; individual family members now laid claim to their own rooms. Hence the conceptual and semantic shift or contrast in the notion of "privacy" (*khalwat*) from its premodern to its intentionally modern meanings and connotations.

71   For example, in addition to Tehran's lending bookstores, the city of Ahwaz too had at least one store with similar arrangements. Reportedly, in the 1930s, a local bookstore in Ahwaz run by a young Jewish bookseller known as "Kolombu" (?) used to offer "rental novels" such as *The Bronze Statues or the Virgin's Kiss*, by George Reynolds, in Persian translation by Seyyed Hosein Khân Sadr al-Ma'âli as *Bouseh-ye 'Azrâ*, and *The Three Musketeers*, by Alexandre Dumas, in Persian translation by Hâj Mohammad Mirzâ Eskandari as *Seh Tofangdâr*, charging "one Qerân per book per night." From personal recollections by Forough al-Zamân Semsârzâdeh of her 1314/1935 trip to Ahwaz, narrated to this author on 27 August 1989.

72   [Seyyed Jalâl al-Din Mu'ayyed al-Islam Hoseini], *Mokâlemeh-ye Sayyâh-e Irani bâ Shakhs-e Hendi* (Discourse of an Iranian Traveler with an Indian Notable), n.n. ([Calcutta], India: Paradise Press, c. 1905). For Mu'ayyed al-Islam (1280 A.H./1863–1309/1930), his writings, and the paper *Habl al-Matin*, see *Press and Poetry*, pp. 28, 73–75; *Jarâ'ed*, Vol. 2, pp. 200–213; *Moshâr*, Vol. 2, pp. 355–356; and Nourollâh Iranparast, "Modir-e Habl al-Matin" (The Proprietor of Habl al-Matin), *Armaghân*, Vol. 10, Nos. 5–6 (1308/1932), pp. 273–284. For reference to several consular reports on the influence of *Habl al-Matin* on Iranian public opinion, see Robert M. Burrell, "Aspects of the Reign of Muzaffar al-Din Shah of Persia 1896–1907" (Ph.D. thesis, University of London, School of Oriental and African Studies, 1979), p. 63.

73   For a brief account of the development of modern translations in Iran, see Mohammad Mohit Tabâtabâ'i, "Seyr-e Tarjomeh dar Iran" (An Overview of Translation in Iran), *Armaghân*, Vol. 36 (1346/1967), pp. 225–237. See further Jamshid Kiânfar, "Tarjomeh dar 'Ahd-e Qajar, az Âghâz tâ Dowreh-ye Nâser al-Din Shah" (Translation in Iran, from the Beginning to the Time of Nâser al-Din Shah), *Nashr-e Dânesh*, Vol. 10, No. 1 (Âzar and Dey 1368/December 1989 and January 1990), pp. 23–28; and Gholâm-Ali Sayyâr, "Negâhi be Vaz'-e Tarjomeh dar Zabân-e Fârsi" (A Note on the State of Translation in Persian Language), *Âyandeh*, Part 1, Vol. 15, Nos. 10–12 (Dey–Esfand 1368/January–March 1990), pp. 685–698; Part 2, Vol. 16, Nos. 1–4 (1369/1990), p. 114 ff.; Part 3, Vol. 16, Nos. 5–8 (Mordâd–Âbân 1369/August–November 1990), pp. 491–506.

74   Persian translations of Georgi Zaidan's narratives by Mohammad-Ali Shirâzi (Naqib al-Mamâlek) include: Jurjî Zaydân, *Amin va Ma'moun* (Amin and Ma'moun, originally *al-Amin wa-al-Ma'mun*) (Tehran: Naqsh-e Jahân Press, n.d.),

138 pp.; *Enteqâm-e Khoun-e Hosein* (Avenging the Murder of Hosein), 3rd edition (Tehran, n.d.), 208 pp.; *Enqelâb-e ʿOsmâni* (The Ottoman Revolution, originally *al-Inqilâb al-ʿUthmani*) (Tehran: Majalleh-ye Mâh-e Now, n.d.), 200 pp.; *Salâh al-Din Ayyoubi* (Saladin, originally *Salah al-Din al-Ayyubi*) (Tehran: Majalleh-ye Mâh-e Now, [1950?]); *Delâvarân-e Arab* (Arab Heroes) (Tehran: Mâh-e Now Press, n.d.), 516 pp.; *Fâjeʿeh-ye Ramadan* (The Tragedy of Ramadan), 3rd edition (Tehran, 1335/1946), 158 pp.; and *Fâjeʿeh-ye Karbala* (The Tragedy of Karbala, originally *Ghadat Karbala*), 7th edition (Tehran, 1337/1948), 206 pp.

75 See Doust-Ali Khân Moʿayyer al-Mamâlek, *Rejâl-e ʿAsr-e Nâseri* (Notables of the Naser al-Din Shah's Period) (Tehran, 1361/1982), pp. 63–64.

76 See *Kolliyât-e Haft-Jeldi-ye Amir Arsalân ibn Malekshah-e Rumi* (A Complete Story in Seven Parts of Amir Arsalân ibn Malekshah-e Rumi), [transcribed] by "a lady from the Court of Nâser al-Din Shah Qajar" (*yeki az bânovân-e darbâri-e Nâser al-Din Shah Qajar*), lithograph edition, calligraphy by Ali-Akbar Mosammem (Tehran, 1329 A.H./1911), 133 pp. Its several later editions include Tehran: Akhavân-e Ketâbchi, 1310/1931, 314 pp.; Tehran: Elmi, n.d., 264 pp.; and a more standard edition, edited with an introduction by Mohammad-Jaʿfar Mahjoub, Tehran, Jibi, 1340/1961. *Amir Arsalân* is a good example of the end of one era and the beginning of another. Both the shah and a commoner could listen to and enjoy *Amir Arsalân*, but with later literature, conflicting tastes and judgments made such unity of enjoyment irrelevant, if not impossible. On the other hand, *Amir Arsalân* itself was not a completely new genre. It is more like the Safavid *naqqâli* works, and also more like the *Arabian Nights*. It can be regarded as the last important popular fiction (i.e., *samar*), in the vein of *Hosein-e Kurd-e Shabestari*, and comparable to earlier works like *Dârâb-Nameh*, *Firouzshah-Nameh*, and the prose *Eskandar-Nameh*s, which always had their discriminating critics (such as Bayhaqi in *Târikh-e Masʿoudi*) who found them shallow. I am grateful to Mohsen Ashtiany for pointing this comparison out to me. For *Amir Arsalân* and Persian popular literature, see the following studies by William L. Hanaway: "*Amir Arsalan* and the Question of Genre," *IS*, Vol. 24, Nos. 1–4 (1991), pp. 55–60; "Formal Elements in the Persian Popular Romances," *Review of National Literatures*, Vol. 2, No. 1 (Spring 1971), pp. 139–60; and "Variety and Continuity in Popular Literature in Iran," in Peter J. Chelkowski, ed., *Iran: Continuity and Variety* (New York, 1971), pp. 59–75.

77 See Ahmad Karimi-Hakkak, "From Translation to Appropriation: Poetic Cross-Breeding in Early Twentieth-Century Iran," *Comparative Literature*, Vol. 47, No. 1 (Winter 1995), pp. 53–78.

78 Seyyed Abd al-Rahim Khalkhâli, *Namâyesh-e Dâstân-e Khounin yâ Sargozasht-e Barmakiân* (The Unfortunate Tale or the Fate of the Barmakids) (Tehran: Matbaʿeh-ye Majles, Tir 1304/June–July 1925), 69 pp. All references in the text are to this edition. On the cover, the title appears as follows: *Dâstân-e Khounin: Dâstânist Târikhi va ʿEshqi beh Sourat-e Namâyesh dar Panj Pardeh dar Bayân-e Sargozasht-e Barmakiân va ʿElal-e Nekbat-e Ânân va Vasf-e Tajammol va*

Ta⁽ayyosh va Fesâd-e Akhlâq-e Darbâr-e Khelâfat va Darbâriân dar ⁽Asr-e Hâroun al-Rashid (The Unfortunate Tale: A Historical Romance in the Form of a Play in Five Acts Depicting the Life of the Barmakids and the Causes of Their Adversity and an Account of the Luxury and Debauchery and Moral Corruption of the Caliphate and the Courtiers during Hâroun al-Rashid's Era). This work has been partially reprinted in Jamshid Malekpour, *Adabiyât-e Namâyeshi dar Iran* (Theatrical Literature in Iran), Vol. 2: *Dowrân-e Enqelâb-e Mashruteh* (The Period of the Constitutional Revolution) (Tehran, 1363/1985), pp. 220–225. Malek-pour suggests that the work was initially written around 1329–1330 A.H./1911–1912. Malek-pour, *Adabiyât-e Namâyeshi*, p. 217.

79   Malekpour, *Adabiyât-e Namâyeshi*, p. 217.

80   Abu Muslim is particularly known for his leadership of an important rebellion he organized among a coalition of discontented Arabs and Iranians in Khorâsân, in June 747, against the Umayyad caliphate. This rebellion later contributed to the downfall of the Umayyads in 750. Both Abu Muslim and the Barmakids (see note 81 below) were frequently regarded as archetypal figures in classical Persian literature and popular legends. For medieval legends centered around Abu Muslim, see Abu Tâher (ibn Ali ibn Hosein) Tartousi, *Abu Muslim-Nâmeh*, edited by Eqbâl Yaghmâ'i (Tehran, 1335/1956). A modern narrative can be found in Jurjî Zaydân, *Abu Muslim Khorâsâni*, Persian translation by Habibol-lâh Âmouzegâr, 3 Vols. (Tehran, 1318/1939), 579 pp.

81   The Barmakids were an ancient Iranian family of clerical background from Balkh, whose Buddhist ancestor was a *barmak* (title of the high priest in the temple of Nowbahâr). Following the Muslim conquest of Persia and the fall of Balkh to the Arab army, the family converted to Islam and moved to Basra (c. 663). During the early Abbasids, they gained prominence as scribes and viziers; they were famous for their administrative skills and cultural patronage. For further information on the Barmakids, see, for example, W. Barthold, "Barmakids," in *EI*, Vol. 1 (1913), pp. 663–666; also D. Sourdel, "al-Barâmika," in *EI2*, Vol. 1, Part 2 (1960), pp. 1033–1036; and Hugh Kennedy, "The Barmakid Revolution in Islamic Government," in Charles Melville, ed., *History and Literature in Iran* (Cambridge, 1990), pp. 89–98.

82   Khalkhâli, *Namâyesh-e Dâstân-e Khounin*, p. 4.

83   Ibid., p. 6. The author further acknowledges that he had greatly benefited from reading Georgi Zaidan. Ibid., p. 6. He also acknowledges the contemporary poet and scholar Gholâm-Reza Rashid Yâsami, who had commented on an earlier draft of the drama and had contributed a few street ballads (*tasnif*), which were later incorporated into the text. Ibid., pp. 7, 39–40.

84   *Shab-nâmeh* was normally an anonymous, clandestine leaflet critical of a given political situation. During the latter part of the Qajar period, *shab-nâmeh* was a common means of expression for political opposition. Especially during the Constitutional movement, various clandestine communiqués, issued by the

pro-Constitutional political societies (or the *anjomans*) and by the opposing parties, were regarded as *shab-nâmeh*. For examples, see Go'el Kohen, *Târikh-e Sânsour dar Matbouʿât-e Iran* (A History of Censorship in the Iranian Press), Vol. 1 (Tehran, 1360/1982), pp. 169–175; Vol. 2 (Tehran, 1362/1983), pp. 433–484.

85 Khalkhâli, *Namâyesh-e Dâstân-e Khounin*, p. 47.

86 Ibid., p. 69.

87 [Muʾayyed al-Islam], *Mokâlemeh-ye Sayyâh Irani bâ Shakhs-e Hendi*, introduction, 2nd page (n.n.).

88 See Mirzâ (Mohammad-) Reza Khân Tabâtabâʾi Nâʾini, *Tiâtr: Majmouʿeh-ye Rouznâmeh* (Theater: A Collection of Papers), edited by Mohammad Golbon and Farâmarz Tâlebi (Tehran: Nashr-e Cheshmeh, 1366/1987). For *Tiâtr* and its editor, see also *Jarâʾed*, Vol. 2, pp. 147–150.

89 Hâj Sheikh Mirzâ (Mohammad-) Hasan Jâberi Ansâri Isfahani (Sadr al-Odabâʾ), *Âftâb-e Derakhshandeh: Az Moʿjezât-e Emrouzeh-ye Islamiyeh* (The Glittering Sun: Of Today's Islamic Miracles), foreword by Hâj Mirzâ Hasan Khân Mohtasham al-Saltaneh (Esfandiâri), then the Minister of Arts, lithograph edition with extensive commentary at the margins, 159 pp. (Tehran, 1302/1923). All references are to this edition. I am grateful to Mohsen Ashtiany for providing me with a copy of this book.

90 Mohammad-Hasan Jâberi (Ansâri), *Târikh-e Isfahan Nesf-e Jahân* (Isfahan, [the city which is worth] One Half of the World: A History) (n.p., 1333 A.H./1915), 214 pp.; reprinted with additions as *Târikh-e Isfahan va Rey va hameh-ye Jahân* (A History of Isfahan and Reyy and the Whole World), edited by Hosein Emâdzâdeh (Tehran, 1321/1942), 449 pp. For a biography of Jâberi and his works, see *Jarâʾed*, Vol. 1, pp. 166–169; and *Moshâr*, Vol. 2, pp. 610–612.

91 Jâberi, *Âftâb-e Derakhshandeh*, p. 4.

92 Ibid., p. 4.

93 Ibid., pp. 26–56.

94 Here Jâberi foreshadows later authors' attempts to argue that the Koran symbolically embodies all scientific discovery. A brief exposition of the ideas of one such later writer, Mehdi Bâzargân, is presented in Chapter 5.

95 Jâberi, *Âftâb-e Derakhshandeh*, pp. 95–96.

96 Ibid., p. 96.

97 Ibid., pp. 96–97.

98 Ibid., p. 100.

99 Ibid., p. 104.

100 Ibid., pp. 112–122. For Arfaʿ al-Dowleh (1267–1356 A.H./1851–1937), see *Moshâr*, Vol. 3, pp. 131–133; and Iraj Afshâr, ed., *Rejâl-e Vezârat-e Khârejeh dar ʿAsr-e Nâseri and Mozaffari az Neveshteh-hâ-ye Mirzâ Mehdi Khân Momtahen al-Dowleh-ye Shaqâqi and Mirzâ Hâshem Khân* (Officials of the Foreign Ministry in the Times of Nâser al-Din Shah and Mozaffar al-Din Shah, documented by Mirzâ Mehdi Khân Momtahen al-Dowleh Shaqâqi and Mirzâ

Hâshem Khân) (Tehran: Asâtir, 1365/1986), pp. 105—108. See further *Rejâl*, Vol. 1, pp. 507—512. For a less sympathetic documentation of Arfaʿal-Dowleh's curriculum vitae, see the editor's note (No. 2) on pp. 173—177, in Mohammad-Hasan Khân Eʿtemâd al-Saltaneh, *Kholseh (Mashhour be Khwâbnâmeh)* (The Book of Dreams), edited by Mahmoud Katirâ'i, 2nd edition (Tehran: Toukâ, 1357/1988).

101   Ibid., p. 113.

102   Ibid., p. 114.

103   Ibid., pp. 131—133.

104   Ibid., pp. 135—159.

105   Ibid., p. 137.

106   From the unpublished Photographic Archive at the Middle East Centre, St. Antony's College, Oxford University, catalogued under No. 1372: Tweedy's hotel in Tabriz, 32(3/204/3). Owen Tweedy was a government employee and journalist working in the Middle East and North Africa from the 1920s to the 1940s. For a study of the urban change and development of modern towns in Russia in the nineteenth century, see Daniel R. Brower, *The Russian City between Tradition and Modernity, 1850—1900* (Berkeley: University of California Press, 1990).

107   For changes in Tehran and European and Ottoman influence in the late nineteenth century, see John Gurney, "The Transformation of Tehran in the Later Nineteenth Century," in Chahryar Adle and Bernard Hourcade, eds., *Téhéran: Capitale bicentenaire* (Paris and Tehran: Institut Français de Recherche en Iran, 1992), pp. 51—71. See also Martin Seger, *Teheran: Eine Stadtgeographische Studies* (Vienna: Springer Verlag, 1978).

108   See Michael Gilsenan, *Recognizing Islam* (London, 1982), "Space, Power, and Tradition," pp. 187—191.

109   Seyyed Mortezâ Moshfeq Kâzemi, *Tehran-e Makhouf* (Tehran, City of Horrors), originally appeared in the paper *Setâreh-ye Iran* (The Star of Iran) (Tehran, 1341 A.H./1922—1923) and was published as a book in 4 Vols. (Tehran and Berlin, 1303—1305/1924—1926); the second part of the book, entitled *Yâdegâr-e Yek Shab* (The Memory of One Night), was initially published in 2 Vols.: Vol. 1 (Berlin: Kâviâni Press, 1342 A.H./1923—1924); Vol. 2 (Tehran, 1342 A.H./1923—1924); 4th edition in 4 Vols. (Tehran, 1320/1941). Moshfeq Kâzemi also wrote *Gol-e Pazhmordeh* (The Drooping Flower) (Tehran, 1308/1929); *Rashk-e Por-Bahâ* (Precious Envy) (Tehran, 1309/1930); and *Rouzgâr va Andishe-hâ* (Times and Thoughts), Vols. 1 and 2 (Tehran, 1971 and 1973). For Moshfeq Kâzemi, see further *S/N*, Vol. 2, pp. 258—264; and Kamil Banák, "Mushfiq Kazimi's Novel The Horrible Tehran—Romantic Fiction or Social Criticism," *Asian and African Studies*, Vol. 13 (1977), pp. 147—152.

110   Mohammad Masʿoud (Dehâti), *Tafrihât-e Shab* (Nocturnal Pleasures) (Tehran, 1313/1934), reprinted (Tehran, 1326/1947). Masʿoud also wrote *Dar Talâsh-e Maʿâsh* (The Struggle for a Living) (Tehran, 1312/1933); *Ashraf-e*

Makhlouqât ([Man,] The Noblest of Creatures) (Tehran, 1313/1934); *Golhâ'ikeh dar Jahannam Mirouyad* (Flowers Blooming in Hell), 2 Vols.: Vol. 1 (Tehran, 1321/1942, reprinted, Tehran, 1337/1958; Vol. 2 as *Bahâr-e 'Omr* (Life's Springtime) (Tehran, 1324/1945); and *Behesht-e Ârezou* (The Paradise of Desire) (Tehran, n.d.). For Mas'oud, see further Kamshad, *Modern Persian Prose Literature*, pp. 66–68.

111 For a pioneering study on forms of imagery in classical Persian poetry, see Mohammad-Reza Shafi'i Kadkani, *Sovar-e Khiâl dar She'r-e Farsi* (Forms of Imagery in Persian Poetry), 3rd edition (Tehran, 1366/1987); an analysis of *Vis va Râmin* is on pp. 564–576.

112 Compare with, for example, the above-mentioned works by Moshfeq Kâzemi and Mohammad Mas'oud; or with Hedâyatollâh Hakim-Elâhi's documentary, *Az Shahr-e Now tâ Dâdgostari* (From the Red Light Quarter to the Court of Justice), 3rd printing (Tehran, 1357–1358/1978–1979).

Chapter 4

1 General Hassan Arfa, *Under Five Shahs* (New York, 1965), p. 305.

2 Ibid.

3 Iran was referred to in wartime rhetoric as "the bridge of victory," since nearly a quarter of the total cargo delivered from the West to the Soviet Union during the war was shipped through the Persian Gulf. See Ali Gheissari, "Persia," in I. C. B. Dear and M. R. D. Foot, eds., *The Oxford Companion to the Second World War* (Oxford and New York: Oxford University Press, 1995), pp. 874–875.

4 For a detailed study of the Iranian cabinets during the period 1941–1953, see Fakhreddin Azimi, *Iran: The Crisis of Democracy (1941–1953)* (London, 1989; see also Zahrâ Shaji'i, *Vezârat va Vazirân dar Iran* (The Ministerial Office and the Ministers in Iran) (Tehran, 2535 [1355]/1976).

5 In his political career Ali Mansour (Mansour al-Molk) twice became prime minister, first from 5 Tir 1319/26 June 1940 to 5 Shahrivar 1320/27 August 1941, and second from 8 Farvardin 1329/28 March 1950 to 5 Tir 1329/26 June 1950. He should not be confused with his son, Hasan-Ali Mansour, who also became prime minister, on 17 Esfand 1342/7 March 1964, and whose career was cut short by his death on 6 Bahman 1343/26 January 1965 following an attempt on his life six days earlier.

6 The 1942 Tripartite Treaty, signed by Iran, Britain, and the Soviet Union, stipulated that the Allied forces would leave Iran within six months of the end of the war with Germany and its associates. This was later adjusted to six months after the end of hostilities with Japan. For the treaty's full text, see George Lenczowski, *Russia and the West in Iran, 1918–1948: A Study in Big-Power Politics* (New York, 1949), Appendix 2, pp. 319–322. For some social reactions to the treaty, see further Arfa, *Under Five Shahs*, pp. 322–323.

7 For political parties, see L. P. Elwell-Sutton, "Political Parties in Iran: 1941–1948," *MEJ*, Vol. 3 (January 1949), pp. 45–62; further information can also be found in Jaleh Pirnazar, "Political Movements and Organizations in Iran: 1890–1953" (Ph.D. dissertation, University of California, Berkeley, 1980). See also Azimi, *Iran: The Crisis of Democracy*.

8 For a list of newspapers and journals, see Vali-Morâd Sâdeqi-Nasab, *Fehrest-e Rouznâme-hâ-ye Farsi: 1320–1332* (An Index of Persian Newspapers: 1941–1953) (Tehran: Tehran University Press, 1360/1982). This index is based on the collection at the Central Library of Tehran University. It includes 1,413 titles of periodicals in Persian published between 1941 and 1953.

9 See the reminiscences of Ahmad Ahrar, Mahshid Amir-Shahi, Daryush Homayoun, Eslam Kazemiyyeh, Mohammad Ja'far Mahjub, Nader Naderpur, and Mehdi Baradaran Qasemi in Foundation for Iranian Studies, *The Oral History Collection of the Foundation for Iranian Studies* catalog edited by Gholam Reza Afkhami and Seyyed Vali Reza Nasr, with a foreword by Elizabeth B. Mason (Bethesda, Md.: Foundation for Iranian Studies, 1991); a brief outline of these reminiscences can be found in the catalog, pp. 15, 19–20, 55–56, 63, 72, and 101, respectively.

10 Several examples of such demonstrations can be found in Mohammad T [Torkamân], *Ettelâ'âti dar-bâreh-ye Tashannojât, Dargirihâ-ye Khiâbâni va Towte'ehâ dar Dowrân-e Hokoumat-e Doktor Mosaddeq* (Some Information about Tensions, Street Confrontations, and Intrigues during the Government of Mosaddeq) (Tehran, 1359/1981).

11 On the arrival of sausage in Iran, see, for example, "Susis va Kâlbâs Chegouneh dar Iran Jâ Bâz Kard?" (How Did the Sausage Open Its Way to Iran?), from *Gozâresh: Vizheh-ye Sanâye'-e Ghazâ'i* (Special Report on the Food Industry), reprinted in *Ettelâ'ât*, No. 181 (11 Bahman 1373/31 January 1995), p. 6. The term *kâlbâs*, current in Persian for mortadella, is in fact an adoption from the Russian *kolbasa* or Polish *kailbas*.

12 The arrival of Polish refugees in the early 1940s and their settlement at a camp east of Tehran was another factor that contributed to further European influence in Tehran's life. See Arfa, *Under Five Shahs*, pp. 313–314.

13 Abrahamian, *Iran between Two Revolutions*, pp. 225–250.

14 See, for example, Bahâr, *Târikh-e Mokhtasar-e Ahzâb-e Siâsi*, p. 27.

15 See, for example, S. R. Shafaq, "Patriotic Poetry in Modern Iran," *MEJ*, Vol. 6, No. 4 (Autumn 1952), pp. 417–428, note pp. 425–426. See also Vera Kubícková, "Persian Literature of the Twentieth Century," in Jan Rypka, *History of Iranian Literature*, edited by Karl Jahn (Dordrecht, The Netherlands, 1968), pp. 353–418, note especially p. 387 in the section on the literary activities of the period 1921–1941, pp. 379–396. A pro-Soviet socialist poet of that period was Ab al-Qâsem Lâhouti. Regarding journalism, key periodicals included *Âzâdi* (Freedom), *Toufân* (Storm), and *Tolou'* (Dawn). For a case study of

Farrokhi Yazdi, the editor of *Toufân*, see Gheissari, "The Poetry and Politics of Farrokhi Yazdi," *IS*, Vol. 26 (1993), pp. 33–50.

16 Second International (1889–1914) was a federation of socialist parties and trade unions that influenced the ideology and programs of the European labor movement from the last decade of the nineteenth century to the beginning of the First World War. Many major figures in both the theory and practice of European socialism were, in varying ways and degrees, associated with the Second International, among them Viktor Adler (1852–1918); August Bebel (1840–1913); Eduard Bernstein (1850–1932); Jules Guesde (1845–1922); Karl Kautsky (1854–1938); Wilhelm Liebknecht (1826–1900), a descendant of Martin Luther; Rosa Luxemburg (1871–1938); William Morris (1834–1896); and G. V. Plekhanov (1856–1918), to name a few. For additional information see G. D. H. Cole, *A History of Socialist Thought*, 5 Vols. (London, 1953–1960), see in particular Vol. 3: *The Second International* (London, 1956); and Leszek Kolakowski, *Main Currents of Marxism: Its Origins, Growth and Dissolution*, 3 Vols. (Oxford: Oxford University Press, 1978), see in particular Vol. 2; *The Golden Age*.

17 Abrahamian, *Iran between Two Revolutions*, p. 162.

18 A more open rivalry in Iran between the West and the Soviets surfaced soon after the war ended. See Stephen L. McFarland, "A Peripheral View of the Origins of the Cold War: The Crises in Iran, 1941–1947," *Diplomatic History*, Vol. 4 (Fall 1980), pp. 333–351. See also Touraj Atabaki, *Azerbaijan: Ethnicity and Autonomy in Iran after the Second World War* (London, I. B. Tauris, 1993).

19 Sepehr Zabih, *The Communist Movement in Iran* (Berkeley: University of California Press, 1966), p. 74. That was a difficult task while the Germans were still advancing, but "as the war progressed, political conversion became easier, so that by early 1944 many Nazi sympathizers of the middle class and the intelligentsia were only too eager to rally to the party's banner, particularly since it had succeeded in creating a substantially nationalistic image." Ibid., p. 74.

20 For the formation of the Tudeh Party, see Abrahamian, *Iran between Two Revolutions*, Chaps. 6–8. See also Zabih, *The Communist Movement in Iran*, Chaps. 3–5; George Lenczowski, "The Communist Movement in Iran," *MEJ*, Vol. 1 (January 1947), pp. 29–45; and Lenczowski, *Russia and the West in Iran*, pp. 223–234.

21 Eighty-seven delegates were from Tehran and thirty-three from the provinces; each delegate represented ten members. The conference met over the course of a week. Abrahamian, *Iran between Two Revolutions*, p. 284.

22 See Abd al-Samad Kâmbakhsh, *Nazari beh Jonbesh-e Kârgari va Komunisti dar Iran* (An Introduction to the Labor and Communist Movement in Iran), collection of articles (n.p. [West Germany]: Tudeh Party, 1972), pp. 56–57.

23 A shortage of grain that had been caused by speculation and a political crisis led to organized protests. The day of 17 Âzar 1321/8 December 1942 be-

gan with a march of high school and university students to the Majles. But the event soon went out of control as supporters of the Shah, in order to challenge the government of the influential prime minister Qavâm, went on a preplanned rampage, attacking shops and damaging property, including the residence of the prime minister. The police intervened only after the riot had spread and tried to disperse the crowd that had assembled opposite the Majles. For further information, see JÂMI (Jebhe-ye Âzâdi-e Mardom-e Iran), *Gozashteh Cherâgh-e Râh-e Âyandeh Ast*, pp. 153–159. For an eyewitness and slightly different account that is critical of the Tudeh Party's lack of resolve in this event, see Anvar Khâmeh'i, *Khâterât-e Doktor Anvar Khâmeh'i* (The Memoirs of Dr. Anvar Khâmehi), Vol. 2, *Forsat-e Bozorg-e Az Dast Rafteh* (A Great Opportunity Lost) (Tehran, 1362/1984), pp. 57–71. See also Stephen L. McFarland, "Anatomy of an Iranian Political Crowd: The Tehran Bread Riot of December 1942," *IJMES*, Vol. 17, No. 1 (February 1985), pp. 51–65; and Azimi, *Iran: The Crisis of Democracy*, pp. 72–74.

24   For the composition of the delegates, see Abrahamian, *Iran between Two Revolutions*, p. 293.

25   *Cheh Bâyad Kard?* (What Is to Be Done?), was prepared in the fall of 1324/1945. A revised version was published in the following year (Tehran, Âzar 1325/December 1946) and was immediately banned by the party and withdrawn from circulation. See also Eprim Eshâq (Âlâtur [pseudonym]), *Hezb-e Tudeh-ye Iran Sar-e Du Râh* (The Tudeh Party of Iran at a Crossroads) edited by Jalâl Âl-Ahmad (Tehran, 1947).

26   Zabih, *The Communist Movement*, pp. 128–131; and Abrahamian, *Iran between Two Revolutions*, pp. 307–308.

27   While in prison, Maleki had developed "reservations about the personalities" of some members of the Group of Fifty-Three. As a result, he did not initially join the Tudeh Party. See Katouzian, *The Political Economy of Modern Iran*, p. 145. Eventually, a group of reformists, headed by Abd al-Hosein Noushin, persuaded Maleki to join. The meeting between this group and Maleki was apparently held in the residence of the writer Sâdeq Hedâyat, a close friend of Noushin but never a party member himself. See Maleki's defense in the military tribunal (Winter 1344/1966), reprinted as "Matn-e Asli-e Modâfe'at-e Âqâ-e Khalil Maleki dar Dâdgâh-e Nezâmi-e Darbasteh, Dar Radd-e Keyfar-Khâst" (The Original Text of Mr. Khalil Maleki's Defense in the Military Court), *Sousialism* (Organ of the Society of Iranian Socialists in Europe), 2nd Series, No. 7 (Mehr 1345/October 1966), pp. 37–56, note p. 41.

28   Khalil Maleki, *Du Ravesh Barâ-e Yek Hadaf* (Two Approaches to the Same Goal) (Tehran, 15 Dey 1326/6 January 1946), 60 pp.

29   For more information on Maleki, see Khalil Maleki, *Khâterât-e Siâsi-e Khalil Maleki* (The Political Memoirs of Khalil Maleki), edited with an introduction by Mohammad-Ali Homâyoun Kâtouziân (Tehran, 1357/1979, distributed 1360/1981).

30   Zabih, *The Communist Movement*, p. 135. Khâmeh'i later published three volumes of his memoirs. See Anvar Khâmeh'i, *Khâterât-e Doktor Anvar Khâmeh'i* (The Memoirs of Dr. Anvar Khâmehi), Vol. 1, *Panjâh Nafar va Seh Nafar* ([The Group of] Fifty and Three) (Tehran, 1352/1983); Vol. 2, *Forsat-e Bozorg-e Az Dast Rafteh* (A Great Opportunity Lost) (Tehran, 1362/1984); Vol. 3, *Az En-she'âb tâ Koudetâ* (From the Split [of the Tudeh Party] to the Coup d'État [of 1953]) (Tehran, reprinted West Germany: Novid, 1363/1984). For a critical review of both Maleki's and Khâmeh'i's memoirs, along with those of Fereydoun Keshâvarz (another Tudeh Party member), see Changiz Pahlevân, "Gozashteh-ye Ghalabeh Nayâftani" (The Unsurpassable Past), in *Ketâbnâmâ-e Iran* [No. 1] (Tehran: Nashr-e Now, 1366/1987), pp. 2–21. Pahlevân is particularly critical of the influence of Soviet Marxism in Iran; see further Changiz Pahlevân, "Leninizm dar Iran" (Leninism in Iran), *Ârash*, 5th Series, No. 7 (Mehr 1360/ October 1981), pp. 25–49.

31   See Abrahamian, *Iran between Two Revolutions*, Table 4, "Early Leaders of the Iran Party," pp. 190–191.

32   Ibid., pp. 256–257.

33   Ibid., p. 258.

34   For a study of the Fadâ'iân-e Islam, see Adele Ferdows, "Religion in Iranian Nationalism: the Study of the Fadayan-i Islam," Ph.D. dissertation, Indiana University, 1967; Y. Richard, "L'Organization des Fedâ'iyân-e eslâm, mouvement intégriste musulman en Iran (1945–1956)," in O. Carré and P. Dumont, eds., *Radicalimes islamiques*, Vol. 1 (Paris: L'Harmattan, 1985), pp. 23–82; and Farhad Kazemi, "Religion and Politics in Iran: The Fadâ'iyân Islâm," *Folia Orientalia*, Vol. 22, 1981–1984 (publication 1985), pp. 191–205. For a study of the society's later activities, see Amir H. Ferdows, "Khomeni and Fadayan's Society and Politics," *IJMES*, Vol. 15 (1983), pp. 241–257. For a documentary collection of Ayatollah Kâshâni's letters, proclamations, and speeches, see M. Dehnavi, ed., *Majmou'eh-i az Maktoubât, Sokhanrânihâ va Payâmhây-e Ayatollah Kâshâni* (A Collection of Writings, Lectures, and Communiqués of Ayatollah Kâshâni), Vol. 1 (1299 to Shahrivar 1330/1921 to September 1951) (Tehran, 1361/1982); Vol. 2 (Mehr 1330 to 30 Tir 1331/October 1951 to 21 July 1952) (Tehran, 1361/1982); and Vol. 3 (1 Mordâd 1331 to 28 Mordâd 1332/23 July 1952 to 19 August 1953) (Tehran, 1362/1983). For Ayatollah Kâshâni, see Y. Richard, "Ayatollah Kashani: Precursor of the Islamic Republic?" In N. R. Keddie, ed., *Religion and Politics in Iran*. New Haven, Conn.: Yale University Press, 1983, pp. 101–124.

35   For a documentary collection of various political agitations and street tensions during Mosaddeq's government, see [Torkamân], *Ettelâ'âti dar-bâreh-ye Tashannojât*; for further discussions, see J. A. Bill and Roger Louis, eds., *Musad-diq, Iranian Nationalism, and Oil* (London, 1988).

36   For a collection of references and material relating to this event, including press coverage and various editorials, photographs, police reports, and po-

ems, see Mohammad Torkamân, ed., *Qiyâm-e Melli-ye Si-ye Tir be Ravâyat-e As-nâd va Tasâvir* (The Popular Uprising of the Thirtieth of Tir [21 July 1952] According to Documents and Photographs) (Tehran: Dehkhodâ, 1361/1982).

37   For the sociolinguistic aspects of Persian, see William O. Beeman, "Status, Style, and Strategy in Iranian Interaction," *Anthropological Linguistics*, Vol. 18, No. 7 (1976), pp. 305–322; William O. Beeman, "What is (Iranian) National Character? A Sociolinguistic Approach," *IS*, Vol. 9, No. 1 (Winter 1976), pp. 22–48; William O. Beeman, *Language, Status, and Power in Iran* (Bloomington: Indiana University Press, 1986); Charles Ferguson, "Word Stress in Persian," *Language*, Vol. 33 (1957), pp. 123–135; Carleton T. Hodge, "Some Aspects of Persian Style," *Language*, Vol. 33 (1957), pp. 355–369; and Mohammad A. Jazayery, "English Loan Words in Persian; A Study in Language and Culture" (Ph.D. dissertation, University of Texas at Austin, 1958). For more technical linguistic studies of Persian, see Jiří Krámsky, "A Study in the Phonology of Modern Persian," *Archiv Orientalni*, Vol. 11 (1939), pp. 66–83; Lotfollah Yarmohammadi, "A Contrastive Study of Modern English and Modern Persian" (Ph.D. dissertation, University of Indiana, Bloomington, 1965); Jalil Towhidi, *Studies in the Phonetics and Phonology of Modern Persian* (Hamburg, 1974); Hessam Tabaian, "Conjunction, Relativization, and Complementation in Persian" (Ph.D. dissertation, University of Colorado, Boulder, 1975); Abdolghasem Soheyli, "Noun Phrase Complementation in Persian" (Ph.D. dissertation, University of Illinois, Urbana, 1976); and Lotfollah Yarmohammadi and Ronayne Cowan, "The Persian Verb Reconsidered," *Archiv Orientalni*, Vol. 46 (1978), pp. 46–60.

38   I have further discussed this topic elsewhere; see Ali Gheissari, "Naqd-e Adab-e Eide'ulozhik: Morouri bar Adabiyât-e Rowshanfekri va Maktabi-ye Iran" (Critique of Ideological Literature: A Review of Intellectual and Doctrinaire Writings in Iran), *Iran Nameh*, Vol. 12, No. 2 (Spring 1994), pp. 233–258.

39   The conference, which was the first of its kind, was held in Tehran from 4 Tir 1325/25 June 1946 until 12 Tir 1326/3 July 1946. For a list of the invitees and a record of the proceedings, see *Nakhostin Kongereh-ye Nevisandegân-e Iran* (The First Congress of Iranian Writers) (Tehran, 1326/1947; reprinted Tehran, 1357/1978). Subsequent references will be to the latter edition. For a fairly detailed account, see Bozorg Alavi, "The First Iranian Writers Congress, 1946," originally published in *Payâm-e Nu*, Vol. 2, No. 9 (Tir 1325/June–July 1946), pp. 1–32 and 101–109, English translation by Thomas M. Ricks and Fariba Amini, in Thomas M. Ricks, ed., *Critical Perspectives on Modern Persian Literature* (Washington, D.C.: Three Continents Press, 1984), pp. 8–25.

40   *Nakhostin Kongereh*, pp. 11–39.

41   *Nakhostin Kongereh*, p. 43.

42   *Nakhostin Kongereh*, pp. 128–175.

43   *Nakhostin Kongereh*, pp. 174–175.

44   For more information on Fâtemeh Sayyâh (b. Moscow, 1903, d. Tehran,

13 Esfand 1326/4 March 1948), together with references and bibliography, see *S/N*, Vol. 3, pp. 171–178.

45 *Nakhostin Kongereh*, p. 183.

46 *Nakhostin Kongereh*, pp. 221–233.

47 *Nakhostin Kongereh*, pp. 233–262.

48 V. G. Belinsky (1811–1848) was an important figure in Russian literary criticism and was considered a pioneer of the radical Russian intelligentsia. In 1832, he was expelled from Moscow University and lived as a journalist. He was first influenced by Schelling's ideas on national character and tried to apply them to his interpretation of Russian culture. Later, he turned to Hegel's ideas on the philosophy of history, but after 1840, he became critical of orthodox Hegelianism. In 1847, he wrote a strong letter to N. V. Gogol (1809–1852) criticizing the latter's suggestion that the Russian people should submit to church and state. N. G. Chernyshevsky (1828–1889) was another influential figure; he stressed the role of social and economic inequalities as the basis for change and argued that artists should not only portray reality but also make judgments and take positions. Later Soviet critics gave both authors an eminent place in the history of modern radical ideas. For Belinsky and Chernyshevsky, see further Herbert E. Bowman, *Vissarion Belinsky, 1811–1848: A Study in the Origins of Social Criticism in Russia* (Cambridge, Mass., 1954); and V. V. Zenkovsky, *A History of Russian Philosophy*, 2 Vols., translated from Russian by George L. Kline (New York and London, 1953).

49 Hasan Âbedini, *Sad-sâl Dâstân-nevisi dar Iran* (Iranian Fiction in the Last Hundred Years), Vol. 1 (1253/1874–1342/1963) (Tehran, 1366/1987), p. 122.

50 *Nakhostin Kongereh*, p. 246.

51 *Nakhostin Kongereh*, p. 262.

52 *Nakhostin Kongereh*, p. 231.

53 Note, for instance, Forouzânfar's blithe reference, in the introduction to his monumental edition of *Kolliyât-e Shams*, to an occasion (in Mashhad, 1339 A.H./1921) when he received a fine Kashmir shawl as a gesture of aristocratic patronage from Qavâm al-Saltaneh (who was then the governor of Khorâsân) in recognition of a *qasida* (lyric) that, as an aspiring young poet, he had composed and in which he had celebrated the coming of spring and had also praised the governor. See Mawlânâ Jalâl al-Din Mohammad Mowlavi, *Kolliyât-e Shams yâ Divân-e Kabir* (The Collected Poetry of Shams or the Greater Divân), Edited with an introduction by Badiᶜ al-Zamân Forouzânfar (1st edition [Tehran: Tehran University Press, 1336]); 2nd edition, 10 Vols. (Tehran: Amir-Kabir, Winter 2535 [1355]/1977), Vol. 1, p. *Alif*, from the introduction.

Chapter 5

1 See Fred Halliday, *Iran, Dictatorship and Development* (London: Penguin Books, 1979), pp. 78–102.

2   This group consisted of about six hundred officers. Twenty-seven of its members were shot and the rest were given long-term sentences. Some of the captives "repented" and were later freed, but some showed exceptional resistance and remained in prison. See Katouzian, *The Political Economy of Modern Iran*, pp. 194–195. See also Bizhan Jazani, *Târikh-e Si Sâleh-ye Iran* (A Thirty-Year History of Iran), Vol. 2, n.p., n.d.; reprinted, n.p. ([Tehran]: Nashr-e Kârgar, n.d. [1358/1979]), pp. 11–16. For more on the Tudeh military network, see Osamu Miyata, "The Tudeh Military Networks during the Oil Nationalization Period," *MES*, Vol. 23, No. 3 (July 1987), pp. 313–328.

3   For a detailed account of Mosaddeq's trials, see Mohammad Mosaddeq, *Mosaddeq dar Mahkameh-ye Nezâmi* (Mosaddeq in the Military Tribunal), edited with an introduction by Jalil Bozorgmehr, 2 Vols. (Tehran, 1363/1985).

4   See H. E. Chehabi, *Iranian Politics and Religious Modernism: The Liberation Movement of Iran under the Shah and Khomeini* (Ithaca and London, 1990).

5   The average influence of landlords in the Majles amounted to about 50 percent during the seventeenth session (1952–1953), the eighteenth session (1953–1956), and the nineteenth session (1956–1960). See Shaji'i, *Namâyandegân-e Majles*, p. 176; and Abrahamian, *Iran between Two Revolutions*, p. 421. However, given the proportionately significant number of absentee landlords and the fact that some bazaar merchants were also landlords (i.e., they owned large estates in the countryside), it is difficult to define with precision their electoral representation. It should also be noted that many major landlords were rather happy with the system because they belonged, generally, to the court circles. Any conflict between them and the shah came after the land reforms. For land reform in Iran, see Ann K. S. Lambton, *The Persian Land Reform 1962–1966* (Oxford, 1969); and Ann K. S. Lambton, "Land Reform and the Rural Cooperative Societies," in Ehsan Yar-Shater, ed., *Iran Faces the Seventies* foreword by John S. Badeau (New York, 1971), pp. 5–43. See further Ahmad Ashraf, "From the White Revolution to the Islamic Revolution," in Saeed Rahnema and Sohrab Behdad, eds., *Iran after the Revolution: Crisis of an Islamic State* (London and New York: I. B. Tauris, 1995), pp. 21–44.

6   See Ashraf, "From the White Revolution to the Islamic Revolution," pp. 33–35. For a social study of the bazaar, see Ahmad Ashraf, "Bazar iii. Socioeconomic and Political Role of the Bazar," in *EIr*, Vol. 4 (1990), pp. 30–44.

7   Abrahamian, *Iran between Two Revolutions*, p. 421.

8   For a detailed account of these events, see Akhavi, *Religion and Politics in Contemporary Iran*, pp. 72–90. The Baghdad Pact was a military alliance between Iraq, Turkey, Britain, Iran, and Pakistan that came into effect in 1955 in order to deter Soviet invasion. Although the United States was not a signatory, it was an active supporter of the alliance. In March 1959, following the republican coup of July 1958, Iraq withdrew from the pact, which was then widely referred to as the Central Treaty Organization. Following the revolution of 1979, Iran pulled out of the treaty and thus disrupted its geographical link and military signifi-

cance. See further Mark J. Gasiorowski, *U.S. Foreign Policy and the Shah: Building a Client State in Iran* (Ithaca, N.Y.: Cornell University Press, 1991).

9 Katouzian, *The Political Economy of Modern Iran*, p. 194.

10 See the introduction to the prison memoirs of Ashraf Dehqâni, a pioneer figure in the Organization of the Iranian People Fedâ'i Guerrillas. Ashraf Dehqâni, *Hamâseh-ye Moqâvemat* (The Legend of Resistance) (n.p., n.d.; reproduced, n.p. [Tehran]: Jonbesh, 1357/1978), pp. 9–15.

11 See Menashri, *Education and the Making of Modern Iran*. See also Peter Avery, "Trends in Iran in the Past Five Years," *World Today*, Vol. 21 (1965), pp. 279–290; and Peter Avery, "Iran 1964–8: The Mood of Growing Confidence," *World Today*, Vol. 24 (1968), pp. 453–466.

12 For the economic development in Iran from the mid-1950s to the late 1960s, see Charles Issawi, "The Economy: An Assessment of Performance," and Jahangir Amuzegar, "Capital Formation and Development Finance," both in Ehsan Yar-Shater, ed., *Iran Faces the Seventies*, foreword by John S. Badeau (New York: Praeger, 1971), pp. 44–65 and pp. 66–87, respectively. See further George B. Baldwin, *Planning and Development in Iran* (Baltimore: Johns Hopkins Press, 1967).

13 For instance, it is estimated that in 1963 there were 1,719,000, 336,000, 9,000, and 25,000 students in schools at the elementary, intermediate, technical, and higher levels of the educational system, respectively; in 1968 these figures rose to 2,900,000, 658,000, 17,000, and 38,000, respectively, with an additional 20,000 university students studying abroad. See Issawi, "The Economy: An Assessment of Performance," Table 2.3, p. 53. The same trend continued during the following decade.

14 See Halliday, *Iran, Dictatorship and Development*, p. 218.

15 For a study of education in Iran, see further Reza Arasteh, *Education and the Social Awakening in Iran* (Leiden: E. J. Brill, 1962). For higher education in particular, see, for example, L. M. Brammer, "Problems of Iranian University Students," *MEJ*, Vol. 18 (1964), pp. 443–450; Arthur Doerr, "An Assessment of Educational Development: The Case Study of Pahlavi University, Iran," *MEJ*, Vol. 22 (1968), pp. 317–323; and Marvin Zonis, "Higher Education and Social Change: Problems and Prospects," in Ehsan Yar-Shater, ed., *Iran Faces the Seventies*, foreword by John S. Badeau (New York: Praeger, 1971), pp. 217–259. For the impact of the White Revolution on the educational situation, see Mansour Delagah, "An Analysis of the Educational Consequences of the 'White Revolution' in Iran from 1962–63 through 1973–74 in Historical Perspective" (Ph.D. dissertation, University of Colorado, Boulder, 1975). For a critical account of the practice of sending students abroad, see Mohammad Derakhshesh, *Hashtâd Sâl Be-Sou-ye Sarâb* (Eighty Years toward a Mirage) (n.p. [Oakton, Va.]: Jâme'eh-ye Mo'alleman-e Iran [Iranian Teachers' Association], Âzar 1362/December 1983), pp. 34–49. See also Ali-Mohammad Hâzeri, *Ravand-e E'zâm-e Dâneshjou dar Iran* (The Trend of Sending Iranian Students Abroad) (Tehran, 1372/1993).

16 See the reminiscences of Jalal Matini, Seyyed Hossein Nasr, and Homa Nateq in Foundation for Iranian Studies, *Oral History Collection*; a brief outline of these reminiscences can be found in the catalog, pp. 75, 88, and 89—90, respectively.

17 See Ervand Abrahamian, *Radical Islam: The Iranian Mojahedin* (London: I. B. Tauris, 1989).

18 In the early 1970s, both the U.S. Central Intelligence Agency and the Israeli intelligence organization, Mossad, were involved in restructuring SAVAK. As the ideology of armed struggle spread among the young generation of political activists, a special joint committee was formed between SAVAK and the police to fight urban underground activities. The unit was under the directorship of Parviz Sâbeti and set up its headquarters at the Central Police's old building in downtown Tehran. It was largely responsible for the arbitrary detention, interrogation, and torture of many university students during that period. For further details on different wings and operations of the Iranian intelligence agencies, see the memoirs of Hosein Fardoust, *Zohour va Soqout-e Saltanat-e Pahlavi* (The Rise and Fall of the Pahlavi Reign), edited by Mo'asseseh-ye Motâle'ât va Pazhouhesh-hâ-ye Siâsi (Institute of Political Studies and Research), 2 Vols. (Vol. 1: *Memoirs*, Vol. 2: *Commentaries of the Editors*) (1st edition, Tehran, Winter 1369/1991; 3rd edition, Tehran, 1370/1991). Fardoust was the shah's long-time associate and top intelligence officer.

19 Asadollah Alam, *The Shah and I: The Confidential Diary of Iran's Royal Court, 1969—1977*, introduced and edited by Alinaghi Alikhani, translated into English by Alinaghi Alikhani and Nicholas Vincent (New York: St. Martin's Press, 1991), p. 361.

20 Alam, *The Shah and I*, pp. 358—359.

21 A good case in point is the Confederation of Iranian Students (CIS). See the reminiscences of Farajollah Ardalan, Hormoz Hekmat, Bahram Khoza'i, Hamid Mohamedi, and Ali Shakeri, in Foundation for Iranian Studies, *Oral History Collection*; a brief outline of the content of these reminiscences can be found in the catalog, pp. 22—23, 53—54, 65—66, 80—81, and 114—115, respectively.

22 Political publications, including newsletters, communiqués, party organs, pamphlets, and translations of radical tracts, are a major source for the study of the intellectual and cultural characteristics of Iranian intellectuals living abroad. For a selective list of such publications, see Wolfgang H. Behn and Willem M. Floor, *Twenty Years of Iranian Power Struggle: A Bibliography of 951 Political Periodicals from 1341/1962 to 1360/1981 with Selective Locations* (Berlin, 1982). See also Wolfgang H. Behn, ed., *The Iranian Opposition to the Shah: 701 Selected Dissident Publications: A Documentary History on Microfiche* (Zug, Switzerland: Inter Documentation Company, n.d.). For a more comprehensive bibliography of Persian underground literature, see Wolfgang H. Behn, *Iranian Opposition in Exile: An Annotated Bibliography of Publications from 1341/1962 to 1357/1978* (Wiesbaden: Harrassowitz, Autumn 1979).

23 For brief accounts by student activists regarding the Iranian student movement and the CIS, which was founded in 1960, see *Jonbesh-e Dâneshjou'i-e Iran* (Iran's Student Movement), a survey of the Iranian student movement, by Ettehâdiyeh-ye Komunist-hâ-ye Iran (Union of Iranian Communists) (n.p.: 1355/1976), 64 pp.; and *Târikh-cheh-ye Konfedrâsioun va Enherâfât-e Mowjoud dar Ân* (A Short History of the Confederation [of Iranian Students] And its Errors), by Konfedrâsioun-e Dâneshjouyân-e Irani (Confederation of Iranian Students) (London: London branch of Confederation of Iranian Students, c. 1977), 22 pp. These documents have been reproduced on microfiche in Wolfgang H. Behn, ed., *The Iranian Opposition to the Shah*, Subject Group 26: Student Affairs, Publ. No. 14, Mf. n. 8, p. 81, and Publ. No. 43, Mf. n. 22, pp. 84–85, respectively. See also interviews of Homayoun Katouzian, Moloud Khanlari, and Khosrow Shakeri, among others, in Habib Lajevardi (Project Director), *Iranian Oral History Collection* (Cambridge, Mass.: Harvard University, Center for Middle Eastern Studies, 1987). Additional references to the CIS can be found in Foundation for Iranian Studies, *Oral History Collection*; for a list of relevant interviews, see the catalog, p. 146. For a more detailed account, see Hamid Showkat, *Târikh-e Bist-Sâleh-ye Konfedrâsioun-e Mohasselin va Dâneshjouyân-e Irani, Ettehâdiyeh-ye Melli* (A Twenty-Year History of the Confederation of Iranian Students, National Union), 2 Vols. (n.p. [Germany]: Châpkhâneh-ye Mortazavi, 1994).

24 A typical method of expressing that opposition was through demonstrations during visits by high-ranking officials or members of the royal family. The news of such protests was also monitored and followed by people within the country. For an account of one such occasion, a visit to Oxford by the shah's sister, Ashraf, in spring 1976, see Parviz Radji, *In the Service of the Peacock Throne: Diaries of the Shah's Last Ambassador to London* (London, 1983), pp. 14–15. Radji also gives several indications of the shah's obsession with promoting the image of his regime in Western countries. See also the memoirs of Radji's counterpart, Sir Anthony Parsons, *The Pride and the Fall: Iran 1974–1979* (London, 1984), pp. 56–57, citing several student protests during a royal visit to Washington in the autumn of 1977 that led to "humiliating" consequences. The shah himself often regarded such demonstrators as paid agents of his enemies. See Mohammad Reza Pahlavi, *Answer to History* (New York: Stein & Day, 1980), pp. 20, 22.

25 Alam, *The Shah and I*, p. 359.

26 In 1976, a group of militant members of the CIS raided the offices of a special branch of SAVAK housed within the Iranian consulate in Geneva. They took away, and later published, a series of letters and documents regarding SAVAK's monitoring of the political activities of Iranian students in Europe. See Konfedrâsioun-e Dâneshjouyân-e Irani—Ettehâdiyeh-ye Melli (Confederation of Iranian Students—National Union, ed., *Pâreh-i az Asnâd-e SAVAK* (Some SAVAK Documents) (Europe [Frankfurt?], 1355/1976–1977; reprinted, Tehran, 1357/1978).

27 During the early 1960s (c. 1963–1964), the number of papers and peri-

odicals published in Iran was as follows: 23 daily newspapers, 113 weekly newspapers, 28 weekly journals, and 34 monthly journals. Tehran's contribution was: 22 daily newspapers, 50 weekly newspapers, 27 weekly journals, and 23 monthly journals. See *Iranshahr*, Vol. 2 (Tehran: Tehran University Press, 1343/1964), p. 1260. For the number of press in other cities, see *Iranshahr*, p. 1262. See further Echo of Iran, *Iran Almanac: 1966* (Tehran: Echo of Iran, 1967). For a brief account of the state of the Iranian press and periodicals in the 1960s, see Amin Banani, "The Role of the Mass Media," in Ehsan Yar-Shater, ed., *Iran Faces the Seventies*, foreword by John S. Badeau (New York: Praeger, 1971), pp. 321–340, note in particular pp. 330–339. For more information on the press and periodicals published in Iran prior to the 1979 revolution, see Shahin Esfandiâri, Ali Atrafi, Jalâl Mosâvât, and Bâqer Mo'meni, eds., *Matbou'ât-e Iran, Fehrest-e Tahlili-e Ketâb-khâneh-ye Majles-e Senâ* (Iranian Press: An Analytical Index of the Library of the Senate) (Tehran: Institute for Research and Planning in Science and Education, Iranian Documentation Centre, 1358/1979); Parvin Abu al-Ziâ', ed., *Râhnamâ-ye Rouznâmehâ-ye Iran* (A Guide to Iranian Newspapers) (Tehran: Institute for Research and Planning in Science and Education, Iranian Documentation Centre, n.d.); and Pouri Soltâni, ed., *A Directory of Iranian Periodicals* (21 March 1972–20 March 1973) (Tehran: Tehran Book Processing Centre, July 1973). For a more descriptive account of the Iranian press, see Mas'oud Barzin, *Matbou'ât-e Iran, 1343–53* (Iranian Press, 1964–74) (Tehran, 1354/1976).

28   Among other important periodicals were *Payâm-e Now*, later *Payâm-e Novin* (both meaning New Message); *Ketâb-e Hafteh (Keyhân-e Hafteh)* (Book of the Week, or Keyhân Weekly) and *Ketâb-e Mâh (Keyhân-e Mâh)* (Book of the Month, or Keyhân Monthly); and the influential *Jahân-e Now* (New World), coedited by Hosein Hejâzi and Amin Âlimard. For *Jahân-e Now* and an obituary of Hejâzi, see Iraj Afshâr, "Hosein Hejâzi," *Âyandeh*, Vol. 6, Nos. 7–8 (Mehr-Âbân 1359/October–November 1980), pp. 922–930.

29   The following are examples of such publications: *Ârash* (literally the Shining One, name of a legendary archer in ancient Iranian mythology) *Jagan* (a kind of rush, a marsh plant with a slender pithy stem used for making mats, baskets, etc.), and *Jong-e Torfeh* (New Journal) in Tehran; *Jong* in Isfahan; *Parcham* (Flag) in Ahwâz; *Mahd-e Âzâdi* (The Cradle of Freedom) and *Sahand* (a mountain peak in Azârbâyjân) in Tabriz; *Hirmand* and *Pârt* in Mashhad; *Âbnous* (Ebony) and *She'r va Qesseh* (Verse and Stories) in Shiraz; *Bazaar* in Rasht; *Honar va Adabiyât* (Art and Literature) in Abadan; and *Jong-e Falak al-Aflâk* (literally Empyrean Heaven, name of a medieval fort in Khorramâbâd, in western Iran, with the mystique of having been occasionally used for the detention of political prisoners) in Khorramâbâd. See Mohammad-Ali Sepânlou, *Nevisandegân-e Pishrow-e Iran: Az Mashrutiyat tâ 1350* (Progressive Writers of Iran: From the Constitutional Movement to 1971) (Tehran, 1362/1983), p. 85, n. 1. For an annotated introduction to this type of periodicals and irregular *jong*s, see Kâzem Sâdât-Eshkevari, *Negâhi beh Nashriyât-e Gahgâhi: Mo'arefi-ye Nashriyât-e*

Nâ-Monazzam-e Gheyr-e Dowlati-ye 1332 tâ 1357 ([Iranian] Periodicals in a Glance: An Introduction of Irregular and non-Governmental Periodicals from 1954 to 1978) (Tehran: Tirâzheh, 1370/1991 [issued 1374/1995]).

30   Persian translation of mostly literary works by foreign writers improved both in quality and volume during the 1950s and 1960s. These translations were, according to one observer, "mostly, although not exclusively, acquired by intellectuals." See Gavin Hambly, "Attitudes and Aspirations of the Contemporary Iranian Intellectual," *Royal Central Asian Journal*, Vol. 51, Part 3 (April, 1964), pp. 127–140, here p. 132. Accordingly a random list of authors whose works were translated and available to Persian readers would include: "Dante, Shakespeare, Goethe, Stendhal, Flaubert, Dumas, Hugo, Tolstoy, Turgenev, Gogol, Dostoievsky, Dickens, Oscar Wilde, Shaw, Ibsen, Chekhov, Gorki, Baudelaire, Thomas Mann, Somerset Maugham, André Gide, Jean-Paul Sartre, Albert Camus, André Maurois, Jack London, Ernest Hemingway, William Faulkner, John Steinbeck, Eugene O'Neil, Aldous Huxley, Bertrand Russell and Agatha Christie." Ibid., p. 132.

31   At the same time, the intellectuals generally disliked the increasingly popular tabloids. See, in particular, Jalâl Âl-Ahmad, *Seh Maqâleh-ye Digar* (Three More Essays), 3rd edition (Tehran: Ravâq, 1356/1977), pp. 19–20.

32   This was particularly true for topics that traditionally had been given less coverage in the academic curriculum, such as the political economy of development and underdevelopment; the politics of the modern Middle East, with special reference to the Arab-Israeli conflict; Marxist literary criticism; and contemporary literature of both the avant-garde and the more politically colored writers from Iran and abroad.

33   *Mehr* and *Yâdegâr* are discussed in the text. *Armaghân* was a monthly journal of literary, historical, and social issues, founded by Hasan Vahid Dastgerdi in Tehran in Bahman 1298/February 1919; it lasted until Esfand 1355/March 1977. For a review of the first twenty-two years of *Armaghân* and a biography of Vahid Dastgerdi, see *Jarâ'ed*, Vol. 1, pp. 121–136. *Bâgh-e Sâ'eb* was a monthly journal of literary studies, founded by Khalil Sâmâni in Tehran in 1959, with subscription free of charge. *Vahid* was a monthly (and biweekly) journal of literature, literary criticism, and social and historical studies founded by Seyfollâh Vahidniâ in Tehran in 1963. He also founded *Vahid (Haftegi)*, a weekly journal of literary and artistic topics edited by Ali-Akbar Kasmâ'i, and, in 1971 in Tehran, *Khâterât-e Vahid* (Memoirs of Vahid) a monthly journal of literary, social, and recent Iranian historical affairs. *Yaghmâ* was a monthly journal of literary, historical, social, and artistic topics (in Persian with occasional articles in Arabic), founded by Habib Yaghmâ'i in Tehran in 1948.

34   Abbas Eqbâl (b. 1314 A.H./1896–1897, d. Rome 1334/1955–1956), who in his youth was an apprentice carpenter, is a good example of upward mobility in the case of an exceptionally gifted and hard-working scholar. He taught, among other places, at Dâr al-Fonoun and the School of Political Science, be-

fore being appointed (in 1304/1925) as secretary to the Iranian military envoy to Paris. While in Paris, he met the literary scholar Mohammad Qazvini (d. 1368 A.H.) and studied at the Sorbonne. On his return to Iran, Eqbâl was appointed professor of history at Tehran University and was a member of the Iranian Academy of Language (Farhangestân-e Zabân-e Iran). He later became Iran's cultural attaché in Turkey and Italy. Eqbâl wrote several works on Iranian history, including a history of the Mongols and a comprehensive history of Iran from the Mongol invasion to the end of the Qajars. He also edited and published a number of important medieval texts. For reference to Eqbâl's impressively long list of publications, see Khânbâbâ Moshâr, ed., *Fehrest-e Ketâbhâ-ye Châppi-ye Fârsi* (An Index of Persian Books in Print), Vol. 2 (Tehran, n.d.), Name Index, pp. 24–25.

35   See Majid Movaqqar's opening note in the first issue of the journal after the interruption, entitled "Tajdid-e ʿAhd" (Renewal of the Pledge), *Mehr*, Vol. 8, No. 1 (Farvardin 1331/April 1952), pp. 1–7.

36   Ibid.

37   For instance, in a single issue (Vol. 8, No. 1), historical and literary articles by the scholars Mohammad Moʿin and Zabiollâh Safâ appear beside pieces on popular science such as "Instinct de reproduction," pp. 47–49, and "Alif-Ba-ye Atom" (The Alphabets of the Atom), pp. 50–52.

38   Majid Movaqqar, "Iran bar Lab-e Partgâh" (Iran on the Verge of a Precipice), *Mehr*, Vol. 8, No. 7 (Mehr 1331/October 1952), pp. 358–390, here p. 386.

39   For instance, Vol. 9, No. 3 (Tir 1332/July 1953), starts with a leading article by Movaqqar, "Darvishân-e Farangi yâ Marâm-e Taslih-e Akhlâq" (European Dervishes or the Doctrine of Moral Rearmament), pp. 97–100, and contains articles such as "Honarmandân-e Khord-Sâl" (Young Artists), by Khosrow Rezâ'i, pp. 106–109, and "'Elm-e Angosht-Negâri" (Science of Dactyloscopy), by Mir-Mohsen Mahdavi, pp. 110–112.

40   "*Sokhan*," like its English equivalent, "speech," has a wide range of meanings such as "language," "talk," "a word," and "discourse." The journal's subtitle was "*Majalleh-ye Adabiyât va Dânesh va Honar-e Emrouz*" (The Journal of Contemporary Literature, Learning, and Art).

41   Parviz Nâtel Khânlari (b. Tehran, 1292/1913, d. Tehran, 1 Shahrivar 1369/22 August 1990) received his doctorate in Persian literature from Tehran University, where he later became a professor. In addition to being a highly prolific scholar, he had an active administrative and public career, which included positions at the Pahlavi Foundation and membership in the Senate and the Ministry of Education (1341/1962 to 1343/1964) in the government of Asadollâh Alam. For a short biography of Khânlari, see Echo of Iran, *Iran Who's Who*, 2nd edition, (Tehran: Echo of Iran, 1974), p. 263. See also Yadollâh Jalâli Pandari, "Khâterât" (Memoirs), *Âyandeh*, Vol. 16, Nos. 5–8 (Mordâd–Âbân 1369/August–November 1990), pp. 427–448. A brief chronology of Khânlari's

life can be found in a posthumously published volume in his memory. See "Târikh-nâmeh-ye Khânlari" (Khânlari's Chronology), in [Parviz Nâtel Khânlari], *Qâfeleh-sâlâr-e Sokhan, Khânlari* (Khânlari, The Beacon of Language) (A Collection of Articles in the Memory of Parviz Nâtel Khânlari), n.n. (Tehran: Nashr-e Alborz, 1370/1991), pp. 11–13. Further biographical information by Khânlari's friends and associates together with excerpts from Khânlari's own memoirs can also be found here. Ibid., pp. 297 ff. and 439 ff. For a list of Khânlari's earlier works, see *Moshâr*, Vol. 2, pp. 168–170. For his articles published until 1350/1971, see Iraj Afshâr, ed., *Fehrest-re Maqâlât-e Farsi* (An Index of Persian Articles), 3 Vols.: Vol. 1 (1328 A.H./1910–1338/1959) (Tehran, 1348/1970); Vol. 2 (1339/1960–1345/1966), 2nd edition (Tehran, 2536 [1356]/1977); Vol. 3 (1346/1967–1350/1971) (Tehran, 2535 [1355]/1976).

42   André Malraux (1901–1976), a renowned French novelist and art historian, was distinguished for his early and politically committed novels such as *La Condition humaine* (Paris, 1933), *L'Espoir* (Paris, 1937), and *Les Voix du silence* (Paris, 1951). He fought against Fascism in the Spanish Civil War and the Second World War. In 1945 he actively supported General Charles de Gaulle (1890–1970) and when, in 1958, de Gaulle was elected president, Malraux served for ten years as France's minister of cultural affairs.

43   An editorial note at the beginning of the twelfth volume (1340/1961) reiterates the journal's policy and objectives:

For years now, the readers of Sokhan *have been familiar with this journal's line. Now that we begin its twelfth volume, there is no need to say too much about its method and style. Our work has always been: To introduce to the Persian-speaking reader the world's meritorious literature. To introduce and interpret the valuable works of national literature to such an extent that they can assist us to improve our standards; we therefore view such works through contemporary eyes. To publish outstanding samples of contemporary Persian literature whether poetry or prose. To try to preserve the rules of the eloquent Persian and at the same time keep the language alive for the expression of contemporary social needs. To introduce various branches of the arts, such as music, painting, and sculpture, to our readers and keep them informed about the progress of science and technology. So far we have met with some success. But there are still miles in between what we have achieved and what we had wished initially. But since we have not yet abandoned our efforts, there is no room for pessimism. From now on we shall try to bring* Sokhan *closer to our initial dream. Our only support in this effort is the encouragement of our perceptive readers. In fact* Sokhan's *rate of circulation does not match its expenses, but given the number of the country's literates and also noting that this journal is useful only to a few, we are therefore quite content with the present level of publication; also bearing in mind that these types of journals in bigger countries with a greater number of literates, do not have a large circulation and demand either.*

We wish to be able to continue publishing Sokhan, *and that the spiritual bond between the writers of this journal and its readers does not break. (Parviz Nâtel Khânlari, [Editorial Note],* Sokhan, *Vol. 12, No. 1 [Ordibehesht 1340/May 1961], pp. 1–2)*

44 A brief reference to some of the material that appeared in the journal during the 1950s, 1960s, and 1970s best indicates its range and quality.
Vol. 9 (1337/1958)

No. 1, Farvardin 1337/April 1958: Shâpour Râsekh (sociologist), an article on the phenomenology of Edmund Husserl (pp. 25–30); Seyyed Mohammad-Ali Jamâlzâdeh (a pioneer of modern Persian prose, residing in Geneva), an article on the state of Iranian students in Europe (pp. 31–47); and a brief correspondence, from London, from Hamid Enayat (a political scientist), noting the state of the arts in London and commenting on D. P. Costello's translation of Hedayat's *The Blind Owl* and Wilfrid Blunt's *A Persian Spring* (pp. 75–77).

No. 2, Ordibehesht 1337/May 1958: Khânlari, on Persian poetics (pp. 97–101); Pazhouhandeh (pseudonym), part of a series on the history of European painting (pp. 111–114); Javâd Imami's translation of a short story by Albert Camus (pp. 115–128); and the first part of an article by Amir-Hosein Jahân-baglou (an economist) on Keynesian economics (pp. 162–167).

No. 3, Khordâd 1337/June 1958: "Sangar va Qomqomeh-hâ-ye Khâli" (The Trench and Empty Flasks), a short story by Bahrâm Sâdeqi (pp. 237–247).

No. 4, Tir 1337/July 1958: Abd al-Hosein Zarrinkoub (a literary scholar), a note on Ta'ziyeh (Shi'i passion play) (pp. 310–314).

No. 5, Mordâd 1337/August 1958: Hamid Enayat, a note on the question of language in India (pp. 465–468).
Vol. 12 (1340/1961)

No. 1, Ordibehesht 1340/May 1961: Khosrow Khosravi (a rural sociologist), first part of an article on the demography and morphology of Tehran (pp. 34–40).

No. 2, Khordâd 1340/June 1961: Amir-Hosein Âryân-pour (translator and sociologist), first part of an article widely read among the left on the origins and social functions of the arts (pp. 182–191).

No. 6, Mehr 1340/October 1961: Esmâ'il Dowlatshâhi's translation of an article on the criticism of poetry by T. S. Eliot (pp. 673–677).
Vol. 14 (1342/1963)

No. 1, Tir 1342/July 1963: Sâdeq Chubak, part of his famous fiction *Tangsir* (pp. 86–92); and reports on a series of lectures delivered at Tehran's Teachers Training College by, for example, Khânlari ("A Dialogue with the Youth," pp. 93–96), Abdollâh Entezâm ("Moderation in Thinking," pp. 104–105), Seyyed Fakhr al-Din Shâdmân ("Cultural Independence of Iran," p. 105), and Manouchehr Bozorgmehr ("The Origins and Goals of Education," pp. 105–107).

No. 2, Mordâd 1342/August 1963: Part of the introduction of Hume's *Enquiry concerning Human Understanding*, translated by Manouchehr Bozorgmehr (pp. 202–207).

Vol. 15 (1343/1964)

No. 1, Âbân 1343/November 1964: Homâ Nowshirvâni's translation of an article on contemporary Indian painting, sculpture, and architecture (pp. 11–18).

No. 7, Tir 1344/July 1965: Fereydoun Âdamiyat's article on the development of parliamentary practices in the First Majles (pp. 702–709); and two poems by Mohammad-Reza Shafi'i Kadkani (Sereshk).

A few samples of works by contemporary poets from Africa, Israel, Brazil, and China are also printed in Persian translation in different issues of the same year.

Vol. 17 (1346/1967)

No. 1, Farvardin 1346/April 1967: Âdamiyat's article on the crisis of historiography in Iran (pp. 18–30).

Parts of joint research by Shâpour Râsekh and Jamshid Behnâm (sociologists) on the sociology of leisure time in Iran are also published in different issues of the same year.

Vol. 18 (1347/1968)

No. 3, Mordâd 1347/August 1968: The introduction of Herbert Marcuse's *One Dimensional Man*, translated by Ahmad Tâheri (pp. 281–287).

No. 5, Mehr 1347/October 1968: A short story by Reza Navvâbpour, "Sag Gorg" (Dog Wolf), (pp. 511–513).

No. 5, Âbân 1347/November 1968: A poem by Mehdi Akhavân Sâles (M. Omid), "Sa'âdat? Âh . . ." (Happiness? Ah . . .) (pp. 605–614); and an article by Gore Vidal on the modern novel, translated by Mostafâ Qarib (pp. 638–646).

No. 7, Âzar 1347/December 1968: An article by Khânlari on the equality of the rights of men and women, praising a recent government bill on this subject given to the Majles for ratification "Vazifeh-ye Melli" (National Duty) (pp. 693–696).

Nos. 8–9, Dey–Bahman 1347/January–February 1969: A few writings from Sâdeq Hedâyat on the Persian language (pp. 815–825).

Vol. 19 (1348/1969)

No. 4, Shahrivar 1348/September 1969: "The Three-Dimensional Young Generation," by Ehsân Narâqi (sociologist), originally published in UNESCO's *Le Courrier*, translated by Bâqer Parhâm (pp. 422–432).

Vol. 20 (1349/1970)

Nos. 9–10, Esfand 1349/March 1971: A note by Khânlari on the debate between the old and new poetry (pp. 845–850); and "What Is Socialism?" an article by Leszek Kolakowski written originally in 1956 and critical of totalitarianism, translated by Zahrâ Kiâ (pp. 861–864).

Vol. 23 (1353/1974)

No. 8, Tir 1353/July 1974: An article assessing university education by Mahmoud Sanâ'i (psychologist) (pp. 819–831).

No. 10, Shahrivar 1353/September 1974: An article by Khânlari urging translation of the works of the Orientalists (pp. 1067–1070).

Vol. 25 (2535 [1355] /1976)

No. 2, Tir 2535 [1355]/July 1976: An article on existential phenomenology by Jamshid Mirfendereski (pp. 133–143).

45 On *Sokhan* and some of its contributors, see further Mahmoud Kiânoush, "Khânlari: 'In-hâ Ki-and?'" (Khânlari: "Who Are These People?"), *Fasl-e Ketâb*, Vol. 3, No. 2 (Serial No. 8) (London, Summer 1370/1991), pp. 114–118; and Parviz Shahriâri, "Nashriyeh-ye 'Elmi-ye Sokhan" (The Scientific Journal Sokhan), in [Nâtel Khânlari], *Qâfeleh-sâlâr-e Sokhan, Khânlari*, pp. 357–362. It is worth noting that in 1337/1958, Khânlari also began a publishing venture, called Enteshârât-e Sokhan (The Sokhan Press). Although the press lasted only three years, it succeeded in publishing some thirty-six titles in Persian as well as world literature, Western philosophy, Qajar history, and children's books. These included Khânlari's *Darbâreh-ye Zabân-e Fârsi* (On Persian Language), as well as his own critical new editions of the *Divân* of Hâfez and Gorgâni's *Samak-e 'Ayyâr*, Âdamiyat's *Fekr-e Âzâdi*, a Persian translation of Bertrand Russell's *A History of Western Philosophy* by Najaf Daryâbandari, and translations of selected poems of Robert Frost by Fatollâh Mojtabâ'i and of Walt Whitman by Sirous Parhâm, as well as translations of Herman Hesse's *Siddharta* by Fereydoun Gorgâni, Irving Stone's *The Agony and the Ecstasy* by Mohammad-Ali Eslâmi-Nadoushan, Pierre La Mure's *Moulin Rouge* by Houshang Pir-Nazar, Jean-Paul Sartre's *Morts sans sépulture* by Sadiq Âzar, Fyodor Dostoyevski's *Netochka Nezvanova* by Mohammad Qâzi, and Anne Morrow Lindbergh's *Gift from the Sea* by Habibeh Foyuzât, among others. For a brief account of the Sokhan Press, see Esmâ'il Sâremi, "Kârnâmeh-ye Enteshârât-e Sokhan" (The Sokhan Press and Its Records), in [Nâtel Khânlari], *Qâfeleh-sâlâr-e Sokhan, Khânlari*, pp. 363–368.

46 During the 1940s, Vosouqi (b. 1922) had been a member of the Tudeh Party and a contributor to the party organ *Mardom* (People). Later, he joined Khalil Maleki's splinter group and contributed to the latter's journal, *'Elm va Zendegi* (Science and Life). Vosouqi graduated from the Faculty of Law at Tehran University and later received his doctorate in law from Paris. He subsequently held various positions in the Ministry of Justice. On Vosouqi, see Echo of Iran, *Iran Who's Who*, p. 578. For his contributions to *Mardom*, see, for example, Nâser Vosouqi, "Karl Marx va Marxizm" (Karl Marx and Marxism), on Marx's biography, ideas, and influence, *Mardom*, Vol. 1, No. 3 (Âzar 1325/December 1946), pp. 48–59. For his contributions to *'Elm va Zendegi* see, for example, Nâser Vosouqi, "Târikh-e Tahavvolât-e Nehzat-e Beynalmelali-e Kârgarân: Kominform bejâ-ye Anternâsiunâl" (History of the Development of the International Labor Movement: The Cominform instead of the International), *'Elm va Zendegi*, Vol. 1, No. 2 (Bahman 1330/February 1952), pp. 151–161; "Pâyeh-

hâ-ye Nehzat-e Konouni-e Mardom-e Chin va Âyandeh-ye Ân" ([Social] Bases of the Present Movement of the Chinese People and Its Future), *'Elm va Zendegi*, Vol. 1, No. 6 (Khordâd 1331/June 1952), pp. 484–493; and "Tarh-e Mârshâl" (The Marshall Plan), a series of articles on the condition of Europe after World War II and the United States' foreign policy toward the European countries, *'Elm va Zendegi*, Vol. 1, No. 7 (Shahrivar 1331/September 1952), pp. 638–646, and No. 8 (Mehr 1331/October 1952), pp. 689–700, and No. 9 (Bahman 1331/February 1953), pp. 779–784, and No. 10 (Esfand 1331/March 1953), pp. 932–941.

47 See, for example, Nâser Vosouqi, "Naqdi az Hameh Chiz" (A Critique of Everything), *Andisheh va Honar*, Vol. 4, No. 3 (Âbân 1340/November 1961), pp. 189–192; this article is a foreword to the issue, see in particular p. 190.

48 The term "Western Marxism" is synonymous with "humanist Marxism"; both refer to an approach that gives special importance to human consciousness and the role of subjectivity, as can be noted in the ideas of such authors as Georg Lukács and Karl Korsch, or even in Marx's own early writings. This emphasis contrasts with a more Leninist, and later Stalinist, approach where human agency was interpreted in deterministic terms of the relations of production and class struggle. The term was first used by the French author Maurice Merleau-Ponty in his book *Adventures of the Dialectic*, English translation by Joseph Bien (London, 1974), pp. 30–58, originally published as *Les Aventures de la dialectique* (Paris: Gallimard, 1955), and was later followed by other works such as Perry Anderson's *Considerations on Western Marxism* (London, 1976). For further discussion, see Martin Jay, *Marxism and Totality: The Adventures of a Concept from Lukács to Habermas* (Berkeley: University of California Press, 1984), especially "Introduction: The Topography of Western Marxism," pp. 1–20.

49 Arthur Koestler (1905–1983) was a Hungarian-born British novelist, journalist, and critic whose writings often reflected the political and ideological issues confronting his generation. He was formerly a Communist but later became widely known for his novel *Darkness at Noon* (London, 1940), in which he dramatically portrayed Stalin's purges and show trials in Moscow in the 1930s.

50 Isaac Deutscher (1907–1967) was a Polish-born British historian who specialized in the Soviet Union. He was highly critical of Stalin but had sympathy with Leon Trotsky (1879–1940), a leader of the Russian Revolution and one of Stalin's chief rivals for power. Deutscher's writings included *Stalin: A Political Biography* (New York, 1949; revised edition, Harmondsworth, 1966) and a three-volume biography of Trotsky that appeared as *The Prophet Armed: Trotsky 1879–1921* (London, 1954), *The Prophet Unarmed: Trotsky 1921–1929* (London, 1959), and *The Prophet Outcast: Trotsky 1929–1940* (London, 1963).

51 Examples of these topics include: a series of five lectures by the British Labour politician and socialist writer John Strachey (1901–1963) on world politics and its prospects between 1955 and 1965, given in 1961 in Singapore and published as *The Great Awakening: From Imperialism to Freedom* (London, 1961).

The Persian translation, "Houshiâri-e Zharf," which began to appear in *Andisheh va Honar* in Vol. 4, No. 5 (Shahrivar 1341/September 1962), was later published by the journal as a special issue. It may be noted that in his early years John Strachey broke with his family's pro-Conservative tradition and, in 1923, while studying at Oxford, he joined the radical Independent Labour Party and subsequently became the editor of its periodical, *The Socialist Review*. In the 1930s he tilted more toward Communism, but after the Second World War he returned to the Labour Party, and in 1946 he became minister of food and introduced a series of austerity measures, including the rationing of bread. In 1950–1951 he became the minister of war and subsequently served as the Labour spokesman in Parliament for defense and Commonwealth matters. In his moderately leftist later publications, such as *Contemporary Capitalism* (London, 1956), *The End of Empire* (London, 1959), and *On the Prevention of War* (London, 1962), Strachey addressed the issue of dealing with tensions between the Soviet Union and the West. Further topics in *Andisheh va Honar* included: "Peydâyesh-e Yek Tabaqeh: Enqelâb-e Pey dar Pey va Tabaqeh-ye Totâliter" (Emergence of a Class: Permanent Revolution and the Totalitarian Class), by K. Papa Ioannou, Vol. 5, No. 9 (Mehr 1345/October 1966), pp. 1288–1294; and "Zanbaq-e Gandideh," a translation of the epilogue of Arthur Koestler's *The Lotus and the Robot* (London, 1969, pp. 276–285), Vol. 5, No. 9 (Mehr 1345/October 1966), pp. 1275–1285. Following the sixtieth anniversary of the Bolshevik Revolution, the journal published a separate volume that contained a translation of Isaac Deutscher's *The Unfinished Revolution: Russia 1917–1967* (New York, 1967).

52   For example, the journal proposed (in Vol. 4, No. 3 [Âbân 1340/November 1961], p. 193) a discussion on the topic "Contemporary Persian Poetry." The first contribution was made by the linguist Shams al-Din Tondar Kiâ; the first part appeared in the same issue, pp. 194–220, and the second part in Vol. 4, No. 1 (Ordibehesht 1341/May 1962), pp. 247–280. An extensive interview with another linguist, Mohammad Moqaddam, together with two of his articles on the Persian language, appeared in Vol. 5, No. 9 (Mehr 1345/October 1966). Both Tondar Kiâ and Moqaddam (who often signed as "Moghdam") were known for their extreme views on purifying Persian of Arabic words.

53   This distinction is difficult to demonstrate in English transliteration. One example would be the omission of the letter *wâv* prior to *alif* in transcribing certain verbs, for instance, using *khâhim* instead of *khwâhim* (meaning "we shall"), or *khâstan* instead of *khwâstan* (meaning "to want"). In the latter case, the word appears similar to another word, *khâstan* (meaning "to rise").

54   *Toyoul*, assignment of land, was a kind of fief.

55   Quoted from Nâser Vosouqi's editorial note to *Andisheh va Honar*, Vol. 5, No. 9 (Mehr 1345/October 1965).

56   Excerpted from Nâser Vosouqi, "Naqdi az Hameh Chiz" (A Critique of Everything), *Andisheh va Honar*, Vol. 4, No. 3 (Âbân 1340/November 1961), pp. 189–192.

57 For further information on *Andisheh va Honar*, see Sâdât-Eshkevari, *Negâhi beh Nashriyât-e Gahgâhi*, pp. 62–106. It is also interesting to note that even such left-oriented journals as *Andisheh va Honar* and *Jahân-e Now* were often viewed by the more radical activists as a kind of intellectual safety valve that the regime had permitted "as a result of its fear from the communist forces." Masʿoud Ahmad-Zâdeh, *Mobârezeh-ye Mosallahâneh: Ham Estrâtezhi ham Tâktik* (Armed Struggle: Both a Strategy and a Tactic) (n.p., n.d.), p. 34.

58 See *Jarâ'ed*, Vol. 3, pp. 184–186.

59 For a biographical sketch of Shâdmân, see *Moshâr*, Vol. 5, pp. 787–788 (originally taken from *Râhnamâ-ye Ketâb*, Vol. 5, pp. 96–100). Further information can be found in the following obituaries: *Keyhân*, 7 Shahrivar 1346/29 August 1967; Manouchehr Khodâyâr Mohebbi, "Doktor Seyyed Fakhr al-Din Shâdmân: Zendegi va Âsâr-e Ou" (Dr. Seyyed Fakhr al-Din Shâdmân: His Life and Works) *Vahid*, Vol. 4 (1346/1967), pp. 873–875; Iraj Afshâr, "Vafât-e Doktor Seyyed Fakhr al-Din Shâdmân" (The Departure of Dr. Seyyed Fakhr al-Din Shâdmân), *Râhnamâ-ye Ketâb*, Vol. 10 (1346/1967), pp. 435–438; also in Iraj Afshâr, *Savâd va Bayâz* (Black and White), Vol. 2 (Tehran, 1349/1970), included in "Vafiât-e Mo'allefin" (Obituaries of Authors), pp. 513–617; and Habib Yaghmâ'i, "Doktor Seyyed Fakhr al-Din Shâdmân," *Yaghmâ*, Vol. 20 (1346/1967), pp. 279–280.

60 Seyyed Fakhr al-Din Shâdmân, *Taskhir-e Tamaddon-e Farangi* (The Capturing of Western Civilization) (Tehran, Winter 1326/1948), 120 pp. All the following references are to this edition. Shâdmân's other works include: *Ketâb-e Bi-Nâm* (Anonymous Book), written in memory of his late friend Hasan Alavi, 1st edition (Tehran, 1307/1928), 136 pp., 2nd edition (Tehran, 1335/1956), 107 pp.; *Dar Râh-e Hend* (On the Road to India), 1st edition (Tehran, 1312/1933), 40 pp., 2nd edition (Tehran, 1335/1956), 83 pp.; and *Shayyâdihâ-ye Yahoud* (Jewish Deceits) (Tehran, n.d.). Among Shâdmân's numerous articles and contributions to literary journals are: "Sefârat-e Mohammad-Reza Beyg" (The Embassy of Mohammad-Reza Beyg), *Mehr*, Vol. 1, No. 4 (Shahrivar 1312/September 1933), pp. 288–297; "Dâneshgâh-e Qom va Dâneshgâh-hâ-ye digar-e Iran" (The University at Qom and Other Iranian Universities), *Mehr*, Vol. 8, No. 9 (Âzar 1331/December 1952), pp. 523–532, Vol. 8, No. 10 (Dey 1331/January 1953), pp. 578–583; "Safiri keh Safir Naboud: Yek Safheh az Târikh-e Ravâbet-e Iran va Engelis" (An Ambassador Who Was Not an Ambassador: A Page from the [Diplomatic] Relations of Iran and Britain), *Ettelâ'ât-e Mâhâneh* (Ettelâ'ât Monthly), Vol. 1, No. 1 (Farvardin 1327/March–April 1948), pp. 18–19; *Târikh va Rowshanâ'i* (History and the Enlightenment) (Tehran: Majles, 1329/1950, reprinted, Tehran, 1344/1965); *Terâzhedi-ye Farang* (The Tragedy of the West) (Tehran: Tahouri, 1346/1967); "Shenâkht-e Melal" (On Peoples and Nations), *Yaghmâ*, Vol. 21, No. 3 (Khordâd 1347/June 1968), pp. 118–124; and S. F. Shadman, "Review of Anglo-Persian Relations, 1798–1815," *Proceedings of the Iran Society*, Vol. 2, Parts 5–6 (London: The Iran Society, 1943), pp. 23–39.

61 Shâdmân, *Taskhir-e Tamaddon-e Farangi*, p. 4.

62 Ibid., p. 4.

63 Ibid., p. 7.

64 Ibid., p. 7.

65 Ibid., p. 8.

66 Ibid., p. 8. In other places (e.g., pp. 10, 12, 75, 78, and 79), the author refers to *âshoftegi-e fekr* (mental confusion), which can be interpreted in terms of a lack of objective, orderly, and systematic knowledge about the self, society, and culture. Later critics have recognized this same state as a major problem of modern Iranian society. Compare with, for example, Fereydoun Âdamiyat, *Âshoftegi dar Fekr-e Târikhi* (Confusion in Historical Thinking) (Tehran, 1360/1981).

67 Shâdmân, *Taskhir-e Tammadon-e Farangi*, p. 9.

68 Ibid., p. 11.

69 Ibid., p. 11.

70 Ibid., p. 12.

71 *Fokol* is the Persian pronunciation of a French term, *faux col*, for the usually detachable collar or necktie. It includes both the ordinary tie (French *cravate*, established in current Persian as *krâvât*) and bow tie (French *papillon*, adopted in modern Persian as *pâpioun*). In a somewhat pejorative usage, *fokoli* delineates men who, mainly since the Reza Shah period, have adopted European dress. Shâdmân uses the term exclusively to refer to pseudomodernists who are more infatuated with appearances than with the substantive underpinnings of modern European civilization. See also Mohammad-Ali Foroughi (Zakâ' al-Molk), "Hoqouq dar Iran" (Law in Iran), reprinted in *Iranshenasi*, Vol. 2, No. 3 (Fall 1369/1990), pp. 619–634, here p. 621.

72 Shâdmân, *Taskhir-e Tamaddon-e Farangi*, p. 13.

73 Ibid., p. 13.

74 Ibid., p. 17.

75 Hosein-Qoli Âqâ was one of the group of five students who were sent by the order of Mohammad Shah to Paris in 1845 to study military subjects, mining, and medicine. See Hosein Mahboubi Ardakâni, "Dovvomin Kârvân-e Ma'refat" (The Second Caravan of Knowledge), *Yaghmâ*, Vol. 18 (1344/1965), pp. 592–598, here p. 592. He was apparently "the first of a series of European-trained students who expressed strong anti-Islamic feelings and who believed that a new Persian society should be constructed on pre-Islamic cultural foundations." See Le Comte de Gobineau's *Les Religions et les philosophies dans l'Asie Centrale*, cited in Farman Farmayan, "The Forces of Modernization in Nineteenth Century Iran," pp. 119–151, here pp. 125–126; also Mahboubi Ardakâni, "Dovvomin Kârvan-e Ma'refat," pp. 596–597.

76 See Afshâr Begeshlu Qazvini's *Parvaz-e Negâresh-e Pârsi*, referred to in Chapter Two.

77   Shâdmân, *Taskhir-e Tamaddon-e Farangi*, pp. 19–20. See Nasrollâh Khân Fadâ'i Isfahani (Dowlat-yâr Jang), *Dâstân-e Torktâzân-e Hend* (The Story of Indian Ramblers), 5 Vols. (Bombay, 1310 A.H./1867).

78   Shâdmân, *Taskhir-e Tamaddon-e Farangi*, p. 21.

79   Ibid., p. 21.

80   Ibid., p. 26.

81   *Farang*, originally the term for ethnic Franks, has long been used in Iran, not only with reference to the French people, but also to delineate Western Europeans or, more generally, to cover all white, developed, and Christian countries. In F. Steingass, *Persian-English Dictionary* (1st edition [London, 1892]; 6th impression [London: Routledge & Kegan Paul, 1977]), *farang* is identified as "A Frank, an Italian, European; a Christian; all nations which wear short garments"; *farangestân* as "Italy, France, or the country of the Franks; Europe"; and *farangi* as "French; Italian; [an] European Christian." The expression *farangi* in reference to northern and western Europeans (and not only the French) was not limited to Iran but was also used in the whole of the Islamic world and even among the Greeks. For a historical review of *farang*, see Bernard Lewis, *Ifrandj*, in *EI2*; and Bernard Lewis, *Islam and the West* (New York: Oxford University Press, 1993), pp. 12–13. For an earlier text, written in the fourteenth century, see Rashid al-Din Fadl Allâh, *Kitâb Târikh-i Ifrandj* (*Histoire universelle de Rashid al-Din, histoire des Frances*), edited with French translation by K. Jahn (Leiden, 1951). A discussion of this work and further references can be found in David Morgan, "Persian Perceptions of Mongols and Europeans," in Stuart B. Schwartz, ed., *Implicit Understandings: Observing, Reporting, and Reflecting on the Encounters between Europeans and Other Peoples in the Early Modern Era* (Cambridge: Cambridge University Press, 1994), pp. 201–217, see in particular pp. 210–216. For a study of the representation of the West in modern Persian prose, see M. R. Ghanoonparvar, *In a Persian Mirror: Images of the West and Westerners in Iranian Fiction* (Austin: University of Texas Press, 1993).

82   Shâdmân, *Taskhir-e Tamaddon-e Farangi*, p. 28.

83   Ibid., pp. 23–24.

84   Ibid., p. 30.

85   Ibid., p. 30.

86   Ibid., p. 35.

87   Ibid., p. 56.

88   Ibid., p. 56.

89   Ibid., p. 109.

90   Ibid., pp. 109–110.

91   See, for example, Shâdmân's essay on theological colleges: "Dâneshgâh-e Qom va Dâneshgâh-hâ-ye digar-e Iran" (The University at Qom and Other Iranian Universities), *Mehr*, Vol. 8, No. 9 (Âzar 1331/December 1952), pp. 523–532; Vol. 8, No. 10 (Dey 1331/January 1953), pp. 578–583.

92   See, for example, Shâdmân, *Taskhir-e Tamaddon-e Farangi*, p. 114.

93   The author regards Mohammad-Ali Foroughi (Zakâ' al-Molk) as a model for those who intend to introduce Western civilization to Iran. He points out that Foroughi was well grounded in Persian history and literature, and his later exposures to European culture and civilization were systematic and measured. Shâdmân singled out Foroughi in view of the latter's prolific literary activities, including editing and publishing works by Ibn Sinâ, Saʿdi, and Umar Khayyâm; translating from Plato; compiling a two-volume book on rhetorics and speech; and writing the three-volume *Seyr-e Hekmat dar Oroupâ* (A History of Western Philosophy). The latter work was written in a well-structured and lucid Persian and, since its first publication in 1310–1320/1931–1941, has remained one of the main and widely read sources on the subject.

94   For further criticism of Shâdmân and of the discourse on *gharbzadegi* (pseudo-Westernism), discussed below, see, for example, Mehrzad Boroujerdi, "Gharbzadegi va Sharq-Shenâsi-ye Vârouneh" (Westoxication and Orientalism in Reverse), *Iran Nameh*, Vol. 8, No. 3 (Summer 1369/1990), pp. 375–390, note in particular pp. 381–385. See further Mehrzad Boroujerdi, *Iranian Intellectuals and the West: The Tormented Triumph of Nativism* (Syracuse, N.Y.: Syracuse University Press, 1996), pp. 52–62.

95   See, for example, Jalâl Âl-Ahmad, "Masalan Sharh-e Ahvâlât" (My So-Called Autobiography), in Jalâl Âl-Ahmad, *Yek Châh va Du Châleh* (One Well and Two Pits) (Tehran, 1343/1964); reprinted in Hamid Tabrizi, ed., *Jalâl Âl-Ahmad, Mardi dar Kash-â-kash-e Târikh-e Moʿâser* (Jalâl Âl-Ahmad: A Man Confronting Contemporary History) (Tabriz, 1357/1978), pp. 62–68; for an English translation of this piece, see Michael C. Hillmann, ed., *Iranian Society: An Anthology of Writings by Jalal Al-e Ahmad* (Lexington, Ky., 1982).

96   Later, Âl-Ahmad held that the journal was censored because it incorporated sections from *Gharbzadegi*. See Jalâl Âl-Ahmad, *Gharbzadegi* (n.p., n.d.), p. 3; 2nd revised edition (Tehran: Ravâq, Winter 1356/1977–1978).

97   It was not until the eve of the revolution of 1979 that the text appeared in a formal, published form. See Jalâl Âl-Ahmad, *Gharbzadegi*, 2nd revised edition (Tehran: Ravâq, Winter 1356/1977–1978). For more information on this work, see Robert Wells, "Jalâl Âl-Ahmad: Writer and Political Activist" (Ph.D. thesis, Faculty of Arts, University of Edinburgh, 1982), Chap. 2.

98   In colloquial Persian, "machine" (pronounced *mâshin*) is widely used for various kinds of mechanical and industrial apparatus, including the motor vehicle. The latter is also referred to as *otomobil* (automobile). By using the term *mâshin*, Âl-Ahmad intended to imply the general notion of industry.

99   See Herbert Marcuse, *One Dimensional Man* (London, 1964 and 1968). A forerunner of Marcuse was Edmund Husserl, whose philosophical teachings and criticism of modern science had a direct impact on both Martin Heidegger and Marcuse. See Edmund Husserl, *The Crisis of European Sciences and Transcendental Phenomenology: An Introduction to Phenomenological Philosophy*, English

translation with an introduction by David Carr (Evanston, Ill.: Northwestern University Press, 1970). See further Enzo Paci, *The Function of the Sciences and the Meaning of Man*, English translation with an introduction by Paul Piccone and James E. Hansen (Evanston, Ill.: Northwestern University Press, 1972).

100   See, respectively, Jalal Al-e Ahmad, *Plagued by the West (Gharbzadegi)*, translated by Paul Sprachman, Modern Persian Literature Series, No. 4 (Delmar, N.Y.: Caravan Books, 1982); Jalal Al-e Ahmad, *Gharbzadegi (Weststruckness)*, translated by John Green and Ahmad Alizadeh (Lexington, Ky.: Mazda, 1982 (the term "Weststruckness" as the most literal, but least appealing, equivalent for *gharbzadegi* was suggested earlier by Michael C. Hillman in his introduction to the English translation of Jalal Al-e Ahmad, *The School Principal*, translated by John K. Newton [Minneapolis and Chicago: Bibliotheca Islamica, 1974]); Brad Hanson, "The 'Westoxication' of Iran: Depictions and Reactions of Behrangi, Al-e Ahmad, and Shari'ati," *IJMES*, Vol. 15 (1983), pp. 1–23; Hamid Enayat, "The State of Social Sciences in Iran," *Middle East Studies Association Bulletin*, Vol. 8, No. 3 (1974), pp. 1–12 (see also Jalal Al-i Ahmad, *Occidentosis: A Plague from the West*, translated by R. Campbell, annotations and introduction by Hamid Algar [Berkeley: Mizan Press, 1984]); Abdol-Ali Dastghayb, "Jalal Al-e Ahmad: His Absence Has Been a Great Loss," originally published in *Ferdowsi*, Vol. 24, No. 1079 (Shahrivar 1351/September 1972), p. 17, English translation by B. Kamgar and Thomas M. Ricks, in Thomas M. Ricks, ed., *Critical Perspectives on Modern Persian Literature* (Washington, D.C.: Three Continents Press, 1984), pp. 343–345; and Roy Mottahedeh, *The Mantle of the Prophet: Learning and Power in Modern Iran* (London: Chatto & Windus, 1986), p. 296. It may also be rendered as "contracting" the West, following Vicente L. Rafael, *Contracting Colonialism: Translation and Christian Conversion in Tagalog Society under Early Spanish Rule* (Ithaca, N.Y.: Cornell University Press, 1988); 2nd edition (Durham, N.C.: Duke University Press, 1993).

101   Ahmad Fardid was interviewed at his home by this author in 1981. At that time, Fardid also argued that the Greek *dysis* and the Persian *doush* (or *dosh* in Old Iranian as well as in Pahlavi), meaning yesternight, share the same origin. As a more linguistically precise Persian equivalent for his *dysiplexia*, he also suggested *"doushingâh-zadeh-[gi]"* (Ali Gheissari, unpublished interview with Ahmad Fardid, in Persian, Tehran, 7 Mehr 1360/29 September 1981). In the 1960s and 1970s, many of the chic among the intelligentsia, especially those with middle-class or upper-middle-class backgrounds, looked upon Fardid as a guru and were both fascinated and repelled by his flights of German metaphysics. Hence the passing infatuation with Heidegger among a section of Iranian intellectuals who often gave an impression as if they were serving caviar to the masses. For a rare occasion in which Fardid, though very briefly, appears on record, see Ahmad Fardid, "Chand Porsesh dar Bâb-e Farhang-e Sharq" ([Answer to] Some Questions Concerning the Oriental Culture), transcribed by Reza Dâvari, *Farhang va Zendegi* (Culture and Life), No. 7, Special Issue on Ori-

ental Culture (Tehran, Dey 1350/January 1972), pp. 32–39. For further discussion on Fardid and Âl-Ahmad, see Mehrzad Boroujerdi, "*Gharbzadegi*: The Dominant Intellectual Discourse of Pre- and Post-Revolutionary Iran," in Samih K. Farsoun and Mehrdad Mashayekhi, eds., *Iran: Political Culture in the Islamic Republic* (London and New York, 1992), pp. 30–56; and Boroujerdi, *Iranian Intellectuals and the West*, pp. 63–65 and 65–76, respectively.

102   The themes of cultural alienation and urban anomie were among the major sociological topics of the 1960s, and many Third World writers and intellectuals began to explore such topics in their writings, both academic and creative.

103   Jalâl Âl-Ahmad, *Khasi dar Miqât* (Tehran, 1345/1966). For an English translation of this work, see Jalâl Âl-e Ahmad, *Lost in the Crowd*, a translation of Jalâl Âl-Ahmad, *Khasi dar Miqât* by John Green and Ahmad Alizadeh et al., with an introduction by Michael C. Hillmann (Washington, D.C.: Three Continents Press, 1985).

104   The title may also be translated as "On the Vices and Virtues of Intellectuals." However, a more literal translation would be: "On the Service and Treachery of the Intellectuals." See Jalâl Âl-Ahmad, *Dar Khedmat va Khiânat-e Rowshanfekrân*, 3rd edition (complete text) (Tehran: Ravâq, n.d. [1356/1977]). This is a collection of studies written between Bahman 1343/February 1965 and Shahrivar 1348/September 1969 and published in book form posthumously. Subsequent references are to this edition. The title is reminiscent of Julien Benda's *La Trahison des clercs* (The Treason of the Intellectuals) (Paris, 1927).

105   Âl-Ahmad, *Dar Khedmat va Khiânat-e Rowshanfekrân*, p. 13.

106   *Kalâm* (literally meaning a word, speech, as well as discourse and conversation) can ordinarily be regarded as similar to the Latin *dictum* (a formal expression of opinion). In a modern context, however, it should be differentiated from *kalâm* in the scholastic sense of Islamic theology.

107   Âl-Ahmad, *Dar Khedmat va Khiânat-e Rowshanfekrân*, p. 21.

108   Ibid., p. 19.

109   Here Âl-Ahmad refers to the fact that the Iranian Constitution of 1906 was in part taken from French and Belgian sources.

110   Âl-Ahmad, *Dar Khedmat va Khiânat-e Rowshanfekrân*, p. 23.

111   Ibid., p. 42.

112   Ibid., p. 48.

113   Ibid., p. 49.

114   Ibid., p. 49.

115   Ibid., p. 50. *Jahân-bini-ye ʿelmi* (literally "scientific worldview") refers exclusively to a materialist conception of history and a causal explanation of social formation in terms of relations of production and class analysis. In leftist discourse, it is often contrasted with the *jahân-bini-ye gheyr-e ʿelmi* ("unscientific worldview") of both the traditionalists and the bourgeoisie. *Jahân-bini-ye ʿelmi* should not be confused with natural scientific or even technocratic perspectives.

I have further discussed this issue in Ali Gheissari, "Truth and Method in Modern Iranian Historiography and Social Sciences," *Critique* (Journal for Critical Studies of the Middle East), No. 5 (Spring 1995), pp. 39–56, note pp. 47–48.

116 Âl-Ahmad, *Dar Khedmat va Khiânat-e Rowshanfekrân*, p. 45.

117 Ibid., p. 46.

118 Ibid., p. 46.

119 Ibid., p. 73.

120 Ibid., p. 73. Nezâmiyeh was the general name for schools built in different corners of the Seljuq territories at the initiative of the Persian vizier Nezâm al-Molk (b. Tous 408 or 409 A.H./1018 or 1019, murdered near Nahâvand 485 A.H./1092). See Nourollâh Kasâ'i, *Madâres-e Nezâmiyeh va Ta'sirât-e ʿElmi va Ejtemâʿi-e Ân* (The Nezâmiyeh Schools and Their Academic and Social Impacts) (Tehran, 1358/1980). Rabʿ-e Rashidi was a complex of buildings in Tabriz built by order of the learned Persian vizier of the Ilkhanids, Rashid al-Din Fazlollâh (b. ca. 645 A.H./1247, murdered 718 A.H./1318). The buildings included a school, library, hospital, mint, and mosque and several workshops such as textile and paper mills. Jondi-Shâpour (or Gondi-Shâpour) was a town in Khouzestân built by the Sassanid Shâpour I (ruled between 241 and 272 or 273) to accommodate Roman slaves and refugees. It had a famous hospital where physicians of different origins (Persian, Indian, and Greek, among others) practiced, and a school where many Greek texts were translated into Pahlavi. In the third century A.H./ninth century, the town lost its prominence to Baghdad.

121 See, in particular, Shâdmân's article "Dâneshgâh-e Qom va Dâneshgâh-hâ-ye digar-e Iran."

122 A more recent case in point is Abd al-Karim Soroush. See Abd al-Karim Soroush, "Taqlid va Tahqiq dar Solouk-e Dâneshjou'i" (Emulation versus [Independent] Research among the [University] Students), and "Entezârât-e Dâneshgâh az Howzeh" (University's Expectations from the Islamic Seminaries), in Abd al-Karim Soroush, *Farbeh-tar az Eide'ulouzhi* (More Corpulent than Ideology), Collection of Essays (Tehran, Winter 1372/1994), pp. 1–20 and 21–43, respectively. See further Boroujerdi, *Iranian Intellectuals and the West*, Chap. 7: "Debates in the Postrevolutionary Era," pp. 156–175.

123 For Âl-Ahmad, see further Hamid Dabashi, *Theology of Discontent: The Ideological Foundation of the Islamic Revolution in Iran* (New York: New York University Press, 1993), pp. 39–101.

124 Ehsân Narâqi is a descendant of Hâj Mollâ Mohammad-Mehdi (Mohaqqeq) Narâqi and of Hâj Mollâ Ahmad (Fâzel) Narâqi (b. 1185 A.H./1771–1772, d. 1244 A.H./1828–1829), who was among the influential ulama of Fath-Ali Shah's period and who was also a poet known by his nom de plume of Safâ'i; see Hâj Mollâ Ahmad Narâqi, *Masnavi-e Tâqdis*, edited by Hasan Narâqi, 2nd edition (Tehran, 1362/1983), where further sources on Mollâ Ahmad are also cited in the introduction, pp. 5–25, see pp. 9–10.

125 Narâqi's appointments included that of consultant to UNESCO's So-

cial Science Department (Paris, 1957) and membership on a research team to study the settlement of nomadic populations and the social consequences of industrialization and urbanization in the Middle East. In the same year, he returned to Iran and began teaching sociology at Tehran University, where, in 1958, he became director of the Institute for Social Research. In the same year he was invited by the National Iranian Oil Company to study aspects of the oil industry. He was also a member of the Showrâ-ye Enqelâb-e Edâri va Âmouzeshi (Council for Administrative Reorganization) (1968) and the head of UNESCO's Youth Administration (December 1969). See Echo of Iran, *Iran Who's Who*, p. 375. After the revolution of 1979, Narâqi was arrested. He later was freed, went to Paris, and renewed his association with UNESCO. For an interview about his imprisonment, see Ehsan Naraghi, Interview, *Esprit*, 129– 130/11, 8–9 (1987), pp. 55– 62. See also Ehsan Naraghi, *Des Palais du chah aux prisons de la révolution* (Paris, 1991); English translation as *From Palace to Prison: Inside the Iranian Revolution*, translated by Nilou Mobasser (London, 1994).

126   Ehsân Narâqi's books in Persian include: *Jâmĕeh, Javânân, Dâneshgâh: Dirouz, Emrouz, Fardâ* (The Society, the Youth, the University: Yesterday, Today, [and] Tomorrow) (Tehran, 1st edition 1350/1971, 2nd edition 1354/1975, 3rd edition 2536 [1356]/1977); *Ghorbat-e Gharb* (Estrangement of the West) (Tehran, 1354/1975; reprinted, Tehran, 2536 [1356]/1977; *Âncheh Khud Dâsht* (One's Own Treasures) (Tehran, 2535 [1355]/1976). Subsequent references to this book are to this edition; and *Tamaʿ-e Khâm* (Vain Greed) (Tehran, Winter 1356/1978). Two interviews with Narâqi conducted by Ali-Asghar Zarrâbi in 1346/ 1967 and 1348/1969, respectively (and published in the journal *Negin*), later appeared in the following collection: Ali-Asghar Zarrâbi, ed., *Majmouʿeh-ye Mobâheseh-hâ* (A Collection of Debates) (Tehran: Bâmdâd, 1351/1972), pp. 229– 282 and pp. 282–303. Narâqi also wrote an introductory textbook on the development of social thought, originally commissioned by UNESCO in 1960; see Ehsân Narâqi, ʿ*Oloum-e Ejtemâʿi va Seyr-e Takvini-e Ân* (The Growth of Social Sciences) (1st edition, Tehran, 1344/1965, 3rd edition, Tehran, 1363/1984). Among his articles are: Ehsân Narâqi, "Moʿammâ-ye Âmouzeshi va Masʾaleh-ye Jahl-e Modâm" (The Dilemma of Education and the Problem of Continuous Ignorance), *Farhang va Zendegi* (Culture and Life), No. 15 (Tehran, Summer 1353/1974), pp. 89–99. Most recently Narâqi has published *Des Palais du chah aux prisons de la révolution*, referred to above.

127   Narâqi, *Âncheh Khud Dâsht*, pp. 5–6.

128   Ibid., p. 6.

129   Ibid., p. 6.

130   Ibid., p. 7. Compare also with introduction to M. Moʿin and H. Corbin's edition of Nâser Khosrow's *Ketâb-e Jâme ʿal-Hekmateyn*, and its title in French: *Le Livre réunissant les deux sagesses ou harmonie de la philosophie grecque et de la théosophie Ismaélienne* (Tehran, 1332/1953).

131   Narâqi, *Âncheh Khud Dâsht*, p. 192.

132 Ibid., p. 192.

133 Ibid., p. 193. Although Narâqi does not refer to any particular person, it is evident that he is implying the trend of thought that had once been represented by Taqizâdeh.

134 Narâqi, *Âncheh Khud Dâsht*, p. 193.

135 Ibid., p. 193. Again, no specific names are mentioned; however, the author's reference is clearly to leftist intellectuals. Although it may sound rather tautological in both English and Persian, "popular democracy" (*demokrâsi-e khalqi*) is a neologism that stresses the populist aspect of democracy and of democratic planning.

136 Ibid., p. 194.

137 Ibid., pp. 194–195.

138 Ibid., p. 195. Narâqi acknowledges the role played by the pro-Constitutional ulama, who, by trying to combine Constitutionalism with the teachings of Islam, aimed to bring about the society's age-old aspirations regarding the "establishment of justice and respect for law." Ibid., p. 195.

139 Ibid., p. 196. The accuracy of this general statement is debatable. In the later stages of their lives, both men concentrated on research, but they remained fully convinced by their earlier belief in an independent and sovereign government. Their resignation from active politics was not a result of their disillusionment with Western ideas; it was a consequence of the political pressures that followed the rise of Reza Khân. Dehkhodâ was encouraged by Mosaddeq's campaign, which he saw as a ray of hope, and he expressed his feelings to Mosaddeq in the strongest terms. See Jalil Bozorgmehr, *Taqrirât-e Mosaddeq dar Zendân* (The Prison Writings of Mosaddeq), edited by Iraj Afshâr (Tehran, 1359/1980), p. 168. For Moshir al-Dowleh's political vision and his subsequent resignation, see Homayoun Katouzian, "Nationalist Trends in Iran, 1921–1926," *IJMES*, Vol. 10 (1979), pp. 533–551, especially pp. 544 and 548.

140 Narâqi, *Âncheh Khud Dâsht*, pp. 194–197.

141 Ibid., p. 197.

142 Ibid., pp. 197–204, under the heading, "The Concept of Evolution in European Civilization and Its Universal Generalization."

143 Ibid., p. 199. In a footnote, Narâqi explains that the idea of a classless society is a mere illusion because, if a class with specific economic advantages should disappear, a new class of bureaucrats would take its place in dominating the society. Ibid., p. 199, n. 1. This view reproduces an earlier criticism of Soviet bureaucracy. Compare with, for example, Milovan Djilas, *The New Class: An Analysis of the Communist System* (New York, 1957).

144 Narâqi, *Âncheh Khud Dâsht*, pp. 199–200.

145 Ibid., p. 200.

146 Narâqi, *Âncheh Khud Dâsht*, p. 198.

147 See, for example, his articles in the collection *Jâmeʿeh, Javânân, Dâneshgâh*.

148   For further criticism of Narâqi's proposal, see, for example, Boroujerdi, "Gharbzadegi va Sharq-Shenâsi-ye Vârouneh," pp. 387–388; and Javâd Tabâtabâ'i, *Ibn Khaldun va ʿOloum-e Ejtemâʿi: Vazʿiyat-e ʿOloum-e Ejtemâʿi dar Tamaddon-e Islami* (Ibn Khaldun and Social Sciences: The State of Social Sciences in Islamic Civilization) (Tehran, 1374/1995), pp. 32–34 and 57–58. See further Boroujerdi, *Iranian Intellectuals and the West*, pp. 136–140.

149   See the interview of Jamshid Behnam in Foundation for Iranian Studies, *Oral History Collection*; for a brief outline of the content of this interview, see the catalog, p. 33.

150   Shariʿati viewed Shiʿism not merely as one sect among others, but as a correct way of recognizing Islam. For him, Shiʿism and Islam were synonymous; the former "originated in the principle of Tawhid [unitarianism], its history began with Adam, and its mission from Abraham through Hosein [the martyred third Shiʿi Imam] and from him to the End of Time." Ali Shariʿati, *Majmouʿeh-ye Âsâr* (Collected Works), Vol. 7 (Tehran, 1362/1983), p. 296.

151   Especially Franz Fanon (1925–1961), the Algerian psychoanalyst, writer, and activist, with whom Shariʿati had collaborated in Paris. He later translated Fanon's *Les Damnés de la terre* (Wretched of the Earth) (1961) into Persian.

152   On this topic, see Janet Afary, "Review Essay—The Pitfalls of National Consciousness in Iran: The Construction of a Militant Muslim Ideology," *Journal of Political and Military Sociology*, Vol. 15 (Fall 1987), pp. 279–282. Afary looks at the ideas of Ali Shariʿati, Ayatollah Seyyed Mahmoud Tâleqâni, and Ayatollah Mortezâ Motahhari.

153   Enayat, *Modern Islamic Political Thought*, p. 155. See also Ervand Abrahamian, "ʿAli Shariʿati: Ideologue of the Iranian Revolution," *Merip Reports*, No. 102 (January 1982), pp. 24–28; and Hamid Algar, *The Islamic Revolution in Iran* (London: Open Press, 1980), p. 47.

154   For Shariʿati's life and works, see Abrahamian, *Radical Islam*, pp. 105–125; Yann Richard, "Contemporary Shiʿi Thought," in Nikki R. Keddie, *Roots of Revolution*, pp. 202–228, note pp. 215–228; Akhavi, *Religion and Politics in Contemporary Iran*, pp. 143–158; Mangol Bayat-Philipp, "Shiʿism in Contemporary Iranian Politics: The Case of Ali Shariʿati," in E. Kedourie and S. G. Haim, eds., *Towards a Modern Iran* (London, 1980), pp. 155–168; and Dabashi, *Theology of Discontent*, pp. 102–146. See further Ali Rahnema, "Ali Shariʿati: Teacher, Preacher, Rebel," in Ali Rahnema, ed., *Pioneers of Islamic Revival* (London: Zed Books, 1994), pp. 208–250; and Boroujerdi, *Iranian Intellectuals and the West*, pp. 105–115.

155   Shariʿati's doctoral thesis, under the direction of the French Iranologist Gilbert Lazard, was a partial translation, with some commentary, of the Persian text *Faza'el-e Balkh* (Scholars of Balkh). See Richard, "Contemporary Shiʿi Thought," p. 294, n. 50. For a critical appraisal of Shariʿati's scholarly achievements, see Jalâl Matini, "Doktor Ali Shariʿati dar Dâneshgâh-e Mashhad (Ferdowsi)" (Remembering Dr. Ali Shariʿati at the Ferdowsi University in Mash-had), *Iranshenasi*, Vol. 5, No. 4 (Winter 1994), pp. 835–899.

156 Shariʿati assisted in opening a Paris branch of Nehzat-e Âzâdi-e Iran (The Liberation Movement of Iran), formed in 1961 by Mehdi Bâzargân and Ayatollah Seyyed Mahmoud Tâleqâni. He also edited *Iran-e Âzâd* (The Free Iran), the organ of the Jebhe-ye Melli (National Front) in Europe. In addition to Fanon he also translated *Guerilla Warfare* (1961), by the Argentinian revolution-ary Che Guevara (1928–1967), a prominent figure in the Cuban Revolution, into Persian, and he was also briefly detained for his support for Patrice Lu-mumba (1925–1961), the leading nationalist politician of the Congo (Zaire). For further information, see Ebrâhim Yazdi, ed., *Yâd-Nâmeh-ye Shahid-e Jâvid, Doktor Ali Shariʿati* (Festschrift of the Eternal Martyr, Dr. Shariʿati) (n.p. [United States]: Nehzat-e Âzâdi, 1977), pp. 23 ff.

157 Hoseiniyeh Ershâd was an Islamic institution and lecture hall built through the special endowment and support of some merchants from the bazaar. Open to the public, the center provided a valuable forum for different types of Muslim activists (such as Mehdi Bâzargân, Ayatollah Motahhari, and Ali Shariʿati) who wanted to reach a wider audience. See Akhavi, *Religion and Poli-tics in Contemporary Iran*, pp. 143–144. In spite of the criticisms made against him by the more conservative members, Shariʿati gradually became very popular at the center. For an example of Shariʿati's response to his critics, see Hoseiniyeh Ershâd, *Miz-e Gerd: Pâsokh beh So'âlât va Enteqâdât* (Roundtable: Reply to Questions and Criticisms) (Participants: Mohammad-Taqi Shariʿati, Sadr al-Din Balâghi, Seyyed Mortezâ Shabastari, and Ali Shariʿati) (Tehran, 1354/1975). See also Rasoul Jaʿfariân, *Nezâʿ-e Sonnat va Tajaddod: Bahsi dar-bâreh-ye Monâsebât-e Fekri-ye Doktor Shariʿati va Ostâd Motahhari* (The Clash of Tradition with Mo-dernity: On the Ideas of Dr. Shariati and Professor Motahhari) (Qom: En-teshârât-e Ra'ouf, 1371/1992. For a controversial book published after the revo-lution highlighting Shariʿati's differences with Ayatollah Motahhari, see Ali Abu al-Hasani (Monzer), *Shahid Motahhari Efshâgar-e Towte'eh* (Martyr Motahhari: Discloser of Conspiracy) (Tehran, 1362/1983); for a critical response to this book, see Hasan Yousefi-Eshkavari, *Naqdi bar Ketâb-e "Shahid Motahhari Efshâ-gar-e Towte'eh"* (A Critique of the Book "Martyr Motahhari: Discloser of Con-spiracy") (Tehran, 1364/1985).

158 See, for example, Mehdi Bâzargân, *Bâd va Bârân dar Qur'ân* (Wind and Rain in the Koran), edited by Seyyed Mohammad-Mehdi Jaʿfari (originally written in 1343/1964), (Tehran: Enteshâr, 1353/1974). This is a two-part study on the causes of wind and rain, where the author discusses meteorology and thermodynamics (his field of speciality) in accordance with matching quotations from the Koran. In his preface, Bâzargân expressed hope that the book would encourage men of religion to accept modern science and would also prompt university students and intellectuals to turn to the Koran. Bâzargân, *Bâd va Bârân*, p. 18. For Bâzargân's role in Islamic modernism in Iran, see Mehdi

Bâzargân, *Modâfeʿât-e Mohandes Bâzargân dar Dâdgâh-e Tajdid-e Nazar-e Nezâmi dar Sâl-e 1343* (The Defense of Engineer Bâzargân at the Military Court of Appeals in 1964) (Tehran: Modarres, n.d.); and Hamid Algar, "Islâh," in *EI2*, Vol. 4, pp. 163–167, here p. 166. See also comments by Abd al-Karim Soroush on Bâzargân, in his article, "Ostâd Motahhari Ehyâ-konandeh-ye Râstin dar ʿAsr-e Jadid" (Professor Motahhari the True Revivalist of the Modern Times), *Nashr-e Dânesh*, Vol. 1, Nos. 5–6 (Tehran, 1360/1981), pp. 34–50, here pp. 40–42; and especially Chehabi, *Iranian Politics and Religious Modernism*.

159 A bibliography of Shariʿati's works prepared by Yann Richard appeared in *Abstracta Iranica*, Vol. 1 (Tehran and Leiden, 1978); Vol. 2 (Tehran and Leiden, 1979). After the revolution of 1979, Shariʿati's works were meticulously compiled and edited in Tehran by Daftar-e Tadvin va Tanzim-e Majmouʿeh-ye Âsâr-e Moʿallem-e Shahid Doktor Ali Shariʿati (The Editorial Office of the Collected Works of the Martyred Teacher Dr. Ali Shariʿati) and have appeared under the general title series of Shariʿati's *Majmouʿeh-ye Âsâr* (Collected Works), 35 Vols. (Tehran, 1357–1364/1978–1985).

160 For a selective list of works by Ali Shariʿati in English, French, and German translations, see Gheissari, "Ideological Formation of the Iranian Intelligentsia," Appendix 3, pp. 369–371.

161 For example, when Bâqer Mo'meni, a noted leftist intellectual, was asked to give his opinion about Shariʿati's ideas, he responded: "Pity I have not read anything from Dr. Shariʿati, because I thought his arguments were irrelevant to history and sociology. In any case my field is socio-historical criticism, and I'd better stay with that." Bâqer Mo'meni, *Dard-e Ahl-e Qalam* (Writers' Anguish) (Tehran, Winter 1357/1979), p. 73. This quote is from a discussion with the audience that followed Mo'meni's address to the Ten Nights of poetry readings and speeches organized by the Iranian Writers Association in Tehran's Goethe Institute (October 1977). Among Marxist student circles, Mo'meni was a well-known author, translator, and occasional speaker. For another leftist criticism of Shariʿati during the years before the revolution, see Ali-Akbar Akbari, *Bar-resi-e Chand Mas'aleh-ye Ejtemâʿi* (An Overview of Some Social Problems) (Tehran, 1349/1970). This is a critical review of Shariʿati's *Islam-shenâsi* (Islamology), 1st edition (Mashhad, Winter 1347/1969). Akbari, then a sociology lecturer at Tabriz University, acknowledges that he based his review on only 100 pages (out of 627) of the first edition of Shariʿati's work. Akbari, *Bar-resi-ye Chand Mas'aleh*, p. 9.

162 On this topic, reference is made exclusively to Ali Shariʿati, *Bâzgasht-e Beh Khish* (Return to One's Own Self) (Tehran, 1356/1977); also reprinted as *Bâz-shenâsi-ye Huviyyat-e Irani-Islami* (Recognizing the Irano-Islamic Identity), (*Majmouʿeh*, Vol. 27) (Tehran: Elhâm, 1361/1983), pp. 79–225 (references in the text are to this edition).

163 Shariʿati, *Bâz-shenâsi-ye Huviyyat-e Irani-Islami* (*Majmouʿeh*, Vol. 27), pp. 81–82.

164   Ibid., p. 83.

165   Ibid., p. 82.

166   Ibid., p. 83.

167   Ibid., p. 83.

168   Ali Shariʿati, *Târikh-e Tamaddon* (History of Civilization), Vol. 2, 2nd edition (*Majmouʿeh*, Vol. 12) (Tehran: Âgâh, 1361/1982), pp. 72–74; and Ali Shariʿati, *Bâzgasht* (Return) (*Majmouʿeh*, Vol. 4) (Tehran, 1361/1982), pp. 100, 106, and 257.

169   Shariʿati described *taʿassob*, which also means zeal, as a powerful means of cultural defense. Compare with the notion of ʿasabiyyah (group solidarity) in Ibn Khaldun (1332–1406).

170   Shariʿati, *Bâz-shenâsi-ye Huviyyat-e Irani-Islami* (*Majmouʿeh*, Vol. 27), p. 85.

171   Ibid., p. 85.

172   Ibid., p. 85.

173   Ibid., p. 85.

174   Here Shariʿati refers to *Les Quarantaines*, a fiction by Fereydoun Hoveyda, originally written in French and published in Paris (Gallimard, 1962), in which the author portrays the life of a young Egyptian who lived and studied in Paris for several years. There he was always viewed, both by himself and by others, as either an Egyptian or simply a foreigner (in any case, an outsider). Upon his return to Egypt, he found that he no longer felt at home, not least because he was now viewed by his own compatriots as semi-French or as someone different. He finally realizes that he belongs to neither place. The author implies that people like this young Egyptian live in a permanent state of quarantine. Shariʿati regarded this story as a literary expression of Âl-Ahmad's *gharbzadegi*. See Shariʿati (*Majmouʿeh*, Vol. 27), pp. 85–86. For a Persian translation of *Les Quarantaines*, see Fereydoun Hoveydâ, *Qarantineh*, translated from the French by Mostafâ Farzâneh (Tehran: Enteshârât-e Iranmehr, 1345/1966); this translation received a negative review by Nâder Ebrâhimi, *Sokhan*, Vol. 17, No. 2 (Ordibehesht 1346/May 1967), pp. 219–225.

175   Shariʿati, *Bâz-shenâsi-ye Huviyyat-e Irani-Islami* (*Majmouʿeh*, Vol. 27), p. 86.

176   Ibid., p. 86.

177   See, for example, by Ali Shariʿati, *Payâm-e Omid beh Rowshanfekr-e Masʾoul* (A Message of Hope to the Committed Intellectual), lecture at Hoseiniyeh Ershâd (5 Âbân 1351/27 October 1972); revised and reprinted in *Darsi az Roum, beh Zamimeh-ye Alienasioun: Ensân-e Bi Khud* (A Lesson from Rumi, plus a Discussion about Alienation: Man without a Self) (Tehran, 1977); *Rowshanfekr va Masʾouliyyat-e Ou dar Jâmeʿeh* (Intellectual's Responsibility in the Society), lecture at Hoseiniyeh Ershâd 30 and 31 Mordâd 1349/21 and 22 August 1970, 1st edition (Tehran, 1981); and *Cheh Bâyad Kard?* (What Is to Be Done?), lecture at Hoseiniyeh Ershâd, revised by Ali Shariʿati and published in Tehran

(1976). These and other texts related to the topic of intellectuals are incorporated in Ali Shariʿati, *Cheh Bâyad Kard?* (What Is to Be Done?) (*Majmouʿeh*, Vol. 20) (Tehran, 1360/1982). All references in the text are to this latter edition, unless stated otherwise.

178 Shariʿati, *Cheh Bâyad Kard?* (*Majmouʿeh*, Vol. 20), p. 54 and p. 125, n. 1.

179 Ibid., pp. 60–69. Shariʿati explains the subsequent evolution of the European intellectual in the following way:

> *The European intellectual class became anti-religious or non-religious in order to liberate itself from the tyrannical domination of* estebdâd-e rowhâni [*clerical despotism*]; *and opposed the God of the church and that of the pope because the God introduced by the pope was the greatest guardian of aristocracy who gave it* ʿezzat [*might*] *while it brought* zellat [*adversity*] *for others.* [*These intellectuals*] *advocated democracy in order to reduce the power of the pope which was the same as* [*the power of*] *the aristocracy;* [*they*] *were nationalist in order to challenge the cosmopolitanism of the pope.* [*They*] *believed in absolute freedom of scientific thought and in the materiality of science because the apparatus of the church, in the name of* maʿnaviyyat [*spirituality*] *had suspended science and thought to be of some service to life and instead was using them to serve its own establishment.* (*Ibid., p. 67*)

180 Shariʿati's reference to "Christianity" is presumably to Catholicism and to reactions to it, i.e., the Reformation.

181 Ibid., pp. 68–69.

182 Shariʿati regarded himself as a sociologist of religion and defined his project as an attempt to "codify a kind of sociology of religion based on Islam and drawing on the terminology of the Koran and Islamic literature." Ali Shariʿati, *On the Sociology of Islam*, translated by Hamid Algar (Berkeley: Mizan Press, 1979), p. 42. For a recent and sympathetic appraisal of Shariʿati as a "sociologist of religion," see Abd al-Karim Soroush, "Shariʿati va Jâmeʿeh-shenâsi-ye Din" (Shariʿati and the Sociology of Religion), in Abd al-Karim Soroush, *Farbeh-tar az Eideʾuluzhi* (More Corpulent than Ideology) (Tehran, Winter 1372/1994), pp. 199–231.

183 See Ali Shariʿati, *Shiʿa, Yek Hezb-e Tamâm* (Shiʿa: A Perfect Party), lecture at Hoseiniyeh Ershâd (2–3 Âbân 1351/24–25 October 1972); reprinted in Ali Shariʿati, *Shiʿeh* (Shiʿism) (*Majmouʿeh*, Vol. 7) (Tehran: Elhâm, 1362/1983), pp. 3–168.

184 Shariʿati, *Shiʿeh* (*Majmouʿeh*, Vol. 7), p. 16.

185 Ibid., pp. 114–115.

186 In response to the objection that Shiʿism (or Islam in general) should not be identified as a party, Shariʿati argues that in the context of the Koran, *hezb* refers to differences in people on the basis of their belief systems, as in, for example, *mellat-e Ebrâhim* (the people of Abraham) and the followers of Islam, who were viewed in the Koran as members of the same *hezb* (party); hence the contrast between *hezb-e khodâ* or Hezbollâh (the party of God) and *hezb-e sheitân* (the party of Satan). Ibid., p. 288.

187 Ali Shariʿati, *Islam-shenâsi* (Islamology) (*Majmouʿeh*, Vol. 16) (Tehran: Shariʿati, 1360/1981), here pp. 11 and 13.

188 For further references, see Ali Shariʿati, *Târikh-e Tamaddon* (History of Civilization), Vol. 1, 2nd edition (*Majmouʿeh*, Vol. 11) (Tehran: Âgâh, 1361/1982), pp. 127–129.

189 Shariʿati, *Shiʿeh* (*Majmouʿeh*, Vol. 7), pp. 90–91.

190 Ibid., pp. 93–95.

191 Ibid., pp. 95–96.

192 Ibid., pp. 96–97.

193 Ibid., p. 97.

194 Shariʿati may have sensed that this idea would have resonance with authors like Louis Massignon (1883–1957) and other Catholic intellectuals. On this theme, see the essay "Figura" by Erich Auerbach, in his *Scenes from the Drama of European Literature* (New York, 1959), note especially p. 57; new edition (Minneapolis: University of Minnesota Press, 1984).

195 Ali ibn Abi Tâlib (d. 40 A.H./661) was the cousin and son-in-law of the Prophet and the First Imam of the Shiʿis; Fatima (d. 11 A.H./632), also called al-Zahrâʾ, the Shining One, was the daughter of the Prophet, wife of Ali, and mother of Hasan (d. 50 A.H.) and Hosein (d. 61 A.H./680), respectively the Second and Third Shiʿi Imams; and Abouzar (or Abu Dharr in Arabic pronunciation) al-Ghaffâri (d. 32 A.H./652) was an early convert to Islam and an ardent supporter of Ali on the question of the succession to Mohammad, known for his radical, somewhat socialist, views concerning the accumulation of wealth and capital. To each, Shariʿati devoted a separate volume. See Ali Shariʿati, *Ali* (*Majmouʿeh*, Vol. 26), 2nd edition (Tehran: Niloufar, 1362/1983); *Hosein Vâres-e Âdam* (Hosein, the Successor of Adam) (*Majmouʿeh*, Vol. 19), 2nd edition (Tehran: Qalam, 1361/1982); *Abouzar* (*Majmouʿeh*, Vol. 3) (Tehran: Elhâm, 1361/1983).

196 This statement was originally attributed to the Sixth Shiʿi Imam, Jaʿfar al-Sâdeq (d. 765). ʿÂshourâ, the tenth day of Moharram, is the anniversary of the martyrdom of Hosein, the Third Shiʿi Imam, in 61 A.H./680 in the plains of Karbalâ in Iraq, by the order of the second Umayyad Caliph, Yazid (r. 680–683). In the wake of the recent Iranian revolution, it was also used by Ayatollah Khomeini and has since been used frequently in the official discourse and propaganda of the Islamic Republic. On the other hand, Shiʿite active remembrance can be compared with the notion of promise and fulfillment in Christian theology. Note also that in Iran before the revolution of 1979, the subject of Hosein's martyrdom was used by different creative writers who had no particular religious conviction in order to highlight the rebellious and nonconformist content of their work. See, for example, Gholâm-Hosein Sâʿedi, "Madkhali bar Yek Dâstân-e Boland" (Foreword to a Long Story), *Negin*, Vol. 12, No. 146 (31 Tir 2536 [1356]/22 July 1977), pp. 13 and 50.

197 Regarding the practice of *ijtihâd* and its four principal sources—the Koran, *sunna* (traditions of the Prophet), *ʿaql* (faculty of reason), and *ijmâʿ* (consent of the majority of experts)—Shariʿati argued that only the first two are universally valid and unchangeable; the latter two should now be replaced, or rather redefined and updated, in accordance with "science" and "time." See Daftar-e Tadvin va Tanzim-e Majmouʿeh-ye Âsâr-e Moʿallem-e Shahid Doktor Ali Shariʿati (The Editorial Office of the Collected Works of the Martyred Teacher Dr. Ali Shariʿati), ed., *Farhang-e Loghât-e Kotob-e Doktor Ali Shariʿati* (A Terminological Guide to the Writings of Dr. Ali Shariʿati) (Tehran: Ferdowsi, 1362/ 1983), pp. 26–29 (based on Shariʿati, *Majmouʿeh*, Vol. 1, pp. 199–201). See also Shariʿati, *Shiʿeh* (*Majmouʿeh*, Vol. 7), pp. 249–250; and Shariʿati, *Cheh Bâyad Kard?* (*Majmouʿeh*, Vol. 20), pp. 393–405.

198 Ali Shariʿati, *Khud-sâzi-e Enqelâbi* (Revolutionary Reconstruction of the Self) (*Majmouʿeh*, Vol. 2) (Tehran, 1357/1978), pp. 131–182.

199 See, for example, Georg Lukács, *History and Class Consciousness: Studies in Marxist Dialectics* (new edition, Berlin, 1968), English translation by Rodney Livingstone (London, Merlin Press, 1971); Jean-Paul Sartre, *Search for a Method*, first published Paris, 1960, translated from the French with an introduction by Hazel E. Barnes (New York, Vintage Books, 1968), note in particular "The Problem of Mediations and Auxiliary Disciplines," pp. 35–84; and Jean-Paul Sartre, *Critique of Dialectical Reason. I: Theory of Practical Ensembles*, first published Paris, 1960, translated by Alan Sheridan-Smith, edited by Jonathan Rée (London: New Left Books, 1976), note in particular "The Mediation of Reciprocity: The Transcendence-Immanence Tension," pp. 374–382.

200 Ali Shariʿati, *Ensân-e Bi Khud* (Man without a Self) (*Majmouʿeh*, Vol. 25) (Tehran: Qalam, 1361/1983), p. 9.

201 Shariʿati, *Islam-shenâsi*, Vol. 1 (*Majmouʿeh*, Vol. 16), pp. 41–50. Abel and Cain represent two contradictory types of moral and practical attitudes: Abel, "the man of faith, peaceable and self-sacrificing," and Cain, "the voluptuous, the transgressor and the fratricide." Enayat, *Modern Islamic Political Thought*, p. 158. Shariʿati further extends the story to the level of philosophy of history and states that Abel and Cain represent not only two different types of social classes (i.e., common ownership of the means of production in the former case, and the system of private ownership in the latter), but also two opposing worldviews: "In predicting the outcome of the conflict between these two poles, Shariʿati replaces Marxian determinism with the Shiʿi millenarian rehabilitation of the universe: the conflict will end, according to him, only with an 'inevitable revolution' which will restore 'the system of Abel' in the world." Enayat, *Modern Islamic Political Thought*, p. 158.

202 Shariʿati, *Islam-shenâsi*, Vol. 1 (*Majmouʿeh*, Vol. 16), p. 45.

203 Compare the status of the past and that of memory in all biblical traditions with the Marxist reference to the origins of social antagonism and economic exploitation, as epitomized in, for example, Marx and Engels's well-known statement, "The history of all hitherto existing society is the history of class struggles." Karl Marx and Frederick Engels, *Manifesto of the Communist Party* (Moscow, 1977), p. 40. It follows that under capitalism, the proletariat is the embodiment of all previous contradictions and should never forget its class enemies. Remembrance is therefore a necessary first step for the proletariat in developing its own ethics, thus transforming its revolutionary potential into practice as it moves toward its historical telos and the construction of a harmonious, classless society.

204   See Franco Ferrarotti, *Time, Memory, and Society* (New York, 1990), p. 6.

205   It was from this perspective that Shari'ati often emphasized the memory of the martyrdom of Imam Hosein, acknowledged the practice of remembrance (*zikr*), and praised the role of *zâkerin* (professional rememberers and praisers of God), *maddâhin* (professional encomiasts of the Prophet and of the Imams), and the *ta'zieh* (passion play in Shi'ism). See Ali Shari'ati, "Naqsh-e Enqelâbi-e Yâd va Yâd-âvarân dar Târikh-e Tashayyo'" ("The Revolutionary Role of Remembrance and of Rememberers in the History of Shi'ism"), in Shari'ati, *Shi'eh (Majmou'eh*, Vol. 7), pp. 169–226; and Auerbach, "Figura," in Auerbach, *Sources from the Drama*.

206   Shari'ati, *Shi'eh (Majmou'eh*, Vol. 7), p. 90.

207   Shari'ati, *Khud-sâzi-e Enqelâbi (Majmou'eh*, Vol. 2), p. 153. See also Ali Shari'ati, *Niâyesh* (Benediction) *(Majmou'eh*, Vol. 8) (Tehran: Elhâm, 1362/1983).

208   For references to *entezâr*, see, in particular, Ali Shari'ati, "Entezâr, Mazhab-e E'terâz" (Anticipation, the Doctrine of Protest), in Ali Shari'ati, *Hosein, Vâres-e Âdam* (Hosein, the Heir to Adam), 2nd edition *(Majmou'eh*, Vol. 19) (Tehran: Qalam, 1361/1982), pp. 253–304.

209   Shari'ati, *Hosein, Vâres-e Âdam (Majmou'eh*, Vol. 19), p. 287.

210   For additional discussion of Shari'ati's approach to Islam as an ideology and a comparison with other ideological treatments of Islam by Iranian Muslim activists both before and after the revolution of 1979, see Ali Rahnema and Farhad Nomani, "Competing Shi'i Subsystems in Contemporary Iran," in Saeed Rahnema and Sohrab Behdad, eds., *Iran after the Revolution: Crisis of an Islamic State* (London and New York: I. B. Tauris, 1995), pp. 65–93.

211   However, the range and volume of Shari'ati's work and his impact on the terminology and discourse of the contemporary revivalist movement far exceed that of Jazani on the left.

212   See Younes Parsa Benab, "Political Organizations in Iran: A Historical Review," *Review of Iranian Political Economy and History*, Vol. 3, No. 1 (Spring 1979), pp. 30–80, here pp. 53–54. See also Akhavi, *Religion and Politics in Contemporary Iran*, p. 144.

213   During 1970 and 1971, some people were arrested in connection with this group. Five of its central figures, Homâyoun Katirâ'i, Houshang Targol,

Bahrâm Tâherzâdeh, Nâser Karimi, and Nâser Madani, after sustaining extensive torture, were executed in October 1971. See Dehqâni, *Hamâseh-ye Moqâvemat*, pp. 292–293, n. 29.

214 Members of the Palestine Group, which was led by Shokrollâh Pâknezhâd, "were arrested whilst trying to cross the border into Iraq and enlist with the Palestinian guerrillas." Halliday, *Iran, Dictatorship and Development*, p. 326, n. 25. See also Jazani, *Târikh-e Si Sâleh*, pp. 151–154. Sentenced to life imprisonment, Pâknezhâd was freed from prison during the recent revolution only to be arrested again later by the authorities of the Islamic Republic on "counterrevolutionary" charges. He was executed in 1982. For more information about the above groups, see Jazani, *Târikh-e Si Sâleh-ye Iran*, pp. 49–61, 122–126, and 150–162; Parsa Benab, "Political Organizations in Iran," pp. 30–80; Abrahamian, *Iran between Two Revolutions*, pp. 481–482; and Halliday, *Iran, Dictatorship and Development*, p. 231 and p. 326, n. 25.

215 For the Islamic groups, see Jazani, *Târikh-e Si-Sâleh*, pp. 129–145; Abrahamian, *Iran between Two Revolutions*, p. 481; and Davâni, *Nehzat-e Rowhânioun-e Iran*, Vol. 5, pp. 97–100.

216 For the Mojâhedin, see the comprehensive study by Abrahamian, *Radical Islam*; and Boroujerdi, *Iranian Intellectuals and the West*, pp. 116–120. For the Fadâ'i guerrillas, see the foreword to Bizhan Jazani, *Capitalism and Revolution in Iran: Selected Writings of Bizhan Jazani*, translated by the Iran Committee (London: Zed Press, 1980); and Parsa Benab, "Political Organizations in Iran," pp. 30–50. For additional background information, see Jazani, *Târikh-e Si Sâleh*; Ali-Akbar Safâ'i Farahâni, *Âncheh Yek Enqelâbi Bâyad Bedânad* (Facts a Revolutionary Must Know), written in summer 1970, reissued in London by Iran Research Group in 1973, reprinted, with an added introduction, under the title *Az Jâme'eh Cheh Midânim?* (What Do We Know about the Society?) (Tehran, 1978); and Dehqâni, *Hamâseh-ye Moqâvemat*.

217 Here internationalist claims should be differentiated from cosmopolitanism; the latter attitude was also absent among Iranian intellectuals.

218 This is true unless the individual has been ideologically convinced, in which case the dominant authority would, for the time being, appear as legitimate.

Epilogue

1 Nâser Mo'azzen, ed., *Dah Shab*. The Iranian Writers Association was founded in the spring of 1968; its major objective was to protest censorship and demand freedom of expression. For a study of the formation and background of the Writers' Association, see Ahmad Karimi-Hakkak, "Protest and Perish: A History of the Writers' Association of Iran," *IS*, Vol. 18, Nos. 2–4 (Spring–Autumn 1985), pp. 189–229.

2   See the interview of Baqer Parham in Foundation for Iranian Studies, *Oral History Collection*, catalog p. 97.

3   For the involvement of writers in the revolution, see Ahmad Karimi-Hakkak, "Revolutionary Posturing: Iranian Writers and the Iranian Revolution of 1979," *IJMES*, Vol. 23, No. 4, 1991, pp. 507–531.

4   This line refers to the traditional practice of burning incense to attract good omens and avert the evil eye.

5   Houshang Ebtehaj (Sâyeh), (Poem), *Keyhân*, 13 Bahman 1357/1 February 1979. Apart from alluding to the welcome ceremony, the poem also refers to the report that, shortly before the Ayatollah's return to Iran, many people in dire anticipation had miraculously seen his face on the moon.

6   Ahmad Shâmlou, "Dar in Bonbast" (In This Blind Alley) (poem composed on 31 Tir 1358/22 July 1979), *Nâmeh-ye Kânoun-e Nevisandegân-e Iran* (Journal of the Writers Association of Iran), Vol. 2, edited by Mohammad-Ali Sepânlou (Tehran, 1358/1979), pp. 9–10; reprinted in Ahmad Shâmlou, *Tarâneh-hâ-ye Kouchak-e Ghorbat* (Little Homesick Songs) (Tehran, 1359/1980), pp. 30–32. The above translation is from Karimi-Hakkak, "Revolutionary Posturing," p. 518. For an earlier English translation of this poem, see Leonardo P. Alishan, "Trends in Modernist Persian Poetry" (Ph.D. dissertation, University of Texas at Austin, 1982), pp. 109–110.

7   That faction was closely associated with the high-profile ayatollah Mohammad Beheshti and his Hezb-e Jomhouri-ye Islami (Islamic Republic Party). Members of the Tudeh Party who were expelled from the Writers' Association were Mahmoud E'temâd-zâdeh (*Behâzin*), Siâvosh Kasrâ'i, Fereydoun Tonekâboni, Houshang Ebtehâj (*Sâyeh*), and Mohammad-Taqi Boroumand.

8   For a detailed account of this episode, see Bâqer Parhâm, "Hezb-e Tudeh va Kânoun-e Nevisandegân" (The Tudeh Party and the Writers' Association), a six-part report that appeared in *Ketâb-e Jom'eh*, Nos. 25 (11 Bahman 1358/31 January 1980) to 30 (23 Esfand 1358/13 March 1980).

9   Some examples include: *Ârash*, new series, monthly, published Esfand 1359 to Mehr 1360 (March 1981 to October 1981); *Âyandeh*, monthly, published Farvardin 1361/April 1982 to c. 1993; *Jong (Isfahan)*, irregular, published Summer 1360/1981; *Ketâb-e Âgâh*, irregular, published Winter 1360/1982 to 1362/1983; *Ketâb-e Cherâgh*, irregular, published 1360/1981 to 1363/1984; *Ketâb-e Jom'eh*, weekly, published 4 Mordâd 1358/26 July 1979 to 1 Khordâd 1359/22 April 1979); *Nâmeh-ye Kânoun-e Nevisandegân-e Iran* (Iranian Writers Association Bulletin), biannual, published Spring 1358/1979 to Spring 1360/1981; *Naqd-e Âgâh*, irregular, published 1361/1982 to 1363/1984; and *Showrâ-ye Nevisandegân va Honarmandân-e Iran* (Council of the Iranian Writers and Artists), quarterly, published Autumn 1359/1980 to Spring 1363/1984. In addition to these publications, Iran University Press (Markaz-e Nashr-e Dâneshgâhi), founded in 1980 by the Council of the Cultural Revolution, launched four scholarly periodicals:

Nashr-e Dânesh, a bimonthly journal begun in 1980 and published regularly, consisting of reviews, lists of new publications, and news about scholarly events and academic publications in Iran and abroad; *Ma'âref*, founded in 1984, published regularly three times a year, which includes articles on philosophy, Islamic studies, history, and literature; *Luqmân*, a semi-annual journal of Islamic studies, history, and Persian literature in French with summaries of articles in Persian, whose first issue appeared in 1984–1985 and which is still published regularly; and *Majalleh-ye Bâstânshenâsi va Târikh* (Iranian Journal of Archaeology and History), whose first issue appeared in the fall of 1365/1986. Contributors to these journals include new authors as well as several established intellectuals who have continued their careers under the new regime.

10   A few examples of the novels and short stories published in Iran since the revolution are: by Mahmoud Dowlatâbâdi, *Kleydar*, which was begun in the 1960s, with two of its books appearing before the revolution, *Jây-e Khâli-e Salouch* (The Empty Place of Salouch) (Tehran, 1358/1979), and *Qoqnous* (Phoenix) (Tehran, 1361/1982); by Ali-Mohammad Afghâni, *Sindokht* (Tehran, 1360/1981), and *Doktor Baktâsh* (Tehran, 1364/1985); by Ahmad Ahrâr, *Shâhin-e Sepid* (White Falcon) (Tehran, 1364/1985); by Mihan Bahrâmi, *Heyvân* (Animal) (Tehran, 1364/1985); by Reza Barâheni, *Ba'd az 'Arousi Cheh Gozasht?* (What Happened after the Wedding?) (Tehran, 1361/1982), *Âvâz-e Koshtegân* (Song of the Slain) (Tehran, 1362/1983), *Châh beh Châh* (Out of One Well, Down to Another) (Tehran, 1362/1983), and *Râzhâ-ye Sarzamin-e Man* (The Mysteries of My Homeland) (Tehran, 1987); by Simin Dâneshvar, *Be Ki Salâm Konam?* (Whom Should I Greet?), short stories (Tehran, 1359/1980), and *Jazireh-ye Sargardâni* (The Island of Bewilderment), Vol. 1 (Tehran, 1372/1993), Vol. 2 (Tehran, in press); by Asghar Elâhi, *Mâdaram Bi-Bi Jân* (My Mother Bi-Bi Jân) (Tehran, n.d.); by Esmâ'il Fasih, *Dâstân-e Jâvid* (Jâvid's Story) (Tehran, 1360/1981), *Sorayyâ dar Eghmâ'* (Sorayya in a Coma) (Tehran, 1362/1983), *Dard-e Siâvosh* (The Pain of Siâvosh) (Tehran, 1364/1985), *Zemestân-e Shast-u Du* (The Winter of Sixty-Two) (Tehran, 1366/1987), and *Asir-e Zamân* (Prisoner of Time) (Tehran, 1373/1994); by Mahmoud Golâbdarreh'i, *Parastou* (Swallow), short stories (Tehran, 1363/1984), *Sahrâ-ye Sard* (The Cold Desert) (Tehran, Winter 1363/1985), and *Sarnevesht-e Bacheh-ye Shemroun* (The Story of the Boy from Shemirân), short stories (Tehran, 1364/1985); by Houshang Golshiri, *Ma'soum-e Panjom* (The Fifth Innocent) (Tehran, Winter 1359/1981), *Jobbeh-Khâneh* (Cloakroom) (Tehran, 1362/1983), *Hadis-e Mâhi-gir va Div* (The Story of the Fisherman and the Demon) (Tehran, 1363/1984), and *Hasht Dâstân* (Eight Stories), a collection of eight short stories by young writers, edited with an introduction by Houshang Golshiri (Tehran, 1363/1984); by Bahrâm Heydari, *Lâli*, short stories (Tehran, 1358/1979); by Ahmad Mahmoud, *Shahr-e Soukhteh* (Burned City) and *Dâstân-e Du Shahr* (The Story of Two Cities) (Tehran: 1361/1982), both works that relate to the events of the war between Iraq and Iran; by Jamâl Mirsâdeqi, *Bâd-hâ Khabar az Taghyir-e Fasl Midâdand* (Winds Her-

alded the Change of Season) (Tehran, Winter 1363/1985), and *Âtash az Âtash* (Fire from Fire) (Tehran, 1363/1984); by Ja'far Modarres Sâdeqi, *Gâv Khouni* (Tehran, 1362/1983), translated to English by Afkham Darbandi as *The Marsh* [*Gavkhouni*], introduction by Dick Davis (Costa Mesa, Calif.: Mazda, forthcoming 1997); by Abbas Ma'roufi, *Samfouni-ye Mordegân* (Symphony of the Dead), 1st edition (Tehran, 1368/1989), *Sâl-e Balvâ* (Year of the Riot), 3rd edition (Tehran, 1371/1992), and *Peykar-e Farhâd* (The Body of Farhâd), 1st edition (Tehran, 1374/1995); by Khosrow Nasimi, *Khabar-e Ân Sâl-hâ* (The Story of Those Years) (Tehran, 1362/ 1983); and Mohammad-Ali Sepânlou, *Ragbâr-hâ* (Torrents) (Tehran, 1363/1984), and *Piâdeh-row-hâ* (Pedestrians) (Tehran, 1363/ 1984).

11   See, for instance, Fasih's *Dâstân-e Jâvid*, where all of these themes are present in one story.

12   See, for example, Golshiri's reliance on Bayhaqi in *Ma'soum-e Panjom*. For a discussion on Golshiri, see M. R. Ghanoonparvar, "Hushang Golshiri and Post-Pahlavi Concerns of the Iranian Writer of Fiction," *IS*, Vol. 18 (Spring–Autumn 1985), pp. 349–373. Further examples can be found in the psychological narrative employed by Dâneshvar in "Soutrâ," in *Beh Ki Salâm Konam?* pp. 267–299; and by Parviz Owsiâ' in *Parseh dar Diâr-e Gharib* (Wanderings in a Strange Land), unpublished typescript (c. 1984), 186 pp., the first part of which appeared as "Parseh" (Wanderings), signed by "A. Parviz," in *Cheshm-Andâz*, No. 1 (Paris, Summer 1365/1986), pp. 9–21. Another example is Barâheni's *Âvâz-e Koshtegân* (Song of the Slain), where the author reports the intellectual and political climate of the early 1970s with easily recognizable twists to real names as if they were fictional. In terms of technique, a predecessor of Barâheni's work is Sa'id Nafisi's *Nimeh-Râh-e Behesht* (Halfway to Paradise), a much celebrated satire critical of the Iranian elite written in the early 1950s (4th edition, Tehran, 1344/1965). For a study of one of Barâheni's novels published after the revolution, *Râzhâ-ye Sarzamin-e Man*, see Ghanoonparvar, *In a Persian Mirror*, pp. 108–117.

13   For example, Esmâ'il Kho'i, a contemporary modernist poet, has published in exile several collections of his recent works in which traditional forms are used for satirical verse; see "Az Khizesh-e Du-bâreh-ye Mâmout" (Revival of the Mammoth) and "Chekâmeh-ye Châleh va Châh" (The Ballad of the Hole and the Well), in Kho'i's *Kâbous-e Khoun-Sereshteh-ye Bidârân* (The Bloody Nightmare of Those Who Are Awake) (London, 1363/1984), pp. 27–32 and 112–117, respectively; or "Imam-e Tâ'oun" (Imam of the Plague) in his *Dar Nâ-behengâm* (Inopportune Time) (London, 1363/1984), pp. 128–132; or two *rubâ'is* and two *ghazals* in his *Zirâ Zamin Zamin Ast* (Because the Earth Is Always the Earth) (London, 1363/1984), pp. 96–100 (the latter poems were written in 1355–1356/1976–1977). Another example is M. Sahar (pseudonym; the word means dawn); see his *Hezb-e Tudeh dar Bâr-gâh-e Khalifeh* (The Tudeh Party at the Caliph's Court) (1st edition, Paris, 1982, 2nd edition, Paris, 1985); *Dar Bi*

Bahâr va Bi Bârân (At the Time of No Spring and No Rain) (Paris, 1362/1984); and *Ghazal-vâreh-hâ* (Odes) (Paris, 1362/1984).

14   See, for example, Vezârat-e Ershâd-e Islami (Ministry of Islamic Guidance), *Mosâbeqeh-ye She'r, Jang* (The Contest of Poetry, War), a collection of poems for the second anniversary of the war between Iraq and Iran (Tehran, 1361/1982); also Akbar Eksir, *Dar Souk-e Sepidârân* (Mourning for White Poplars) (Tehran, 1361/1982).

15   See especially, the editorial columns of semiofficial newspapers such as *Keyhân*, *Ettelâ'ât*, and *Jomhouri-e Islami* and the proceedings of the new Majles. Further references can also be found in Ayatollah Khomeini's speeches and proclamations; for an English translation of these, see Ruhollah Khomeini, *Islam and Revolution: Writings and Declarations of Imam Khomeini*, translated and annotated by Hamid Algar (Berkeley: Mizan Press, 1981).

16   Among these government-sponsored plays were: Reza Sâberi's *Mazloum-e Panjom* (The Fifth Subdued) (Tehran, 1362/1984); Esmâ'il Soltâniân's *Khoun-e Sabz* (Green Blood) (Tehran, 1362/1984); Hosein Mokhtâri's *Abâzar* (Tehran, 1362/1984); Mortezâ Sâdeq-kâr's *Dâdgâh* (Court) (Tehran, 1362/1984); and Seyyed Abbas Ma'roufi's *Ân Shast Nafar, Ân Shast Hezâr* (Those Sixty People, Those Sixty Thousand) (Tehran, 1362/1984). Among the *maktabi* short stories, some examples include Reza Rahgozar, *Asil-Âbâd* (Tehran: Daftar-e Nashr-e Farhang-e Islami, n.d.); Mohsen Soleymâni, *Âshnâ-ye Penhân* (Hidden Companion), a collection of short stories (Tehran: Howzeh-ye Andisheh va Honar-e Islami, 1361/1982); and Mohsen Makhmalbâf, *Bâgh-e Bolour* (Crystal Garden), a novel (Tehran, 1365/1986).

17   Among the official publishing institutions are: Sâzmân-e Tabliqât-e Islami (Organization for Islamic Propagations), Daftar-e Nashr-e Farhang-e Islami (Bureau for the Publication of Islamic Culture), Enteshârât-e Vezârat-e Ershâd-e Islami (Publications of the Ministry of Islamic Guidance), Enteshârât-e Bonyâd-e Shahid (Publications of the Martyrs Foundation), and Daftar-e Enteshârât-e Islami (Bureau for Islamic Publications), which is attached to the influential theological seminaries of Qom.

18   I have elsewhere discussed this topic in further detail: see Gheissari, "Naqd-e Adab-e Eide'oluzhik."

19   As two examples of the manifestos published during the early 1980s on how to write *maktabi* works and what the main ingredients of *maktabi* aesthetic perception would be, see Mohsen Makhmalbâf, *Yâd-dâshthâ'i dar bâreh-ye Qesseh-Nevisi va Namâyesh-nâmeh-Nevisi* (Notes on Short Story and Play Writing) (Tehran, 1360/1982); and Mohsen Makhmalbâf, *Moqaddameh'i bar Honar-e Islami* (An Introduction to Islamic Art) (Tehran, 1361/1982). Before the decade's end, however, Makhmalbaf displayed remarkable talent in film production and was recognized at home and abroad for a number of works such as *Bâysikel-rân* (The Bicycle Man), *Nâser al-Din Shah Aktor-e Sinemâ* (Nâser al-Din Shah the Movie Actor), and, more recently, *Salâm Sinemâ* (Hello Cinema) and *Gabbeh* (a

nomadic rug that uses images to tell a personal story from the weaver's family history), none of which carry the ideological dogmatism of his earlier writings.

20   See Michael M. J. Fischer, *Iran: From Religious Dispute to Revolution* (Cambridge, Mass.: Harvard University Press, 1980), pp. 13–21 and 21–27. The symbolism of Hosein's martyrdom was repeatedly alluded to by Ayatollah Khomeini and other leading ulama during the revolution. The following is a typical example:

> *Moharram, the month of courage and sacrifice, has arrived. This is the month during which the blood of martyrs defeated the sword and Truth overcame falsehood, rendering the satanic rule of tyrants futile. Moharram has taught generations of people throughout history how to defeat oppression and it has been remembered as the month in which Truth prevailed over secular super-powers. In this month, our Imam Hossein taught us how to fight against tyranny. He showed us how the clenched fists of freedom fighters can crush the tanks and guns of the oppressors, ultimately giving the victory to Truth. . . . Islam is for the oppressed and the peasants and the poor. . . . Today nobody has any excuse to be passive, and silence or withdrawal is suicidal, aiding the oppressors. . . . I consider martyrdom for truth an everlasting honour.*

Rouhollah Khomeini, "The Message of Ayatollah Khomaini to the Brave People of Iran on the Occasion of Moharram," in Ali-Reza Nobari, ed., *Iran Erupts* (Stanford, Calif.: Iran-America Documentation Group, 1978), pp. 229–231; quoted in Farhad Kazemi, *Poverty and Revolution in Iran: The Migrant Poor, Urban Marginality and Politics* (New York: New York University Press, 1980), p. 94.

21   For a discussion of conspiracy theory in Iranian political culture, see Ahmad Ashraf, "Conspiracy Theories," in *EIr*, Vol. 6, pp. 138–147. See further Ervand Abrahamian, *Khomeinism: Essays on the Islamic Republic* (Berkeley: University of California Press, 1993), especially "The Paranoid Style in Iranian Politics," pp. 111–131. It should also be noted that the Islamic state itself is vexed with factionalism and does not represent ideological homogeneity. See Ali Banuazizi, "Iran's Revolutionary Impasse: Political Factionalism and Societal Resistance," *Middle East Report* (November–December 1994), pp. 2–8.

22   This attitude is clear in the condemnation of Salman Rushdie for allegedly blaspheming Islam in his *Satanic Verses*. A similar attitude also existed among the earlier communist writers: note the warnings about the intrigues of the liberals, and the idea that true Communism (or, in the case of *maktabi* writers, true Islam) has not yet arrived and we are only moving toward it. Ayatollah Khomeini repeatedly stated that the ultimate duty of the Islamic government is to prepare the country for its "veritable owner" (*sâheb-e asli*), the Mahdi.

23   See, for example, Kazemi, *Poverty and Revolution in Iran*, pp. 88–96; and

Mohsen M. Milani, *The Making of Iran's Islamic Revolution: From Monarchy to Islamic Republic* Boulder, Colo.: Westview Press (1st edition, 1988; 2nd edition, 1994), pp. 110–133.

24 For a study of the emerging young Muslim intellectuals in neighboring Turkey, who share many similarities with their Iranian counterparts, see Michael E. Meeker, "The New Muslim Intellectuals in the Republic of Turkey," in Richard Tapper, ed., *Islam in Modern Turkey: Religion, Politics and Literature in a Secular State* (London, 1994), pp. 189–219; and Michael Meeker, "The Muslim Intellectual and His Audience: A New Configuration of Writer and Reader among Believers in the Republic of Turkey," in Serif Mardin, ed., *Cultural Transitions in the Middle East* (Leiden: E. J. Brill, 1994), pp. 153–188.

25 See Meskoob, *Melliyat va Zabân*; English edition, Meskoob, *Iranian Nationality and the Persian Language*.

26 On the distinction between *content* and *intent* in literary theory, see Paul De Man, *Blindness and Insight: Essays in the Rhetoric of Contemporary Criticism* (New York: Oxford University Press, 1971).

27 For further theoretical and political discussions on this topic, see, for example, Robert J. Brym, *Intellectuals and Politics* (London: George Allen and Unwin, 1980); and Dick Flacks, "Making History and Making Theory: Notes on How Intellectuals Seek Relevance," in Charles C. Lemert, ed., *Intellectuals and Politics: Social Theory in a Changing World* (Newbury Park, Calif.: Sage, 1991), pp. 3–18.

28 For several recent studies on different aspects of the political commitment of intellectuals, see Ian Maclean, Alan Montefiore, and Peter Winch, eds., *The Political Responsibility of Intellectuals* (Cambridge: Cambridge University Press, 1990).

29 For the concept of generation, see Karl Mannheim, "The Problem of Generations," in his *Essays in the Sociology of Knowledge* (London: Routledge and Kegan Paul, 1952), pp. 276–322.

30 For an analysis of different types of knowledge-constitutive interests, see Jürgen Habermas, *Knowledge and Human Interests*, translated by Jeremy J. Shapiro (Boston: Beacon Press, 1971).

31 Compare with, for example, the argument put forward by Walter Benjamin on the functions of history and theology, with the former implying a sense of political continuity and the latter referring to a break with any given order of things. See Walter Benjamin, "Theologico-Political Fragment" and "The Destructive Character," both in his *One Way Street*, translated by Edmund Jephcott and Kingsley Shorter (London, NLB, 1979), pp. 155–156 and 157–159, respectively.

32 Here "objective spirit" represents what in the social sciences is often called "culture." A major philosophical contribution to this topic can be searched in G. W. F. Hegel, *The Phenomenology of Mind*, translated from the Ger-

man with an introduction and notes by J. B. Baillie, 2nd edition (revised), 7th impression (London: George Allen and Unwin, 1966), note in particular "Culture and Its Realm of Actual Reality," pp. 514–548. For an elucidation of Hegelian arguments, see W. T. Stace, *The Philosophy of Hegel: A Systematic Exposition* (New York: Dover, 1955), pp. 374–438. See further Georg Simmel, *The Philosophy of Money*, translated from the German by Tom Bottomore and David Frisby (London: Routledge & Kegan Paul, 1978), especially "The Concept of Culture," pp. 446–470.

33 For a few samples of classical Marxist statements on morality and ethics, see Howard Selsam and Harry Martel, eds., *Reader in Marxist Philosophy: From the Writings of Marx, Engels, and Lenin* (New York: International Publishers, 1963; 7th printing, 1973), Part 7, "Ethics," pp. 248–274. See further Leon Trotsky, *Their Morals and Ours* (New York, 1942). For a critical remark on cultural relativism, see Ramin Jahanbagloo, *Conversations with Isaiah Berlin: Recollections of an Historian of Ideas* (London, 1992), pp. 37–40.

34 I have borrowed this expression from Isaiah Berlin; see Jahanbagloo, *Conversations with Isaiah Berlin*, pp. 108–109. For some Kantian ideas on intuitive and moral certainty, see Immanuel Kant, *Grundlegung zur Metaphysik der Sitten*, edited by Karl Vorländer (Hamburg: Verlag von Felix Meiner, 1962); translated into English by, among others, H. J. Paton, as *Groundwork of the Metaphysic of Morals* (reprinted, New York, 1964).

— BIBLIOGRAPHY —

I. Works in Persian and Arabic

Âbedini, Hasan. *Sad-sâl Dâstân-nevisi dar Iran* (Iranian Fiction in the Last Hundred Years). Vol. 1 (1253/1874–1342/1963), Tehran, 1366/1987.

Abu al-Hasani (Monzer), Ali. *Shahid Motahhari Efshâgar-e Towte'eh* (Martyr Motahhari: Discloser of Conspiracy). Tehran, 1362/1983.

Abu al-Ziâ' Parvin, ed. *Râhnamâ-ye Rouznâmehâ-ye Iran* (A Guide to Iranian Newspapers). Tehran: Institute for Research and Planning in Science and Education, Iranian Documentation Centre, n.d.

Âdamiyat, Fereydoun, *Eide'uluzhi-ye Nehzat-e Mashrutiyat-e Iran. Jeld-e Dovvom: Majles-e Avval va Bohrân-e Âzâdi* (The Ideology of the Iranian Constitutional Movement. Vol. 2: The First Majles and the Crisis of Freedom [*Âzâdi* can also be translated here as "civil liberties" or simply as "democracy"]). Tehran, n.d.

———. *Fekr-e Âzâdi va Moqaddameh-ye Nehzat-e Mashrutiyat-e Iran* (The Idea of Liberty and the Beginning of the Iranian Constitutional Movement). Tehran, 1340/1961–1962.

———. *Andishehâ-ye Mirzâ Âqâ Khân Kermâni* (The Ideas of Mirzâ Âqâ Khân Kermâni). Tehran, 1346/1967.

———. *Amir Kabir va Iran* (Amir Kabir and Iran). 4th edition, Tehran, 1354/1975.

———. *Fekr-e Demokrâsi-ye Ejtemâ'i dar Nehzat-e Mashrutiyat-e Iran* (The Idea of Social Democracy in the Iranian Constitutional Movement). Tehran, 1355/1976.

———. *Eide'uluzhi-ye Nehzat-e Mashrutiyat-e Iran* (The Ideology of the Iranian Constitutional Movement). Vol. 1, Tehran, 2535 [1355]/1976.

———. *Andishehâye Mirzâ Fath-Ali Âkhoundzâdeh* (The Ideas of Mirzâ Fath-Ali Âkhoundzâdeh). Tehran, 1349/1970–1971.

———. *Andisheh-ye Taraqqi va Hokoumat-e Qânoun: 'Asr-e Sepahsâlâr* (The Idea of Progress and the Rule of Law: The Period of Sepahsâlâr). Tehran, 1351/1972.

———. "Barkhurd-e Afkâr va Takâmol-e Pârlemâni dar Majles-e Avval" (Exchange of Ideas and Parliamentary Development in the First Majles). In Fereydoun Âdamiyat, *Maqâlât-e Târikhi* (Historical Essays). Tehran, 1352/1973, pp. 109–118.

———. "'Aqâyed va Ârâ-ye Sheikh Fazlollâh Nouri" (The Ideas of Sheikh Fazlollâh Nouri). *Ketâb-e Jom'eh*, Vol. 1, No. 31, Tehran (28 Farvardin 1359/17 April 1980), pp. 52–61.

———. *Âshoftegi dar Fekr-e Târikhi* (Confusion in Historical Thinking). Tehran, 1360/1981.

———. *Shouresh bar Emtiâz-Nâmeh-ye Rezhi: Tahlil-e Siâsi* (Protest against the Régie Concession: A Political Analysis). Tehran, 1360/1981.

————. *Andishehâ-ye Tâlebuf Tabrizi* (The Ideas of Tâlebuf Tabrizi). 2nd edition, Tehran, 1363/1984.

Âdamiyat, Fereydoun, and Homâ Nâteq. *Afkâr-e Ejtemâ'i va Siâsi va Eqtesâdi dar Âsâr-e Montasher-Nashodeh-ye Dowrân-e Qajar* (Social and Political and Economic Ideas in the Unpublished Sources of the Qajar Period). Tehran, 2536 [1356]/1977.

Afghâni, Ali-Mohammad. *Sindokht*. Tehran, 1360/1981.

————. *Doktor Baktâsh*. Tehran, 1364/1985.

Afkhami, Gholam Reza, and Seyyed Vali Reza Nasr, eds. *The Oral History Collection of the Foundation for Iranian Studies*. See Foundation for Iranian Studies.

Afshâr, Iraj. "Vafât-e Doktor Seyyed Fakhr al-Din Shâdmân" (The Departure of Dr. Seyyed Fakhr al-Din Shâdmân). *Râhnamâ-ye Ketâb*, Vol. 10 (1346/1967), pp. 435–438. Also in Iraj Afshâr, *Savâd va Bayâz* (Black and White). Vol. 2, Tehran, 1349/1970, included in "Vafiât-e Mo'allefin" (Obituaries of Authors), pp. 513–617.

Afshâr, Iraj. "Hosein Hejâzi." *Âyandeh*, Vol. 6, Nos. 7–8 (Mehr–Âbân 1359/October– November 1980), pp. 922–930.

Afshâr, Iraj, ed. *Fehrest-re Maqâlât-e Farsi* (An Index of Persian Articles). 3 vols.: Vol. 1 (1328 A.H./1910–1338/1959), Tehran, 1348/1970; Vol. 2 (1339/1960–1345/ 1966), 2nd edition, Tehran, 2536 [1356]/1977; Vol. 3 (1346/1967–1350/1971), Tehran, 2535 [1355]/1976.

————. *Rejâl-e Vezârat-e Khârejeh dar 'Asr-e Nâseri and Mozaffari az Neveshteh-hâ-ye Mirzâ Mehdi Khân Momtahen al-Dowleh-ye Shaqâqi and Mirzâ Hâshem Khân* (Officials of the Foreign Ministry in the Times of Nâser al-Din Shah and Mozaffar al-Din Shah, documented by Mirzâ Mehdi Khân Momtahen al-Dowleh Shaqâqi and Mirzâ Hâshem Khân) (Tehran: Asâtir, 1365/1986).

Afshâr Begeshlu Qazvini, Mirzâ Reza Khân. *Parvaz-e Negâresh-e Pârsi* (The Principal Method of Writing Persian). Istanbul: Akhtar, 1300 A.H./1883.

Ahmad-Zâdeh, Mas'oud. *Mobârezeh-ye Mosallahâneh: Ham Estrâtezhi ham Tâktik* (Armed Struggle: Both a Strategy and a Tactic). N.p., n.d.

Ahrâr, Ahmad. *Shâhin-e Sepid* (White Falcon). Tehran, 1364/1985.

Akbari, Ali-Akbar. *Bar-resi-ye Chand Mas'aleh-ye Ejtemâ'i* (An Overview of Some Social Problems). Tehran, 1349/1970.

Âlâtur. See Eshâq, Eprim.

Alavi, Seyyed Abd al-Hasan. *Rejâl-e 'Asr-e Mashrutiyat*. Edited by Habib Yaghmâ'i, reprinted by Iraj Afshâr, Tehran, 1363/1984.

Alizâdeh, Mobârez. "Pirâmoun-e Jahânbini-e Mirzâ Malkam Khân" (On the World Outlook of Mirzâ Malkam Khan). In Hosein Mohammadzâdeh (H. Sadiq), ed. and trans., *Masâ'el-e Adabiyât-e Nuvin-e Iran* (Problems of Modern Persian Literature). Tehran, 1354/1975, pp. 99–121.

Âl-Ahmad, Jalâl. "Masalan Sharh-e Ahvâlât" (My So-Called Autobiography). In Jalâl Âl-Ahmad, *Yek Châh va Du Châleh* (One Well and Two Pits). Tehran, 1343/1964. Reprinted in Hamid Tabrizi, ed., *Jalâl Âl-Ahmad, Mardi dar Kash-â-kash-e Târikh-e Mo'âser* (Jalâl Âl-Ahmad: A Man Confronting Contemporary History). Tabriz, 1357/1978, pp. 62–68.

————. *Khasi dar Miqât*. Tehran, 1345/1966.

————. *Dar Khedmat va Khiânat-e Rowshanfekrân* (The Intellectuals: How They

Serve or Betray Their Country). 3rd edition (complete text), Tehran: Ravâq, n.d. (1356/1977).

———. *Gharbzadegi*. N.p., n.d.; 2nd revised edition, Tehran: Ravâq, Winter 1356/1977–1978.

———. *Seh Maqâleh-ye Digar* (Three More Essays). 3rd edition, Tehran: Ravâq, 1356/1977.

Algar, Hamid. "Islâh." *EI2*, pp. 163–167.

Amir Arsalân. See *Kolliyât-e Haft-Jeldi-ye Amir Arsalân*.

Andisheh va Honar. See Vosouqi, Nâser.

Âref Qazvini, Abul-Qâsem. *Divân-e 'Âref*. Edited by Seyf Âzâd, Tehran, 1327/1948.

Âryan-pour, Yahyâ. *Az Sabâ tâ Nimâ: Târikh-e 150 Sâl Adab-e Fârsi* (From Sabâ to Nimâ: A History of 150 Years of Persian Literature). 2 Vols. (Tehran, 1350/1971), 4th edition, Tehran: Jibi, 1354/1975; 3rd additional volume, published posthumously as *Az Nimâ tâ Rouzegâr-e Mâ: Târikh-e Adab-e Fârsi-ye Mo'âser* (From Nimâ to Our Time: A History of Contemporary Persian Literature), Tehran: Zavvâr, 1374/1995.

Asad-Âbâdi, Mirzâ Lotfollâh Khân. *Sharh-e Hâl va Âsâr-e Seyyed Jamâl al-Din Asad-Âbâdi* (The Life and Works of al-Afghani). Vol. 1, Berlin, 1304/1926; reprinted, Tehran, 2536 [1356]/1977.

Asad-Âbâdi, Mirzâ Lotfollâh Khân, ed., *Maqâlât-e Jamâliyeh* (al-Afghani's Essays). Tehran, 1312/1933.

Âshouri, Dâriush, Karim Emâmi, and Hosein Ma'soumi-Hamedâni, eds. *Payâmi dar Râh: Nazari be She'r va Naqqâshi-ye Sohrâb Sepehri* (A Message in the Way: Glancing at Sepehri's Poetry and Paintings). Tehran: Tahouri, Winter 1359/1982.

Âshtiâni, Seyyed Jalâl al-Din. *Montakhebâti az Âsâr-e Hokamâ-ye Elâhi-e Iran (Anthologie des philosophes iraniens)*. Vol. 1, 2nd edition, Qom, 1363/1984.

Atrafi, Ali. *Matbou'ât-e Iran*. See Esfandiâri, Shahin, Ali Atrafi, Jalâl Mosâvat, and Bâqer Mo'meni, eds., *Matbou'ât-e Iran*.

Azod al-Dowleh, Ahmad Mirzâ. *Târikh-e Azodi* (The Azodi History). Bombay, Sha'ban 1306 A.H./April 1888; edited and reprinted by H. Kouhi Kermâni, Tehran, 1328/1949 (reprinted, Karaj, 1362/1984); new edition edited by Abd al-Hosein Navâ'i, Tehran, 1355/1976.

Bahâr, Mohammad-Taqi (Malek al-Sho'arâ). *Sabk-Shenâsi* (Stylistics). Vol. 3, 4th edition, Tehran, 2535 [1355]/1976.

———. *Târikh-e Mokhtasar-e Ahzâb-e Siâsi* (A Short History of Political Parties in Iran). Vol. 1, 3rd edition, Tehran, 1357/1978.

Bahrâmi, Mihan. *Heyvân* (Animal). Tehran, 1364/1985.

Bâmdâd, Mehdi. *Sharh-e Hâl-e Rejâl-e Iran dar Qarn-e 12 va 13 va 14 Hejri* (Iranian National Biography in the Nineteenth and Twentieth Centuries). 6 Vols., Tehran, 1347–1353/1968–1974; reprinted, Tehran, 1357/1978.

Baqâ'i, Mozaffar. *Cheh Kasi Monharef Shod, Doktor Mosaddeq Yâ Doktor Baqâ'i?* (Who Deviated? Dr. Mosaddeq or Dr. Baqâ'i?). N.n., Tehran, 1363/1985.

Barâheni, Reza. *Ba'd az 'Arousi Cheh Gozasht?* (What Happened after the Wedding?). Tehran, 1361/1982.

———. *Âvâz-e Koshtegân* (Song of the Slain). Tehran, 1362/1983.

———. *Châh beh Châh* (Out of One Well, Down to Another). Tehran, 1362/1983.

————. *Qesseh-Nevisi* (Writing Fiction). 3rd edition, Tehran, 1362/1983.

————. *Târikh-e Mozakkar* (Masculine History). Tehran, 1363/1984.

————. *Râzhâ-ye Sarzamin-e Man* (The Mysteries of My Homeland). Tehran, 1987.

Barzin, Mas'oud. *Matbou'ât-e Iran, 1343–53* (Iranian Press, 1964–74). Tehran, 1354/1976.

Bâstâni Pârizi, Mohammad Ebrâhim. *Talâsh-e Âzâdi (Mohit-e Siâsi va Zendegâni-e Moshir al-Dowleh Pirniâ)* (Struggle for Liberty: The Political Environment and the Life of Moshir al-Dowleh Pirniâ). 4th edition, Tehran, 2536 [1356]/1977.

Bâzargân, Mehdi. *Modâfe'ât-e Mohandes Bâzargân dar Dâdgâh-e Tajdid-e Nazar-e Nezâmi dar Sâl-e 1343* (The Defense of Engineer Bâzargân at the Military Court of Appeals in 1964). Tehran: Modarres, n.d.

————. *Bâd va Bârân dar Qur'ân* (Wind and Rain in the Koran). Edited by Seyyed Mohammad-Mehdi Ja'fari (originally written in 1343/1964). Tehran: Enteshâr, 1353/1974.

Behnam, Jamshid. "Manzelgâhi dar Râh-e Tajaddod-e Iran: Istanbul" (Istanbul: A "Way Station" to the Modernization of Iran). *Iran Nameh*, Vol. 11, No. 2 (Spring 1993), pp. 271–282.

Bidgoli Kâshâni (pen name "Sobhi," also known as "Mu'bed"), Sheikh Abd al-Ali (ibn Mohammad). *Majmou'eh-ye Mu'bed*. Tehran, 1320 A.H./1902–1903.

Boroujerdi, Mehrzad. "Gharbzadegi va Sharq-Shenâsi-ye Vârouneh" (Westoxication and Orientalism in Reverse). *Iran Nameh*, Vol. 8, No. 3 (Summer 1369/1990), pp. 375–390.

Bozorg Omid, Abu al-Hasan. *Az Mâst keh Bar Mâst: Mohtavi-e Khâterât va Moshâhedât* (We Have Only Ourselves to Blame: Memoirs). 2nd edition, Tehran, 1363/1984.

Bozorgmehr, Jalil. *Taqrirât-e Mosaddeq dar Zendân* (The Prison Writings of Mosaddeq). Edited by Iraj Afshâr, Tehran, 1359/1980.

Daftar-e Nashr-e Mirâs-e Maktoub (Written Heritage Press). *Kârnâmeh-ye Mirâs: Fehrest-e Âsâr va Motoun-e Dar Dast-e Tas-hih va Enteshâr* (The Heritage Records: A List of Works and Manuscripts in Editorial Preparation for Publication). Tehran, Fall 1374/1995.

Daftar-e Tadvin va Tanzim-e Majmou'eh-ye Âsâr-e Mo'allem-e Shahid Doktor Ali Shari'ati (The Editorial Office of the Collected Works of the Martyred Teacher Dr. Ali Shari'ati), ed., *Farhang-e Loghât-e Kotob-e Doktor Ali Shari'ati* (A Terminological Guide to the Writings of Dr. Ali Shari'ati). Tehran: Ferdowsi, 1362/1983.

Dâneshvar, Simin. *Be Ki Salâm Konam?* (Whom Should I Greet?). (Short stories), Tehran, 1359/1980.

————. *Jazireh-ye Sargardâni* (The Island of Bewilderment). Vol. 1, Tehran, 1372/1993; Vol. 2, Tehran, in press.

Davâni, Ali. *Nehzat-e Rowhânioun-e Iran* (The Movement of the Iranian Clergy). 10 vols. Tehran, n.d. (1360/1981).

Dâvari, Reza. *Vaz'-e Konouni-ye Tafakkor dar Iran* (The Present Status of Thought in Iran). Tehran, 1357/1978.

Dehâti. See Mas'oud, Mohammad.

Dehkhodâ, Ali-Akbar. *Loghat-Nâmeh* (Persian Lexicon). Tehran, 1351/1972.

Dehnavi, M., ed. *Majmou'eh-i az Maktoubât, Sokhanrânihâ va Payâmhây-e Ayatollah Kâshâni* (A Collection of Writings, Lectures, and Communiqués of Ayatollah Kâshâni). Vol. 1 (1299–Shahrivar 1330/1921–September 1951), Tehran, 1361/

1982; Vol. 2 (Mehr 1330–30 Tir 1331/October 1951–21 July 1952), Tehran, 1361/1982; Vol. 3 (1 Mordâd 1331–28 Mordâd 1332/23 July 1952–19 August 1953), Tehran, 1362/1983.

Dehqâni, Ashraf. *Hamâseh-ye Moqâvemat* (The Legend of Resistance). N.p., n.d.; reproduced, n.p. Tehran: Jonbesh, 1357/1978.

Derakhshesh, Mohammad. *Hashtâd Sâl Be-Sou-ye Sarâb* (Eighty Years toward a Mirage). N.p. (Oakton, Va.: Jâme'eh-ye Mo'allemân-e Iran (Iranian Teachers' Association), Âzar 1362/December 1983.

Dowlatâbâdi, Mahmoud. *Jây-e Khâli-e Salouch* (The Empty Place of Salouch). Tehran, 1358/1979.

———. *Qoqnous* (Phoenix). Tehran, 1361/1982.

———. *Kleydar.* 10 Vols. in 5 Books, 3rd edition, Tehran, 1363/1984.

Dowlatâbâdi, Yahyâ. *Hayât-e Yahyâ* (Yahyâ's Life). 4 Vols., 2nd edition, Tehran, 1361/1982.

Ebrâhimi, Nâder. Review of Fereydoun Hoveydâ, *Qarantineh.* Tehran: Enteshârât-e Iranmehr, 1345/1966. *Sokhan,* Vol. 17, No. 2 (Ordibehesht 1346/May 1967), pp. 219–225.

Ebtehâj (Sâyeh), Houshang. (Poem). *Keyhân* (13 Bahman 1357/1 February 1979).

Eksir, Akbar. *Dar Souk-e Sepidârân* (Mourning for White Poplars). Tehran, 1361/1982.

Elâhi, Asghar. *Mâdaram Bi-Bi Jân* (My Mother Bi-Bi Jân). Tehran, n.d.

Emâmi, Karim. *Payâmi dar Râh.* See Âshouri, Dariush, Karim Emâmi, and Hosein Ma'soumi-Hamedani, eds., *Payâmi dar Râh.*

Enâyat, Hamid. "Din va Donyâ" (Sacred and Secular). *Negin* (31 Mordâd 1347/22 August 1968); reprinted in Hamid Enâyat, *Jahâni Az Khud Bigâneh: Majmu'eh-ye Maqâlât* (An Alienated World: Collection of Essays). Tehran, 1351/1972, pp. 75–102.

———. *Jahâni Az Khud Bigâneh: Majmu'eh-ye Maqâlât* (An Alienated World: Collection of Essays). Tehran, 1351/1972.

———. *Seyri dar Andisheh-ye Siâsi-ye Arab: Az Hamleh-ye Nâpole'oun beh Mesr tâ Jang-e Jahâni-ye Dovvom* (A Survey of Arab Political Thought: From Napoleon's Incursion into Egypt to the Second World War). 1st edition, Tehran, 1356/1977; 2nd edition, Tehran: Amir Kabir, 1358/1979.

Esfandiâri, Shahin, Ali Atrafi, Jalâl Mosâvât, and Bâqer Mo'meni, eds. *Matbou'ât-e Iran, Fehrest-e Tahlili-e Ketâb-khâneh-ye Majles-e Senâ* (Iranian Press: An Analytical Index of the Library of the Senate). Tehran: Institute for Research and Planning in Science and Education, Iranian Documentation Centre, 1358/1979.

Eshâq, Eprim. *Cheh Bâyad Kard?* (What Is to be Done?). Reprinted, Tehran, Âzar 1325/December 1946.

Eshâq, Eprim (Âlâtur [pseudonym]). *Hezb-e Tudeh-ye Iran Sar-e Du Râh* (The Tudeh Party of Iran at a Crossroads). Edited by Jalâl Âl-Ahmad, Tehran, 1947.

Eshqi, Seyyed Mohammad-Reza (Mirzâdeh). See Moshir-Salimi, Ali-Akbar, ed. *Kolliyât-e Mosavvar-e Mirzâdeh 'Eshqi* (Collected Works of Mirzâdeh Eshqi).

E'temâd al-Saltaneh, Mohammad-Hasan Khân. *Kholseh (Mashhour be Khwâbnâmeh)* (The Book of Dreams). Edited by Mahmoud Katirâ'i, 2nd edition. Tehran, Toukâ, 1357/1988.

Ettehâdiyeh (Nezâm Mâfi), Mansoureh. *Peydâyesh va Tahavvol-e Ahzâb-e Siâsi-e Mash-*

rutiyat: *Dowreh-ye Avval va Dovvom-e Majles-e Showrâ-ye Melli* (The Rise and Development of Political Parties in the Constitutional Movement during the First and Second Sessions of the Majles). Tehran, 1361/1982.

Ettehâdiyeh-ye Komunist-hâ-ye Iran (Union of Iranian Communists). *Jonbesh-e Dâneshjou'i-e Iran* (Iran's Student Movement). N.p.: Ettehâdiyeh-ye Komunist-hâ-ye Iran, 1355/1976, 64 pp.; reproduced on microfiche in Wolfgang H. Behn, *The Iranian Opposition to the Shah*, Subject Group 26: Student Affairs, Publ. No. 14, Mf. n. 8, p. 81.

Fadâ'i Isfahani (Dowlat-yâr Jang), Nasrollâh Khân. *Dâstân-e Torktâzân-e Hend* (The Story of Indian Ramblers). 5 Vols. Bombay, 1310 A.H./1867.

Farhangestân-e Iran (Iranian Academy). *Vâzhehâ-ye Now* (New Words). Vols. 6 and 7, Tehran (n.d.).

―――. *Nâmeh-ye Farhangestân* (The [Iranian] Academy's Newsletter), Vol. 1, No. 1, Tehran (Ordibehesht 1322/April–May 1943).

Fardid, Ahmad. "Chand Porsesh dar Bâb-e Farhang-e Sharq" ([Answer to] Some Questions concerning the Oriental Culture). Transcribed by Reza Dâvari. *Farhang va Zendegi* (Culture and Life), No. 7, Special Issue on Oriental Culture, Tehran (Dey 1350/January 1972), pp. 32–39.

Fardid, Ahmad. Unpublished interview. See Gheissari, Ali. Unpublished interview with Ahmad Fardid.

Fardoust, Hosein. *Zohour va Soqout-e Saltanat-e Pahlavi* (The Rise and Fall of the Pahlavi Reign). Edited by Mo'asseseh-ye Motâle'at va Pazhouhesh-hâ-ye Siâsi (Institute of Political Studies and Research). 2 Vols. (Vol. 1: *Memoirs*, Vol. 2: *Commentaries of the Editors*), 1st edition, Tehran, Winter 1369/1991; 3rd edition, Tehran, 1370/1991.

Farhangestân. *Farhangestân-e Iran: Vâzheha-ye Now* (Iranian Academy: New Terms), Vols. 6 and 7, Tehran (n.d.).

―――. *Nâmeh-ye Farhangestân* (The [Iranian] Academy's Newsletter), Vol. 1, No. 1, Tehran (Ordibehesht 1322/April–May 1943).

Farrokhi Yazdi, Mohammad. *Divân-e Farrokhi Yazdi*. Edited with an introduction by Hosein Makki, 7th edition, Tehran, 1363/1984.

Farzâd, Hosein. *Târikh-e Enqelâb va Tahavvul-e Âzarbâyjân dar Dowreh-ye Mashrutiyat yâ Târikh-e Sattâr Khân Sardâr-e Melli* (A History of Revolution in Azerbaijan during the Constitutional Period or a History of Sattar Khan the National Commander). Tabriz, 1324/1945.

Fasih, Esmâ'il. *Dâstân-e Jâvid* (Jâvid's Story). Tehran, 1360/1981.

―――. *Sorayyâ dar Eghmâ'* (Sorayya in a Coma). Tehran, 1362/1983.

―――. *Dard-e Siâvosh* (The Pain of Siâvoush). Tehran, 1364/1985.

―――. *Zemestân-e Shast-u Du* (The Winter of Sixty-Two). Tehran, 1366/1987.

―――. *Asir-e Zamân* (Prisoner of Time). Tehran, 1373/1994.

Fathi, Asghar. *Menbar, Yek Rasâneh-ye 'Omoumi dar Islam* (The Minbar as a Medium of Public Communication in Islam). Tehran, 1358/1980.

Forouhi, Ali. "Arâmaneh-ye Gilân va Nehzat-e Mashroutiyat" (The Armenians of Gilân and the Constitutional Movement). *Âyandeh*, Vol. 19, Nos. 7–9 (Mehr–Âzar 1372/October–December 1993), pp. 695–711.

Foroughi (Zakâ' al-Molk), Mohammad-Ali. "Hoqouq dar Iran" (Law in Iran). Reprinted in *Iranshenasi*, Vol. 2, No. 3 (Fall 1369/1990), pp. 619–634.

Forouzânfar, Badiʿ al-Zamân. *Kolliyât-e Shams.* See Mowlavi, Mawlânâ Jalâl al-Din Mohammad. *Kolliyât-e Shams.*

Gheissari, Ali. Unpublished interview with Ahmad Fardid. Tehran, 7 Mehr 1360/29 September 1981.

Gheissari, Ali. "Naqd-e Adab-e Eideʾulozhik: Morouri bar Adabiyât-e Rowshan-fekri va Maktabi-ye Iran" (Critique of Ideological Literature: A Review of Intellectual and Doctrinaire Writings in Iran). *Iran Nameh,* Vol. 12, No. 2 (Spring 1994), pp. 233–258.

Golâbdarrehʾi, Mahmoud. *Parastou* (Swallow). (Short stories). Tehran, 1363/1984.

———. *Sahrâ-ye Sard* (The Cold Desert). Tehran, Winter 1363/1985.

———. *Sarnevesht-e Bacheh-ye Shemroun* (The Story of the Boy from Shemirân). (Short stories). Tehran, 1364/1985.

Golestân, Lili, ed. *Sohrâb Sepehri: Shâʿer, Naqqâsh* (Sohrâb Sepehri: Poet, Painter). Tehran: Amir-Kabir, 1359/1980.

Golshiri, Houshang. "Javânmargi dar Nasr-e Moʿâser-e Fârsi" (Premature Death in Contemporary Persian Prose). In Nâser Moʾazzen, ed., *Dah Shab* (Ten Nights). Tehran: Iranian Writers Association, 1357/1978, pp. 346–356.

———. *Maʿsoum-e Panjom* (The Fifth Innocent). Tehran, 1359/1981.

———. "Hâshiyehʾi bar Român-hâ-ye Moʿâser: Hâshiyehʾi bar Kleydar" (A Commentary on Contemporary Novels: A Commentary on Kleydar). In *Naqd-e Âgâh* (No. 1). Tehran: Enteshârât-e Âgâh, 1361/1982, pp. 38–62.

———. *Jobbeh-Khâneh* (Cloakroom). Tehran, 1362/1983.

———. *Hadis-e Mâhi-gir va Div* (The Story of the Fisherman and the Demon). Tehran, 1363/1984.

Golshiri, Houshang, ed. *Hasht Dâstân* (Eight Stories). (Collection of short stories). Edited with an introduction by Houshang Golshiri, Tehran, 1363/1984.

Hâʾeri, ʿAbd al-Hâdi. "Sokhani Pirâmoun-e Vâzheh-ye Mashruteh" (A Note on the Term *Mashruteh*). *Vahid,* Vol. 12 (1353/1974), pp. 287–300.

———. *Nakhostin Rouyârouʾihâ-ye Andisheh-garân-e Iran bâ Du Rouyeh-ye Tamaddon-e Bourzhovâzi-ye Gharb* (Early Encounters of Iranian Thinkers with the Two Faces of Modern Western Civilization). Tehran, 1367/1988.

Hâfez, Shams al-Din Mohammad. *Divân.* Edited by Mohammad Qazvini and Qâsem Ghani, Tehran, 1320/1941.

Hakim-Elâhi, Hedâyatollâh. *Az Shahr-e Now tâ Dâdgostari* (From the Red Light Quarter to the Court of Justice). 3rd printing, Tehran, 1357–1358/1978–1979.

Halabi, Ali-Asghar. *Zendegi va Safarhâ-ye Seyyed Jamâl al-Din Asad-Âbâdi* (The Life and Travels of al-Afghani). Tehran, 2536 [1356]/1977–1978.

Hamedâni (Kowsar-Alishâh), Mollâ Mohammad-Reza. *Irshâd al-Muzellin fi Ithbât-i Nobuuwwat-i Khâtam al-Nabiʾin* (Directing the Misguided to the Path by Proving the Prophethood of the Seal of the Prophets). N.p., Persian manuscript transcribed in 1229 A.H./1814 by Mohammad-Hosein al-Mâzandarâni, Tehran.

———. *Meftâh al-Nobuuwwat* (The Opening of Prophecy), with an introduction by Mirzâ Abu al-Qâsem Qâʾem-Maqâm Farâhâni. Tehran, 1240 A.H./1824–1825; reprinted, Tehran 1340 A.H.(?)/1921–1922(?).

Haqq-e Dafʿ-e az Sharr va Qiâm bar Zedd-e Zolm (The Right to Repulse Evil and Rise against Injustice). N.n., Istanbul, 1326 A.H./1908.

Hâshem Khân, Mirzâ. See Afshâr, Iraj, ed. *Rejâl-e vezârat-e Khârejeh.*

Hâzeri, Ali-Mohammad. *Ravand-e E'zâm-e Dâneshjou dar Iran* (The Trend of Sending Iranian Students Abroad). Tehran, 1372/1993.

Hedâyat, Sâdeq, ed. *Tarânehâ-ye Khayyâm* (Khayyâm's Poems). Introduction by Sâdeq Hedâyat, 6th edition, Tehran, 1353/1974.

Heydari, Bahrâm. *Lâli*. (Short stories), Tehran, 1358/1979.

Hoseiniyeh Ershâd. *Miz-e Gerd: Pâsokh beh So'âlât va Enteqâdât* (Roundtable: Reply to Questions and Criticisms). (Participants: Mohammad-Taqi Shari'ati, Sadr al-Din Balâghi, Seyyed Mortezâ Shabastari, and Ali Shari'ati), Tehran, 1354/1975.

Hoveydâ, Fereydoun. *Qarantineh*. Translated from the French by Mostafâ Farzâneh, Tehran: Entesharât-e Iranmehr, 1345/1966.

Iranparast, Nourollâh. "Modir-e Habl al-Matin" (The Proprietor of Habl al-Matin). *Armaghân*, Vol. 10, Nos. 5–6 (1308/1932), pp. 273–284.

Iranshahr. Vol. 2, Tehran: Tehran University Press, 1343/1964.

Iranski, S. *Seh Maqâleh*. See Pavlovitch, M., V. Teria, and S. Iranski, *Seh Maqâleh*.

Ivanov, M. S. *Enqelâb-e Mashrutiyat-e Iran* (Iranian Constitutional Revolution). Persian translation by Kâzem Ansâri, Tehran, n.d.

Ja'fariân, Rasoul. *Nezâ'-e Sonnat va Tajaddod (Bahsi dar-bâreh-ye Monâsebât-e Fekri-ye Doktor Shari'ati va Ostâd Motahhari)* (The Clash of Tradition with Modernity: On the Ideas of Dr. Shariati and Professor Motahhari). Qom: Entesharât-e Ra'ouf, 1371/1992.

Jâberi (Ansâri), Mohammad-Hasan. *Târikh-e Isfahan Nesf-e Jahân* (Isfahan, [the city which is worth] One Half of the World: A History). N.p., 1333 A.H./1915, 214 pp.; reprinted with additions as *Târikh-e Isfahan va Rey va hameh-ye Jahân* (A History of Isfahan and Reyy and the Whole World). Edited by Hosein 'Emâdzâdeh, Tehran, 1321/1942, 449 pp.

Jâberi Ansâri Isfahani (Sadr al-Odabâ'), Hâj Sheikh Mirzâ (Mohammad-) Hasan. *Âftâb-e Derakhshandeh: Az Mo'jezât-e Emrouzeh-ye Islamiyeh* (The Glittering Sun: Of Today's Islamic Miracles). Foreword by Hâj Mirzâ Hasan Khân Mohtasham al-Saltaneh (Esfandiâri), lithograph edition, Tehran, 1302/1923.

Jalâli Pandari, Yadollah. "Khâterât" (Memoirs). *Âyandeh*, Vol. 16, Nos. 5–8 (Mordâd–Âban 1369/August–November 1990), pp. 427–448.

JÂMI (Jebhe-ye Âzâdi-e Mardom-e Iran) (Front for the Liberation of the Iranian People). *Gozashteh Cherâgh-e Râh-e Âyandeh Ast: Târikh-e Iran dar Fâseleh-ye Du Koudetâ* (The Past Shows the Road to the Future: A History of Iran between the Two Coups d'État). N.p., n.d. (1st edition, 1355/1976); reprinted, Tehran, 1357/1978–1979.

Jazani, Bizhan. *Târikh-e Si Sâleh-ye Iran* (A Thirty-Year History of Iran). Vol. 2, n.p., n.d.; reprinted, n.p. (Tehran): Nashr-e Kârgar, n.d. (1358/1979).

Kâmbakhsh, Abd al-Samad. *Nazari beh Jonbesh-e Kârgari va Komunisti dar Iran* (An Introduction to the Labor and Communist Movement in Iran). N.p. (West Germany?): Tudeh Party, 1972.

Kasâ'i, Nourollâh. *Madâres-e Nezâmiyeh va Ta'sirât-e 'Elmi va Ejtemâ'i-e Ân* (The Nezâmiyeh Schools and Their Academic and Social Impacts). Tehran, 1358/1980.

Kâshâni, Mollâ Abd al-Rasoul. *Resâleh-ye Ensâfiyeh* (Treatise on Impartiality and Justice). Kâshân, 1328 A.H./1910.

Kâshâni, Ayatollah Abu al-Qâsem. *Majmou'eh'i az Maktoubât, Sokhanrânihâ va Payâm-hay-e Ayatolla Kâshâni*. Edited by Mohammad Dehnavi, Vol. 1 (1299–Shahrivar

1330/1921–September 1951), Tehran, 1361/1982; Vol. 2 (Mehr 1330–30 Tir 1331/October 1951–21 July 1952), Tehran, 1361/1982; Vol. 3 (1 Mordâd 1331– 28 Mordâd 1332/23 July 1952–19 August 1953), Tehran, 1362/1983.

Kâshef, Mohammad. *Favâyed-e Râh-Âhan* (Benefits of the Railway). Edited by Mohammad-Javâd Sâhebi, Tehran, 1374/1995.

Kasravi, Ahmad. *Târikh-e Mashruteh-ye Iran* (A History of the Iranian Constitutional Movement). 13th edition, Tehran, 2536 [1356]/1978.

Katirâ'i, Mahmoud, ed. *Kholseh (Mashhour be Khwâbnâmeh)*. See Eʿtemâd al-Saltaneh, Mohammad-Hasan Khân. *Kholseh (Mashhour be Khwâbnâmeh)* (The Book of Dreams).

Kâtouziân, Mohammad-Ali Homâyoun. "Yâd-dâshti dar bâreh-ye Mellat, Melli, Melli-gerâ va Nâsiounâlism" (A Note on Nation, National, Nationalist, and Nationalism). *Fasl-e Ketâb*, London, Nos. 2 and 3 (Summer and Fall 1367/1988).

———. *Estebdâd, Demukrâsi va Nehzat-e Melli* (Democracy, Arbitrary Rule, and the Popular Movement of Iran). Washington, D.C.: Mehregan, 1372/1993.

Kâtouziân, Mohammad-Ali Homâyoun, and Amir Pishdâd. *Melli Kist va Nehzat-e Melli Chist?* (Who Is Nationalist and What Is the National Movement?). Europe (Paris?), January 1981.

Kermâni, Âqâ Khân Mirzâ. *Ketâb-e Reyhân-e Boustân Afrouz bar Tarz va Tarbiyat-e Adabiyât-e Farangestân-e Emrouz* (The Book of Garden Dazzling Herbs on the Manners and Formation of Modern Western Culture). 1st edition, 1313 A.H./1894.

Khalkhâli, Seyyed Abd al-Rahim. *Namâyesh-e Dâstân-e Khounin yâ Sargozasht-e Barmakiân* (The Unfortunate Tale or the Fate of the Barmakids). Tehran: Matbaʿeh-ye Majles, Tir 1304/June–July 1925, 69 pp.

Khâmeh'i, Anvar. *Khâterât-e Doktor Anvar Khâmeh'i* (The Memoirs of Dr. Anvar Khâmehi). Vol. 1, *Panjâh Nafar va Seh Nafar* ([The Group of] Fifty and Three), Tehran, 1352/1983; Vol. 2, *Forsat-e Bozorg-e Az Dast Rafteh* (A Great Opportunity Lost), Tehran, 1362/1984; Vol. 3, *Az Ensheʿâb tâ Koudetâ* (From the Split [of the Tudeh Party] to the Coup d'État [of 1953]), Tehran, reprinted, West Germany: Novid, 1363/1984.

Khânlari, Parviz Nâtel. See Nâtel Khânlari, Parviz.

Kho'i, Esmâʿil. *Âzâdi, Haqq, va ʿEdâlat: Monâzereh-ye Esmâʿil Kho'i bâ Ehsân Narâqi* (Liberty, Rights, and Justice: A Debate between Esmâʿil Kho'i and Ehsân Narâqi). 2nd edition, Tehran, 1357/1978.

———. *Dar Nâ-behengâm* (Inopportune Time). London, 1363/1984.

———. *Kâbous-e Khoun-Sereshteh-ye Bidârân* (The Bloody Nightmare of Those Who Are Awake). London, 1363/1984.

———. *Zirâ Zamin Zamin Ast* (Because the Earth Is Always the Earth). London, 1363/1984.

Khodâyâr Mohebbi, Manouchehr. "Doktor Seyyed Fakhr al-Din Shâdmân, Zendegi va Âsâr-e Ou" (Dr. Seyyed Fakhr al-Din Shâdmân: His Life and Works). *Vahid*, Vol. 4 (1346/1967), pp. 873–875.

Kiânfar, Jamshid. "Tarjomeh dar ʿAhd-e Qajar, az Âghâz tâ Dowreh-ye Nâser al-Din Shah" (Translation in Iran, from the Beginning to the Time of Nâser al-Din Shah). *Nashr-e Dânesh*, Vol. 10, No. 1 (Âzar and Dey 1368/December 1989 and January 1990), pp. 23–28.

Kiânoush, Mahmoud. "Khânlari: 'In-hâ Ki-and?'" (Khânlari: "Who Are These

People?"). *Fasl-e Ketâb*, Vol. 3, No. 2 (Serial No. 8), London (Summer 1370/1991), pp. 114–118.

Kohen, Go'el. *Târikh-e Sânsour dar Matbou'ât-e Iran* (A History of Censorship in the Iranian Press). Vol. 1, Tehran, 1360/1982; Vol. 2, Tehran, 1362/1983.

Kolliyât-e Haft-Jeldi-ye Amir Arsalân ibn Malekshah-e Rumi (A Complete Story in Seven Parts of Amir Arsalân ibn Malekshah-e Rumi), [transcribed] by "a lady from the Court of Nâser al-Din Shah Qajar" (*yeki az bânovân-e darbâri-e Nâser al-Din Shah Qajar*). Lithograph edition, calligraphy by Ali-Akbar Mosammem, Tehran, 1329 A.H./1911, 133 pp. Its several later editions include: Tehran: Akhavân-e Ketâbchi, 1310/1931, 314 pp.; Tehran: 'Elmi, n.d., 264 pp.; and a more standard edition edited with an introduction by Mohammad-Ja'far Mahjoub, Tehran: Jibi, 1340/1961.

Kolliyât-e Mosayyeb-Nâmeh: Sâmel-e Behtarin Revâyât va Akhbâr va Janghâ-ye Vâqe'i bâ Qataleh-ye Hazrat-e Seyyed al-Shohadâ va Koshteh-Shodan-e Ân-hâ bedast-e Ân Nâmdâr-e Vafâdâr (A Collection of Mosayyeb-Nâmeh: Including the Fullest Narrative of Campaigns with the Murderers of Imam Hosein and Their Death in the Hands of the Acclaimed and Loyal Mosayyeb). Tehran: Elmi, n.n., n.d., 178 pp.

Konfedrâsioun-e Dâneshjouyân-e Irani (Confederation of Iranian Students). *Târikh-cheh-ye Konfedrâsioun va Enherâfât-e Mowjoud dar Ân* (A Short History of the Confederation [of Iranian Students] and Its Errors). London: Confederation of Iranian Students, London branch, c. 1977, 22 pp.; reproduced on microfiche in Wolfgang H. Behn, ed., *The Iranian Opposition to the Shah*, Subject Group 26: Student Affairs, Publ. No. 43, Mf. n. 22, pp. 84–85.

Konfedrâsioun-e Dâneshjouyân-e Irani—Ettehâdiyeh-ye Melli (Confederation of Iranian Students—National Union), ed. *Pâreh-i az Asnâd-e SAVAK* (Some SAVAK Documents). Europe (Frankfurt?), 1355/1976–1977; reprinted, Tehran, 1357/1978.

Kotobi, Mortezâ. "Pazhouheshi Pirâmoun-e Voroud-e Dâneshjou beh Dâneshgâh" (A Survey on Student Entry to the Universities). *Nâmeh-ye 'Oloum-e Ejtemâ'i*, Vol. 1, no. 4 (Tir 1353/June 1974), pp. 57–76.

Ladjevardi, Habib (Project Director). *Iranian Oral History Collection*. Cambridge, Mass.: Harvard University, Center for Middle Eastern Studies, 1987.

Lesân al-Molk (Sepehr), Mirzâ Mohammad-Taqi. *Nâsekh al-Tawârikh: Salâtin-e Qâjâriyeh* (The Conclusion of All Histories: On Qajar Rulers). 4 Books in 2 Vols., edited by Mohammad-Bâqer Behboudi, Tehran, 1353/1974–1975.

Mahboubi Ardakâni, Hosein. "Dovvomin Kârvân-e Ma'refat" (The Second Caravan of Knowledge). *Yaghmâ*, Vol. 18 (1344/1965), pp. 529–598.

———. *Târikh-e Mu'assesât-e Tamaddoni-e Jadid dar Iran* (A History of Modern Institutions in Iran). Vol. 1, Tehran, 1354/1975; Vol. 2, Tehran, 2537 [1357]/1978; Vol. 3, edited by Karim Isfahaniân and Jahângir Qajariyeh, Tehran, 1368/1989.

Mahdavi, Asghar, and Iraj Afshâr, eds. *Majmou'eh-ye Asnâd va Madârek-e Châp-Nashodeh dar bâreh-ye Seyyed Jamâl al-Din mashhour beh Afghani* (A Collection of Formerly Unpublished Material on al-Afghani). Tehran, 1342/1963.

Mahmoud, Ahmad. *Dâstân-e Du Shahr* (The Story of Two Cities). Tehran, 1361/1982.

———. *Shahr-e Soukhteh* (Burned City). Tehran, 1361/1982.

Majâles-e Shahnâmeh (Ferdowsi Shahnameh Album). Tehran: Kolâleh-ye Khâvar, 1354/1975.

Makhmalbâf, Mohsen. *Moqaddameh'i bar Honar-e Islami* (An Introduction to Islamic Art). Tehran, 1361/1982.

———. *Yâd-dâshthâ'i dar bâreh-ye Qesseh-Nevisi va Namâyesh-nâmeh-Nevisi* (Notes on Short Story and Play Writing). Tehran, 1360/1982.

———. *Bâgh-e Bolour* (Crystal Garden). (Novel), Tehran, 1365/1986.

Makki, Hosein. *Târikh-e Bist Sâleh-ye Iran* (A Twenty-Year History of Iran). 8 Vols., Tehran, 1323–1363/1944–1984.

Maleki, Khalil. *Du Ravesh Barây-e Yek Hadaf* (Two Approaches to the Same Goal). Tehran, 15 Dey 1326/6 January 1946, 60 pp.

———. "Matn-e Asli-e Modâfe'ât-e Âqây-e Khalil Maleki dar Dâdgâh-e Nezâmi-e Darbasteh, Dar Radd-e Keyfar-Khâst" (The Original Text of Mr. Khalil Maleki's Defense in the Military Court). *Sousialism* (Organ of the Society of Iranian Socialists in Europe), 2nd Series, No. 7 (Mehr 1345/October 1966), pp. 37–56.

———. *Khâterât-e Siâsi-e Khalil Maleki* (The Political Memoirs of Khalil Maleki). Edited with an introduction by Mohammad-Ali Homâyoun Kâtouziân, Tehran, 1357/1979 (distributed 1360/1981).

Malekpour, Jamshid. *Adabiyât-e Namâyeshi dar Iran* (Theatrical Literature in Iran). Vol. 2: *Dowrân-e Enqelâb-e Mashruteh* (The Period of the Constitutional Revolution). Tehran, 1363/1985.

Malekzâdeh, Mehdi. *Târikh-e Enqelâb-e Mashrutiyat-e Iran* (A History of the Iranian Constitutional Revolution). Tehran, 1351/1972–1973.

Malkam Khân, Mirzâ. *Kolliyât* (Collected Works). Edited by Hâshem Rabi'zâdeh, Vol. 1, Tehran, 1325/1946–1947.

———. *Majmou'eh-ye Âsâr-e Mirzâ Malkam Khân* (Collected Works). Vol. 1: *Nazm-e Jadid* (New Order). Edited with an introduction by Mohammad Mohit Tabâtabâ'i, Tehran, 1327/1948.

———. *Rouznâmeh-ye Qânoun*. 2nd edition, collected and reprinted with an introduction by Homâ Nâteq, Tehran, 2535 [1355]/1976.

Mamaqâni, Asadollâh. *Maslak al-Imam fi Salâmat al-Islam* (The Doctrine of Imam for the Well-Being of Islam). Istanbul: Matba'eh-ye Shams, 1328 A.H./1910, 61 pp.; reprinted, Tabriz, 1329 A.H./1911; new edition, Tehran: Nashr-e Târikh-e Iran, 1363/1984.

———. *Din va Sho'oun va Tarz-e Hokoumat dar Mazhab-e Shi'a* (Religion, Functions and the Method of Government in Shi'ism). Istanbul, 1334 A.H./1916, 191 pp.; 2nd edition, Tehran: Majles, 1335/1956.

Mândegâr, Mehrdâd. [pseudonym]. "Parirouyân-e Bitâb va Asâtir-e Motevarrem: Jor'at-e 'Na' Nagoftan" (Impatient Fairies and Inflated Myths: The Courage Not to Say "No"). *Iran va Jahân*, No. 93, Paris (24–31 Khordâd 1361/14–21 June 1982).

Ma'roufi, Seyyed Abbas. *Ân Shast Nafar, Ân Shast Hezâr* (Those Sixty People, Those Sixty Thousand). Tehran, 1362/1984.

Ma'roufi, Abbas. *Samfouni-ye Mordegân* (Symphony of the Dead). 1st edition, Tehran, 1368/1989.

———. *Sâl-e Balvâ* (Year of the Riot). 3rd edition, Tehran, 1371/1992.

————. *Peykar-e Farhâd* (The Body of Farhâd). 1st edition, Tehran, 1374/1995.

Mas'oud (Dehâti), Mohammad. *Behesht-e Ârezou* (The Paradise of Desire). Tehran, n.d.

————. *Dar Talâsh-e Ma'âsh* (The Struggle for a Living). Tehran, 1312/1933.

————. *Ashraf-e Makhlouqât* ([Man,] the Noblest of Creatures). Tehran, 1313/1934.

————. *Tafrihât-e Shab* (Nocturnal Pleasures). Tehran, 1313/1934; reprinted, Tehran, 1326/1947.

————. *Golhâ'ikeh dar Jahannam Mirouyad* (Flowers Blooming in Hell). 2 Vols.: Vol. 1, Tehran, 1321/1942, reprinted, Tehran, 1337/1958; Vol. 2: *Bahâr-e 'Omr* (Life's Springtime). Tehran, 1324/1945.

Ma'soumi-Hamedâni, Hosein. *Payâmi dar Râh*. See Âshouri, Dâriush, Karim Emâmi, and Hosein Ma'soumi-Hamedani, eds., *Payâmi dar Râh*.

Matini, Jalâl. "Doktor Ali Shari'ati dar Dâneshgâh-e Mashhad (Ferdowsi)" (Remembering Dr. Ali Shari'ati at the Ferdowsi University in Mashhad). *Iranshenasi*, Vol. 5, No. 4 (Winter 1994), pp. 835–899.

Mehr. See Movaqqar, Majid.

Mesbâhi-pour Iranian, Jamshid. *Vâqe'iyat-e Ejtemâ'i va Jahân-e Dâstân* (Social Reality and the World of the Novel). Tehran, 1358/1979–1980.

Meskoob, Shahrokh. *Melliyat va Zabân: Naqsh-e Divân, Din, va 'Erfân dar Nasr-e Fârsi* (Nationality and Language: The Role of the Court, Religion, and Mysticism in the Development of Persian Prose). Paris: Ferdowsi, n.d. (1360/1981).

————. "Qesseh-ye Ghosseh yâ Român-e Haqiqi" (A Tale of Grief or the True Story). *Iran Nameh*, Vol. 11, No. 3 (Summer 1993), pp. 451–480.

Minovi, Mojtabâ. "Avvalin Kârvân-e Ma'refat." *Yaghmâ*, Vol. 6 (1332/1953).

————. *Târikh va Farhang* (History and Culture). 2nd edition, Tehran, 2536 [1356]/1977.

Mirsâdeqi, Jamâl. *Âtash az Âtash* (Fire from Fire). Tehran, 1363/1984.

————. *Bâd-hâ Khabar az Taghyir-e Fasl Midâdand* (Winds Heralded the Change of Season). Tehran, Winter 1363/1985.

Mo'ayyer al-Mamâlek, Doust-Ali Khân. *Rejâl-e 'Asr-e Nâseri* (Notables of the Naser al-Din Shah's Period). Tehran, 1361/1982.

Mo'azzen, Nâser, ed. *Dah Shab* (Ten Nights). Tehran: Iranian Writers Association, 1357/1978, 694 pp.

Mo'meni, Bâqer. *Matbou'ât-e Iran*. See Esfandiâri, Shahin, Ali'Atrafi, Jalâl Mosâvat, and Bâqer Mo'meni, eds., *Matbou'at-e Iran*.

————. *Dard-e Ahl-e Qalam* (Writers' Anguish). Tehran, Winter 1357/1979.

————. *Iran dar Âstâneh-ye Enqelâb-e Mashrutiyat* (Iran at the Threshold of the Constitutional Revolution). 6th edition, Tehran, 1359/1980.

Mo'in, Mohammad. *Mazdiasnâ va Adab-e Pârsi* (Mazdiasnâ and Persian Literature). 3rd edition, Tehran, 2535 [1355]/1976.

————. *Farhang-e Mo'in* (Persian Dictionary). 6 Vols., 5th edition, Tehran, 1362/1983.

Modarres Sâdeqi, Ja'far. *Gâv Khouni*. Tehran, 1362/1983, translated into English by Afkham Darbandi as *The Marsh [Gavkhouni]*, introduction by Dick Davis. Costa Mesa, Calif.: forthcoming, 1997.

Modarresi, Chahârdehi, Nour al-Din. *Seyri dar Tasavvof* (A Study in Persian Sufism). 2nd edition, Tehran, 1361/1982.

Modarresi-Chahârdehi, Mortezâ. *Seyyed Jamâ al-Din va Andishehâ-ye Uo* (al-Afghani's Ideas). 6th edition, Tehran, 1360/1981.

Moghtader, Reza. "Dowrân-e Sad-Sâleh-ye Tajaddod dar Shahr-sâzi va Meʿmâri-ye Iran" (A Hundred Years of Modernization in Iran's Architecture). *Iran Nameh*, Vol. 11, No. 2 (Spring 1993), pp. 259–282.

Mohammadi-Malâyeri, Mohammad. "Negâhi beh darbâr-e Sâsâni az Khelâl-e Maʾâkhez-e Islami" (A View of the Sassanian Court in Islamic Historical Sources). Article in three parts in *Iranshenasi*, Vols. 3 and 4 (1991–1992).

Mohammadzâdeh, Hosein (H. Sadiq), ed. and trans. *Masâʾel-e Adabiyât-e Nuvin-e Iran* (Problems of Modern Persian Literature). Tehran, 1354/1975.

Mohit Tabâtabâ'i, Mohammad. "Farmân-e Mashruteh az Kist?" (Who Proclaimed *Mashruteh*?). *Mohit*, Vol. 1, No. 1 (1323/1942), pp. 9–18; 2nd Series, Vol. 2, No. 4 (1326/1947), pp. 18–20, 23.

———. "Risheh-ye Mashruteh" (The Origin of *Mashruteh*). *Mohit*, 2nd Series, Vol. 1, No. 3 (1326/1947), p. 24.

———. "Seyr-e Tarjomeh dar Iran" (An Overview of Translation in Iran). *Armaghân*, Vol. 36 (1346/1967), pp. 225–237.

———. *Târikh-e Tahlili-e Matbouʿât-e Iran* (An Analytical History of the Iranian Press). Tehran, Winter 1366/1988.

Mohtasham al-Saltaneh Esfandiâri, Hâj Mirzâ Hasan Khân. *ʿElal-e Badbakhti-e Mâ va ʿAlâj-e Ân* (Causes of Our Misery and Its Cure). [Tehran], 1340 A.H./1921.

Mojtahedi, Karim. *Seyyed Jamâl al-Din Asad-Âbâdi va Tafakkor-e Jadid* (al-Afghani and Modern Thought). Tehran, 1363/1984.

Mojtahedi, Mehdi. *Rejâl-e Âzarbâyjân dar ʿAsr-e Mashrutiyat* (Azarbâyjâni Figures in the Time of the Constitutional Movement). Tehran, 1327/1948.

Mokhtâri, Hosein. *Abâzar*. Tehran, 1362/1984.

Momtahen al-Dowleh Shaqâqi, Mirzâ Mehdi Khân. See Afshâr, Iraj, ed. *Rejâl-e Vezârat-e Khârejeh.*

Mosaddeq, Mohammad. *Mosaddeq dar Mahkameh-ye Nezâmi* (Mosaddeq in the Military Tribunal). Edited with an introduction by Jalil Bozorgmehr, 2 Vols., Tehran, 1363/1985.

Mosâvât, Jalâl. *Matbouʿât-e Iran*. See Esfandiâri, Shahin, Ali ʿAtrafi, Jalâl Mosâvat, and Bâqer Moʾmeni, eds., *Matbouʿât-e Iran.*

Mosayyeb-Nâmeh. See *Kolliyât-e Mosayyeh-Nâmeh.*

Moshâr, Khânbâbâ. *Moʿallefin-e Kotob-e Châppi-e Fârsi va Arabi az Âghâz-e Châpp tâ Konoun* (Persian and Arabic Books in Print and Their Authors from the Beginning of the Print Industry in Iran to the Present). 5 Vols., Tehran, 1340–1342/1961–1963.

Moshâr, Khânbâbâ, ed. *Fehrest-e Ketâbhâ-ye Châppi-ye Fârsi* (An Index of Persian Books in Print). Vol. 2, Tehran, n.d.

Moshfeq Kâzemi, Seyyed Mortezâ. *Tehran-e Makhouf* (Tehran, City of Horrors). Part 1, 4 Vols., Tehran, 1303–1305/1924–1926; Part 2 entitled *Yâdegâr-e Yek Shab* (The Memory of One Night), 2 Vols.: Vol. 1, Berlin: Kâviâni Press, 1342 A.H./1923–1924; Vol. 2, Tehran, 1342 A.H./1923–1924; 4th edition in 4 Vols., Tehran, 1320/1941.

———. *Gol-e Pazhmordeh* (The Drooping Flower). Tehran, 1308/1929.

———. *Rashk-e Por-Bahâ* (Precious Envy). Tehran, 1309/1930.

————. *Rouzgâr va Andishe-hâ* (Times and Thoughts). Vols. 1 and 2, Tehran, 1971 and 1973.

Moshir-Salimi, Ali-Akbar, ed. *Kolliyât-e Mosavvar-e Mirzâdeh Eshqi* (Collected Works of Mirzâdeh Eshqi). 7th edition, Tehran, 1357/1978.

Movaqqar, Majid. "Iran bar Lab-e Partgâh" (Iran on the Verge of a Precipice). *Mehr*, Vol. 8, No. 7 (Mehr 1331/October 1952), pp. 358–390.

————. "Tajdid-e ʿAhd" (Renewal of the Pledge). *Mehr*, Vol. 8, No. 1 (Farvardin 1331/April 1952), pp. 1–7.

Mowlavi, Mawlânâ Jalâl al-Din Mohammad. *Kolliyât-e Shams yâ Divân-e Kabir* (The Collected Poetry of Shams or the Greater Divân). Edited with an introduction by Badiʿ al-Zamân Forouzânfar (1st edition, Tehran: Tehran University Press, 1336); 2nd edition, 10 Vols., Tehran: Amir-Kabir, Winter 2535 [1355]/1977.

[Muʾayyed al-Islam Hoseini, Seyyed Jalâl al-Din]. *Mokâlemeh-ye Sayyâh-e Irani bâ Shakhs-e Hendi* (Discourse of an Iranian Traveler with an Indian Notable). N.n., (Calcutta), India: Paradise Press, c. 1905.

Nafisi, Saʿid. *Nimeh-Râh-e Behesht* (Halfway to Paradise). 4th edition, Tehran, 1344/1965.

Nâʾini, Mirzâ Mohammad-Hosein. *Tanbih al-Umma va Tanzih al-Milla* (Awakening the Community and Purifying the Nation). 3rd edition, Tehran, 1374 A.H./ 1955.

Nâʾini, Mirzâ Reza Khân (Tabâtabâʾi). *Rouznâmeh-ye Tiâtr* (Theater News). Edited by Mohammad Golbon and Farâmarz Tâlebi, Tehran, 1366/1987.

Najmâbâdi Tehrani, Hâj Sheikh Hâdi. *Tabaqeh-bandi-e Ers* (Classification of Inheritance). Lithograph edition, Tehran, 1308 A.H./1890–1891.

Najmâbâdi Tehrani, Hâj Sheikh Hâdi (ibn Mehdi). *Tahrir al-ʿOqalâ*. Foreword by Mirzâ Mohammad-Hosein Foroughi (Zakâʾ al-Molk), edited by Sheikh Mortezâ Najm-Âbâdi, Tehran, 1352 A.H./1933–1934, 295 pp. This volume also contains the author's *Resâleh dar Radd-e Ferqeh-ye Bahâʾiyeh* (Refutation of the Bahâʾi Sect).

Najmi, Nâser. *Iran dar Miân-e Toufân yâ Sharh-e Zendegâni-ye ʿAbbâs Mirzâ Nâyeb al-Saltaneh va Janghâ-ye Iran va Rous* (Iran in the Storm, or the Biography of the Crown Prince Abbas Mirzâ and the Perso-Russian Wars). Tehran: Kânoun-e Maʿrefat, 1336/1957.

Nakhostin Kongereh-ye Nevisandegân-e Iran (The First Congress of Iranian Writers). Tehran, 1326/1947; reprinted Tehran, 1357/1978.

Naqavi, Ali-Mohammad. *Jâmeʿeh-shenâsi-ye Gharb-gerâʾi* (The Sociology of Westernism). 2 Vols., Tehran, Vol. 1, 1361/1982; Vol. 2, 1363/1984.

Narâqi, Hâj Mollâ Ahmad, *Masnavi-e Tâqdis*. Edited by Hasan Narâqi, 2nd edition, Tehran, 1362/1983.

Narâqi, Ehsân. *Jâmeʿeh, Javânân, Dâneshgâh: Dirouz, Emrouz, Fardâ* (The Society, the Youth, the University: Yesterday, Today, [and] Tomorrow). Tehran, 1st edition 1350/1971; 2nd edition 1354/1975; 3rd edition 2536 [1356]/1977.

————. "Moʿammâ-ye Âmouzeshi va Masʾaleh-ye Jahl-e Modâm" (The Dilemma of Education and the Problem of Continuous Ignorance). *Farhang va Zendegi* (Culture and Life), No. 15, Tehran (Summer 1353/1974), pp. 89–99.

————. *Âncheh Khud Dâsht* (One's Own Treasures). Tehran, 2535 [1355]/1976.

————. *Ghorbat-e Gharb* (Estrangement of the West). Tehran, 1354/1975; reprinted, Tehran, 2536 [1356]/1977.

————. *Tamaʿ-e Khâm* (Vain Greed). Tehran, Winter 1356/1978.

————. *ʿOloum-e Ejtemâʿi va Seyr-e Takvini-e Ân* (The Growth of Social Sciences). 1st edition, Tehran, 1344/1965; 3rd edition, Tehran, 1363/1984.

Nâser Khosrow Qobâdiâni, Abou Moʿin. *Ketâb-e Jâmeʿ al-Hekmateyn* (Title in French: *Le livre réunissant les deux sagesses ou harmonie de la philosophie grecque et de la théosophie ismaélienne*). Edited by M. Moʿin and H. Corbin, Tehran, 1332/1953.

Nasimi, Khosrow. *Khabar-e Ân Sâl-hâ* (The Story of Those Years). Tehran, 1362/1983.

Nâtel Khânlari, Parviz. (Editorial Note). *Sokhan*, Vol. 12, No. 1 (Ordibehesht 1340/May 1961), pp. 1–2.

[Nâtel Khânlari, Parviz]. *Qâfeleh-sâlâr-e Sokhan, Khânlari* (Khânlari, The Beacon of Language). (Collection of articles in the memory of Parviz Nâtel Khânlari), n.n., Tehran: Nashr-e Alborz, 1370/1991.

Nâteq, Homâ. "Mâ va Mirzâ Malkam Khân-hâ-ye Mâ" (Us and Our Mirzâ Malkam Khans). In Homâ Nâteq, *Az Mâst Keh Bar Mâst: Chand Maqâleh* (We Have Only Ourselves to Blame: Essays). Tehran, 2537 [1357]/1978, pp. 163–199.

————. *Mosibat-e Vabâ va Balâ-ye Hokoumat: Majmouʿeh-ye Maqâlât* (The Tragedy of Cholera and the Calamity of Government: A Collection of Essays). Tehran, 1358/1979.

————. "Jang-e Ferqeh-hâ dar Enqelâb-e Mashrutiyat-e Iran" (Factional Disputes in the Iranian Constitutional Revolution). *Alif-Bâ*. New Series, No. 3, Paris (Summer 1983), pp. 30–52.

Navvâb Tehrâni (Badâyeʿ-Negâr), Mirzâ Mohammad-Ebrâhim. Persian translation of Seyyed ibn Tâvous, *Faiz al-Domouʿ* (Munificence of Tears). Lithograph edition, Tehran, 1286 A.H./1869; new edition, edited by Akbar Irani, Tehran: forthcoming.

Nâzem al-Islam Kermâni, Mirzâ Mohammad. *Târikh-e Bidâri-e Iranian* (History of the Iranian Awakening). Edited by Ali-Akbar Saʿidi Sirjâni, Parts 1 and 2, Tehran, 1349/1971.

Nourâʾi, Fereshteh. *Tahqiq dar Afkâr-e Mirzâ Malkam Khân Nâzem al-Dowleh* (Mirza Malkam Khan: An Intellectual Study). Tehran, 1352/1973.

Nouri, Mollâ Ali. *Borhân al-Milla* (The Proof of Faith). Edited by Gholâm-Hosein Ebrâhimi-Dinâni, associate editor Sahl-Ali Madadi. Tehran: forthcoming.

Obituary of Seyyed Fakhr al-Din Shâdmân. *Keyhân* (7 Shahrivar 1346/29 August 1967).

Omrâni, Noushin, ed. *Ketâb-Shenasi-ye Owqât-e Farâghat* (A Bibliography of Leisure Time). Tehran, 1368/1989.

Owsiâʾ, Parviz. *Parseh dar Diâr-e Gharib* (Wanderings in a Strange Land). Unpublished typescript, c. 1984, 186 pp.; its first part appeared as "Parseh" (Wanderings), under the name "A. Parviz." *Cheshm-Andâz*, No. 1, Paris (Summer 1365/1986), pp. 9–21.

Pahlevân, Changiz. "Leninizm dar Iran" (Leninism in Iran). *Ârash*, 5th Series, No. 7 (Mehr 1360/October 1981), pp. 25–49.

————. "Gozashteh-ye Ghalabeh Nayâftani" (The Unsurpassable Past). *Ketâbnamây-e Iran*, No. 1, Tehran (1366/1987), pp. 2–21.

Parhâm, Bâqer. "Hezb-e Tudeh va Kânoun-e Nevisandegân" (The Tudeh Party and the Writers Association). Six-part report that appeared in *Ketâb-e Jomʿeh*, Nos. 25 (11 Bahman 1358/31 January 1980) to 30 (23 Esfand 1358/13 March 1980).

————. (Interview). In Foundation for Iranian Studies, *The Oral History Collection of the Foundation for Iranian Studies*. Interviewer Seyyed Vali Reza Nasr, catalog edited by Gholam Reza Afkhami and Seyyed Vali Reza Nasr, with a foreword by Elizabeth B. Mason. Bethesda, Md.: Foundation for Iranian Studies, 1991, catalog, p. 97.

Pavlovitch, M., V. Teria, and S. Iranski, *Seh Maqâleh Dar-bâreh-ye Enqelâb-e Mashruteh-ye Iran* (Three Essays on the Iranian Constitutional Revolution). Originally written in 1926, translated into Persian (1329/1951) by M. Houshyâr, 1st edition, Tehran, 1339/1960; 2nd and 3rd editions, Tehran, 1357/1978.

Pourdâvoud, Ebrâhim. "Dasâtir." Reprinted in the introduction to Mohammad-Hosein ibn Khalaf Tabrizi, *Borhân-e Qâteʿ* (Definite Proof). Persian dictionary written in 1062 A.H./1652, edited by Mohammad Moʿin. 3rd edition, Tehran, 1357/1978, pp. 52–59.

Qâʾem-Maqâm Farâhâni, Mirzâ Abu al-Qâsem. *Monshaʾât* (Writings). Edited by Mohammad Abbasi, Tehran, 1356/1977–1978.

Qâfeleh-sâlâr-e Sokhan, Khânlari (Khânlari, The Beacon of Language). See Nâtel Khânlari, Parviz.

Qajar, Jalâl al-Din Mirzâ. *Nâmeh-ye Khosrovân* (The Book of Kings). 3 Vols., Tehran, 1285–1288 A.H./1868–1871.

Râʾin, Esmâʿil. *Mirzâ Malkam Khân: Zendegi va Koushesh-hâ-ye Siâsi-ye Ou* (Mirzâ Malkam Khân: His Life and Political Activities). Tehran, 1350/1971.

Rahgozar, Reza. *Asil-Âbâd*. Tehran: Daftar-e Nashr-e Farhang-e Islami, n.d.

Rashid al-Din Fadl Allâh. *Kitâb Târikh-i Ifrandj* (*Histoire universelle de Rashid al-Din, histoire des Frances*). Edited with French translation by K. Jahn, Leiden, 1951.

Rezazâdeh Shafaq, Sâdeq. *Khâterât-e Majles, va Demokrâsi Chist?* (Majles Memoirs, and What Is Democracy?). Tehran, 1334/1955.

Roshdiyeh, Shams al-Din. *Savâneh-e ʿOmr* (Life's Events: The Life and Works of Mirzâ Hasan Roshdiyeh). Tehran, 1364/1985.

Rouh al-Amini, Mahmoud, ed. *Bâvarhâ-ye ʿÂmiâneh dar-bâreh-ye Fâl-e Hâfez* (Popular Beliefs on Seeking Augury from Hâfez). Tehran, 1369/1990.

Rouh-Bakhshân, A. "Nakhostin Âshnâʾi-hâ-ye Irâniân bâ Enqelâb-e Farânseh" (Early Iranian Encounters with the French Revolution). *Nashr-e Dânesh*, Vol. 9, No. 4 (Khordâd–Tir 1368/June–July 1989), pp. 4–11.

Rumi, Jalâl al-Din Mohammad. See Mowlavi, Mawlânâ Jalâl al-Din Mohammad. *Kolliyât-e Shams*.

Sâberi, Reza. *Mazloum-e Pajom* (The Fifth Subdued). Tehran, 1362/1984.

Sâdât-Eshkevari, Kâzem. *Negâhi beh Nashriyât-e Gahgâhi: Moʿarrefi-ye Nashriyât-e Nâ-Monazzam-e Gheyr-e Dowlati-ye 1332 tâ 1357* ([Iranian] Periodicals in a Glance: An Introduction to Irregular and non-Governmental Periodicals from 1954 to 1978). Tehran: Tirâzheh, 1370/1991 (issued 1374/1995).

Sâdeq-kâr, Mortezâ. *Dâdgâh* (Court). Tehran, 1362/1984.

Sâdeqi-Nasab, Vali-Morâd. *Fehrest-e Rouznâmeh-hâ-ye Fârsi: 1320–1332* (An Index of Persian Newspapers: 1941–1953). Tehran: Tehran University Press, 1360/1982.

Sadr-Hâshemi, Mohammad. *Târikh-e Jarâʾed va Majallât-e Iran* (A History of the Iranian Press and Periodicals). 4 Vols., Isfahan, 1327–1331/1948–1952; reprinted Isfahan, 1364/1985.

Sâ'edi, Gholâm-Hosein. "Madkhali bar Yek Dâstân-e Boland" (Foreword to a Long Story). *Negin*, Vol. 12, No. 146 (31 Tir 2536 [1356]/22 July 1977), pp. 13 and 50.

Safâ'i Farahâni, Ali-Akbar. *Âncheh Yek Enqelâbi Bâyad Bedânad* (Facts a Revolutionary Must Know). Written in the summer of 1970; reissued, London, Iran Research Group, 1973; reprinted, with an added introduction, under the title *Az Jâme'eh Cheh Midânim?* (What Do We Know about the Society?). Tehran, 1978.

Sahar, M. [pseudonym]. *Dar Bi Bahâr va Bi Bârân* (At the Time of No Spring and No Rain). Paris, 1362/1984.

———. *Ghazal-vâreh-hâ* (Odes). Paris, 1362/1984.

———. *Hezb-e Tudeh dar Bâr-gâh-e Khalifeh* (The Tudeh Party at the Caliph's Court). 1st edition, Paris, 1982; 2nd edition, Paris, 1985.

Sâremi, Esmâ'il. "Kârnâmeh-ye Enteshârât-e Sokhan" (The Sokhan Press and Its Records). In [Parviz Nâtel Khânlari], *Qâfeleh-sâlâr-e Sokhan, Khânlari* (Khânlari, The Beacon of Language). (Collection of articles in the memory of Parviz Nâtel Khânlari), n.n., Tehran: Nashr-e Alborz, 1370/1991, pp. 363–368.

Sâsâni, (Ahmad) Khân Malak. *Yâd-boud-hâ-ye Sefârat-e Istanbul* (Memoirs of the Embassy in Istanbul). Tehran, 1345/1965.

SAVAK. *Pâreh'i az Asnâd-e SAVAK* (Some SAVAK Documents). Edited by Confederation of Iranian Students (National Union), first published in Europe [Frankfurt?], 1355/1976–1977; reprinted, Tehran, 1357/1978.

Sayyâr, Gholâm-Ali. "Negâhi be Vaz'-e Tarjomeh dar Zabân-e Fârsi" (A Note on the State of Translation in Persian Language). *Âyandeh*, Part 1, Vol. 15, Nos. 10–12 (Dey–Esfand 1368/January–March 1990), pp. 685–698; Part 2, Vol. 16, Nos. 1–4 (1369/1990), p. 114 ff.; Part 3, Vol. 16, Nos. 5–8 (Mordâd–Âbân 1369/August–November 1990), pp. 491–506.

Sepânlou, Mohammad-Ali. *Nevisandegân-e Pishrow-e Iran: Az Mashrutiyat tâ 1350* (Progressive Writers of Iran: From the Constitutional Movement to 1971). Tehran, 1362/1983.

———. *Piâdeh-row-hâ* (Pedestrians). Tehran, 1363/1984.

———. *Ragbâr-hâ* (Torrents). Tehran, 1363/1984.

Seyrafizâdeh, Mahmoud (Javâd Sadiq [pseudonym]). *Melliyat va Enqelâb dar Iran* (Nationality and Revolution in Iran). 1st edition, New York, 1352/1973; 2nd edition, Tehran, 1358/1980.

Shâdmân, Seyyed Fakhr al-Din. *Taskhir-e Tamaddon-e Farangi* (The Capturing of Western Civilization). Tehran, Winter 1326/1948, 120 pp.

———. "Dâneshgâh-e Qom va Dâneshgâh-hâ-ye digar-e Iran" (The University at Qom and Other Iranian Universities). *Mehr*, Vol. 8, No. 9 (Âzar 1331/December 1952), pp. 523–532; Vol. 8, No. 10 (Dey 1331/January 1953), pp. 578–583.

Shafi'i Kadkani, Mohammad-Reza. Review of *Az Sabâ tâ Nimâ*. *Ketâb-e Emrouz*, Tehran (Khordâd 1351/June 1972), p. 16.

———. "Talaqqi-e Qodamâ az Vatan" (Predecessors' View of Nation). *Alif-Bâ*, Vol. 2, Tehran (1352/1973), pp. 1–26.

———. *Advâr-e She'r-e Farsi az Mashrutiyat tâ Soqout-e Saltanat* (Periods of Persian Poetry from the Constitutional Movement to the Fall of the Monarchy). Tehran, 1359/1980.

————. *Sovar-e Khiâl dar She'r-e Farsi* (Forms of Imagery in Persian Poetry). 3rd edition, Tehran, 1366/1987.

Shahriâri, Parviz. "Nashriyeh-ye 'Elmi-ye Sokhan" (The Scientific Journal Sokhan). In [Parviz Nâtel Khânlari], *Qâfeleh-sâlâr-e Sokhan, Khânlari* (Khânlari, The Beacon of Language). (Collection of articles in the memory of Parviz Nâtel Khânlari), n.n., Tehran: Nashr-e Alborz, 1370/1991, pp. 357–362.

Shaji'i, Zahrâ. *Namâyandegân-e Majles-e Showrâ-ye Melli dar Bist va Yek Dowreh-ye Qânoun-gozâri* (Majles Deputies during Its Twenty-One Sessions). Tehran, 1344/1965.

————. *Vezârat va Vazirân dar Iran* (The Ministerial Office and the Ministers in Iran). Vol. 1: *Vezârat va Tatavvor-e Ân: Motâle'eh az Nazar-e Jâme'eh-Shenâsi-e Siâsi* (The Development of the Ministerial Office: From the Perspective of Political Sociology). Tehran, 2535 [1355]/1976.

Shâmlou, Ahmad. "Dar in Bonbast" (In This Blind Alley). (Poem composed on 31 Tir 1358/22 July 1979). In *Nâmeh-ye Kânoun-e Nevisandegân-e Iran* (Journal of the Writers Association of Iran), Vol. 2, edited by Mohammad-Ali Sepânlou, Tehran (1358/1979), pp. 9–10; reprinted in Ahmad Shâmlou, *Tarâneh-hâ-ye Kouchak-e Ghorbat* (Little Homesick Songs). Tehran, 1359/1980, pp. 30–32.

Shaqâqi (Momtahen al-Dowleh), Mirzâ Mehdi Khân. See Afshâr, Iraj, ed. *Rejâl-e Vezârat-e Khârejeh.*

Shari'ati, Ali. *Islam-shenâsi* (Islamology). 1st edition, Mashhad: Tous, 1347/1969; Vol. 1, reprinted (*Majmou'eh*, Vol. 16), Tehran: Shari'ati, 1360/1981.

————. *Rowshanfekr va Mas'ouliyyat-e Ou dar Jâme'eh* (Intellectuals' Responsibility in the Society). Lecture at Hoseiniyeh Ershâd, 30 and 31 Mordâd 1349/21 and 22 August 1970. 1st edition, Tehran, 1981.

————. *Payâm-e Omid beh Rowshanfekr-e Mas'oul* (A Message of Hope to the Committed Intellectual). Lecture at Hoseiniyeh Ershâd, 5 Âbân 1351/27 October 1972, revised and reprinted in *Darsi az Roum, beh Zamimeh-ye Alienasioun: Ensân-e Bi Khud* (A Lesson from Rumi, plus a Discussion about Alienation: Man without a Self). Tehran, 1977.

————. *Khud-sâzi-e Enqelâbi* (Revolutionary Reconstruction of the Self) (*Majmou'eh*, Vol. 2). Tehran, 1357/1978.

————. *Bâzgasht* (Return) (*Majmou'eh*, Vol. 4). Tehran, 1361/1982.

————. *Cheh Bâyad Kard?* (What Is to Be Done?) (*Majmou'eh*, Vol. 20). Tehran, 1360/1982.

————. *Hosein Vâres-e Âdam* (Hosein, the Successor of Adam). 2nd edition (*Majmou'eh*, Vol. 19). Tehran: Qalam, 1361/1982.

————. *Târikh-e Tamaddon* (History of Civilization). Vol. 1, 2nd edition (*Majmou'eh*, Vol. 11). Tehran: Âgâh, 1361/1982.

————. *Târikh-e Tamaddon* (History of Civilization). Vol. 2, 2nd edition (*Majmou'eh*, Vol. 12). Tehran: Âgâh, 1361/1982.

————. *Abouzar* (*Majmou'eh*, Vol. 3). Tehran: Elhâm, 1361/1983.

————. *Ali* (*Majmou'eh*, Vol. 26). 2nd edition. Tehran: Niloufar, 1362/1983.

————. *Bâz-shenâsi-ye Huviyyat-e Irani-Islami* (Recognizing the Irano-Islamic Identity) (*Majmou'eh*, Vol. 27). Tehran: Elhâm, 1361/1983.

————. *Ensân-e Bi Khud* (Man without a Self) (*Majmou'eh*, Vol. 25). Tehran: Qalam, 1361/1983.

————. *Niâyesh* (Benediction) (*Majmou'eh*, Vol. 8). Tehran: Elhâm, 1362/1983.

————. *Shi'eh* (Shi'ism) (*Majmou'eh*, Vol. 7). Tehran: Elhâm, 1362/1983.

————. *Majmou'eh-ye Âsâr* (Collected Works). Edited by Daftar-e Tadvin va Tanzim-e Majmou'eh-ye Âsâr-e Mo'allem-e Shahid Doktor Ali Shari'ati (The Editorial Office of the Collected Works of the Martyred Teacher Dr. Ali Shari'ati). 35 Vols. Tehran, 1357–1364/1978–1985.

Shirouyeh Nâmdâr: Kolliyât-e Haft-Jeldi-ye Shahzâdeh Shirouyeh ibn Malekshah-e Rumi Barâdar-e Kâmkâr-e Shahzadeh Amir Arsalân-e Rumi va Malakeh-ye Simin-'Ozâr va Ghoncheh-Lab va 'Eshqbâzihâ-ye Ânhâ (Glorious Shirouyeh: A Complete Story in Seven Parts of Prince Shirouyeh ibn Malekshah-e Rumi the August Brother of the Prince Amir Arsalân-e Rumi, and His Amorous Affairs with the Silver Cheeks and Rose-bud Lips Queen). Tehran: 'Elmi, n.n., n.d., 288 pp.

Showkat, Hamid. *Târikh-e Bist-Sâleh-ye Konfedrâsioun-e Mohasselin va Dâneshjouyân-e Irani, Ettehâdiyeh-ye Melli* (A Twenty-Year History of the Confederation of Iranian Students, National Union). 2 Vols., n.p. (Germany): Châpkhâneh-ye Mortazavi, 1994.

Sokhan. See Nâtel Khânlari, Parviz.

Soleymâni, Mohsen. *Âshnâ-ye Penhân* (Hidden Companion). (Collection of short stories). Tehran: Howzeh-ye Andisheh va Honar-e Islami, 1361/1982.

Soltâni, Pouri, ed. *A Directory of Iranian Periodicals* (21 March 1972–20 March 1973). Tehran: Tehran Book Processing Centre, July 1973.

Soltâniân, Esmâ'il. *Khoun-e Sabz* (Green Blood). Tehran, 1362/1984.

Soroush, Abd al-Karim. "Ostâd Motahhari Ehyâ-konandeh-ye Râstin dar 'Asr-e Jadid" (Professor Motahhari the True Revivalist in the Modern Times). *Nashr-e Dânesh*, Vol. 1, Nos. 5–6, Tehran (1360/1981), pp. 34–50.

————. *Farbeh-tar az Eide'ulouzhi* (More Corpulent than Ideology). (Collection of essays), Tehran, Winter 1372/1994.

————. "Shari'ati va Jâme'eh-shenâsi-ye Din" (Shari'ati and the Sociology of Religion). In Abd al-Karim Soroush, *Farbeh-tar az Eide'ulouzhi* (More Corpulent than Ideology). (Collection of essays), Tehran, Winter 1372/1994, pp. 199–231.

"Susis va Kâlbâs Chegouneh dar Iran Jâ Bâz Kard?" (How Did the Sausage Open Its Way to Iran?). In *Gozâresh: Vizheh-ye Sanâye'-e Ghazâ'i* (Special Report on the Food Industry), reprinted in *Ettelâ'ât*, No. 181 (11 Bahman 1373/31 January 1995), p. 6.

T [Torkamân], Mohammad. See Torkamân, Mohammad. *Ettelâ'âti dar-bâreh-ye Tashannojât*.

Tabari, Ehsân. *Forou-pâshi-e Nezâm-e Sonnati va Zâyesh-e Sarmâyeh-dâri dar Iran: Az Âghâz-e Tamarkoz-e Qajar tâ Âstâneh-ye Enqelâb-e Mashrutiyat* (Disintegration of Traditional Society and the Birth of Capitalism in Iran: From the Beginnings of Qajar Centralization to the Eve of the Constitutional Revolution). Stockholm: Tudeh Party, 1354/1975.

Tabâtabâ'i, Javâd. *Darâmadi Falsafi bar Târikh-e Andisheh-ye Siâsi dar Iran* (A Philosophical Prologue to the History of Political Thought in Iran). Tehran, 1367/1988.

————. *Ibn Khaldun va 'Oloum-e Ejtemâ'i: Vaz'iyat-e 'Oloum-e Ejtemâ'i dar Tamaddon-e Islami* (Ibn Khaldun and Social Sciences: The State of Social Sciences in Islamic Civilization). Tehran, 1374/1995.

Tabâtabâ'i Nâ'ini, Mirzâ (Mohammad-) Reza Khân. *Tiâtr: Majmou'eh-ye Rouznâmeh* (Theater: A Collection of Papers). Edited by Mohammad Golbon and Farâmarz Tâlebi, Tehran: Nashr-e Cheshmeh, 1366/1987.

Tabrizi, Hamid, ed. *Jalâl Âl-Ahmad, Mardi dar Kash-â-kash-e Târikh-e Mo'âser* (Jalâl Âl-Ahmad: A Man Confronting Contemporary History). Tabriz, 1357/1978.

Tabrizi, Mohammad-Hosein ibn Khalaf. *Borhân-e Qâte'* (Definite Proof). Persian dictionary written in 1062 A.H./1652, edited by Mohammad Mo'in. 3rd edition, Tehran, 1357/1978.

Taqizâdeh, Seyyed Hasan. "Lozoum-e Hefz-e Farsi-e Fasih" (The Necessity of Preserving Eloquent Persian). *Yâdegâr*, Vol. 4, No. 6 (Esfand 1326/February–March 1948), pp. 1–40.

————. *Khatâbeh: Moshtamel bar Shammeh'i az Târikh-e Avâ'el-e Enqelâb va Mashrutiyat-e Iran* (Lecture: Early Days of the Iranian Constitutional Revolution). Tehran, 1338/1959.

————. "Târikh-e Mokhtasar-e Majles-e Melli-ye Iran" (A Short History of the Iranian National Assembly). In Iraj Afshâr, ed., *Maqâlât-e Taqi-Zâdeh* (Taqizâdeh's Essays). Vol. 5, Tehran, 2535 [1355]/1976, pp. 241–337.

————. *Owrâq-e Tâzeh-yâb-e Mashrutiyat va Naqsh-e Taqi-Zâdeh: 1325–1330 A.H.* (Newly Found Papers concerning the Constitutional Movement and the Role of Taqi-Zâdeh: 1907–1912). Edited by Iraj Afshâr, Tehran, 1359/1980.

————. "Akhz-e Tamaddon-e Khâreji" (Adoption of Foreign [i.e., Western] Civilization). *Yaghmâ*, Vol. 13, Nos. 9 and 10 (Âzar and Dey 1339/December 1960 and January 1961).

Tartousi, Abu Tâher (ibn Ali ibn Hosein). *Abu Muslim-Nâmeh*. Edited by Eqbâl Yaghmâ'i, Tehran, 1335/1956.

Tashayyod, Ali-Akbar. "Hâji Mohtasham al-Saltaneh-ye Esfandiâri. *Khâterât-e Vahid*, No. 5 (1350/1971), pp. 73–76.

Tavakoli-Targhi, Mohammad. "Asar-e Âgâhi az Enqelâb-e Farânseh dar Shekl-giri-ye Engâreh-ye Mashrutiyat dar Iran" (Constitutionalist Imagery in Iran and the Ideals of the French Revolution). *Iran Nameh*, Vol. 8, No. 3 (Summer 1369/1990), pp. 411–439.

Teria, V. See Pavlovitch, M., V. Teria, and S. Iranski, *Seh Maqâleh*.

Teymourtâsh (Sardâr Mo'azzam-e Khorâsâni), Abd al-Hosein. "Nâmeh'i beh Seyyed Hasan Taqizâdeh" (A Letter to Taqizâdeh). (Introductory note by Iraj Afshâr). *Âyandeh*, Vol. 14, Nos. 9–12 (1367/1988–1989), pp. 657–660.

Tiâtr: Majmou'eh-ye Rouznâmeh (Theater: A Collection of Papers). See Tabâtabâ'i Nâ'ini, Mirzâ (Mohammad-) Reza Khân.

[Torkamân], Mohammad T. *Ettelâ'âti dar-bâreh-ye Tashannojât, Dargirihâ-ye Khiâbâni va Towte'ehâ dar Dowrân-e Hokoumat-e Doktor Mosaddeq* (Some Information about Tensions, Street Confrontations, and Intrigues during the Government of Mosaddeq). Tehran, 1359/1981.

Torkamân, Mohammad, ed. *Qiyâm-e Melli-ye Si-ye Tir be Ravâyat-e Asnâd va Tasâvir* (The Popular Uprising of the Thirtieth of Tir [21 July 1952] According to Documents and Photographs). Tehran: Dehkhodâ, 1361/1982.

Valâyati, Ali-Akbar. *Moqaddameh-ye Fekri-ye Nehzat-e Mashrutiyat* (The Intellectual Background of the Constitutional Movement). 3rd edition, Tehran, 1365/1986.

Vezârat-e Ershâd-e Islami (Ministry of Islamic Guidance). *Mosâbeqeh-ye She'r, Jang* (The Contest of Poetry, War). Tehran, 1361/1982.

Vosouq, Hasan (Vosouq al-Dowleh). *Divân-e Vosouq*. Edited by Iraj Afshâr, Tehran, 1363/1984.

Vosouqi, Nâser. "Karl Marx va Marxizm" (Karl Marx and Marxism). *Mardom*, Vol. 1, No. 3 (Âzar 1325/December 1946), pp. 48–59.

————. "Pâyeh-hâ-ye Nehzat-e Konouni-e Mardom-e Chin va Âyandeh-ye Ân" ([Social] Bases of the Present Movement of the Chinese People and Its Future). *'Elm va Zendegi*, Vol. 1, No. 6 (Khordâd 1331/June 1952), pp. 484–493.

————. "Tarh-e Mârshâl" (The Marshall Plan) (a series of articles). *'Elm va Zendegi*, Vol. 1, No. 7 (Shahrivar 1331/September 1952), pp. 638–646, and No. 8 (Mehr 1331/October 1952), pp. 689–700, and No. 9 (Bahman 1331/February 1953), pp. 779–784, and No. 10 (Esfand 1331/March 1953), pp. 932–941.

————. "Târikh-e Tahavvolât-e Nehzat-e Beynalmelali-e Kârgarân: Kominform bejâ-ye Anternâsiunâl" (History of the Development of the International Labor Movement: the Cominform instead of the International). *'Elm va Zendegi*, Vol. 1, No. 2 (Bahman 1330/February 1952), pp. 151–161.

————. "Naqdi az Hameh Chiz" (A Critique of Everything). *Andisheh va Honar*, Vol. 4, No. 3 (Âbân 1340/November 1961), pp. 189–192.

————. (Editorial Note). *Andisheh va Honar*, Vol. 5, No. 9 (Mehr 1345/October 1965).

Yaghmâ'i, Habib. "Doktor Seyyed Fakhr al-Din Shâdmân." *Yaghmâ*, Vol. 20 (1346/1967), pp. 279–280.

Yaghmâ'i (Toghrâ), Abu al-Qâsem. "Soufiân-e Jandaq" (Sufis of Jandaq). *Âyandeh*, Vol. 15, Nos. 10–12 (Dey–Esfand 1368/1990), pp. 824–828.

Yaghmâ-ye Jandaqi, Mirzâ Rahim. *Majmu'eh-ye Âsâr-e Yaghmâ-ye Jandaqi* (Collected Works of Yaghmâ of Jandaq). Edited and with an introduction and commentary by Seyyed Ali Âl-Dâvoud, 2 Vols., Vol. 1: Poetry, Tehran, 1357/1978; Vol. 2: Prose, Tehran, 1362/1983.

Yazdi, Ebrâhim, ed. *Yâd-Nâmeh-ye Shahid-e Jâvid, Doktor Ali Shari'ati* (Festschrift of the Eternal Martyr, Dr. Shari'ati). N.p. (United States): Nehzat-e Âzâdi, 1977.

Yousefi-Eshkavari, Hasan. *Naqdi bar Ketâb-e "Shahid Motahhari Efshâgar-e Towte'eh"* (A Critique of the Book "Martyr Motahhari: Discloser of Conspiracy"). Tehran, 1364/1985.

Zaidan, Georgi. See Zaydân, Jurjî.

Zargari-nezhâd, Gholâm-Hosein, ed. *Rasâ'el-e Mashrutiyat: 18 Resâleh va Lâyeheh dar-bâreh-ye Mashrutiyat* (Constitutional Treatises: Eighteen Treatises and Tracts about Constitutionalism). Tehran: Enteshârât-e Kavir, 1374/1995.

Zarrâbi, Ali-Asghar, ed. *Majmou'eh-ye Mobâheseh-hâ* (A Collection of Debates). Tehran: Bâmdâd, 1351/1972.

Zarrinkoub, Abd al-Hosein. *Naqd-e Adabi* (Literary Criticism). Vol. 2, 3rd edition, Tehran, 1361/1982.

Zaydân, Jurjî. *Amin va Ma'moun* (Amin and Ma'moun, originally *al-Amin wa-al-Ma'mun*). Persian translation by Mohammad-Ali Shirâzi (Naqib al-Mamâlek), Tehran, Naqsh-e Jahân Press, n.d., 138 pp.

————. *Delâvarân-e Arab* (Arab Heroes). Persian translation by Mohammad-Ali Shirâzi (Naqib al-Mamâlek), Tehran, Mâh-e Now Press, n.d., 516 pp.

————. *Enqelâb-e ʿOsmâni* (The Ottoman Revolution, originally *al-Inqilâb al-ʿUth-mani*). Persian translation by Mohammad-Ali Shirâzi (Naqib al-Mamâlek), Teh-ran: Majalleh-ye Mâh-e Now, n.d., 200 pp.

————. *Enteqâm-e Khoun-e Hosein* (Avenging the Murder of Hosein). Persian trans-lation by Mohammad-Ali Shirâzi (Naqib al-Mamâlek), 3rd edition, Tehran, n.d., 208 pp.

————. *Salâh al-Din Ayyoubi* (Saladin, originally *Salah al-Din al-Ayyubi*), Persian translation by Mohammad-Ali Shirâzi (Naqib al-Mamâlek). Tehran: Majalleh-ye Mâh-e Now, n.d. [1950?].

————. *Abu Muslim Khorâsâni*. Persian translation by Habibollâh Âmouzegâr, 3 Vols., Tehran, 1318/1939, 579 pp.

————. *Fâjeʿeh-ye Ramadan* (The Tragedy of Ramadan). Persian translation by Mohammad-Ali Shirâzi (Naqib al-Mamâlek), 3rd edition, Tehran, 1335/1946, 158 pp.

————. *Fâjeʿeh-ye Karbala* (The Tragedy of Karbala, originally *Ghadat Karbala*). Per-sian translation by Mohammad-Ali Shirâzi (Naqib al-Mamâlek), 7th edition, Tehran, 1337/1948, 206 pp.

II. Works in European Languages

Abrahamian, Ervand. "Kasravi: The Integrative Nationalist of Iran." *MES*, Vol. 9, No. 3 (October 1973), pp. 271–295.

————. "ʿAli Shariʿati: Ideologue of the Iranian Revolution." *Merip Reports*, No. 102 (January 1982), pp. 24–28.

————. *Iran between Two Revolutions*. Princeton, N.J.: Princeton University Press, 1982.

————. *Radical Islam: The Iranian Mojahedin*. London: I. B. Tauris, 1989.

————. *Khomeinism: Essays on the Islamic Republic*. Berkeley: University of California Press, 1993.

Adle, Chahryar, and Bernard Hourcade, eds. *Téhéran: Capitale bicentenaire*. Paris and Tehran, Institut Français de Recherche en Iran, 1992.

Afary, Janet. "Review Essay—The Pitfalls of National Consciousness in Iran: The Construction of a Militant Muslim Ideology." *Journal of Political and Military Soci-ology*, Vol. 15 (Fall 1987), pp. 279–289.

Afkhami, Gholam Reza. See Foundation for Iranian Studies.

Akhavi, Shahrough. *Religion and Politics in Contemporary Iran: Clergy-State Relations in the Pahlavi Period*. Albany: State University of New York, 1980.

Alam, Asadollah. *The Shah and I: The Confidential Diary of Iran's Royal Court, 1969–1977*. Introduced and edited by Alinaghi Alikhani, translated into English by Ali-naghi Alikhani and Nicholas Vincent. New York: St. Martin's Press, 1991.

Alavi, Bozorg. "From Modern Persian Literature." In *Yâdnâme-ye Jan Rypka* (Col-lection of Articles on Persian and Tajik Literature). Prague: Academia, 1967, pp. 167–172.

————. "The First Iranian Writers Congress, 1946." English translation by Thomas M. Ricks and Fariba Amini. In Thomas M. Ricks, ed., *Critical Perspectives on Modern Persian Literature*. Washington, D.C.: Three Continents Press, 1984, pp. 8–25.

Algar, Hamid. "Islâh," *EI2*, Vol. 4, 1973, pp. 163–167.

———. *Mirza Malkam Khan: A Biographical Study in Iranian Modernism.* Berkeley, 1973.

———. *The Islamic Revolution in Iran.* London: Open Press, 1980.

Alishan, Leonardo P. "Trends in Modernist Persian Poetry." Ph.D. dissertation, University of Texas at Austin, 1982, pp. 109–110.

Al-e Ahmad, Jalal. *The School Principal.* Translated by John K. Newton, introduction by Michael C. Hillman. Minneapolis and Chicago: Bibliotheca Islamica, 1974.

———. *Gharbzadegi (Weststruckness).* Translated by John Green and Ahmad Alizadeh. Lexington, Ky.: Mazda, 1982.

———. *Iranian Society: An Anthology of Writings by Jalal Al-e Ahmad.* Edited by Michael C. Hillmann. Lexington, Ky.: 1982.

———. *Plagued by the West (Ghabzadegi).* Translated by Paul Sprachman. Modern Persian Literature Series, No. 4. Delmar, N.Y.: Caravan Books, 1982.

———. *Lost in the Crowd,* a translation of Jalal Âl-Ahmad, *Khasi dar Miqât* by John Green and Ahmad Alizadeh, et al., with an introduction by Michael C. Hillmann. Washington, D.C.: Three Continents Press, 1985.

Al-i Ahmad, Jalal. *Occidentosis: A Plague from the West.* Translated by R. Campbell, annotations and introduction by Hamid Algar. Berkeley, Calif.: Mizan Press, 1984.

Amanat, Abbas. *Resurrection and Renewal: The Making of the Babi Movement in Iran, 1844–1850.* Ithaca, N.Y.: Cornell University Press, 1989.

Amuzegar, Jahangir. "Capital Formation and Development Finance." In Ehsan Yar-Shater, ed., *Iran Faces the Seventies.* Foreword by John S. Badeau. New York: Praeger, 1971, pp. 66–87.

Anderson, Perry. *Considerations on Western Marxism.* London, 1976.

Arasteh, Reza. *Education and the Social Awakening in Iran.* Leiden: E. J. Brill, 1962.

Arfa, General Hassan. *Under Five Shahs.* New York, 1965.

Arjomand, Said Amir. "The ʿUlamâʾa Traditionalist Opposition to Parliamentarism: 1907–1909." *MES,* Vol. 17, No. 2 (1981), pp. 174–190.

———. *The Shadow of God and the Hidden Imam: Religion, Political Order, and Societal Change in Shiʿite Iran from the Beginning to 1890,* Chicago: University of Chicago Press, 1984.

———. "Ideological Revolution in Shiʿism." In Said Amir Arjomand, ed., *Authority and Political Culture in Shiʿism.* Albany: State University of New York Press, 1988, pp. 178–209.

Arjomand, Said Amir, ed. *Authority and Political Culture in Shiʿism.* Albany: State University of New York Press, 1988.

Ashraf, Ahmad. "Bazar iii. Socio-economic and Political Role of the Bazar." In *EIr,* Vol. 4, 1990, pp. 30–44.

———. "Conspiracy Theories." In *EIr,* Vol. 6, Fascicle 2, 1992, pp. 138–147.

———. "From the White Revolution to the Islamic Revolution." In Saeed Rahnema and Sohrab Behdad, eds., *Iran after the Revolution: Crisis of an Islamic State.* London and New York: I. B. Tauris, 1995, pp. 21–44.

Atabaki, Touraj. *Azerbaijan: Ethnicity and Autonomy in Iran after the Second World War.* London: I. B. Tauris, 1993.

Auerbach, Erich. *Scenes from the Drama of European Literature.* New York, 1959; new edition, Minneapolis: University of Minnesota Press, 1984.

Avery, Peter. "Trends in Iran in the Past Five Years." *World Today*, Vol. 21 (1965), pp. 279–290.

———. "Iran 1964–8: The Mood of Growing Confidence." *World Today*, Vol. 24 (1968), pp. 453–466.

Avery, Peter W. "An Enquiry into the Outbreak of the Second Russo-Persian War, 1826–28." In C. E. Bosworth, ed., *Iran and Islam: In Memory of the Late Vladimir Minorsky*. Edinburgh, 1971, pp. 17–45.

Azimi, Fakhreddin. *Iran: The Crisis of Democracy (1941–1953)*. London, 1989.

Baddeley, John F. *The Russian Conquests of the Caucasus*. London, 1908.

Bakhash, Shaul. *Iran: Monarchy, Bureaucracy and Reform under the Qajars: 1858–1896*. London: Ithaca Press, 1978.

———. "The Failure of Reform: The Prime Ministership of Amin al-Dawla, 1897–8." In Edmund Bosworth and Carole Hillenbrand, eds., *Qajar Iran: Political, Social and Cultural Change 1800–1925*. Edinburgh, 1983, pp. 14–33.

Baldwin, George B. *Planning and Development in Iran*. Baltimore: Johns Hopkins Press, 1967.

Banák, Kamil. "Mushfiq Kazimi's Novel The Horrible Tehran—Romantic Fiction or Social Criticism." *Asian and African Studies*, Vol. 13 (1977), pp. 147–152.

Banani, Amin. *The Modernization of Iran (1921–1941)*. Stanford, Conn., 1961.

———. "The Role of the Mass Media." In Ehsan Yar-Shater, ed., *Iran Faces the Seventies*. Foreword by John S. Badeau. New York: Praeger, 1971, pp. 321–340.

Banuazizi, Ali. "Iranian 'National Character': A Critique of Some Western Perspectives." In L. Carl Brown and Norman Itzkowitz, eds., *Psychological Dimensions of Near Eastern Studies*. Princeton, N.J.: Darwin Press, 1977, pp. 210–239.

———. "Iran's Revolutionary Impasse: Political Factionalism and Societal Resistance." *Middle East Report* (November–December 1994), pp. 2–8.

Baraheni, Reza. *The Crowned Cannibals: Writings on Repression in Iran*. New York, 1977.

Barthold, W. "Barmakids." In *EI*, Vol. 1, 1913, pp. 663–666.

Bayat, Mangol. *Mysticism and Dissent: Socioreligious Thought in Qajar Iran*. Syracuse, N.Y.: Syracuse University Press, 1982.

———. *Iran's First Revolution: Shi'ism and the Constitutional Revolution of 1905–1909*. New York and Oxford, 1991.

Bayat-Philipp, Mangol. "Shi'ism in Contemporary Iranian Politics: The Case of Ali Shari'ati." In E. Kedourie and S. G. Haim, eds., *Towards a Modern Iran*. London, 1980, pp. 155–168.

Beeman, William O. "Status, Style, and Strategy in Iranian Interaction." *Anthropological Linguistics*, Vol. 18, No. 7 (1976), pp. 305–322.

Beeman, William O. "What Is (Iranian) National Character? A Sociolinguistic Approach." *IS*, Vol. 9, No. 1 (Winter 1976), pp. 22–48.

Beeman, William O. *Language, Status, and Power in Iran*. Bloomington: Indiana University Press, 1986.

Behdad, Sohrab. *Iran after the Revolution*. See Rahnema, Saeed, and Sohrab Behdad, eds., *Iran after the Revolution*.

Behn, Wolfgang H. *Iranian Opposition in Exile: An Annotated Bibliography of Publications from 1341/1962 to 1357/1978*. Autumn 1979.

Behn, Wolfgang H., ed. *The Iranian Opposition to the Shah: 701 Selected Dissident Publications: A Documentary History on Microfiche*. Zug, Switzerland: Inter Documentation Company, n.d.

Behn, Wolfgang H., and Willem M. Floor. *Twenty Years of Iranian Power Struggle: A Bibliography of 951 Political Periodicals from 1341/1962 to 1360/1981 with Selective Locations*. Berlin, 1982.

Behnam, Djamshid. "Le rôle de la communauté iranienne d'Istanbul dans le processus de modernisation de l'Iran." In Thierry Zarcone and Fariba Zarinebaf-Shahr, eds., *Les Iraniens d'Istanbul*. Paris and Tehran, 1993.

Benda, Julien. *La trahison des clercs*. Paris, 1927.

Benjamin, Walter. *One Way Street*. Translated by Edmund Jephcott and Kingsley Shorter. London, NLB, 1979.

Berger, Peter L., and Thomas Luckmann. *The Social Construction of Reality: A Treatise in the Sociology of Knowledge*. London, 1967 and 1976.

Berkes, Niyazi. *The Development of Secularism in Turkey*. Montreal, 1964.

Berlin, Isaiah. *Conversations with Isaiah Berlin*. See Jahanbagloo, Ramin.

Berque, Jacques. *Cultural Expression in Arab Society Today*. Translated by Robert W. Stookey. Austin and London: University of Texas Press, 1978.

Bharier, Julian. "A Note on the Population of Iran 1900–66." *Population Studies*, Vol. 22, No. 2 (July 1968), pp. 273–279.

———. *Economic Development in Iran, 1900–1970*. London: Oxford University Press, 1971.

———. "The Growth of Towns and Villages in Iran, 1900–66." *MES*, Vol. 8, No. 1 (January 1972), pp. 51–61.

Bill, J. A., and Roger Louis, eds. *Musaddiq, Iranian Nationalism, and Oil*. London, 1988.

Boroujerdi, Mehrzad. "*Gharbzadegi*: The Dominant Intellectual Discourse of Pre- and Post-Revolutionary Iran." In Samih K. Farsoun and Mehrdad Mashayekhi, eds., *Iran: Political Culture in the Islamic Republic*. London and New York, 1992, pp. 30–56.

———. *Iranian Intellectuals and the West: The Tormented Triumph of Nativism*. Syracuse, N.Y.: Syracuse University Press, 1996.

Bosworth, C. E. "The Heritage of Rulership in Early Islamic Iran and the Search for Dynastic Connections with the Past." *Iran*, Vol. 11 (1973), pp. 51–62.

Bosworth, Edmund, and Carole Hillenbrand, eds. *Qajar Iran: Political, Social and Cultural Change 1800–1925*. Edinburgh, 1983.

Bowman, Herbert E. *Vissarion Belinsky, 1811–1848: A Study in the Origins of Social Criticism in Russia*. Cambridge, Mass., 1954.

Boyce, Mary. *Zoroastrians: Their Religious Beliefs and Practices*. London: 1979.

Brammer, L. M. "Problems of Iranian University Students." *MEJ*, Vol. 18 (1964), pp. 443–450.

Brower, Daniel R. *The Russian City between Tradition and Modernity, 1850–1900*. Berkeley: University of California Press, 1990.

Browne, E. G. *A Brief Narrative of Recent Events in Persia*. (Followed by a translation of "The Four Pillars of the Persian Constitution"). London, 1909.

———. *A Literary History of Persia*. Vol. 4. Reprinted, Cambridge, 1959.

————. *The Persian Revolution of 1905–1909.* 1st edition, Cambridge, 1910; new impression, London, 1966.

Browne, E. G., and M. A. Tarbiyat. *The Press and Poetry of Modern Persia.* Cambridge, 1914.

Brym, Robert J. *Intellectuals and Politics.* London: George Allen and Unwin, 1980.

Burrell, Robert M. "Aspects of the Reign of Muzaffar al-Din Shah of Persia 1896–1907." Ph.D. thesis, University of London, School of Oriental and African Studies, 1979.

Busse, H. "The Revival of Persian Heritage under the Bûyids." In D. H. Richards, ed., *Islamic Civilisation 950–1150.* Oxford, 1975, pp. 47–70.

Calder, Norman. "The Structure of Authority in Imami Shiʿi Jurisprudence." Ph.D. thesis, University of London, School of Oriental and African Studies, (1980).

Cannadine, David, and Simon Price, eds. *Rituals of Royalty: Power and Ceremonies in Traditional Societies.* Cambridge, 1987.

Carrithes, M., S. Collins, and S. Lukes, eds. *The Category of the Person.* Cambridge, 1985.

Chehabi, H. E. *Iranian Politics and Religious Modernism: The Liberation Movement of Iran under the Shah and Khomeini.* Ithaca and London, 1990.

Chehabi, Houchang, E. "Staging the Emperor's New Clothes: Dress Codes and Nation-Building under Reza Shah." *IS*, Vol. 26, Nos. 3–4 (Summer–Fall 1993), pp. 209–229.

Chelkowski, Peter J., ed. *Iran: Continuity and Variety.* New York, 1971.

————. *Taʿziyeh, Ritual and Drama in Iran.* New York: New York University Press, 1979.

Clawson, Patrick. "Knitting Iran Together: The Land Transport Revolution, 1920–1940." *IS*, Vol. 26, Nos. 3–4 (Summer–Fall 1993), pp. 235–250.

Cole, G. D. H. *A History of Socialist Thought.* 5 Vols. London, 1953–1960.

Cole, Juan R. I. "Shiʿi Clerics in Iraq and Iran, 1722–1780: The Akhbari-Usuli Conflict Reconsidered," *IS*, Vol. 18, No. 1 (1985), pp. 3–34.

————. "Ideology, Ethics, and Philosophical Discourses in Eighteenth Century Iran," *IS*, Vol. 22, No. 1 (1989), pp. 7–34.

Corbin, Henri. *L'École Shaykhie en Théologie Shiʿite.* Paris: Annuaire de l'École Pratique des Hautes Études, Section des Sciences Religieuses, 1960–1961. Reprinted with Persian translation by Ferydoun Bahmanyâr. Tehran: Tâbân, 1964.

Cottam, Richard W. *Nationalism in Iran.* 2nd ed., updated through 1978. Pittsburgh: University of Pittsburgh Press, 1979.

Dabashi, Hamid. *Theology of Discontent: The Ideological Foundation of the Islamic Revolution in Iran.* New York: New York University Press, 1993.

Dastghayb, Abd al-Ali. "Jalal Al-e Ahmad: His Absence Has Been a Great Loss." English translation by B. Kamgar and Thomas M. Ricks, in Thomas M. Ricks, ed., *Critical Perspectives on Modern Persian Literature.* Washington, D.C.: Three Continents Press, 1984, pp. 343–345.

De Man, Paul. *Blindness and Insight: Essays in the Rhetoric of Contemporary Criticism.* New York: Oxford University Press, 1971.

Delagah, Mansour. "An Analysis of the Educational Consequences of the 'White Revolution' in Iran from 1962–63 through 1973–74 in Historical Perspective." Ph.D. dissertation, University of Colorado, Boulder, 1975.

Djilas, Milovan. *The New Class: An Analysis of the Communist System.* New York, 1957.

Djoudaki, Hodjatollah. "*L'Anjoman-e Saʿâdat* des Iraniens d'Istanbul." In Thierry Zarcone and Fariba Zarinebaf-Shahr, eds., *Les Iraniens d'Istanbul.* Paris and Tehran, 1993.

Doerr, Arthur. "An Assessment of Educational Development: The Case Study of Pahlavi University, Iran." *MEJ,* Vol. 22 (1968), pp. 317–323.

Echo of Iran. *Iran Almanac: 1966.* Tehran: Echo of Iran, 1967.

———. *Iran Who's Who.* 2nd edition. Tehran: Echo of Iran, 1974.

Ehlers, Eckart, and Willem Floor. "Urban Change in Iran, 1920–1941." *IS,* Vol. 26, Nos. 3–4 (Summer–Fall 1993), pp. 251–275.

Ekhtiar, Maryam D. "The Dar al-Funun: Educational Reform and Cultural Development in Qajar Iran." Ph.D. dissertation, New York University, 1994.

Elwell-Sutton, L. P. "Political Parties in Iran: 1941–1948." *MEJ,* Vol. 3 (January 1949), pp. 45–62.

———. *Persian Oil: A Study in Power Politics.* London, 1955.

Enâyat, Hamid. Review of Nikki R. Keddie's *Sayyid Jamâl al-Dîn "al-Afghâni," A Political Biography* (Berkeley: University of California Press, 1972), in *IS,* Vol. 6, No. 4 (Autumn 1973), pp. 246–255.

———. "The State of Social Sciences in Iran." *Middle East Studies Association Bulletin,* Vol. 8, No. 3 (1974), pp. 1–12.

———. *Modern Islamic Political Thought: The Response of the Shiʿi and Sunni Muslims to the Twentieth Century.* London: Macmillan, 1982.

Ettehadieh Nezam Mafi, M. "The Origin and Development of Political Parties in Persia (1906–1911)." Ph.D. thesis, Edinburgh University, 1980.

Ettehadieh Nezam-Mafi, Mansoureh. "The Council for the Investigation of Grievances: A Case Study of Nineteenth Century Iranian Social History." *IS,* Vol. 22, No. 1 (1989), pp. 51–61.

Faghfoory, Mohammad H. "The Ulama-State Relations in Iran: 1921–1941." *IJMES,* Vol. 19 (November 1987), pp. 413–432.

———. "The Impact of Modernization on the Ulama in Iran, 1925–1941." *IS,* Vol. 26, Nos. 3–4 (Summer–Fall 1993), pp. 277–312.

Fahd, T., ed. *Le Shîʿsme imâmite.* Paris: Presses Universitaires de France, 1970.

Farman Farmayan, Hafez. "The Forces of Modernization in Nineteenth Century Iran: A Historical Survey." In William R. Polk and Richard L. Chambers, eds., *Beginnings of Modernization in the Middle East: The Nineteenth Century.* Chicago: University of Chicago Press, 1968, pp. 119–151.

Ferdows, Adele. "Religion in Iranian Nationalism: The Study of the Fadayan-i Islam." Ph.D. dissertation, Indiana University, Urbana, 1967.

Ferdows, Amir H. "Khomeini and Fadayan's Society and Politics." *IJMES,* Vol. 15 (1983), pp. 241–257.

Ferguson, Charles. "Word Stress in Persian." *Language,* Vol. 33 (1957), pp. 123–135.

Ferrarotti, Franco. *Time, Memory, and Society.* New York, 1990.

Field, Henry. *Contributions to the Anthropology of Iran.* Anthropological Series, Vol. 29, Nos. 1 and 2. Publication 458, No. 1, "Jews of Isfahan" and "Comparative Data on Jews from Southwestern Asia and the Caucasus," pp. 290–315 and 316–330, respectively. Chicago: Field Museum of Natural History, December 15, 1939.

Fischel, Walter J. "The Jews of Persia, 1795–1940." *Jewish Social Studies*, Vol. 12, No. 2, April 1950, pp. 119–160.

Fischer, Michael M. J. *Iran: From Religious Dispute to Revolution.* Cambridge, Mass.: Harvard University Press, 1980.

Flacks, Dick. "Making History and Making Theory: Notes on How Intellectuals Seek Relevance." In Charles C. Lemert, ed., *Intellectuals and Politics: Social Theory in a Changing World.* Newbury Park, Calif.: Sage, 1991, pp. 3–18.

Floor, Willem, and Eckart Ehlers. "Urban Change in Iran, 1920–1941." *IS*, Vol. 26, Nos. 3–4 (Summer–Fall 1993), pp. 251–275.

Foundation for Iranian Studies. *The Oral History Collection of the Foundation for Iranian Studies.* Catalog edited by Gholam Reza Afkhami and Seyyed Vali Reza Nasr, with a foreword by Elizabeth B. Mason. Bethesda, Md.: Foundation for Iranian Studies, 1991.

Fraser, James B. *An Historical and Descriptive Account of Persia from the Earliest Ages to the Present Time: With a Detailed View of Its Resources, Government, Population, Natural History, and the Character of Its Inhabitants, Particularly the Wandering Tribes, including a Description of Afghanistan and Beloochistan.* Edinburgh: Oliver & Boyd, 1834.

Gable, Richard W. "Culture and Administration in Iran." *MEJ*, Vol. 13, No. 4 (Autumn 1959), pp. 407–421.

Gardanne, A. de. *Mission du Général Gardanne en Perse sous le premier empire.* London, 1865.

Gasiorowski, Mark J. *U.S. Foreign Policy and the Shah: Building a Client State in Iran.* Ithaca, N.Y.: Cornell University Press, 1991.

Ghanoonparvar, M. R. "Hushang Golshiri and Post-Pahlavi Concerns of the Iranian Writer of Fiction." *IS*, Vol. 18 (Spring–Autumn 1985), pp. 349–373.

———. *In a Persian Mirror: Images of the West and Westerners in Iranian Fiction.* Austin: University of Texas Press, 1993.

Gheissari, Ali. "The Ideological Formation of the Iranian Intelligentsia: From the Constitutional Movement to the Fall of the Monarchy." D.Phil. thesis, Oxford University, Oxford, 1989.

———. "The Poetry and Politics of Farrokhi Yazdi." *IS*, Vol. 26, Nos. 1–2 (Winter–Spring 1993), pp. 33–50.

———. "Persia." In I. C. B. Dear and M. R. D. Foot, eds., *The Oxford Companion to the Second World War.* Oxford and New York: Oxford University Press, 1995, pp. 874–875.

———. "Truth and Method in Modern Iranian Historiography and Social Sciences." *Critique* (Journal for Critical Studies of the Middle East), No. 5 (Spring 1995), pp. 39–56.

Gilbar, Gad G. "The Big Merchants (*tujjâr*) and the Persian Constitutional Revolution of 1906." *Asian and African Studies*, Vol. 11, No. 1 (Summer 1976), pp. 275–303.

Gilsenan, Michael. *Recognizing Islam.* London, 1982.

Goitein, S. D. "The Origin and Nature of the Muslim Friday Worship." In S. D. Goitein, *Studies in Islamic History and Institutions.* Leiden: E. J. Brill, 1966, pp. 111–125.

Graham-Brown, Sarah. *Images of Women: The Portrayal of Women in Photography of the Middle East, 1860–1950.* London: Quartet Books, 1988.

Gurney, John. "The Transformation of Tehran in the Later Nineteenth Century." In Chahryar Adle and Bernard Hourcade, eds., *Téhéran: Capitale bicentenaire*. Paris and Tehran: Institut Français de Recherche en Iran, 1992, pp. 51–71.

————. "E. G. Browne and the Iranian Community in Istanbul." In Thierry Zarcone and Fariba Zarinebaf-Shahr, eds., *Les Iraniens d'Istanbul*. Paris and Tehran, 1993, pp. 149–175.

Gurney, John, and Negin Nabavi. "Dâr al-Fonûn." In *EIr*, Vol. 6, 1993, pp. 662–668.

Habermas, Jürgen. *Knowledge and Human Interests*. Translated by Jeremy J. Shapiro. Boston: Beacon Press, 1971.

Habibi, Mohsen. "Réza Chah et le développement de Téhéran (1925–1941)." In Chahryar Adle and Bernard Hourcade, eds., *Téhéran: Capitale bicentenaire*. Paris and Tehran: Institut Français de Recherche en Iran, 1992, pp. 199–206.

Hairi, A. H. "The Idea of Constitutionalism in Persian Literature prior to the 1906 Revolution." In *Akten des VII Kongresses für Arabistik und Islamwissenschaft: Götingen, August 15–22, 1974*. Edited by Albert Dietrich. Götingen: Vandenhoeck & Ruprecht, 1976, pp. 189–207.

————. "Shaykh Fazl Allah Nuri's Refutation of the Idea of Constitutionalism." *MES*, Vol. 13, No. 3 (1977), pp. 327–339.

Hairi, Abdul-Hadi. *Shiʿism and Constitutionalism in Iran: A Study of the Role Played by the Persian Residents of Iraq in Iranian Politics*. Leiden: E. J. Brill, 1977.

Halliday, Fred. *Iran, Dictatorship and Development*. London: Penguin Books, 1979.

Hambly, Gavin. "Attitudes and Aspirations of the Contemporary Iranian Intellectual." *Royal Central Asian Journal*, Vol. 51, Part 3 (April 1964), pp. 127–140.

Hamzavi, A. H. [Abd al-Hosein]. *Persia and the Powers: An Account of Diplomatic Relations, 1941–1946*. London: Hutchinson & Co., n.d. [1947].

Hanaway, William L. "Formal Elements in the Persian Popular Romances." *Review of National Literatures*, Vol. 2, No. 1 (Spring 1971), pp. 139–160.

————. "Variety and Continuity in Popular Literature in Iran." In Peter J. Chelkowski, ed., *Iran: Continuity and Variety*. New York, 1971, pp. 59–75.

————. "*Amir Arsalan* and the Question of Genre." *IS*, Vol. 24, Nos. 1–4 (1991), pp. 55–60.

Hanson, Brad. "The 'Westoxication' of Iran: Depictions and Reactions of Behrangi Al-e Ahmad, and Shariʿati." *IJMES*, Vol. 15 (1983), pp. 1–23.

Hegel, G. W. F. *The Phenomenology of Mind*. Translated from the German with an introduction and notes by J. B. Baillie. 1st edition, London, 1910; 2nd edition (revised), London: George Allen and Unwin, 1931; 7th impression, London: George Allen and Unwin, 1966.

Hillmann, Michael C., ed. *Iranian Society: An Anthology of Writings by Jalal Al-e Ahmad*. Lexington, Ky., 1982.

Hodge, Carleton T. "Some Aspects of Persian Style." *Language*, Vol. 33 (1957), pp. 355–369.

Hourani, Albert. *Minorities in the Arab World*. London, 1947.

————. *Arabic Thought in the Liberal Age, 1798–1939*. London and Oxford, 1962 and 1967.

————. *The Emergence of the Modern Middle East*. London, 1981.

Hourcade, Bernard, and Chahryar Adle, eds. *Téhéran: Capitale bicentenaire*. See Adle, Chahryar.

Hoveyda, Fereydoun. *Les Quarantines*. Paris: Gallimard, 1962.

Husserl, Edmund. *The Crisis of European Sciences and Transcendental Phenomenology: An Introduction to Phenomenological Philosophy*. English translation with an introduction by David Carr. Evanston, Ill.: Northwestern University Press, 1970.

Hyppolite, Jean. *Genesis and Structure of Hegel's* Phenomenology of Spirit. Translated from the French by Samuel Cherniak and John Heckman. Evanston, Ill.: Northwestern University Press, 1974.

Iran Who's Who. See Echo of Iran.

Ishaque, Mohammad. *Modern Persian Poetry*. Calcutta, 1943.

Issawi, Charles. "Economic Change and Urbanization in the Middle East." In Ira M. Lapidus, ed., *Middle Eastern Cities: A Symposium on Ancient, Islamic, and Contemporary Middle Eastern Urbanism*. Berkeley: University of California Press, 1969, pp. 102–121.

———. "The Economy: An Assessment of Performance." In Ehsan Yar-Shater, ed., *Iran Faces the Seventies*. Foreword by John S. Badeau. New York: Praeger, 1971, pp. 44–65.

Jahanbagloo, Ramin. *Conversations with Isaiah Berlin: Recollections of an Historian of Ideas*. London, 1992, pp. 37–40.

Jay, Martin. *Marxism and Totality: The Adventures of a Concept from Lukács to Habermas*. Berkeley: University of California Press, 1984.

Jazani, Bizhan. *Capitalism and Revolution in Iran: Selected Writings of Bizhan Jazani*. Translated by the Iran Committee. London: Zed Press, 1980.

Jazayery, Mohammad A. "English Loan Words in Persian: A Study in Language and Culture." Ph.D. dissertation, University of Texas at Austin, 1958.

Jernudd, Björn H. "The Texture of Language Purism: An Introduction." In Björn H. Jernudd and Michael J. Shapiro, eds., *The Politics of Language Purism*. Berlin and New York, 1989, pp. 1–19.

Kamshad, H. *Modern Persian Prose Literature*. Cambridge: Cambridge University Press, 1966.

Kant, Immanuel. *Grundlegung zur Metaphysik der Sitten*. Edited by Karl Vorländer. Hamburg: Verlag von Felix Meiner, 1962; translated into English by H. J. Paton, as *Groundwork of the Metaphysic of Morals*. Reprinted, New York, 1964.

Karimi-Hakkak, Ahmad. "Protest and Perish: A History of the Writers' Association of Iran." *IS*, Vol. 18, Nos. 2–4 (Spring–Autumn 1985), pp. 189–229.

———. "Language Reform Movement and Its Language: The Case of Persian." In Björn H. Jernudd and Michael J. Shapiro, eds., *The Politics of Language Purism*. Berlin and New York, 1989, pp. 81–104.

———. "Revolutionary Posturing: Iranian Writers and the Iranian Revolution of 1979." *IJMES*, Vol. 23, No. 4 (1991), pp. 507–531.

———. "From Translation to Appropriation: Poetic Cross-Breeding in Early Twentieth-Century Iran." *Comparative Literature*, Vol. 47, No. 1 (Winter 1995), pp. 53–78.

Karny, A. "The Premiership of Mirza Hosein Khan and His Reforms in Iran." *Asian and African Studies*, Vol. 10 (1974), pp. 127–158.

Katouzian, Homa. "Nationalist Trends in Iran, 1921–1926." *IJMES*, Vol. 10 (1979), pp. 533–551.

Katouzian, Homa. *The Political Economy of Modern Iran: Despotism and Pseudo-Modernism, 1926–1979.* London, 1981.

———. "The Aridosoladic Society: A Model of Long-Term Social and Economic Development in Iran." *IJMES*, Vol. 15 (1983), pp. 259–281.

Kazemi, Farhad. *Poverty and Revolution in Iran: The Migrant Poor, Urban Marginality and Politics.* New York: New York University Press, 1980.

———. "Religion and Politics in Iran: The Fadâ'iyân Islâm." *Folia Orientalia,* Vol. 22 (*Iranica:* Studies in Memory of Professor Franciszek Machalski) (1981–1984 [publication 1985]), pp. 191–205.

Keddie, Nikki R. "The Origins of the Religious-Radical Alliance in Iran." *Past and Present,* Vol. 34 (April 1966), pp. 70–80; reprinted in Nikki R. Keddie. *Iran: Religion, Politics and Society.* London: Frank Cass, 1980, pp. 53–79.

———. *An Islamic Response to Imperialism: Political and Religious Writings of Sayyid Jamâl ad-Dîn "al-Afghânî."* Includes a translation of "Refutation of the Materialists" from the Original Persian by Nikki R. Keddie and Hamid Algar. Berkeley: University of California Press, 1968.

———. *Seyyid Jamal al-Din "al-Afghani": A Political Biography.* Berkeley: University of California Press, 1972.

———. *Iran: Religion, Politics and Society.* London: Frank Cass, 1980.

———. *Roots of Revolution: An Interpretive History of Modern Iran.* Includes a section by Yann Richard. New Haven: Yale University Press, 1981.

———. "Sayyid Jamal al-Din 'al-Afghani'. In Ali Rahnema, ed., *Pioneers of Islamic Revival.* London: Zed Books, 1994, pp. 11–29.

Kennedy, Hugh. "The Barmakid Revolution in Islamic Government." In Charles Melville, ed., *History and Literature in Iran.* Cambridge, 1990, pp. 89–98.

Khomeini, Ruhollah. *Islam and Revolution: Writings and Declarations of Imam Khomeini.* Translated and annotated by Hamid Algar. Berkeley, Calif.: Mizan Press, 1981.

Klyucheskiy, V. O. "The Murder of Griboyedov." See Petrov, G. M., V. Minorskiy, M. N. Pokrovskiy, and V. O. Klyucheskiy, "The Murder of Griboyedov."

Kolakowski, Leszek. *Main Currents of Marxism: Its Origins, Growth and Dissolution.* 3 Vols. Oxford: Oxford University Press, 1978.

Kologlu, Orhan. "*Akhtar,* journal persan d'Istanbul." In Thierry Zarcone and Fariba Zarinebaf-Shahr, eds., *Les Iraniens d'Istanbul.* Paris and Tehran, 1993.

Krámsky, Jiří. "A Study in the Phonology of Modern Persian." *Archiv Orientalni,* Vol. 11 (1939), pp. 66–83.

Kubícková, Vera. "Persian Literature of the Twentieth Century." In Jan Rypka, *History of Iranian Literature.* Edited by Karl Jahn. Dordrecht, The Netherlands, 1968, pp. 417–428.

Lahidji, Abdol Karim. "Constitutionalism and Clerical Authority." In Said Amir Arjomand, ed., *Authority and Political Culture in Shi'ism.* Albany: State University of New York Press, 1988, pp. 133–158.

Lambton, A. K. S. *Landlord and Peasant in Persia.* Oxford, 1953.

———. "The Tobacco Régie: Prelude to Revolution." *Studia Islamica,* Vol. 22 (1965), pp. 119–157, and Vol. 23 (1966), pp. 71–90; reprinted in A. K. S. Lambton, *Qajar Persia: Eleven Studies.* London, 1987, pp. 223–276.

———. *Qajar Persia: Eleven Studies.* London, 1987.

————. "Concepts of Authority in Persia: Eleventh to Nineteenth Centuries A.D." *Iran* (Journal of the British Society of Persian Studies), Vol. 26 (1988), pp. 95–103.

Lambton, Ann K. S. "Quis Custodiet Custodes: Some Reflections on the Persian Theory of Government." *Studia Islamica*, Vol. 5 (1956), pp. 125–148, and Vol. 6 (1957), pp. 125–146.

————. "Secret Societies and the Persian Revolution of 1905–1906," in *St. Antony's Papers*, No. 4, Middle Eastern Affairs: No. 1. London, 1958, pp. 43–60. Reprinted in Ann K. S. Lambton, *Qájár Persia: Eleven Studies*. London, 1987, pp. 301–318.

————. "Persian Political Societies 1906–11." In *St. Antony's Papers*, No. 16, Middle Eastern Affairs: No. 3. London, 1963, pp. 41–89.

————. *The Persian Land Reform 1962–1966*. Oxford, 1969.

————. "The Persian 'Ulamâ' and the Constitutional Reform." In T. Fahd, ed., *Le Shî'sme imâmite*. Paris: Presses Universitaires de France, 1970, pp. 245–269; reprinted in Ann K. S. Lambton, *Qajar Persia: Eleven Studies*. London, 1987, pp. 277–300.

————. "Land Reform and the Rural Cooperative Societies." In Ehsan Yar-Shater, ed., *Iran Faces the Seventies*. Foreword by John S. Badeau. New York, 1971, pp. 5–43.

————. "Some New Trends in Islamic Political Thought in late Eighteenth and early Nineteenth Century Persia." *Studia Islamica*, Vol. 32 (1974), pp. 95–128.

Lane-Poole, Stanley. "Rawlinson, Sir Henry Creswicke." In Sir Leslie Stephen and Sir Sidney Lee, eds., *The Dictionary of National Biography*. Vol. 16. Oxford, 1959–1960, pp. 771–774.

Lapidus, Ira M., ed. *Middle Eastern Cities: A Symposium on Ancient, Islamic, and Contemporary Middle Eastern Urbanism*. Berkeley: University of California Press, 1969.

Lemert, Charles C., ed. *Intellectuals and Politics: Social Theory in a Changing World*. Newbury Park, Calif.: Sage, 1991.

Lenczowski, George. "The Communist Movement in Iran." *MEJ*, Vol. 1 (January 1947), pp. 29–45.

————. *Russia and the West in Iran, 1918–1948: A Study in Big-Power Politics*. New York, 1949.

Lewis, Bernard. *Ifrandj*. In *EI2*. Vol. 3, Fasciculus 57–58. Edited by B. Lewis, J. L. Ménage, Ch. Pellat, and J. Schacht. Leiden: E. J. Brill, 1970.

————. *Islam and the West*. New York: Oxford University Press, 1993.

Lorentz, J. H. "Iran's Greatest Reformer of the Nineteenth Century: An Analysis of Amir Kabir's Reforms." *IS*, Vol. 4 (1971), pp. 85–103.

Luckmann, Thomas. *The Social Construction of Reality*. See Berger, Peter L., and Thomas Luckmann, *The Social Construction of Reality*.

Lukács, Georg. *History and Class Consciousness: Studies in Marxist Dialectics*. New edition, Berlin, 1968; English translation by Rodney Livingstone. London: Merlin Press, 1971.

Lukes, Steven. "Political Rituals and Social Integration." In Steven Lukes, *Essays in Social Theory*. London, 1977.

Machalski, Franciszek. "Notes on the Intellectual Movement in Iran, 1921–1941." In *Yadname-ye Jan Rypka*. (A collection of articles on Persian and Tajik literature). Prague: Academia Prague, 1967, pp. 179–185.

Maclean, Ian, Alan Montefiore, and Peter Winch, eds. *The Political Responsibility of Intellectuals.* Cambridge: Cambridge University Press, 1990.

Mahdavi, Shireen. "Taj al-Saltaneh, an Emancipated Qajar Princess." *MES,* Vol. 23, No. 2 (April 1987), pp. 188–193.

Malkaum Khan, [Mirzâ]. "Persian Civilization." *Contemporary Review,* Vol. 59 (February 1891), pp. 238–244.

Mannheim, Karl. *Essays in the Sociology of Knowledge.* Edited by Paul Kecskemeti. London: Routledge and Kegan Paul, 1952.

————. *Ideology and Utopia: An Introduction to the Sociology of Knowledge.* Reprinted, London, 1972.

Marcuse, Herbert. *One Dimensional Man.* London, 1964 and 1968.

Marefat, Mina. "The Protagonists Who Shaped Modern Tehran." In Chahryar Adle and Bernard Hourcade, eds., *Téhéran: Capitale bicentenaire.* Paris and Tehran: Institut Français de Recherche en Iran, 1992, pp. 95–125.

Martel, Harry. *Reader in Marxist Philosophy.* See Selsam, Howard, and Harry Martel, eds., *Reader in Marxist Philosophy.*

Martin, V. A. "The Anti-Constitutionalist Arguments of Shaikh Fazlallah Nuri." *MES,* Vol. 22, No. 2 (April 1986), pp. 181–196.

————. "Shaikh Fazlallah Nuri and the Iranian Revolution 1905–09." *MES,* Vol. 23, No. 1 (January 1987), pp. 39–53.

Martin, Vanessa. *Islam and Modernism: The Persian Revolution of 1906.* London, 1989.

Marx, Karl, and Frederick Engels. *Manifesto of the Communist Party.* Moscow, 1977.

Matthee, Rudi. "Jamal al-Din al-Afghani and the Egyptian National Debate." *IJMES,* Vol. 21 (1989), pp. 151–169.

McFarland, Stephen L. "A Peripheral View of the Origins of the Cold War: The Crisis in Iran, 1941–1947." *Diplomatic History,* Vol. 4 (Fall 1980), pp. 333–351.

————. "Anatomy of an Iranian Political Crowd: The Tehran Bread Riot of December 1942." *IJMES,* Vol. 17, No. 1 (February 1985), pp. 51–65.

Meeker, Michael. "The Muslim Intellectual and His Audience: A New Configuration of Writer and Reader among Believers in the Republic of Turkey." In Serif Mardin, ed., *Cultural Transitions in the Middle East.* Leiden: E. J. Brill, 1994, pp. 153–188.

Meeker, Michael E. "The New Muslim Intellectuals in the Republic of Turkey." In Richard Tapper, ed., *Islam in Modern Turkey: Religion, Politics and Literature in a Secular State.* London, 1994, pp. 189–219.

Melikian-Chirvani, A. S. "Le Royaume de Salomon les inscriptions persanes de sites achéménides." *Le Monde iranien et Islam,* Vol. 1, Geneva and Paris (1971), pp. 1–41.

Menashri, David. *Education and the Making of Modern Iran.* Ithaca, N.Y.: Cornell University Press, 1992.

Merleau-Ponty, Maurice. *Adventures of the Dialectic.* English translation by Joseph Bien. London, 1974; originally published as *Les Aventures de la dialectique.* Paris: Gallimard, 1955.

Meskoob, Shahrokh. *Iranian Nationality and the Persian Language.* Washington, D.C.: Mage, 1992.

Milani, Mohsen M. *The Making of Iran's Islamic Revolution: From Monarchy to Islamic*

Republic. Boulder, Colo.: Westview Press, 1st edition, 1988; 2nd edition, 1994.

Minorskiy, V. "The Murder of Griboyedov." See Petrov, G. M., V. Minorskiy, M. N. Pokrovskiy, and V. O. Klyucheskiy, "The Murder of Griboyedov."

Miyata, Osamu. "The Tudeh Military Networks during the Oil Nationalization Period." *MES,* Vol. 23, No. 3 (July 1987), pp. 313–328.

Montefiore, Alan. *The Political Responsibility of Intellectuals.* See Maclean, Ian, Alan Montefiore, and Peter Winch, eds., *The Political Responsibility of Intellectuals.*

Moore, Barrington, Jr. *Privacy: Studies in Social and Cultural History.* New York: M. E. Sharpe, 1984.

Morgan, David. "Persian Perceptions of Mongols and Europeans." In Stuart B. Schwartz, ed., *Implicit Understandings: Observing, Reporting, and Reflecting on the Encounters between Europeans and Other Peoples in the Early Modern Era.* Cambridge: Cambridge University Press, 1994, pp. 201–217.

Mottahedeh, R. P. "The Shuʿūbîyah Controversy and the Social History of Early Islamic Iran." *IJMES,* Vol. 7 (1976), pp. 161–182.

Mottahedeh, Roy. *The Mantle of the Prophet: Learning and Power in Modern Iran.* London: Chatto & Windus, 1986.

Nabavi, Negin, and John Gurney. "Dâr al-Fonûn." See Gurney, John, "Dâr al-Fonûn."

Naraghi, Ehsan. Interview. *Esprit,* 129–130/11, 8–9 (1987), pp. 55–62.

———. *Des palais du chah aux prisons de la révolution.* Paris, 1991; English translation as *From Palace to Prison: Inside the Iranian Revolution.* Translated by Nilou Mobasser. London, 1994.

Nasr, Seyyed Vali Reza. See Foundation for Iranian Studies.

Nomani, Farhad. "Competing Shiʿi Subsystems." See Rahnema, Ali, and Farhad Nomani, "Competing Shiʿi Subsystems."

Nouraie, Fereshteh M. "The Constitutional Ideas of a Shiʿite Mujtahid: Muhammad Husayn Nâ'inî." *IS,* Vol. 8 (1975), pp. 234–247.

Paci, Enzo. *The Function of the Sciences and the Meaning of Man.* English translation with an introduction by Paul Piccone and James E. Hansen. Evanston, Ill.: Northwestern University Press, 1972.

Pahlavi, Mohammad Reza. *Answer to History.* New York: Stein & Day, 1980.

Paidar, Parvin. *Women and the Political Process in Twentieth-Century Iran.* Cambridge: Cambridge University Press, 1995.

Pal, Dharm. *Campaign in Western Asia: Official History of the Indian Armed Forces in the Second World War 1939–45.* General editor Bisheshwar Prasad. Calcutta, 1957.

Parsa Benab, Younes. "Political Organizations in Iran: A Historical Review." *Review of Iranian Political Economy and History,* Vol. 3, No. 1, Washington, D.C. (Spring 1979), pp. 30–80.

Parsons, Sir Anthony. *The Pride and the Fall: Iran 1974–1979.* London, 1984.

Pennock, J. Roland, and John W. Chapman, eds. *Privacy.* Vol. 8 of *Nomos* (Yearbook of the American Society for Political and Legal Philosophy). New York: Atherton Press, 1971.

Perry, John R. "Language Reform in Turkey and Iran." *IJMES,* Vol. 17 (1985), pp. 295–311.

Petrov, G. M., V. Minorskiy, M. N. Pokrovskiy, and V. O. Klyucheskiy. Four separate sources on "The Murder of Griboyedov," introduced in *Central Asian Review*, Vol. 7, No. 4 (1959), pp. 382–386.

Pirnazar, Jaleh. "Political Movements and Organizations in Iran: 1890–1953." Ph.D. dissertation, University of California, Berkeley, 1980.

Pistor-Hatem, Anja. *Iran und die Reformbewegung im Osmanischen Reich.* Berlin, 1992.

———. "The Persian Newspaper *Akhtar* as a Transmitter of Ottoman Political Ideas." In Thierry Zarcone and Fariba Zarinebaf-Shahr, eds., *Les Iraniens d'Istanbul.* Paris and Tehran, 1993.

Pokrovskiy, M. N. "The Murder of Griboyedov." See Petrov, G. M., V. Minorskiy, M. N. Pokrovskiy, and V. O. Klyucheskiy, "The Murder of Griboyedov."

Porter, Sir Robert Ker. *Travels in Georgia, Persia, Armenia, Ancient Babylonia, &c. &c. During the Years 1817, 1818, 1819, and 1820.* 2 Vols. London, 1821–1822.

Radji, Parviz. *In the Service of the Peacock Throne: Diaries of the Shah's Last Ambassador to London.* London, 1983.

Rafael, Vicente L. *Contracting Colonialism: Translation and Christian Conversion in Tagalog Society under Early Spanish Rule.* Ithaca, N.Y.: Cornell University Press, 1988; 2nd edition, Durham, N.C.: Duke University Press, 1993.

Rahman, M. "Post-revolution Persian Verse, with Special Reference to the Poetry of Lahuti, Bahar, 'Arif, Iraj, 'Ishqi and Parvin." Ph.D. thesis, School of Oriental and African Studies, University of London, 1953–1954.

Rahnema, Ali. "Ali Shari'ati: Teacher, Preacher, Rebel." In Ali Rahnema, ed., *Pioneers of Islamic Revival.* London: Zed Books, 1994, pp. 208–250.

Rahnema, Ali, and Farhad Nomani. "Competing Shi'i Subsystems in Contemporary Iran." In Saeed Rahnema and Sohrab Behdad, eds., *Iran after the Revolution: Crisis of an Islamic State.* London and New York: I. B. Tauris, 1995, pp. 65–93.

Rahnema, Ali, ed. *Pioneers of Islamic Revival.* London: Zed Books, 1994.

Rahnema, Saeed, and Sohrab Behdad, eds. *Iran after the Revolution: Crisis of an Islamic State.* London and New York, I. B. Tauris, 1995.

Rashid al-Din Fadl Allâh. *Kitâb Târikh-i Ifrandj (Histoire universelle de Rashid al-Din, histoire des Frances).* Edited with French translation by K. Jahn. Leiden, 1951.

Rawlinson, George. *A Memoir of Major-General Sir Henry Creswicke Rawlinson.* London, 1898.

Richard, Y. "Ayatollah Kashani: Precursor of the Islamic Republic?" In N. R. Keddie, ed., *Religion and Politics in Iran.* New Haven, Conn.: Yale University Press, 1983, pp. 101–124.

———. "L'Organization des Fedâ'iyân-e eslâm, mouvement intégriste musulman en Iran (1945–1956). In O. Carré and P. Dumont, eds., *Radicalimes islamiques.* Vol. 1. Paris: L'Harmattan, 1985, pp. 23–82.

Richard, Yann. "Contemporary Shi'i Thought." In Nikki R. Keddie, *Roots of Revolution: An Interpretive History of Modern Iran.* New Haven: Yale University Press, 1981, pp. 202–228.

———. "Le Radicalisme islamique du Sheykh Fazollâh Nuri et son impact dans l'histoire de l'Iran contemporain." *Laïcité,* n.s. 29, 2 (*Les Intégrismes,* Brussels, 1986, pp. 60–86.

Richard, Yann, ed. (A bibliography of the writings of Ali Shari'ati). *Abstracta Iranica,* Vol. 1, Tehran and Leiden, 1978; Vol. 2, Tehran and Leiden, 1979.

Ricks, Thomas M., ed. *Critical Perspectives on Modern Persian Literature*. Washington, D.C.: Three Continents Press, 1984.

Sabri-Tabrizi, G. R. "Human Values in the Works of Two Persian Writers." In Congrés d'Études Arabes Islamiques (Brussels, 1970). *Vᵉ Congrés International d'Arabisants et d'Islamisants, Brussels, 31 August–6 September 1970 (actes)*. Series: Correspondance d'Orient, No. 11. Brussels: Centre pour l'Étude des Problèmes du Monde Musulman Contemporain, 1971, pp. 411–418.

Sadiq, Issa Khan. *Modern Persia and Her Educational System*. New York, 1931.

Said, Edward W. *Representations of the Intellectuals: The 1993 Reith Lectures*. New York: Pantheon House, 1994.

Sandjabi, K. *Essai sur l'économie rurale et le régime agraire de la Perse*. Paris, 1934.

Sartre, Jean-Paul. *Critique of Dialectical Reason. I: Theory of Practical Ensembles*. First published Paris, 1960; translated by Alan Sheridan-Smith, edited by Jonathan Rée. London: New Left Books, 1976.

Sartre, Jean-Paul. *Search for a Method*. First published Paris, 1960; translated from the French with an introduction by Hazel E. Barnes. New York: Vintage Books, 1968.

Sass, Hans-Martin. "Hegel's Concept of Philosophy and the Meditations of Objective Spirit." In Donald Phillip Verene, ed., *Hegel's Social and Political Thought: The Philosophy of Objective Spirit*. Atlantic Highlands, N.J.: Humanities Press, 1980, pp. 1–26.

Sassani, A. H. K. "Higher Education in Iran." *College and University*, Vol. 24 (October 1948), pp. 78–96.

Scheler, Max. *Ressentiment*. Edited with an introduction by Lewis A. Coser, translation by William W. Holdhem. New York, [1961], 1972.

Schwartz, Stuart B., ed. *Implicit Understandings: Observing, Reporting, and Reflecting on the Encounters between Europeans and Other Peoples in the Early Modern Era*. Cambridge: Cambridge University Press, 1994.

Seccombe, Thomas. "Porter, Sir Robert Ker." In Sir Leslie Stephen and Sir Sidney Lee, eds., *The Dictionary of National Biography*. Vol. 16. Oxford, 1959–1960, pp. 190–192.

Seger, Martin. *Teheran: Eine Stadtgeographische Studies*. Vienna: Springer Verlag, 1978.

Selsam, Howard, and Harry Martel, eds. *Reader in Marxist Philosophy: From the Writings of Marx, Engels, and Lenin*. New York: International Publishers, 1963; 7th printing, 1973.

Shadman, S. F. "Review of Anglo-Persian Relations, 1798–1815." *Proceedings of the Iran Society*. Vol. 2, Parts 5/6. London: The Iran Society, 1943, pp. 23–39.

Shafaq, S. R. "Patriotic Poetry in Modern Iran." *MEJ*, Vol. 6, No. 4 (Autumn 1952), pp. 417–428.

Shafi'i Kadkani, Mohammad-Reza. "Persian Literature (Belles-Lettres) from the Time of Jâmi to the Present Day." In G. Morrison, ed., *History of Persian Literature from the Beginnings of the Islamic Period to the Present Day*. Leiden: E. J. Brill, 1981, pp. 135–206.

Shapiro, Michael J. "A Political Approach to Language Purism." In Björn H. Jernudd and Michael J. Shapiro, eds., *The Politics of Language Purism*. Berlin and New York, 1989, pp. 21–29.

Shari'ati, Ali. *On the Sociology of Islam.* Translated by Hamid Algar. Berkeley, Calif.: Mizan Press, 1979.

Shils, Edward. "Intellectuals." In *International Encyclopedia of the Social Sciences.* Vol. 7. New York: Macmillan and Free Press, 1968, pp. 399–413.

Siassi, Ali Akbar. *La Perse au contact de l'Occident: Étude historique et sociale.* Paris, 1931.

Simmel, Georg. *The Philosophy of Money.* Translated from the German by Tom Bottomore and David Frisby. London: Routledge & Kegan Paul, 1978.

Simon, Jules-François. *La Politique radicale.* Paris, 1868.

Skalmowski, Wojciech. "Remarks on Daulat in Hafiz." *Folia Orientalia,* Vol. 22 (*Iranica*: Studies in Memory of Professor Franciszek Machalski), 1981–1984 (publication 1985), pp. 131–137.

Soheyli, Abdolghasem. "Noun Phrase Complementation in Persian." Ph.D. dissertation, University of Illinois, Urbana, 1976.

Sourdel, D. "al-Barâmika." In *EI2*, Vol. 1, Pt. 2, 1960, pp. 1033–1036.

Stace, W. T. *The Philosophy of Hegel: A Systematic Exposition.* First published London: Macmillan, 1924; New York: Dover, 1955.

Stern, S. M. "Ya'qûb the Coppersmith and Persian National Sentiment." In C. E. Bosworth, ed., *Iran and Islam.* Edinburgh, 1971, pp. 535–555.

Tabaian, Hessam. "Conjunction, Relativization, and Complementation in Persian." Ph.D. dissertation, University of Colorado, Boulder, 1975.

Tarbiyat, M. A., and E. G. Browne. *The Press and Poetry of Modern Persia.* Cambridge, 1914.

Tavakoli-Targhi, Mohammad. "Refashioning Iran: Language and Culture during the Constitutional Revolution." *IS*, Vol. 23, Nos. 1–4 (1990), pp. 77–101.

Taylor, Charles. *Hegel and Modern Society.* Cambridge, Mass.: Cambridge University Press, 1979.

———. *Sources of the Self: The Making of the Modern Identity.* Cambridge, Mass.: Harvard University Press, 1989.

Towhidi, Jalil. *Studies in the Phonetics and Phonology of Modern Persian.* Hamburg, 1974.

Trotsky, Leon. *Their Morals and Ours.* New York, 1942.

Tweedy, Owen. "Tweedy's Hotel in Tabriz." (Photo and note, dated 1931). In the unpublished Photographic Archive, Middle East Centre, St. Antony's College, Oxford University, catalogued under No. 1372: 32 (3/204/3).

Tynianov, Yuri. *Death and Diplomacy in Persia.* Translated from the Russian by Alec Brown. First published London: Boriswood, 1938; reprint edition, Westport, Conn.: Hyperion Press, 1975 (translation of *Smert' Vazir-Mukhtara*).

Vatandoust, G. "Sayyed Hasan Taqizadeh and Kaveh: Modernism in Post-Constitutional Iran (1916–1921)." Ph.D. dissertation, University of Washington, Seattle, 1977.

Vaziri, Mostafa. *Iran as Imagined Nation: The Construction of National Identity.* New York: Paragon House, 1993.

Verene, Donald Phillip, ed. *Hegel's Social and Political Thought: The Philosophy of Objective Spirit.* Atlantic Highlands, N.J.: Humanities Press, 1980.

Waterfield, Robin E. *Christians in Persia: Assyrians, Armenians, Roman Catholics and Protestants.* London: George Allen and Unwin, 1973.

Weber, Max. "Politics as a Vocation." In *From Max Weber: Essays in Sociology*, translated, edited, and with an introduction by H. H. Gerth and C. Wright Mills. London and Boston: Routledge and Kegan Paul, 1948; reprinted, 1974, pp. 77–128.

Weiker, Walter F. *The Modernization of Turkey: From Ataturk to the Present Day*. New York and London, 1981.

Weiss, Paul. *Privacy*. Carbondale: Southern Illinois University Press, 1983.

Wells, Robert. "Jalâl Âl-Ahmad: Writer and Political Activist." Ph.D. thesis, Faculty of Arts, University of Edinburgh, 1982.

Wilber, Donald N. *Riza Shah Pahlavi: The Resurrection and Reconstruction of Iran*. New York, 1975.

Winch, Peter. *The Political Responsibility of Intellectuals*. See Maclean, Ian, Alan Montefiore, and Peter Winch, eds., *The Political Responsibility of Intellectuals*.

Wright, Sir Denis. *The English Amongst the Persians: During the Qajar Period 1787–1921*. London, 1977.

Yar-Shater, Ehsan, ed. *Iran Faces the Seventies*. Foreword by John S. Badeau. New York: Praeger, 1971.

Yarmohammadi, Lotfollah. "A Contrastive Study of Modern English and Modern Persian." Ph.D. dissertation, University of Indiana, Bloomington, 1965.

Yarmohammadi, Lotfollah, and Ronayne Cowan. "The Persian Verb Reconsidered." *Archiv Orientalni*, Vol. 46 (1978), pp. 46–60.

Zabih, Sepehr. *The Communist Movement in Iran*. Berkeley: University of California Press, 1966.

Zarcone, Thierry, and Fariba Zarinebaf-Shahr, eds. *Les Iraniens d'Istanbul*. Paris and Tehran, 1993.

Zarinebaf-Shahr, Fariba. "The Iranian Merchant Community in the Ottoman Empire and the Constitutional Revolution." In Thierry Zarcone and Fariba Zarinebaf-Shahr, eds., *Les Iraniens d'Istanbul*. Paris and Tehran, 1993, pp. 203–212.

Zenkovsky, V. V. *A History of Russian Philosophy*. 2 Vols., translated from Russian by George L. Kline. New York and London, 1953.

Zonis, Marvin. "Higher Education and Social Change: Problems and Prospects." In Ehsan Yar-Shater, ed., *Iran Faces the Seventies*. Foreword by John S. Badeau. New York: Praeger, 1971, pp. 217–259.

— INDEX —

Eliot, T. S., 80
Enayat, Hamid, 138nn.84,86
Enâyat, Mahmoud, 78
Enlightenment, 14, 70, 101, 123n.4
Eqbâl Âshtiâni, Abbas, 79
Eshâq, Eprim, 66, 67
'Eshqi, Seyyed Mohammad-Reza
　Mirzâdeh, 17
Eskandari, Soleymân Mirzâ, 15
Estebdâd. See Despotism
E'temâdzâdeh, Mahmoud, 193n.7
Ethics, 107, 118. See also Morality
Europe, 58, 77, 78
Existentialism, 97, 98, 104

Fadâ'iân-e Islam, 69, 75
Fadâ'iân-e Khalq, 76, 107
Fakhr al-Dawleh, Tourân Âghâ, 53
Fanon, Franz, 184n.151
Farang and *Farangestân* (Europe), 42,
　176–177n.81. See also Shâdmân
Fardid, Ahmad, 89
Farhangestân (Iranian Academy), 46, 84,
　123n.3, 146n.43, 167n.34
Farmânfarmâ, Mohammad, 64
Farrokhi Yazdi, Mohammad, 17, 18, 84
Farzâd, Hosein, 124n.7
Fâtemi, Hosein, 75
Fatima, 104
Fâzel Ardakâni, Mollâ Hosein, 124n.7
Fiqh (Islamic jurisprudence), 14
Firouz, Mozaffar, 64
Flammarion, Camille, 57
Foroughi (Zakâ' al-Molk), Moham-
　mad-Ali, 62, 178n.93
Forouzânfar, Badi' al-Zamân, 72, 73
Fraser, James, 129n.28
French Revolution, 25, 27

Geneva: Iranian Consulate in, 165n.26;
　University of, 92
Germany, 155n.6
Gharbzadegi (superficial Westernism), 6,
　89. See also Âl-Ahmad
Gilân, 66
Golestân, 51, 86
Golshiri, Houshang, 39, 122n.4, 195n.12

Gorgâni, *Vis va Râmin*, 59
Gowharshâd Mosque, 48–49
Greek: early philosophers (Fardid's
　assessment of), 89; early philoso-
　phers (Narâqi's depiction of), 95;
　medicine and philosophy, teaching
　of in Tabriz (Âl-Ahmad on), 91; rule
　in Iran (Shari'ati on) 99;
Griboyedov, A. S., 23

Hasibi, Kâzem, 68
Hedâyat, Sâdeq, 59, 62, 71, 83, 126n.20,
　158n.27
Heidegger, Martin, 178n.99, 179n.101
Hekmat, Ali-Asghar, 72, 73
Hekmat, Sardâr Fâkher, 64
Hezb-e Jomhouri-ye Islami. See Islamic
　Republic party
Hezb-e Mardom, 64
Hezb-e Melliyoun, 64
Hezb-e Rastâkhiz, 64
Hezb-e Tudeh. See Tudeh Party
Hezbollâh (Party of God), 101, 188n.186
Hidden Imam, 106. See also Mahdi
Hosein, Imam, 104, 128n.26, 189n.196,
　191n.205, 197n.20
Hoseiniyeh Ershâd, 98
Hoveydâ, Amir-Abbâs, 76
Hoveydâ, Fereydoun, 187n.174
Hugo, Victor, 53

Ideology, 1, 69, 70, 71, 73, 79, 90,
　92, 102, 103, 112, 115; of armed
　struggle, 76, 83, 107–108, 163n.18;
　"collectivist," 65; constitutional, 14;
　culture as, 82; Islam as, 101–105;
　maktabi, 113–115; Marxist, 100;
　modern materialist, 101; nationalist,
　xi; of the Second International, 65;
　social function of, 98; socialist, 16,
　45, 60, 65, Stalinist, 66
Ijtihâd, 14, 104
Imam-Jom'eh (of Tehran), Mirzâ Abu
　al-Qâsem, 35
India, 17, 133n.52; politics of, 80
Individual rights. See Rights
Institutionalization, 2; of constitutional